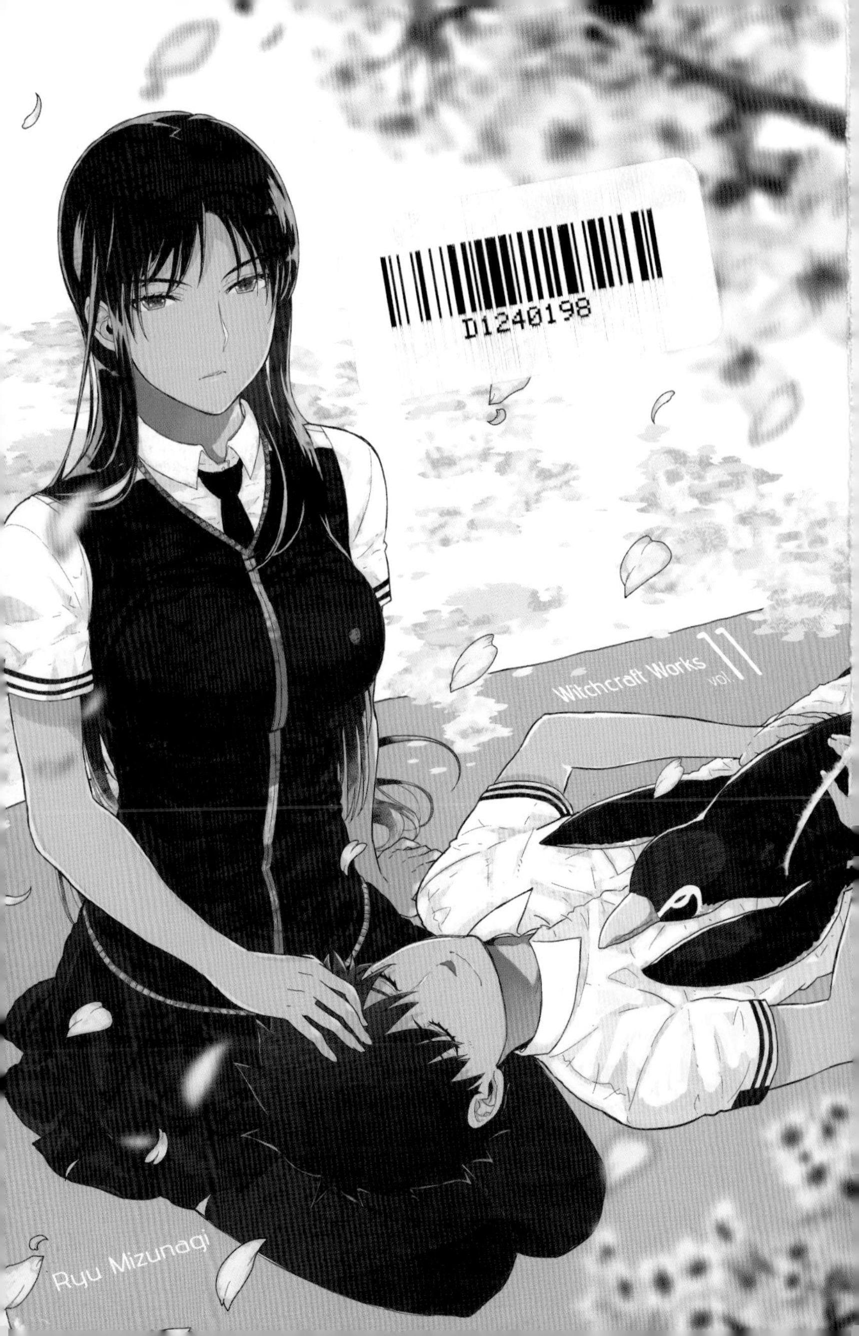
Witchcraft Works vol. 11
Ryu Mizunagi

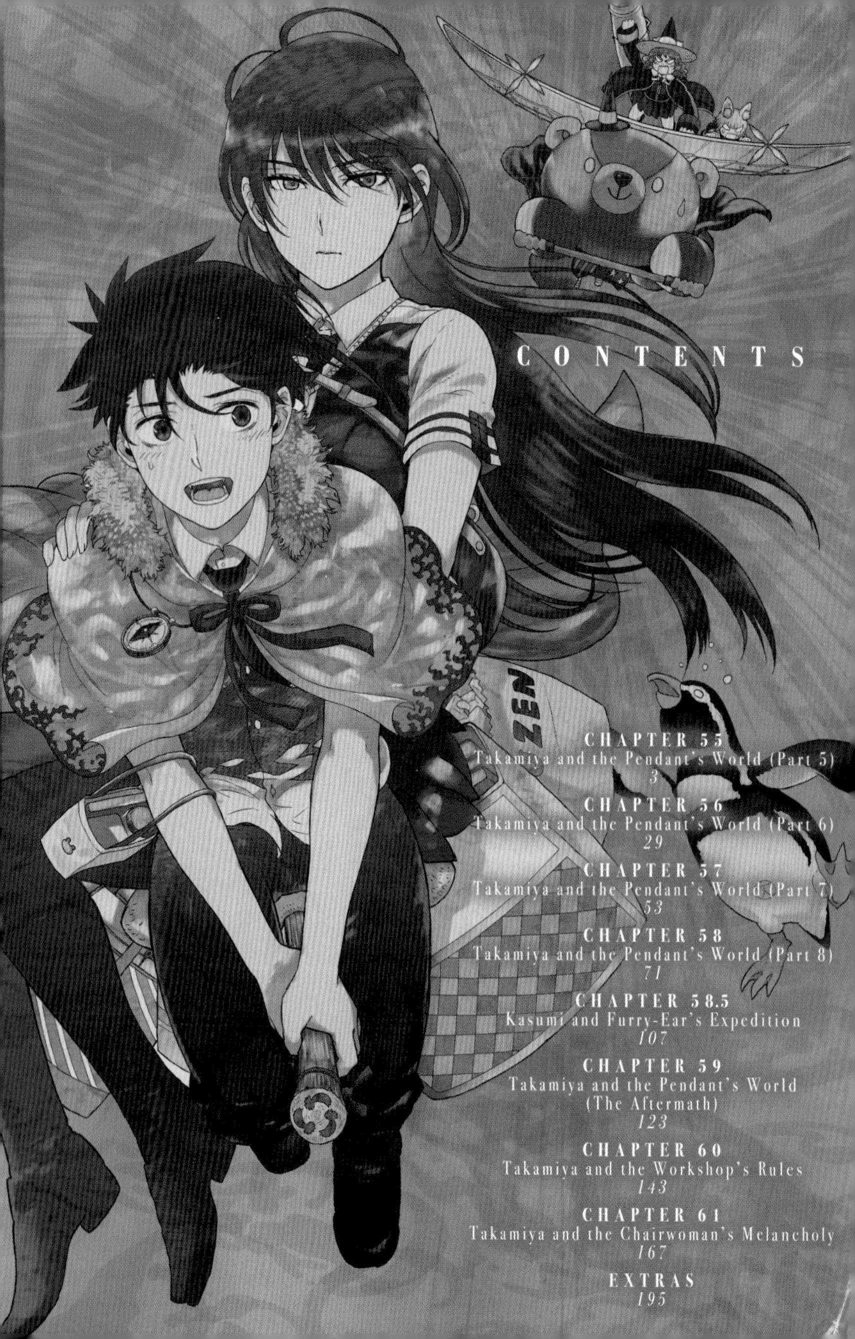

CONTENTS

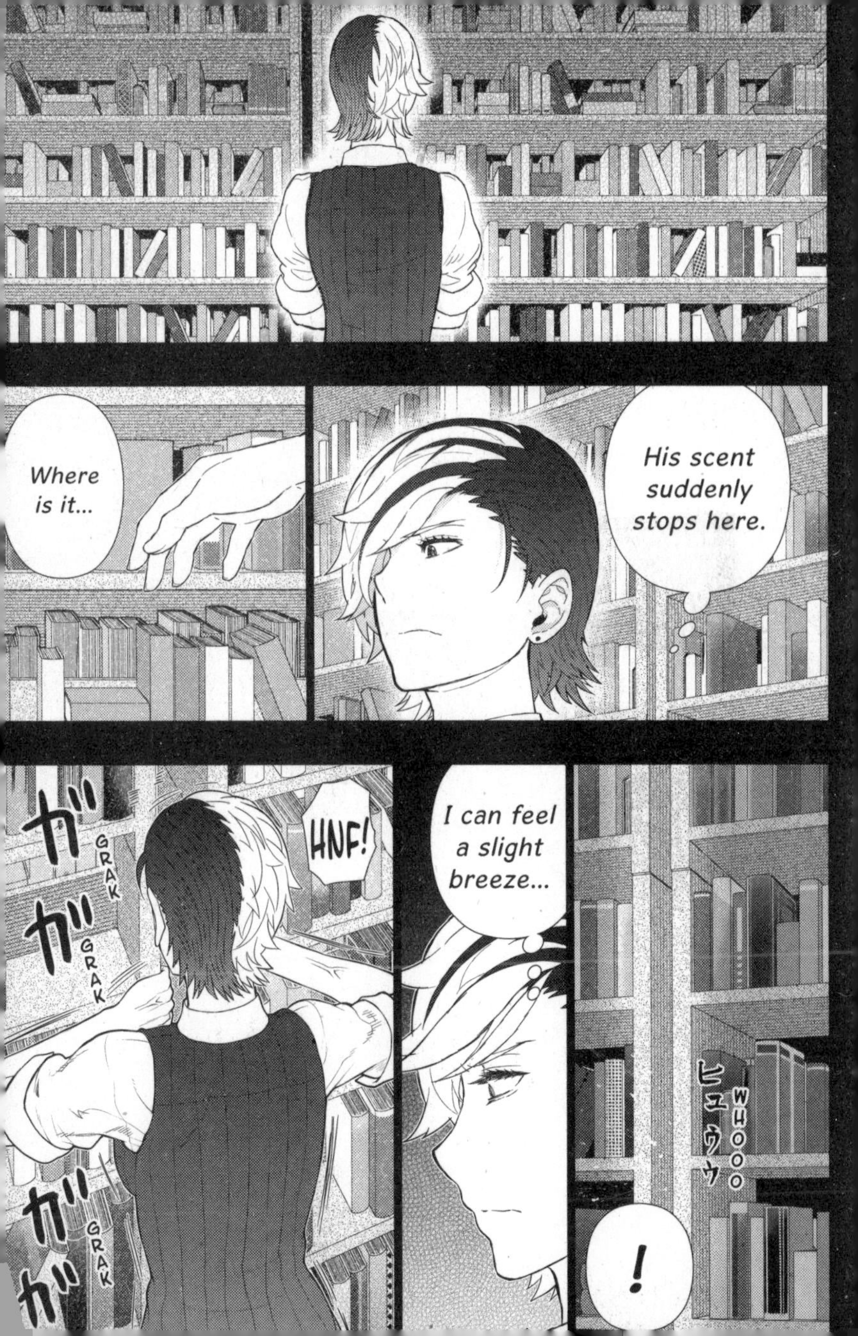
His scent suddenly stops here.
Where is it...
I can feel a slight breeze...
ヒュウウ
WHOOOO
!
HNF!
ガ GRAK
ガ GRAK
ガ GRAK
ガ

CHAPTER 55 Takamiya and the Pendant's World (Part 5)

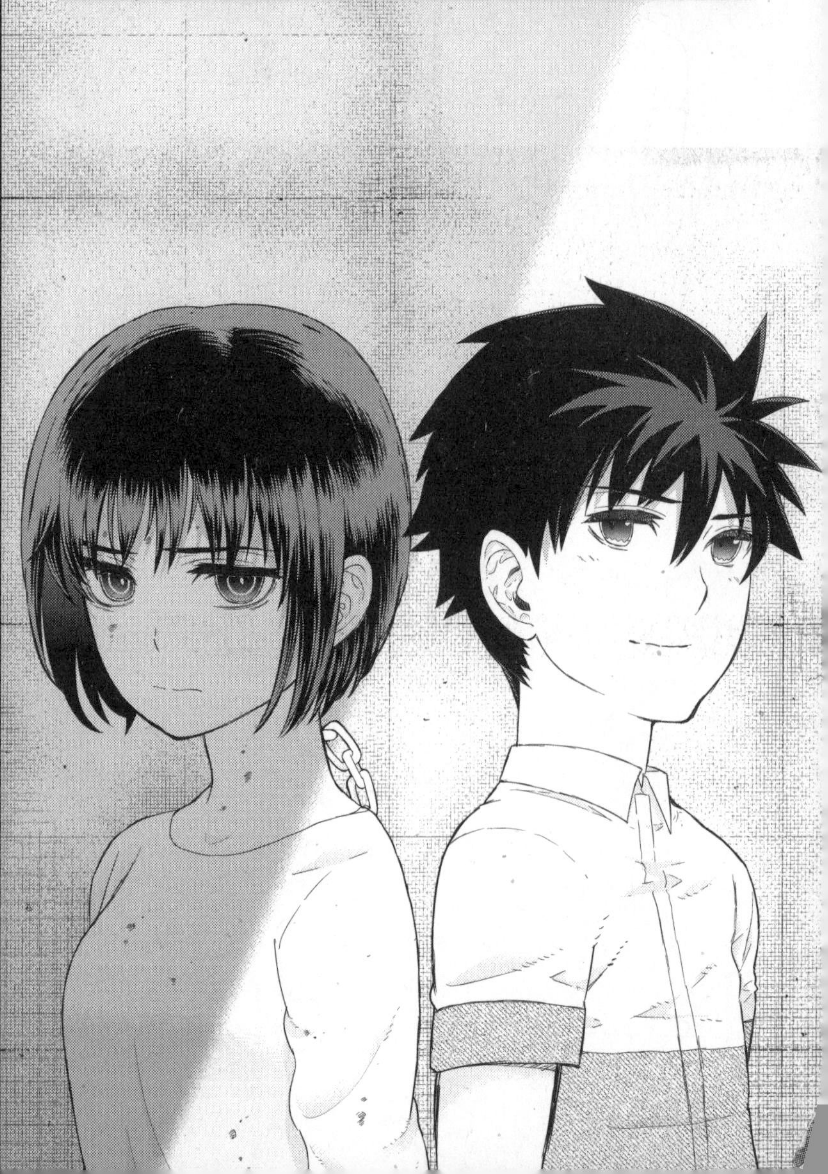

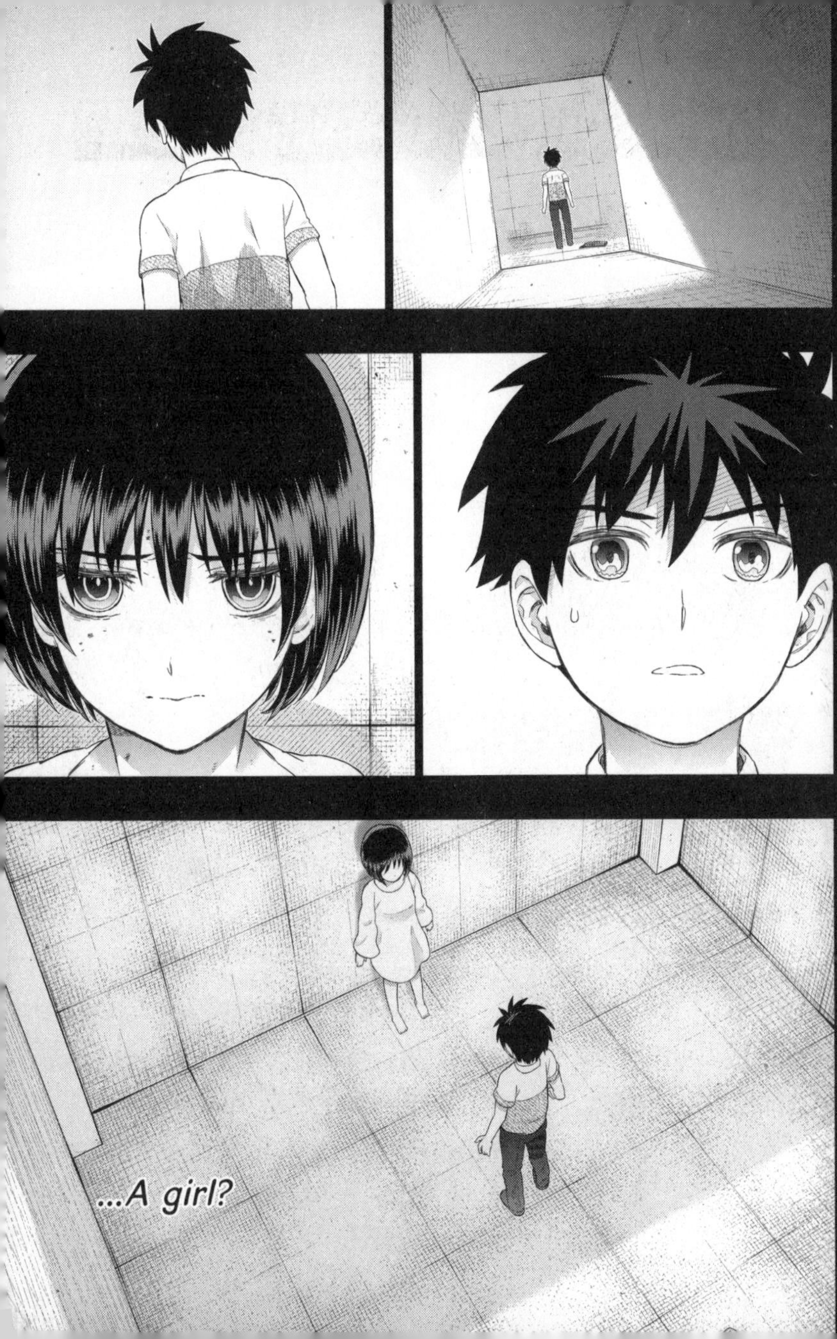
...A girl?

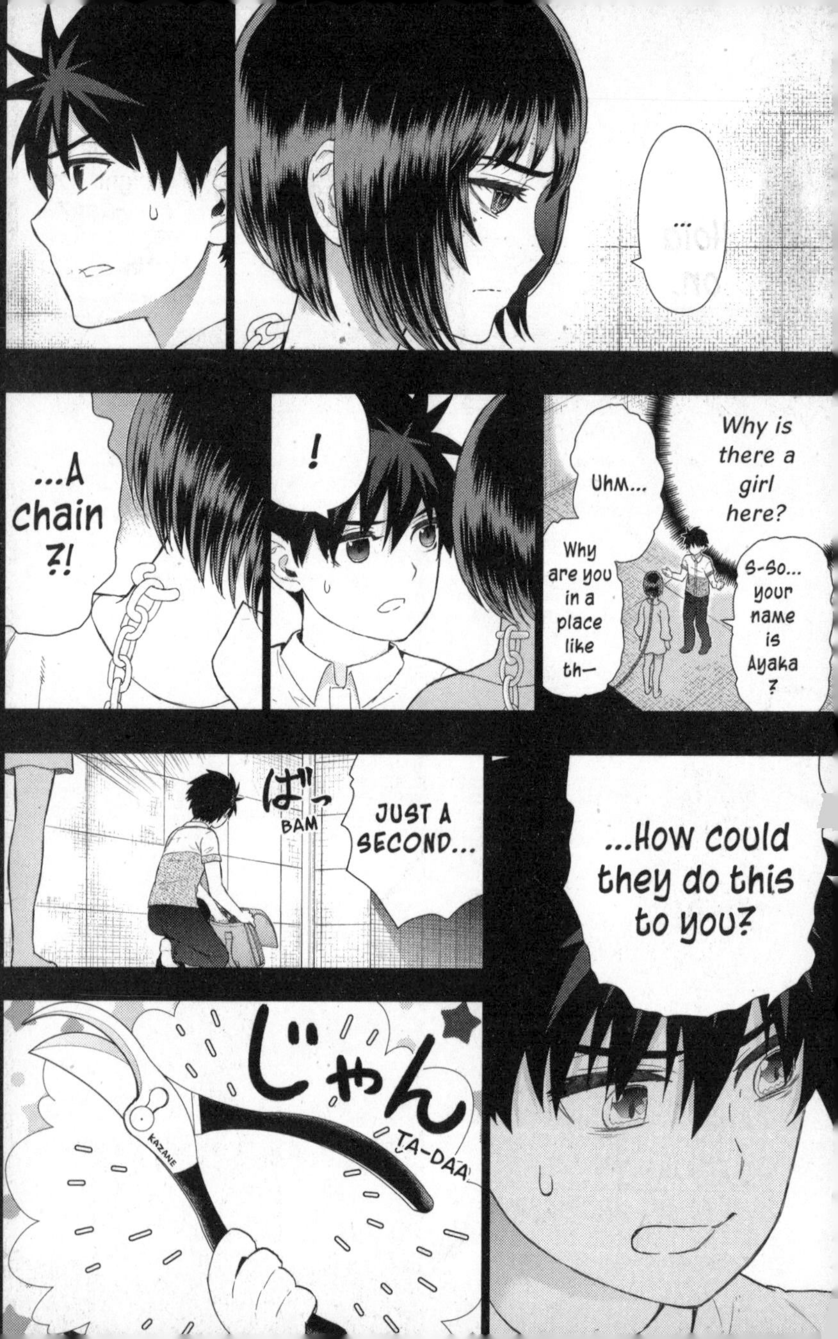
...
Why is there a girl here?
Uhm...
S-So... your name is Ayaka?
Why are you in a place like th—
!
...A chain?!
...How could they do this to you?
JUST A SECOND...
ばっ
BAM
じゃん
TA-DAA
KAZANE

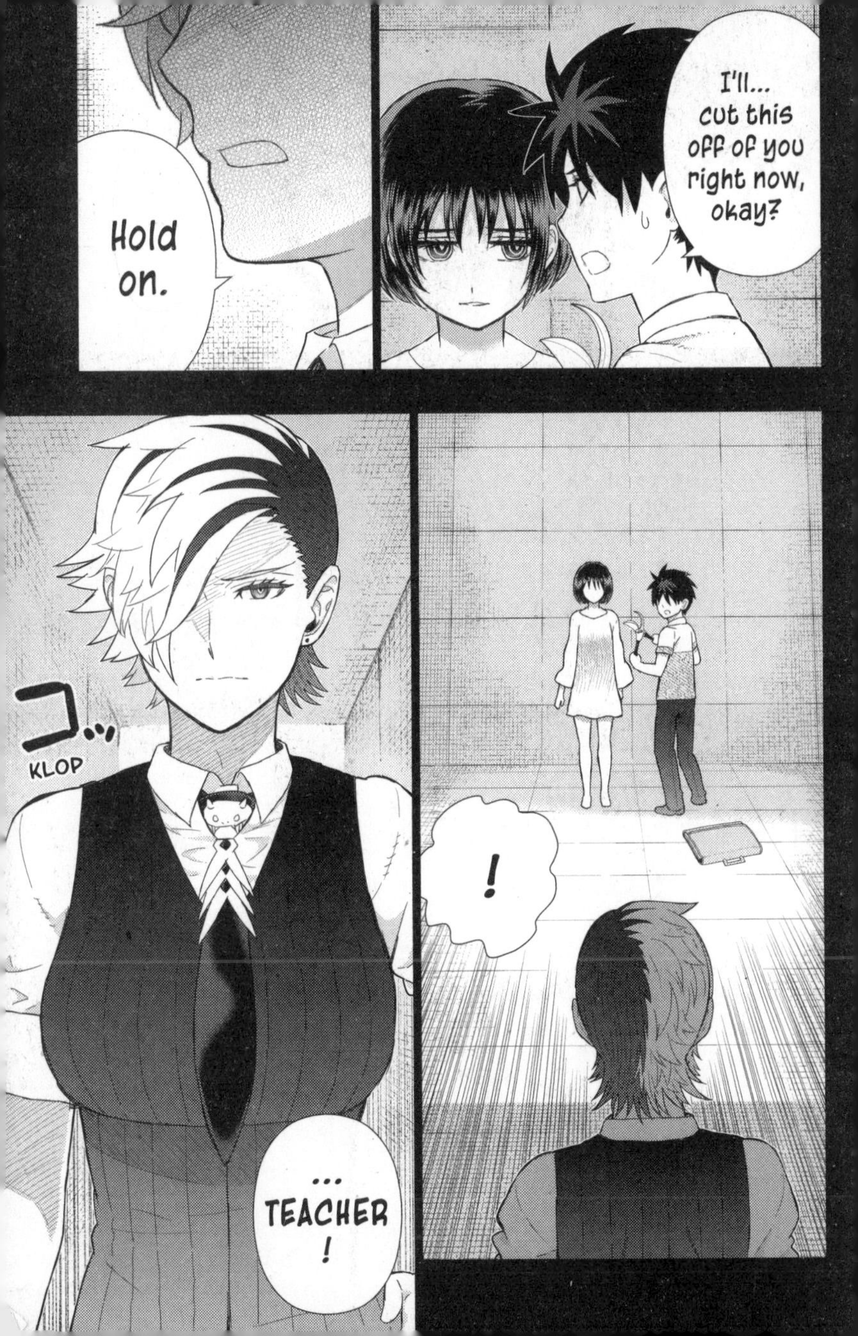
I'll... cut this off of you right now, okay?
Hold on.
!
... TEACHER !
コッ
KLOP

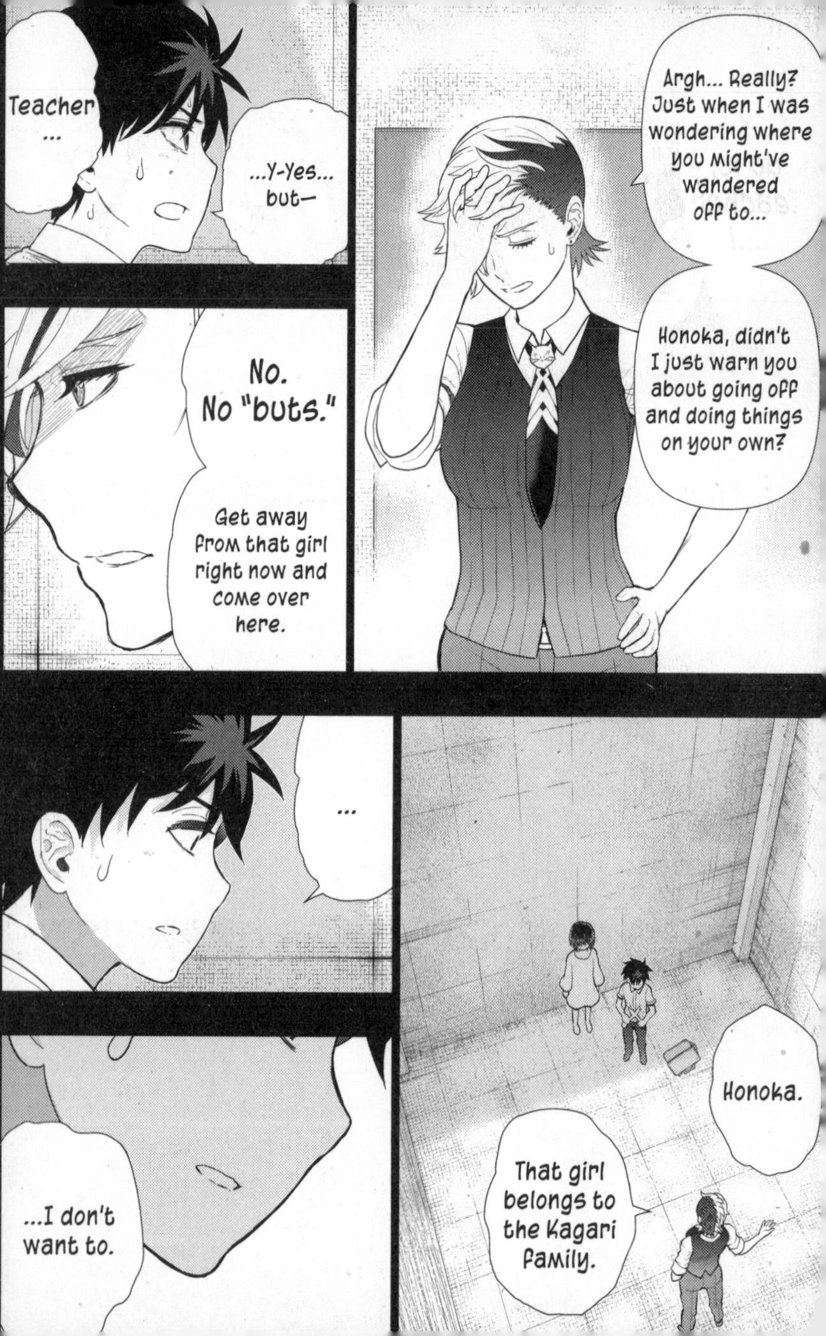
Argh... Really? Just when I was wondering where you might've wandered off to...
Honoka, didn't I just warn you about going off and doing things on your own?
Teacher ...
...Y-Yes... but—
No. No "buts."
Get away from that girl right now and come over here.
Honoka.
That girl belongs to the Kagari family.
...
...I don't want to.

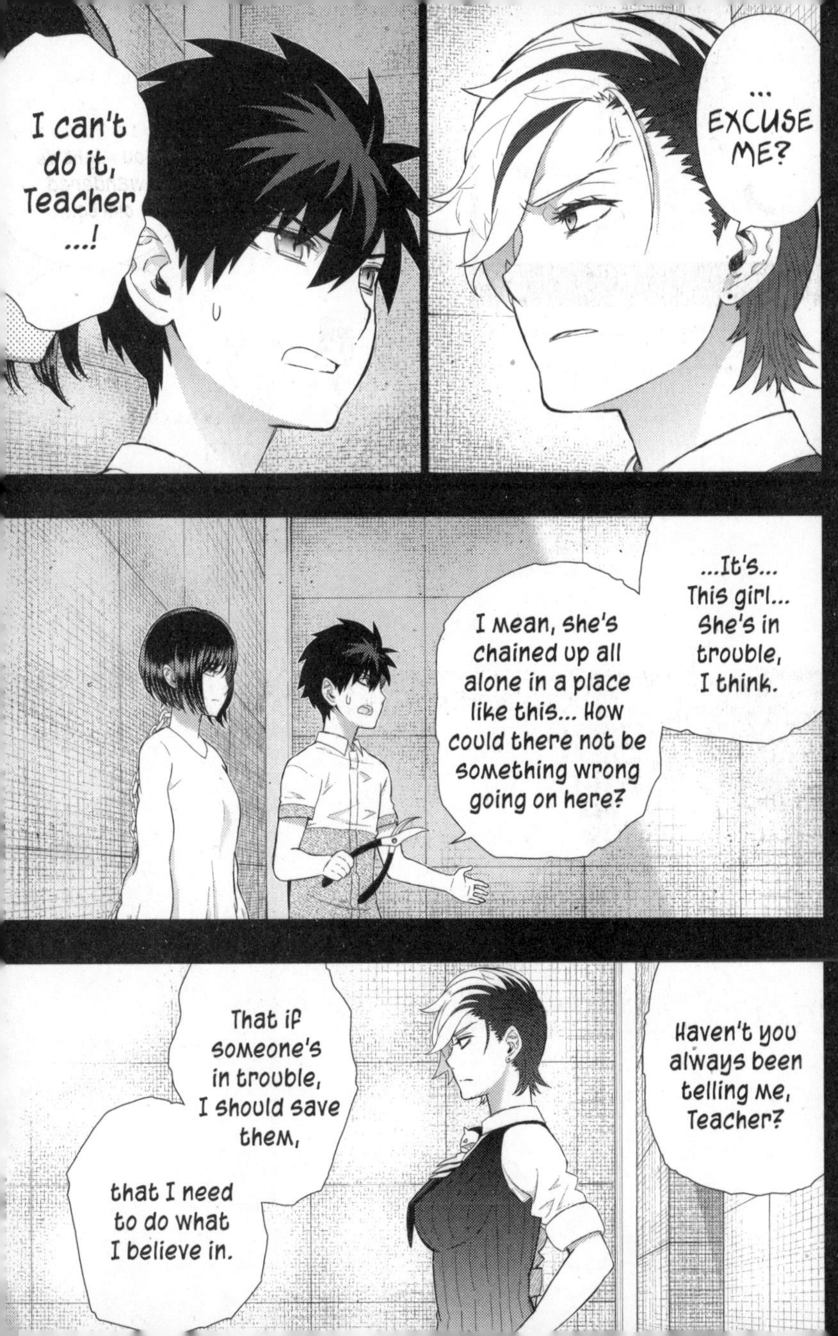
...EXCUSE ME?
I can't do it, Teacher...!
...It's... This girl... She's in trouble, I think.
I mean, she's chained up all alone in a place like this... How could there not be something wrong going on here?
Haven't you always been telling me, Teacher?
That if someone's in trouble, I should save them,
that I need to do what I believe in.

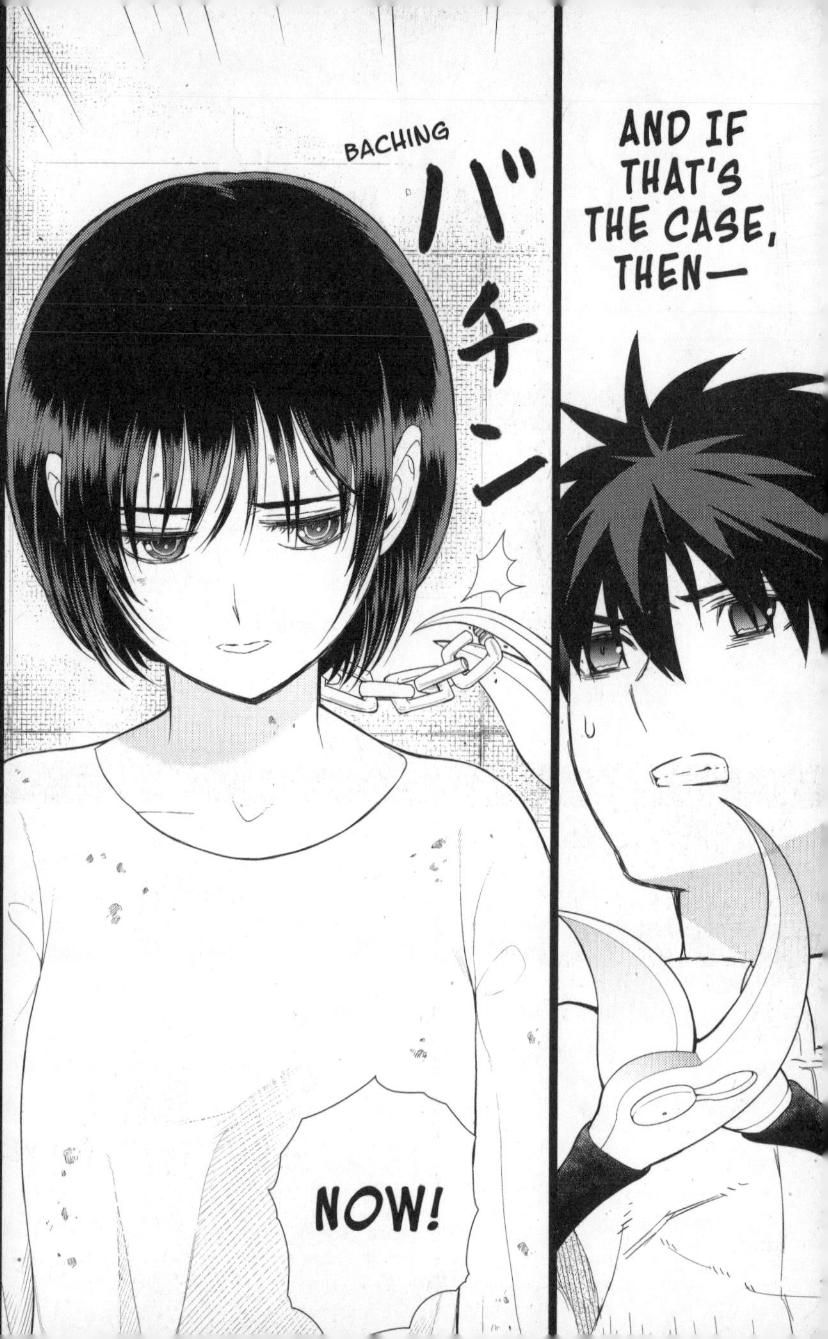
AND IF THAT'S THE CASE, THEN—
BACHING
バチーン
NOW!

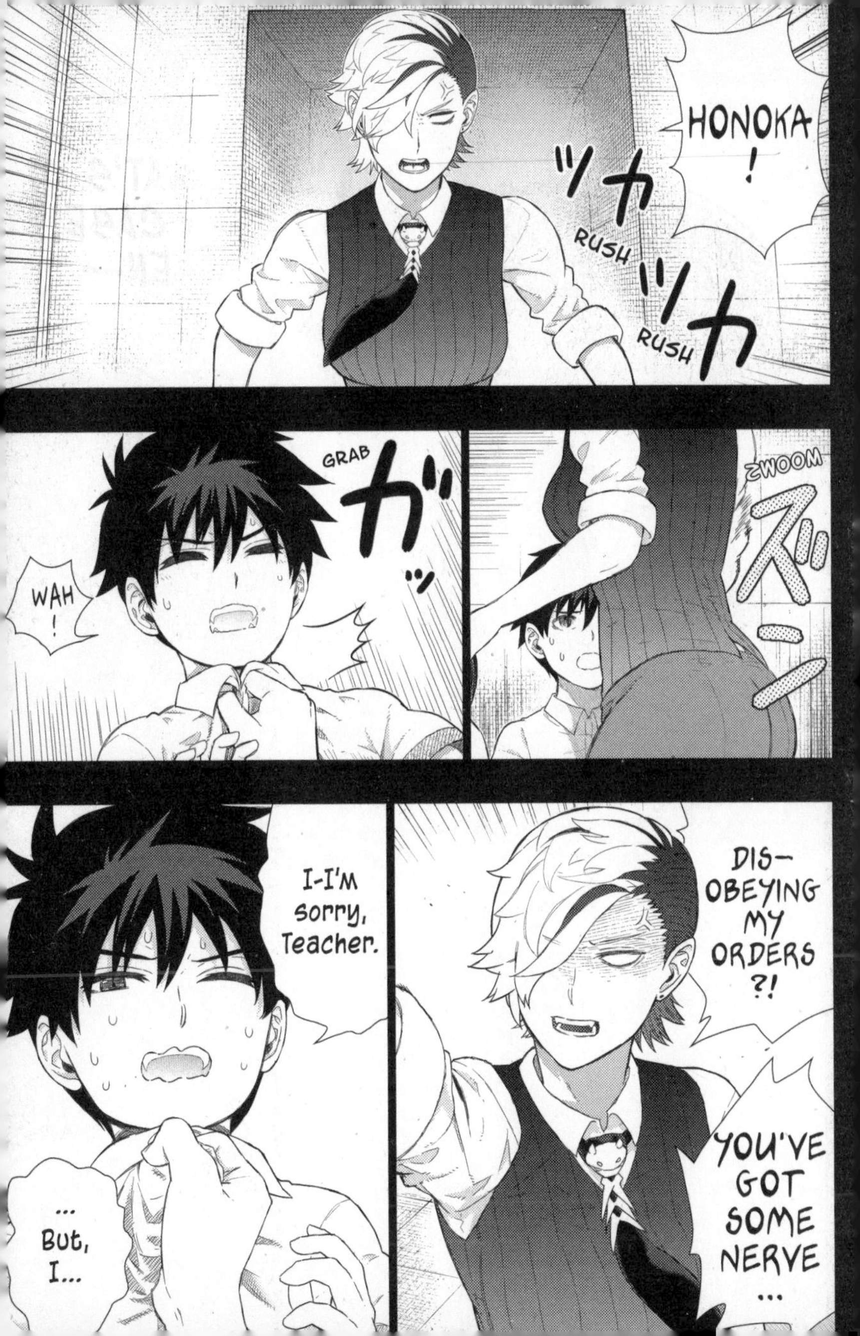
HONOKA!
ツカ
RUSH
ツカ
RUSH
ZWOOM
ズッ
GRAB
ガッ
WAH!
DIS—OBEYING MY ORDERS?!
YOU'VE GOT SOME NERVE...
I-I'M sorry, Teacher.
...But, I...

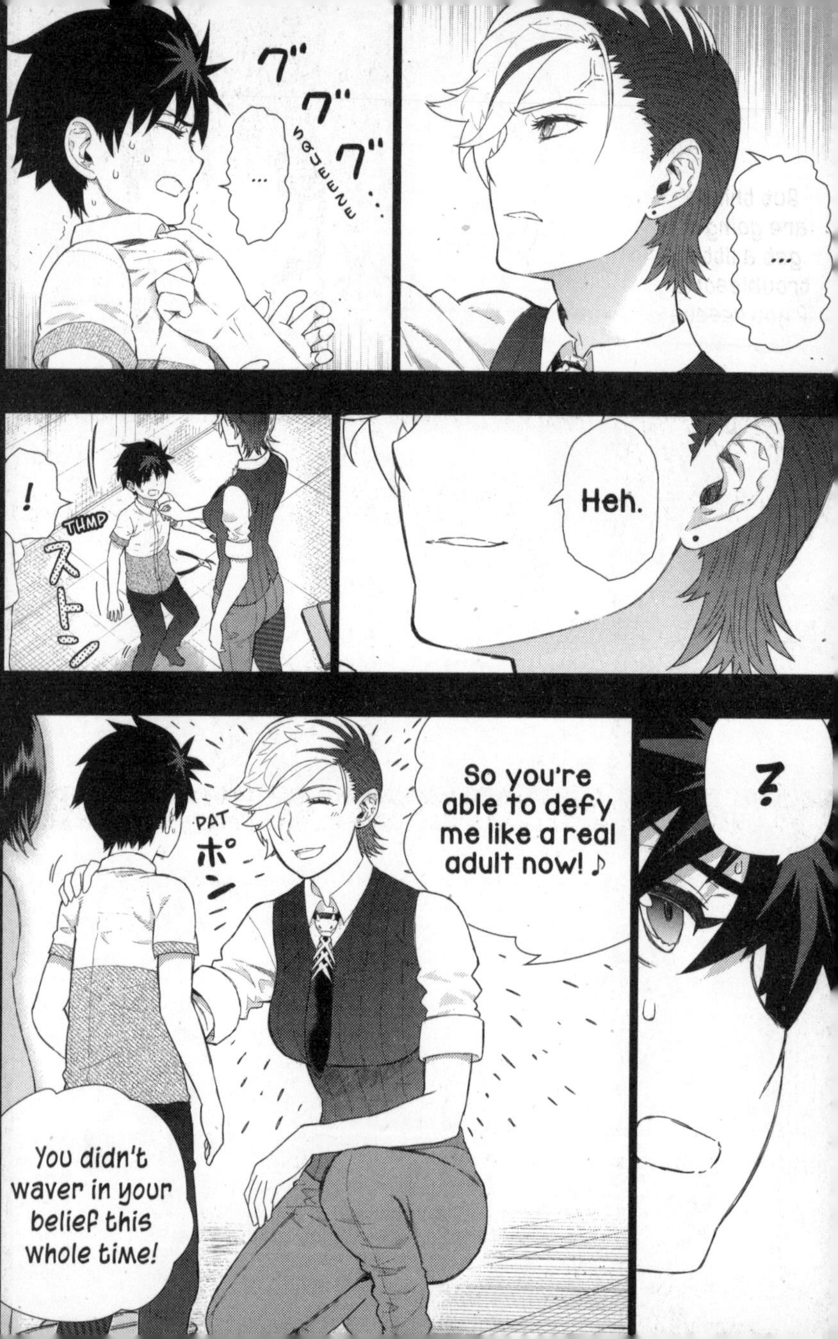
...
グ グ グ
SQUEEZE
...
Heh.
!
THMP
ストン
?
So you're able to defy me like a real adult now! ♪
PAT
ポン
You didn't waver in your belief this whole time!

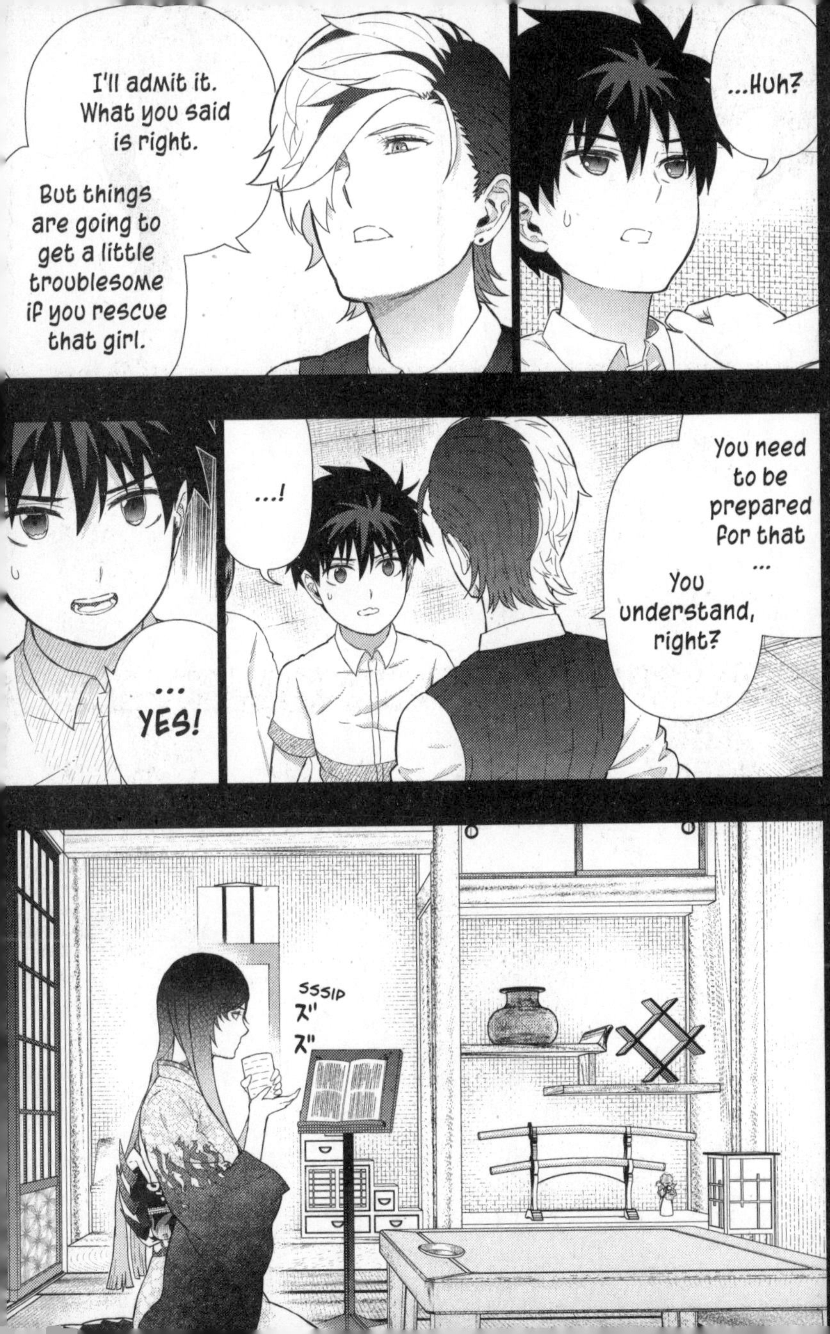
...Huh?
I'll admit it. What you said is right.
But things are going to get a little troublesome if you rescue that girl.
You need to be prepared for that ...
You understand, right?
...!
... YES!
SSSIP
ズズ

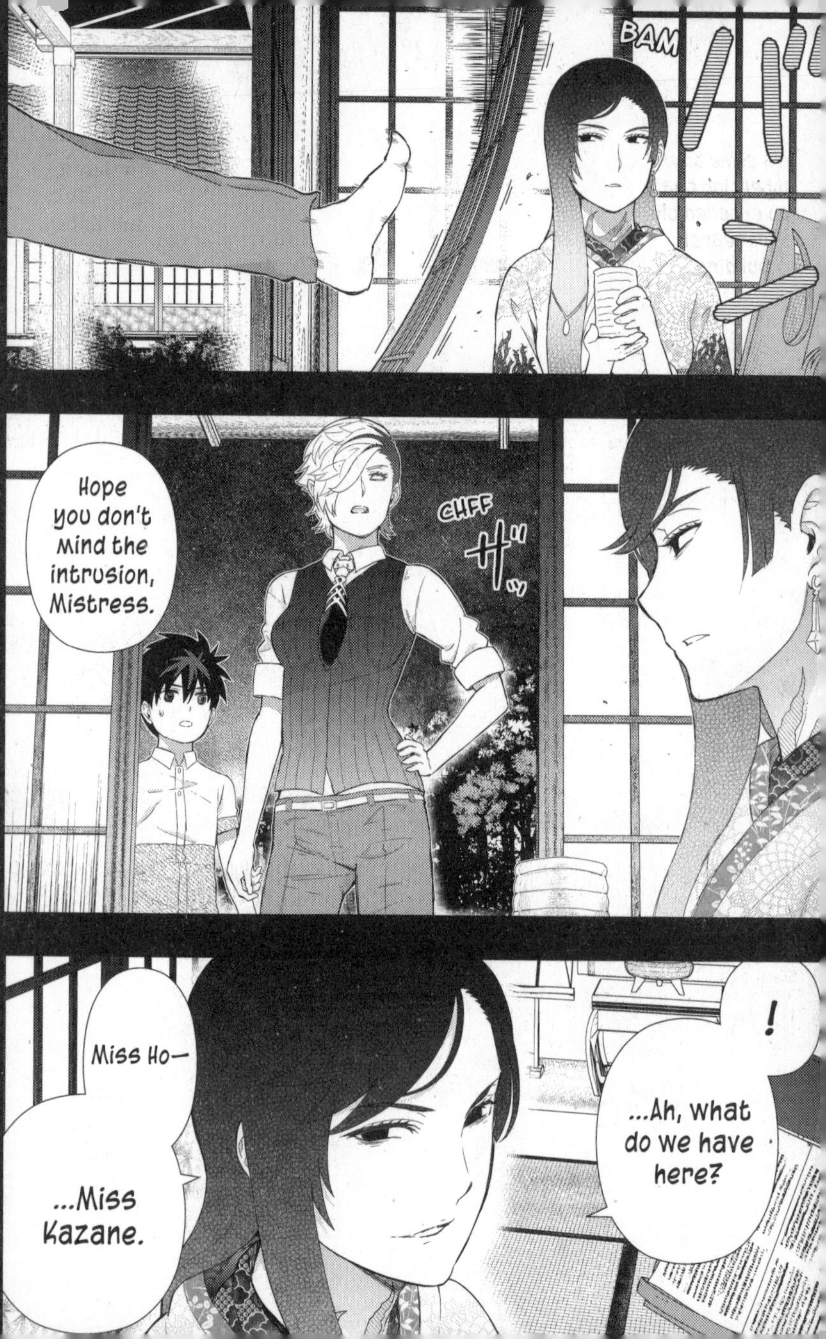
BAM
Hope you don't mind the intrusion, Mistress.
CHFF
!
...Ah, what do we have here?
Miss Ho—
...Miss Kazane.

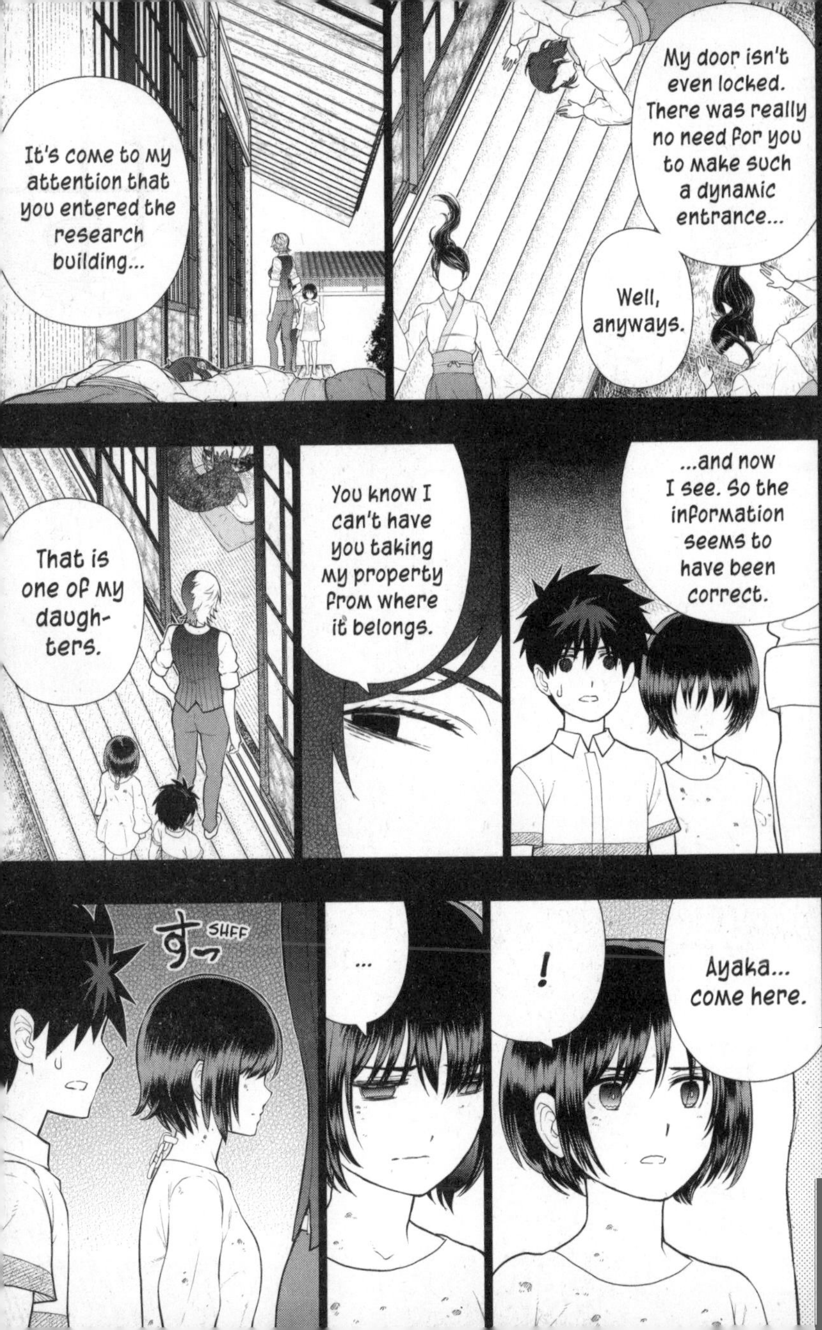
My door isn't even locked. There was really no need for you to make such a dynamic entrance...
Well, anyways.
It's come to my attention that you entered the research building...
...and now I see. So the information seems to have been correct.
You know I can't have you taking my property from where it belongs.
That is one of my daughters.
Ayaka... come here.
!
...
すっ
SHFF

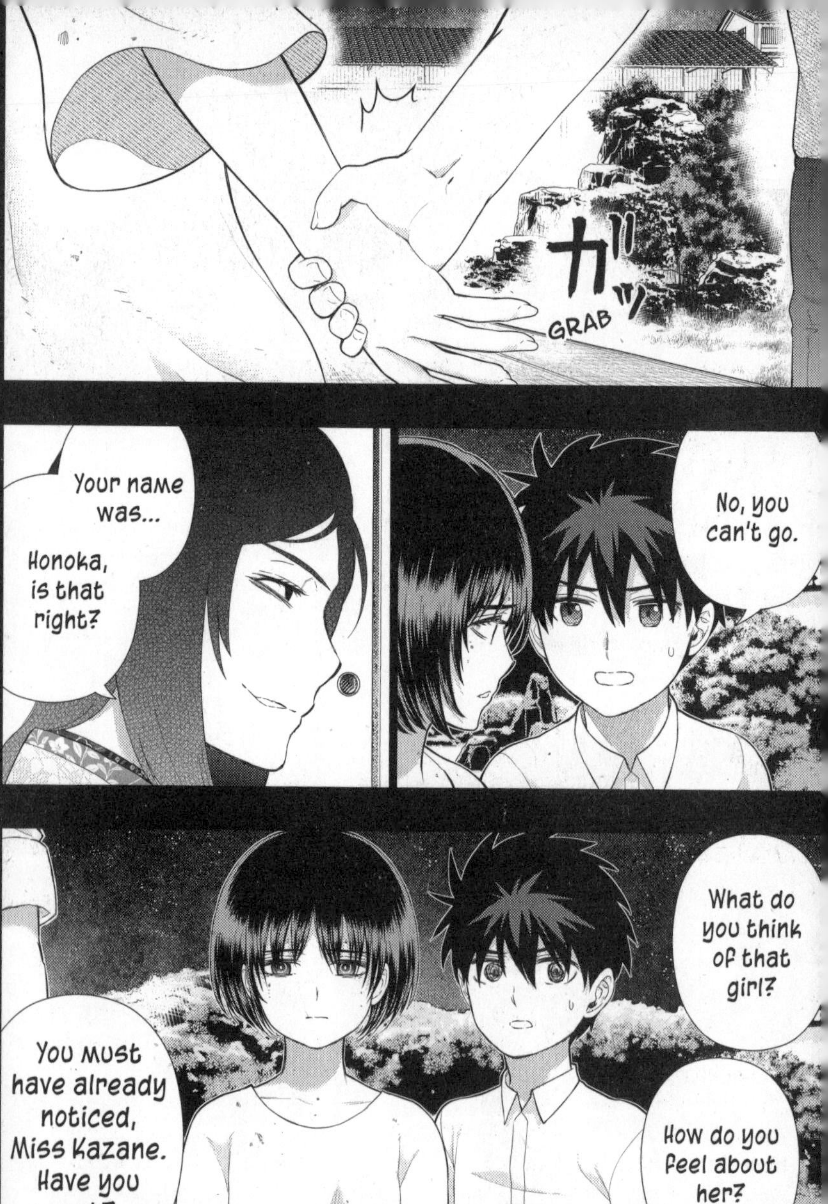
カッ
GRAB
No, you can't go.
Your name was...
Honoka, is that right?
What do you think of that girl?
How do you feel about her?
You must have already noticed, Miss Kazane. Have you not?

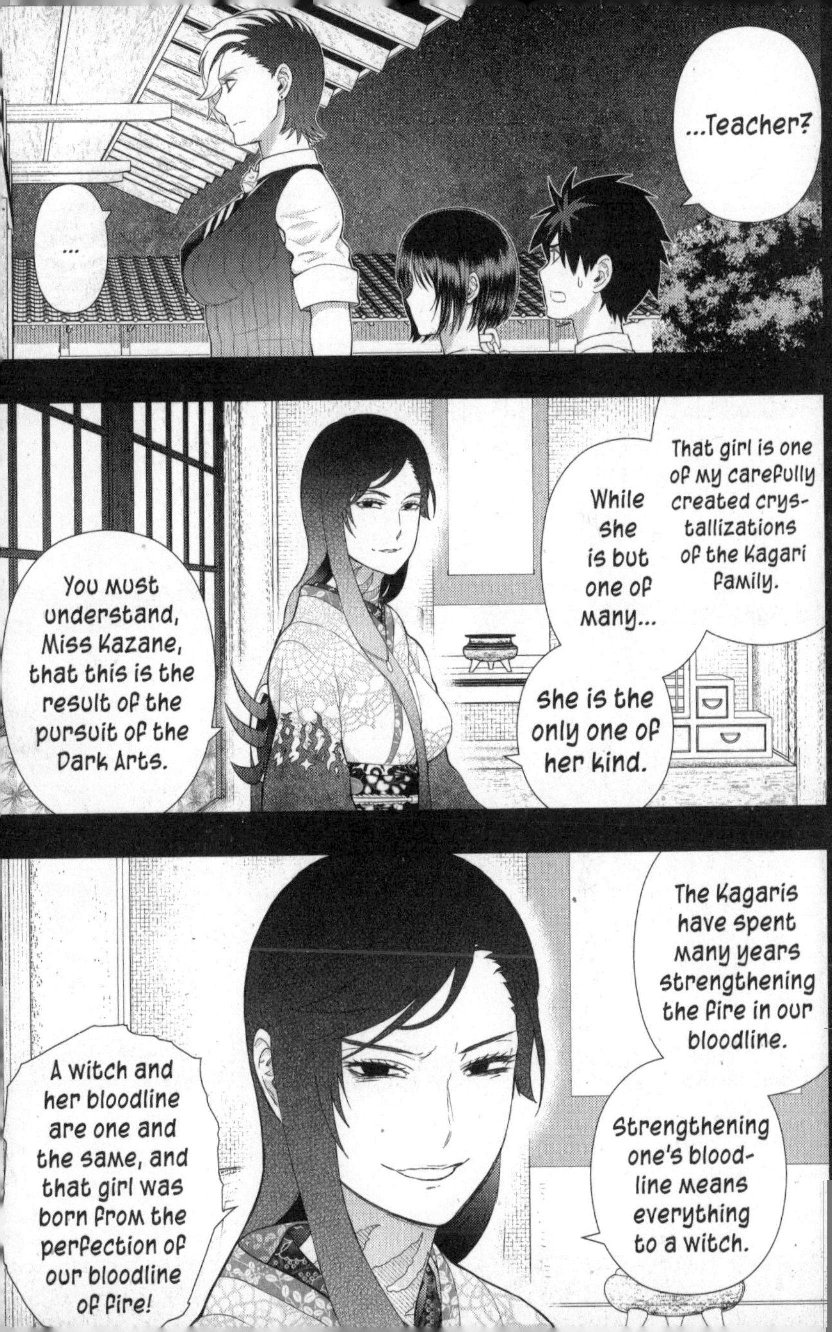
...Teacher?
...
That girl is one of my carefully created crys-tallizations of the Kagari family.
While she is but one of many...
She is the only one of her kind.
You must understand, Miss Kazane, that this is the result of the pursuit of the Dark Arts.
The Kagaris have spent many years strengthening the fire in our bloodline.
Strengthening one's blood-line means everything to a witch.
A witch and her bloodline are one and the same, and that girl was born from the perfection of our bloodline of fire!

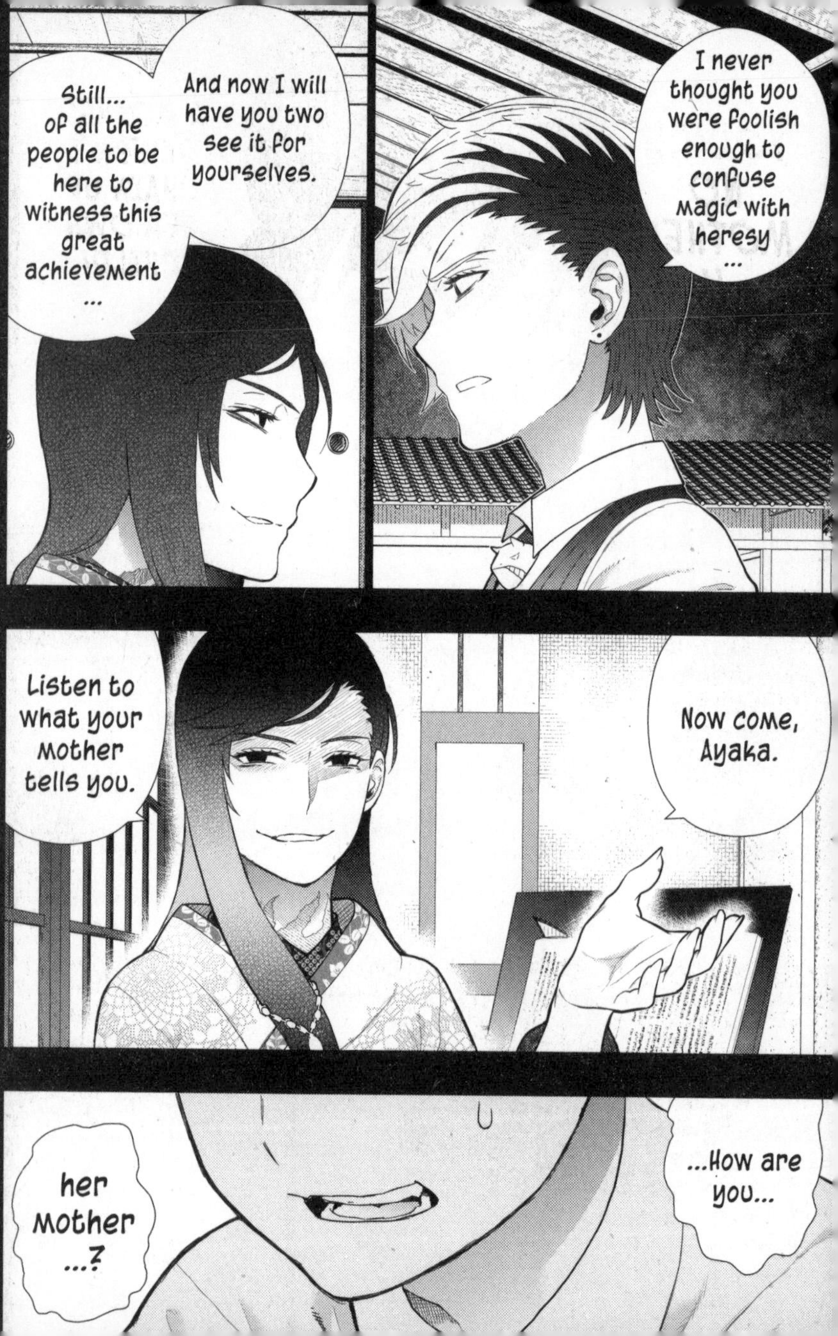
I never thought you were foolish enough to confuse magic with heresy...
And now I will have you two see it for yourselves.
Still... of all the people to be here to witness this great achievement...
Now come, Ayaka.
Listen to what your mother tells you.
...How are you...
her mother ...?

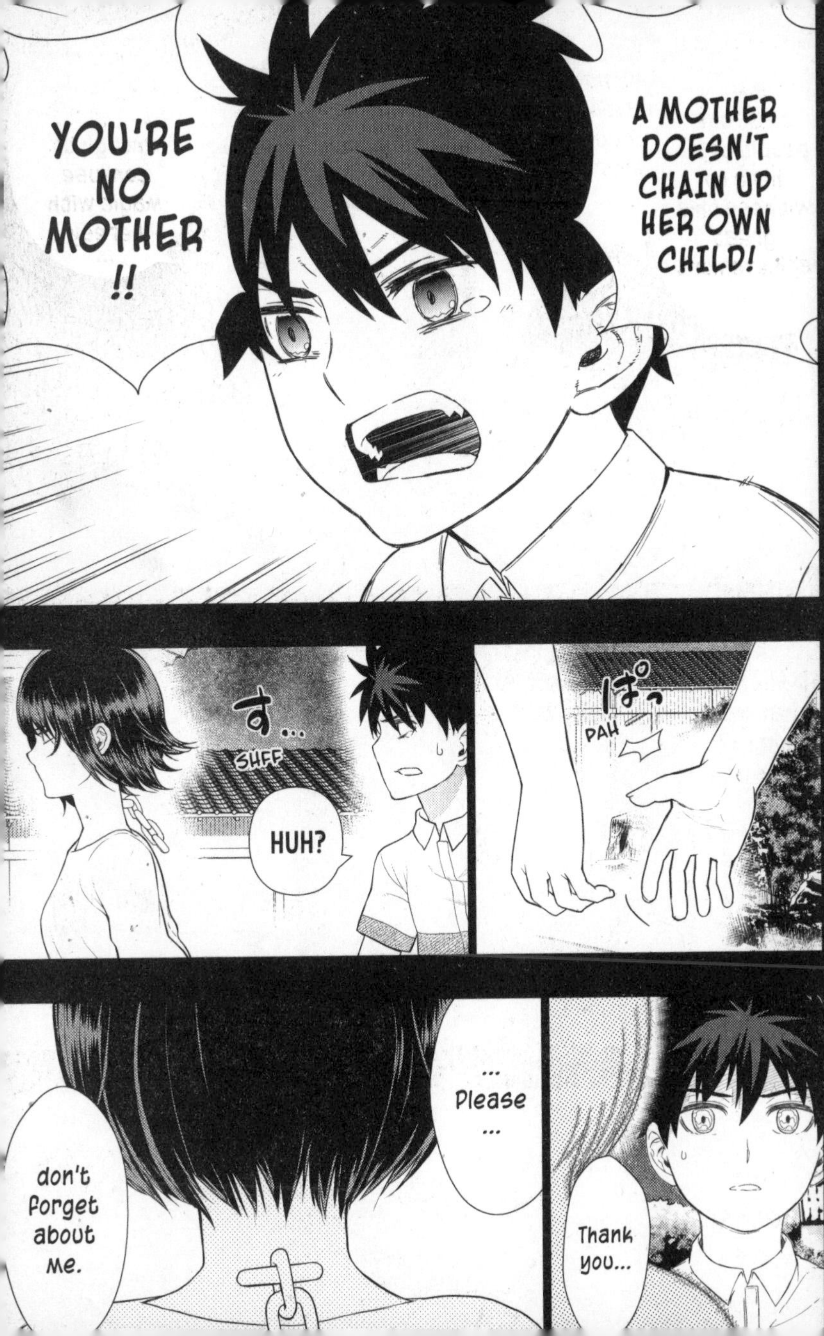
A MOTHER DOESN'T CHAIN UP HER OWN CHILD!
YOU'RE NO MOTHER !!
ぱっ
PAH
す...
SHFF
HUH?
Thank you...
... Please ...
don't forget about me.

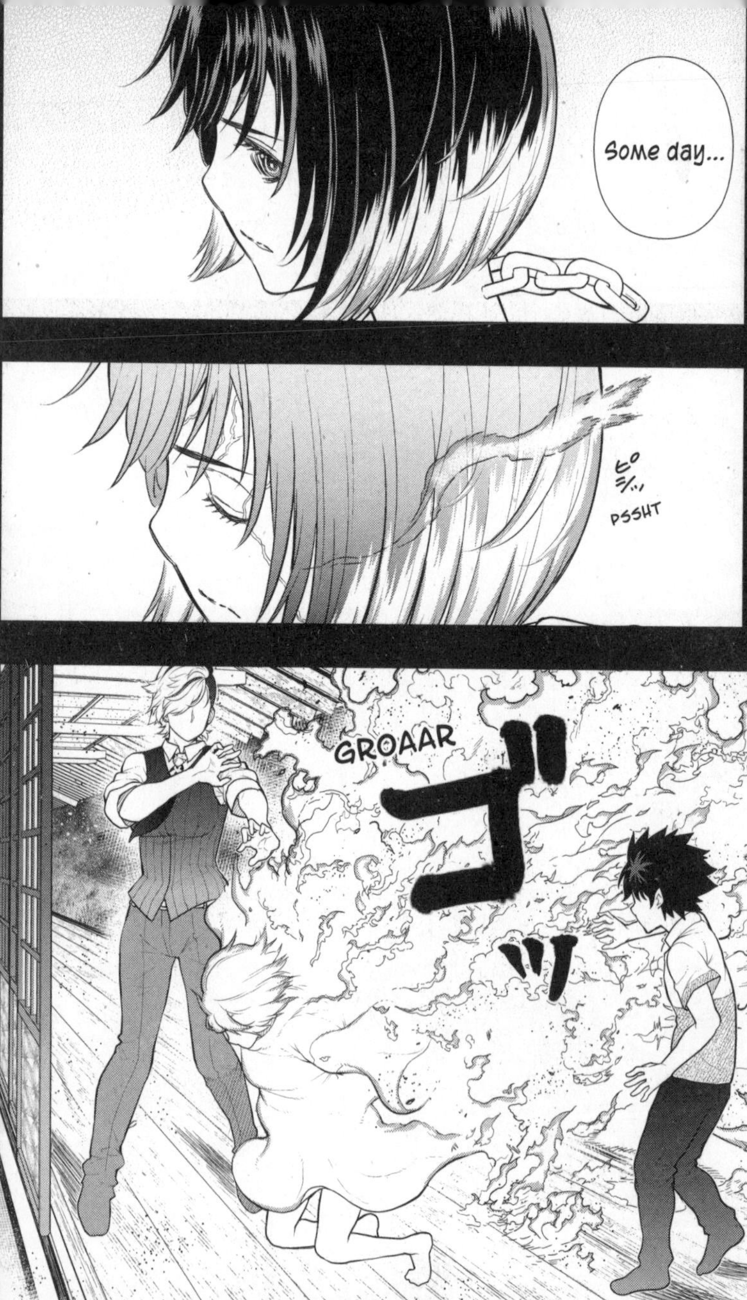
Some day...
ピシッ
PSSHT
ゴッ
GROAAR

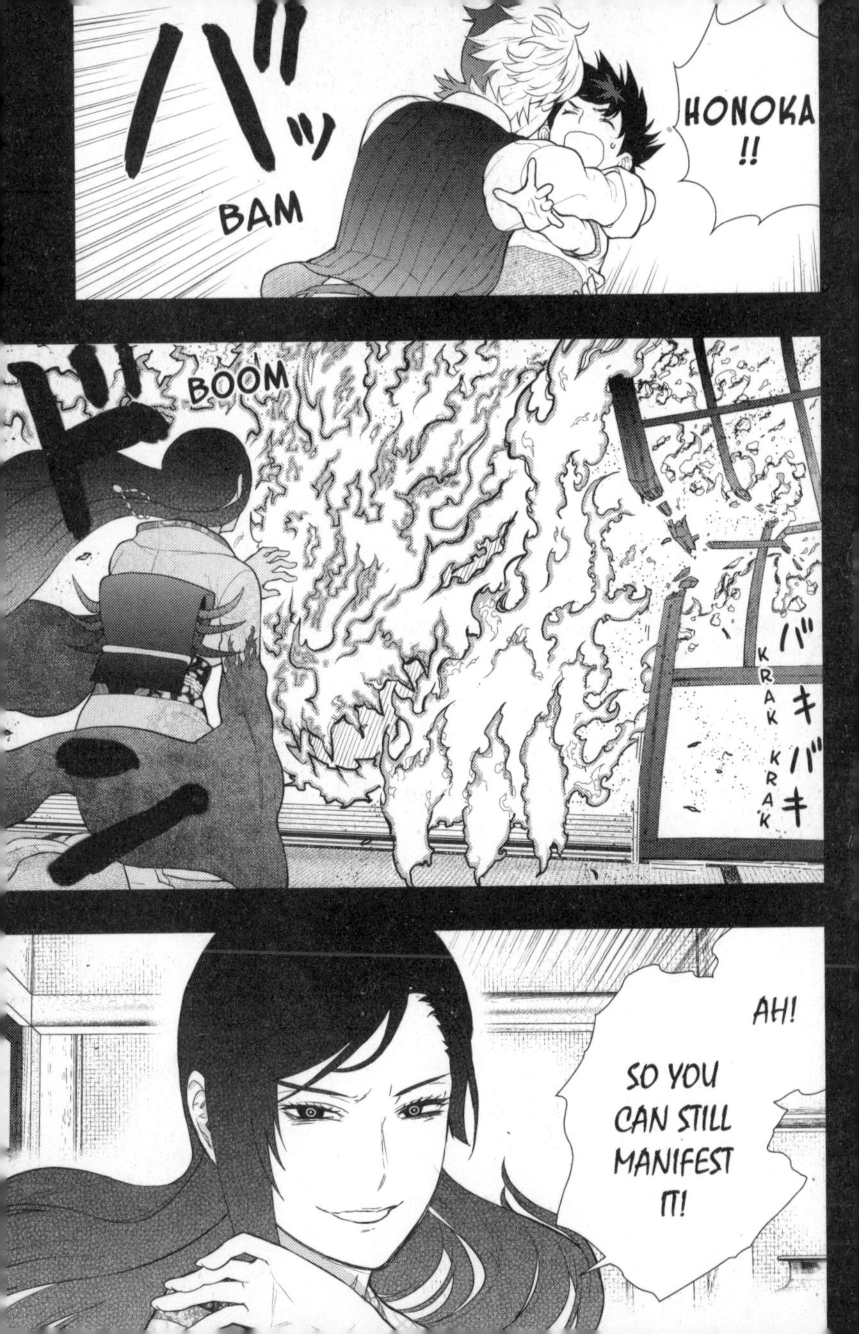
HONOKA !!
バッ
BAM
バキバキ
KRAK KRAK
ドッ
BOOM
AH!
SO YOU CAN STILL MANIFEST IT!

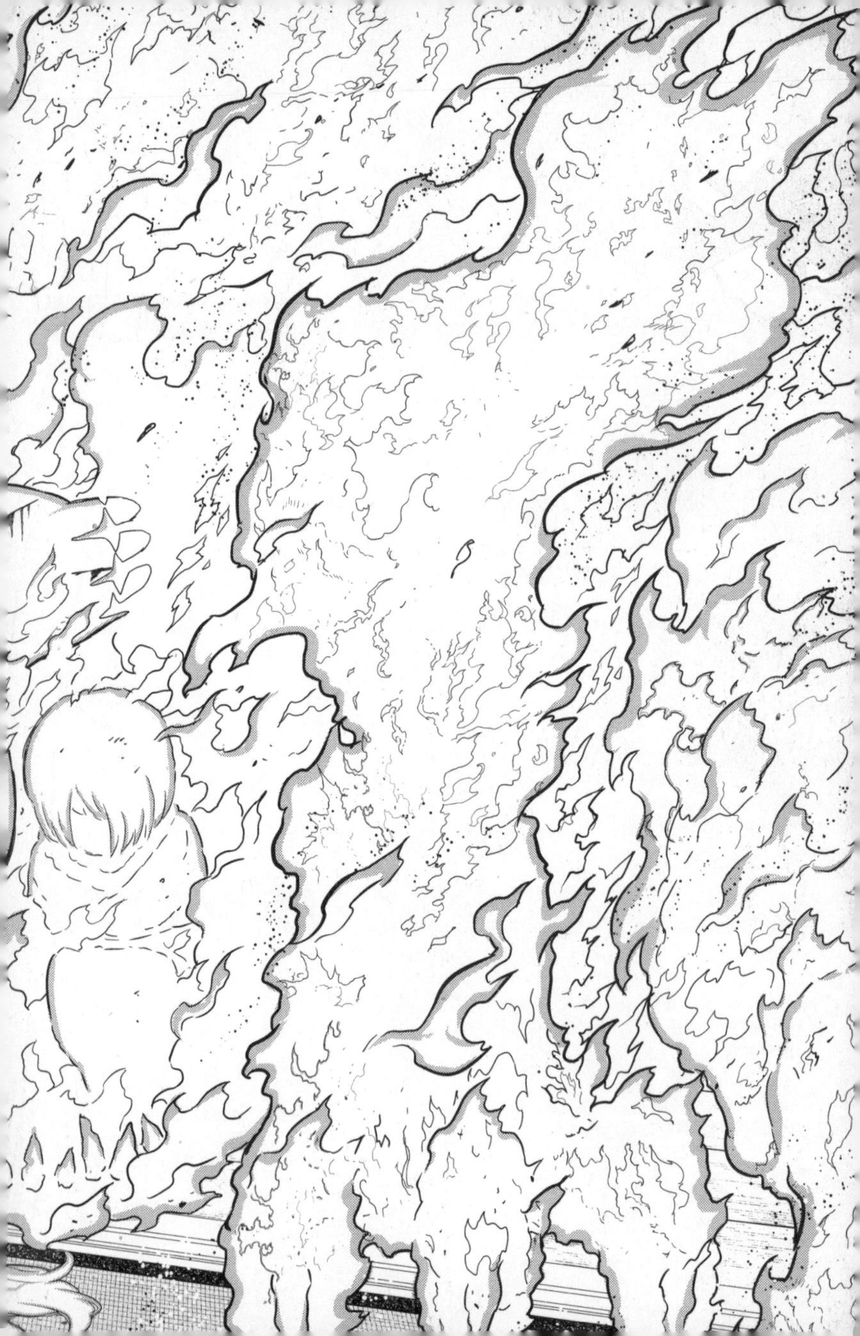

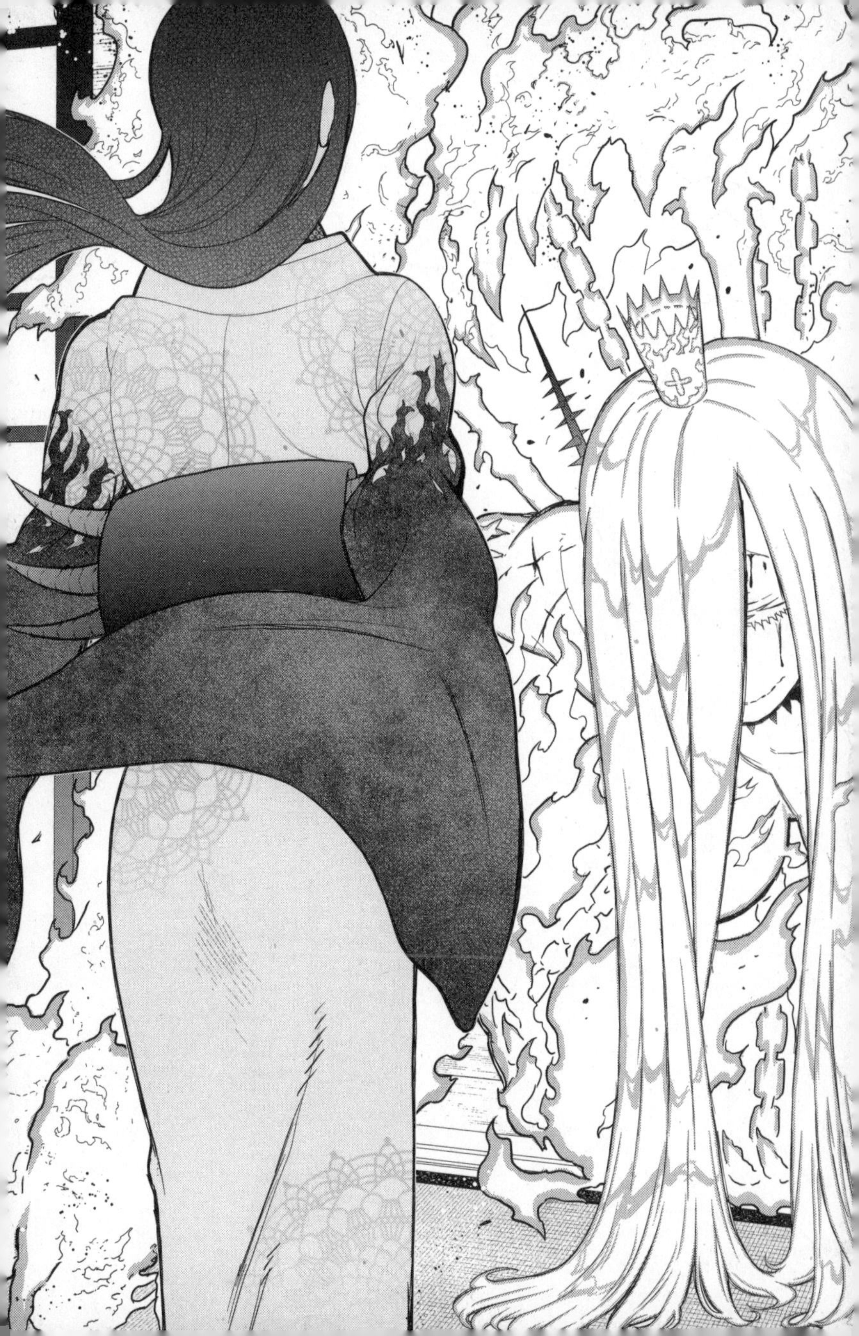

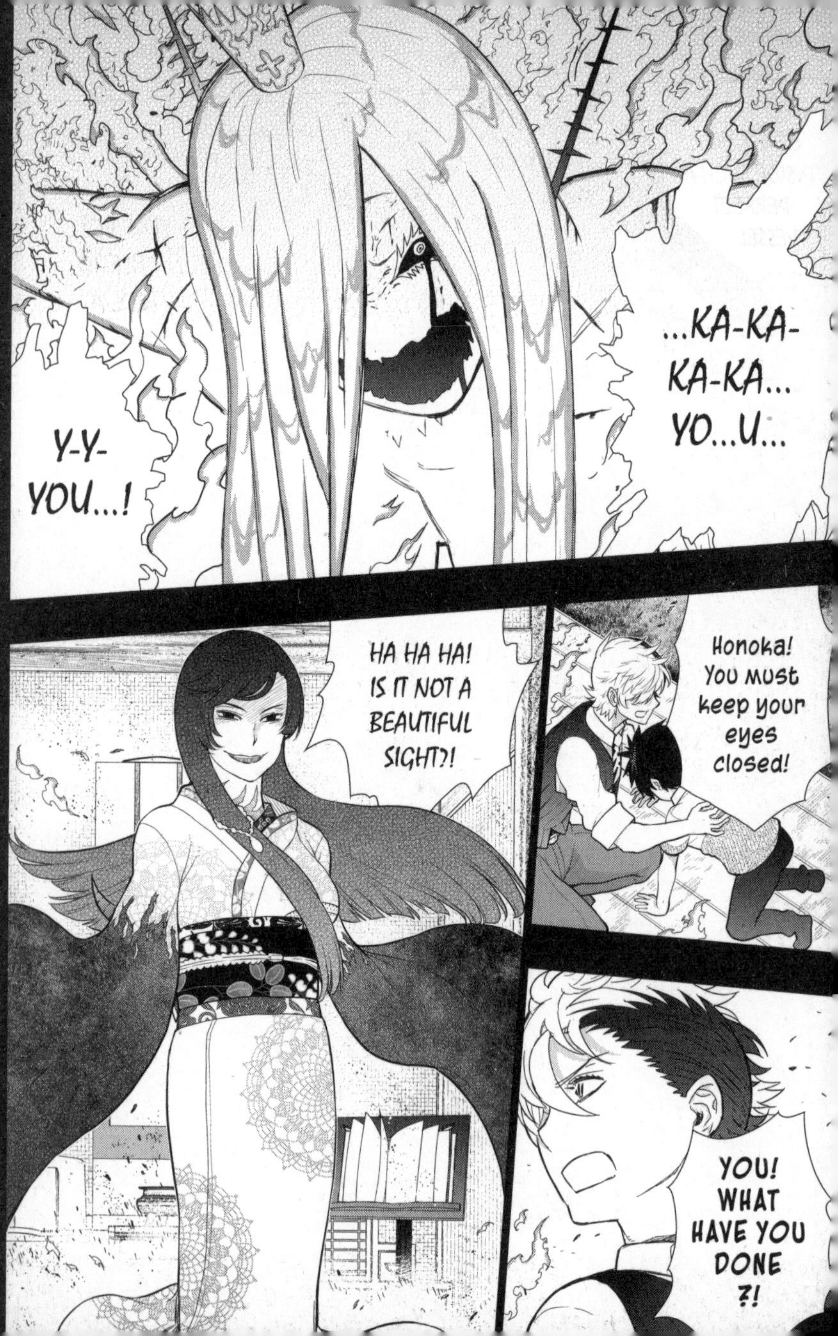
...KA-KA-KA-KA... YO...U...
Y-Y-YOU...!
Honoka! You must keep your eyes closed!
YOU! WHAT HAVE YOU DONE?!
HA HA HA! IS IT NOT A BEAUTIFUL SIGHT?!

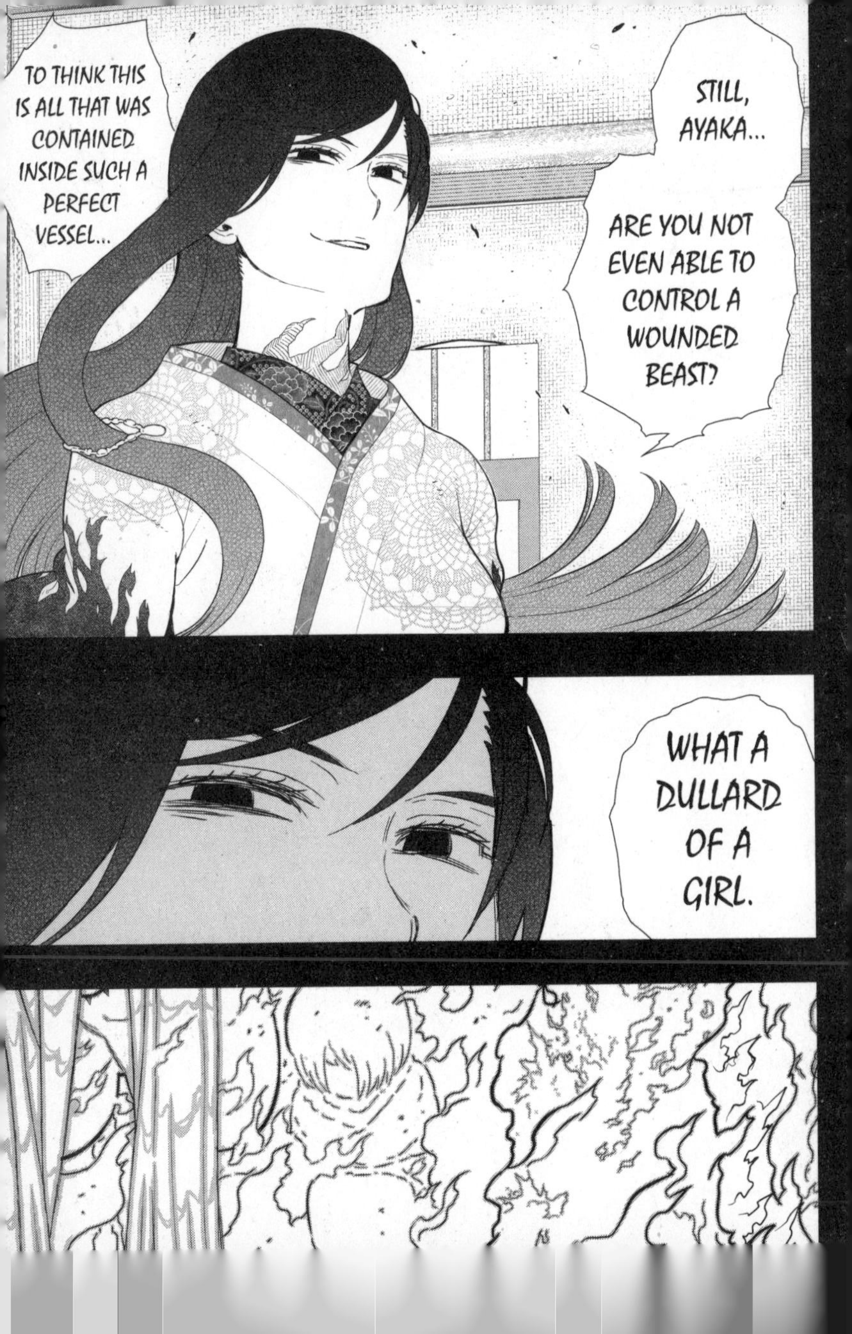
STILL, AYAKA...
ARE YOU NOT EVEN ABLE TO CONTROL A WOUNDED BEAST?
TO THINK THIS IS ALL THAT WAS CONTAINED INSIDE SUCH A PERFECT VESSEL...
WHAT A DULLARD OF A GIRL.

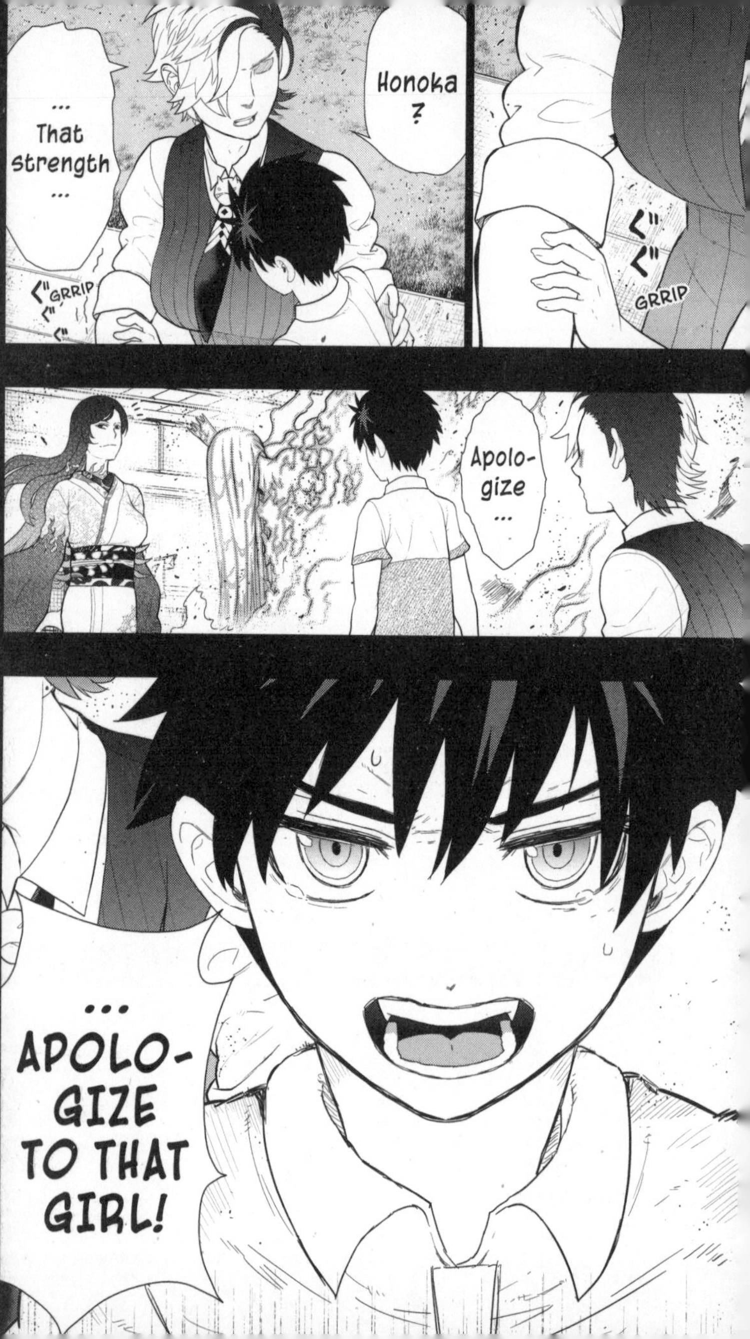
ぐ"
ぐ"
GRRIP
Honoka?
... That strength ...
ぐ" ぐ" ぐ" GRRIP
Apolo-gize ...
... APOLO-GIZE TO THAT GIRL!

CHAPTER 55 END

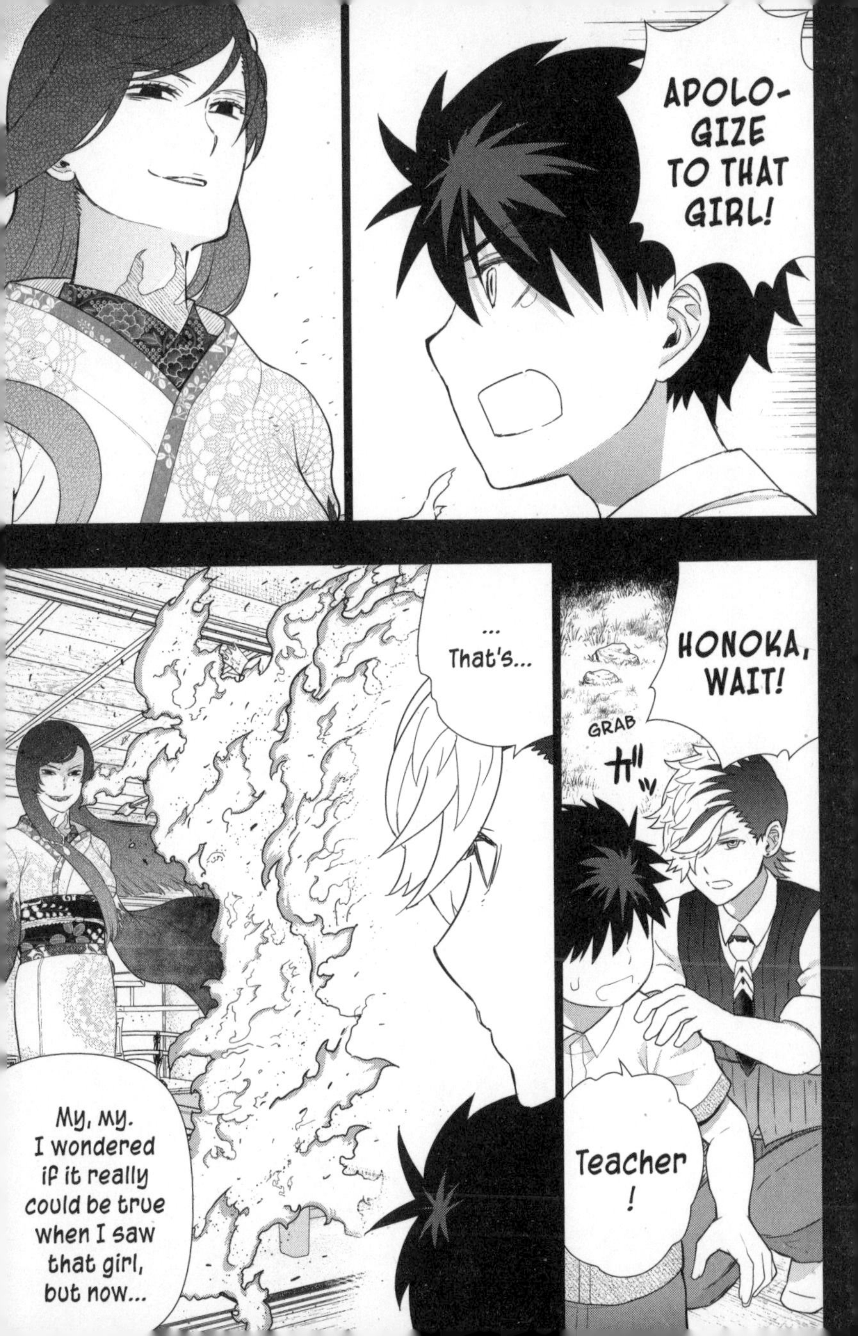
APOLO-GIZE TO THAT GIRL!
HONOKA, WAIT!
GRAB
ガッ
Teacher!
... That's...
My, my. I wondered if it really could be true when I saw that girl, but now...

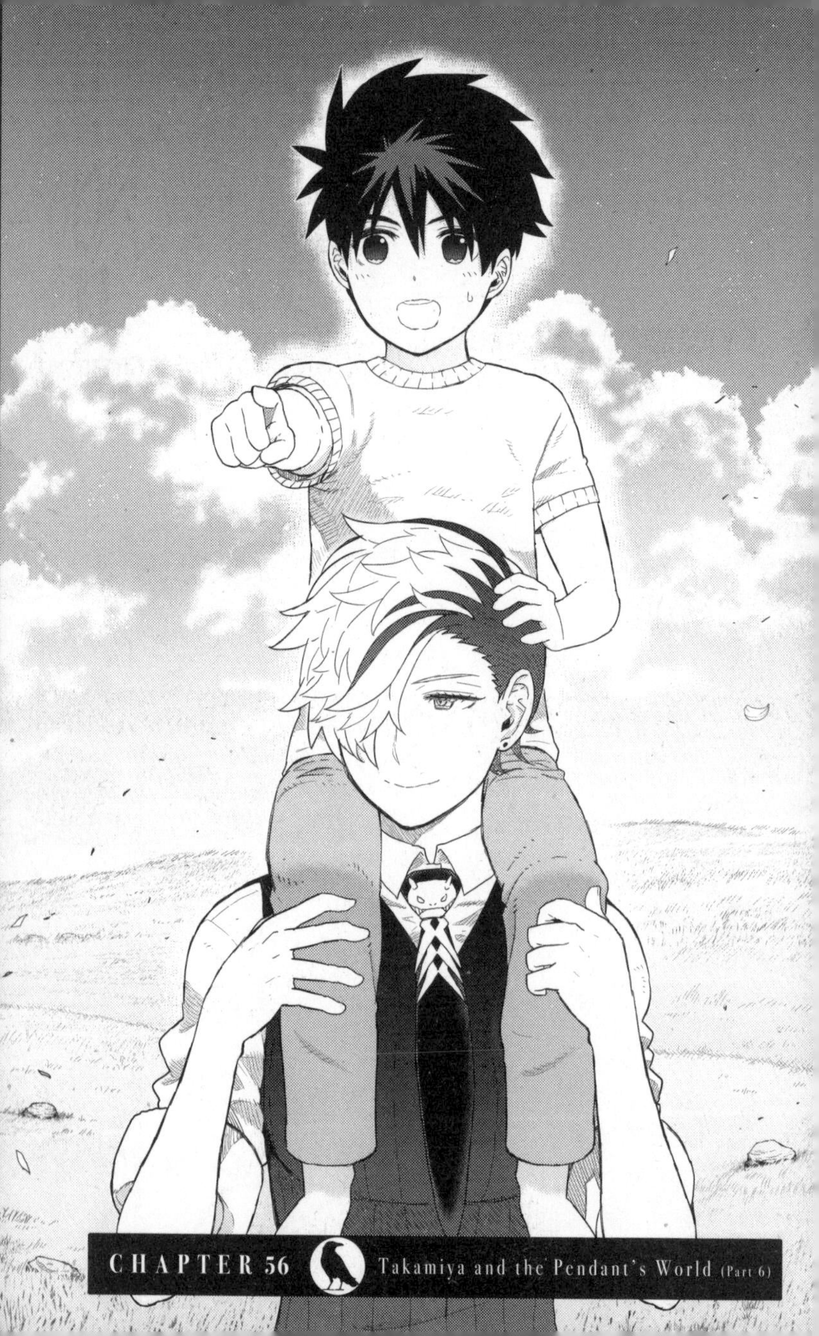

CHAPTER 56 Takamiya and the Pendant's World (Part 6)

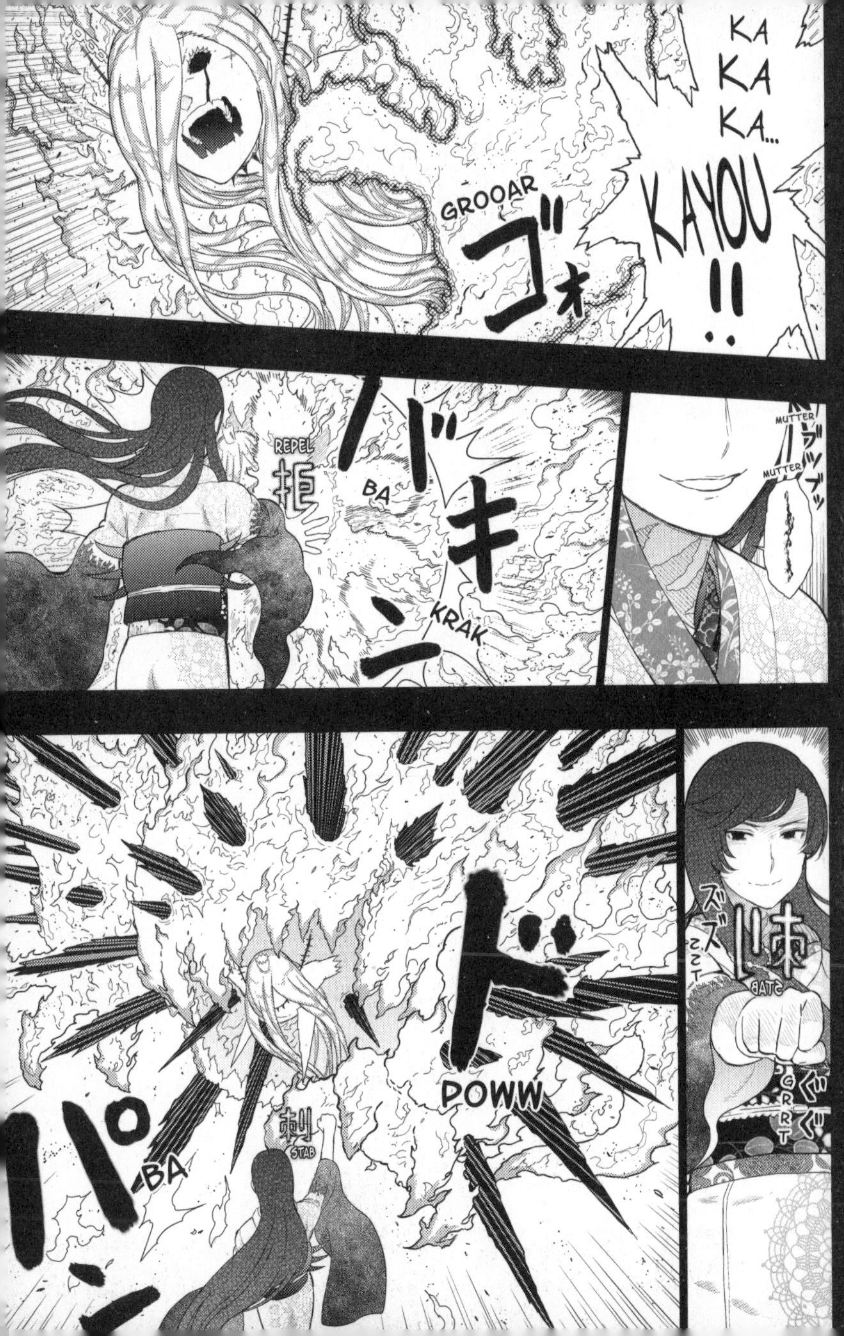
KA
KA
KA...
KAYOU!!
GROOAR
MUTTER
MUTTER
BA
KRAK
REPEL
拒
STAB
ZZT
GRRT
POWW
BA
刺
STAB

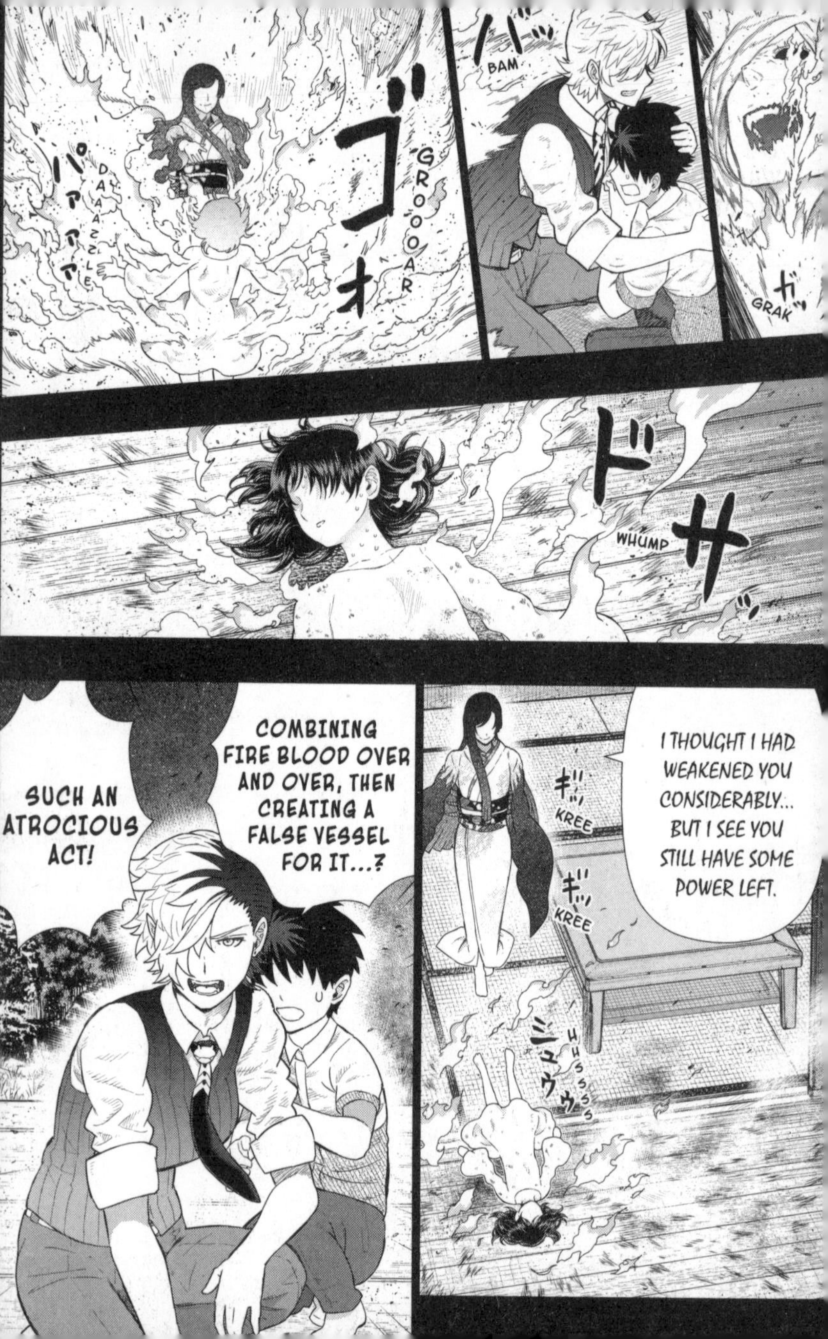
ガッ
GRAK
バッ
BAM
パアア
DAAAZZLE
ゴオ
GROOOAR
ドサッ
WHUMP
I THOUGHT I HAD WEAKENED YOU CONSIDERABLY... BUT I SEE YOU STILL HAVE SOME POWER LEFT.
ギッ
KREE
ギッ
KREE
ジュウウ
HHSSSS
COMBINING FIRE BLOOD OVER AND OVER, THEN CREATING A FALSE VESSEL FOR IT...?
SUCH AN ATROCIOUS ACT!

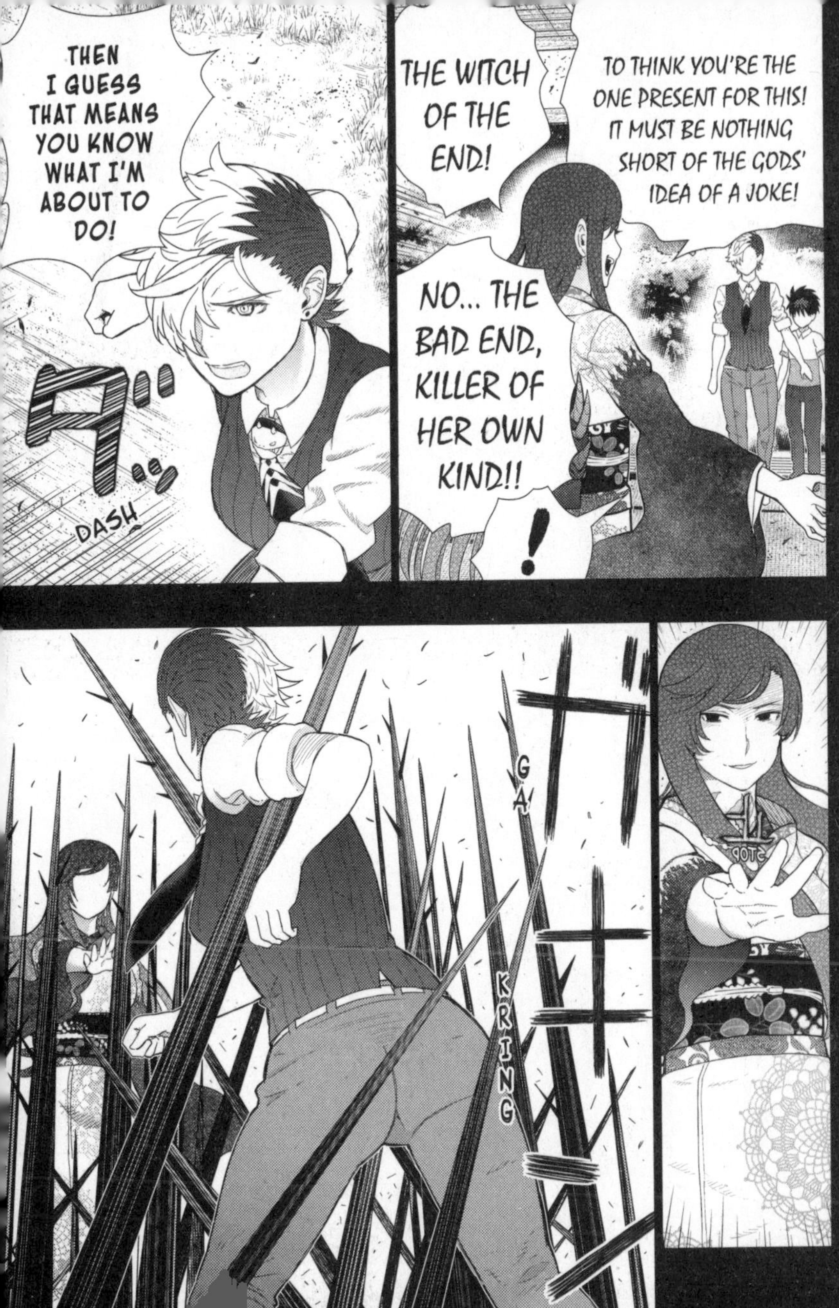
TO THINK YOU'RE THE ONE PRESENT FOR THIS! IT MUST BE NOTHING SHORT OF THE GODS' IDEA OF A JOKE!
THE WITCH OF THE END!
NO... THE BAD END, KILLER OF HER OWN KIND!!
!
THEN I GUESS THAT MEANS YOU KNOW WHAT I'M ABOUT TO DO!
DASH
GA
KRING

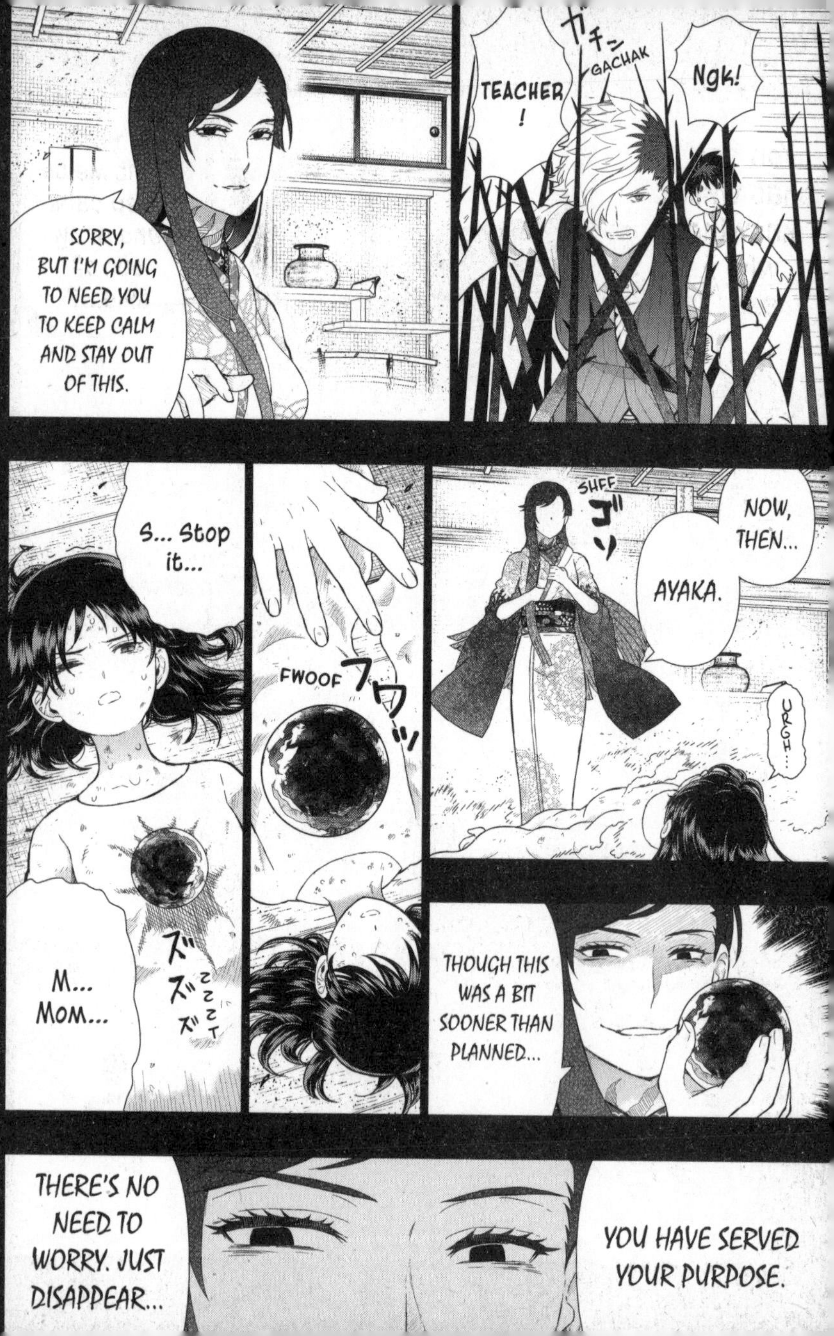
Ngk!
ガチン
GACHAK
TEACHER!
SORRY, BUT I'M GOING TO NEED YOU TO KEEP CALM AND STAY OUT OF THIS.
NOW, THEN...
SHFF
ゴソ
AYAKA.
URGH...
THOUGH THIS WAS A BIT SOONER THAN PLANNED...
FWOOF
フワーッ
S... Stop it...
ズズズ
ZZZT
M... MOM...
YOU HAVE SERVED YOUR PURPOSE.
THERE'S NO NEED TO WORRY. JUST DISAPPEAR...

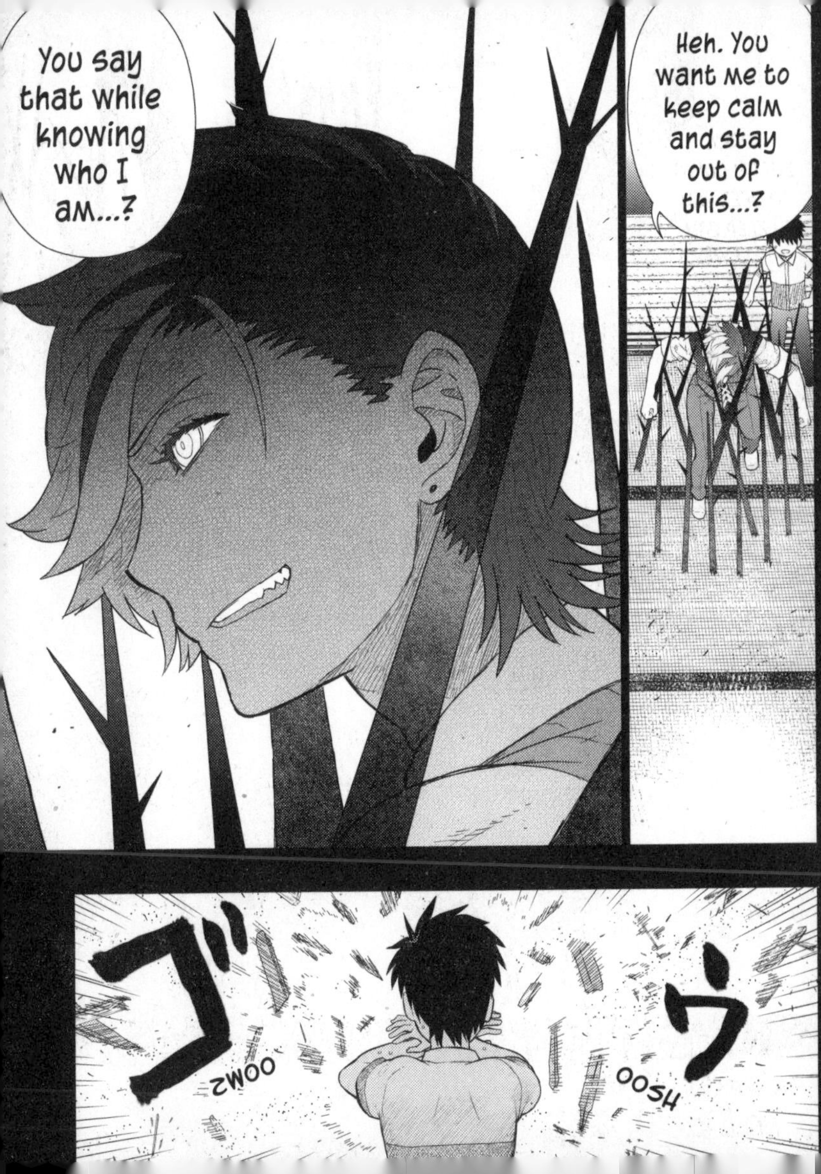
Heh. You want me to keep calm and stay out of this...?
You say that while knowing who I am...?
ゴウ
ZWOO
OOSH

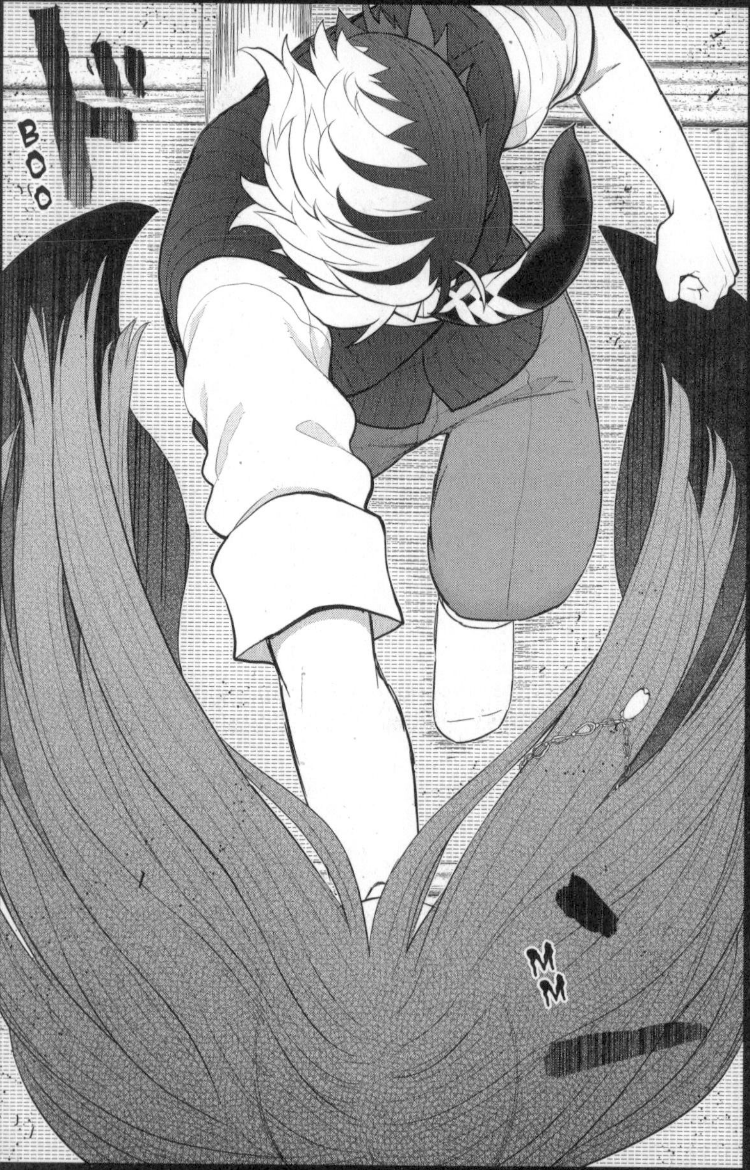
BOO
MM

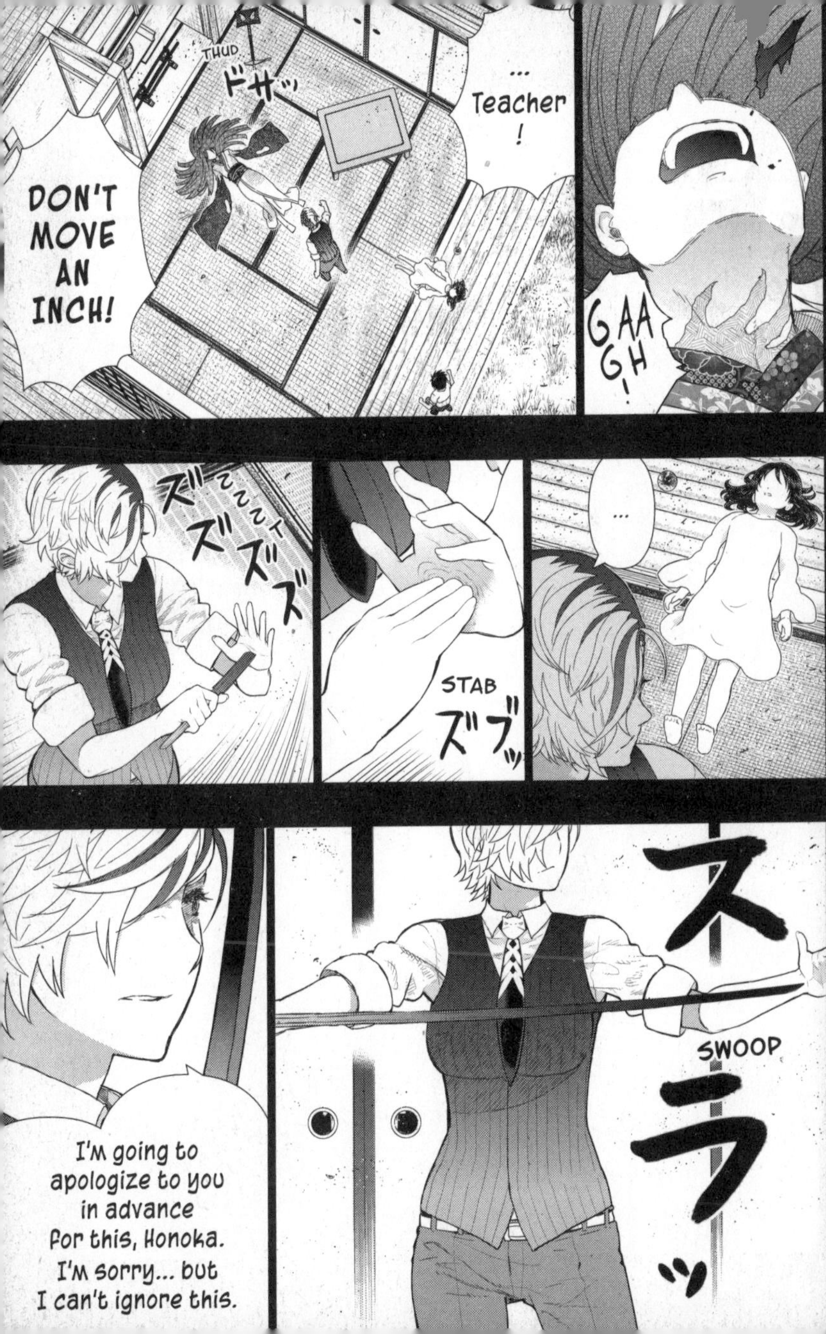
GAAGH!
...Teacher!
THUD
ドサッ
DON'T MOVE AN INCH!
...
STAB
ズブッ
ズズズズ
スラッ
SWOOP
I'm going to apologize to you in advance for this, Honoka. I'm sorry... but I can't ignore this.

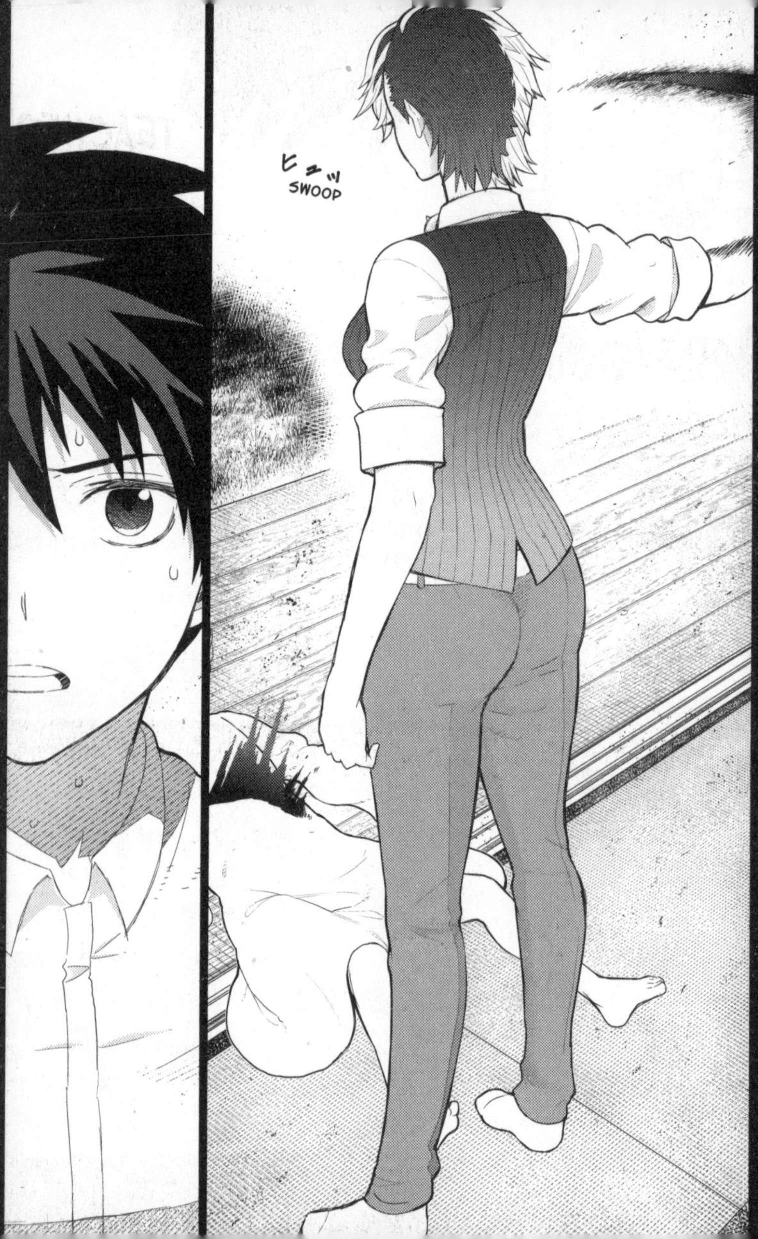
ヒュッ
SWOOP

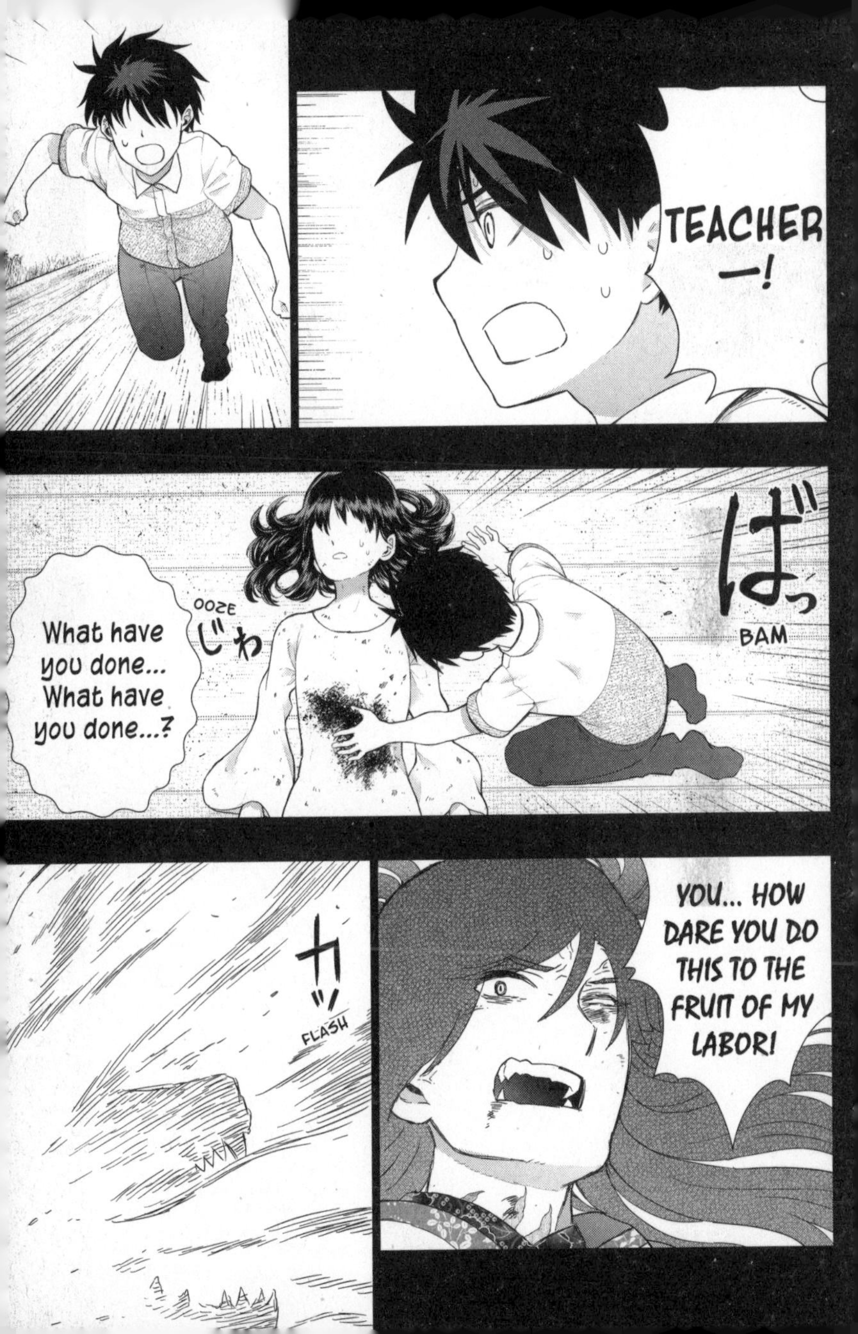
TEACHER —!
ばっ
BAM
じわ
OOZE
What have you done... What have you done...?
YOU... HOW DARE YOU DO THIS TO THE FRUIT OF MY LABOR!
カッ
FLASH

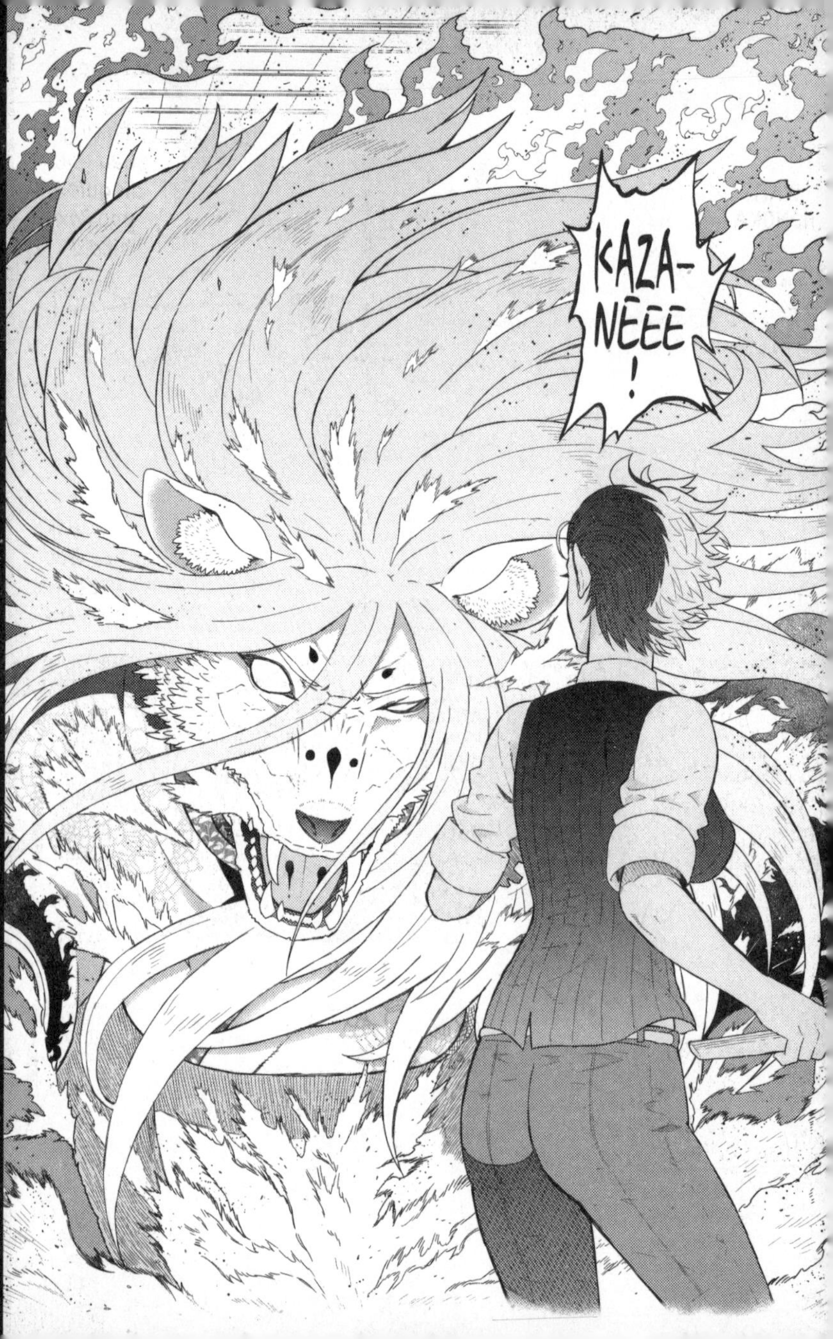
KAZA-NEEE!

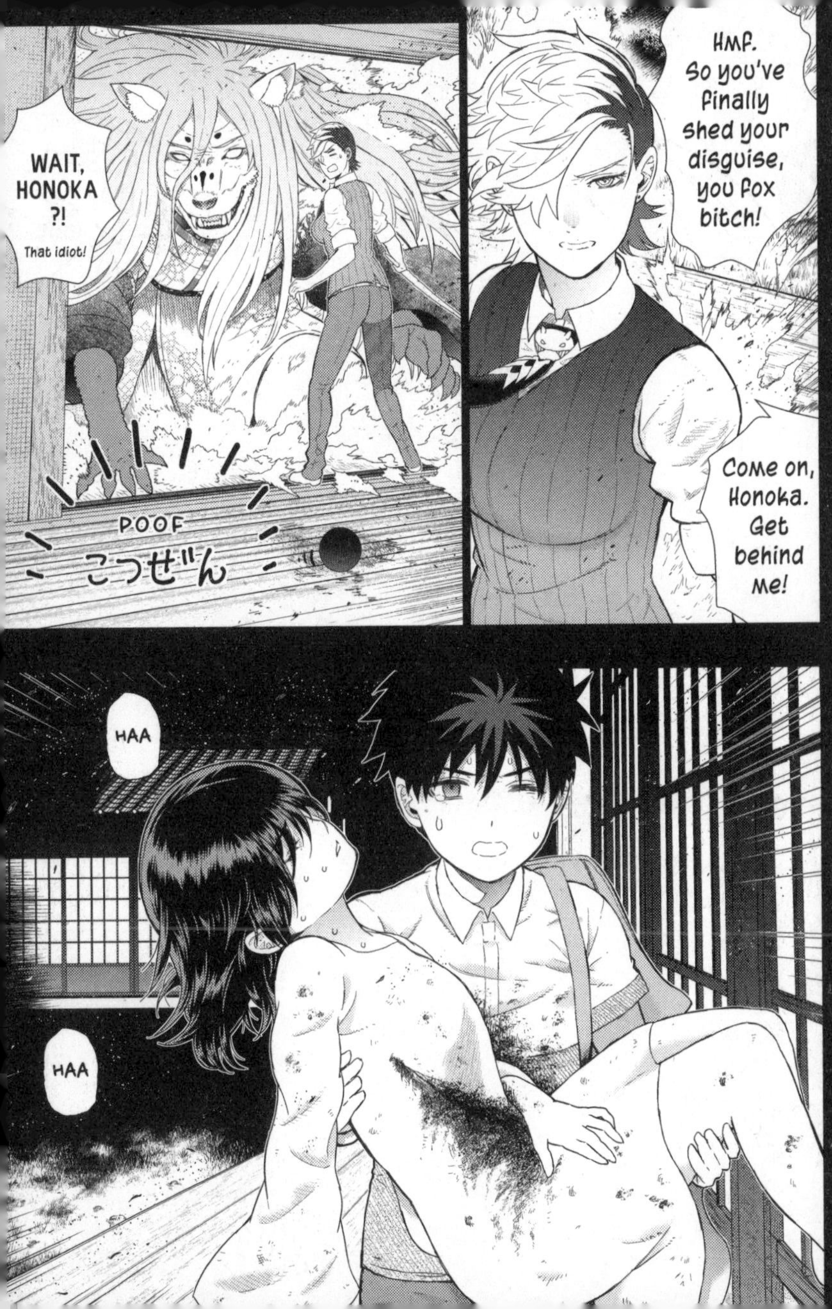
Hmf. So you've finally shed your disguise, you fox bitch!
Come on, Honoka. Get behind me!
WAIT, HONOKA ?!
That idiot!
POOF
こつぜん
HAA
HAA

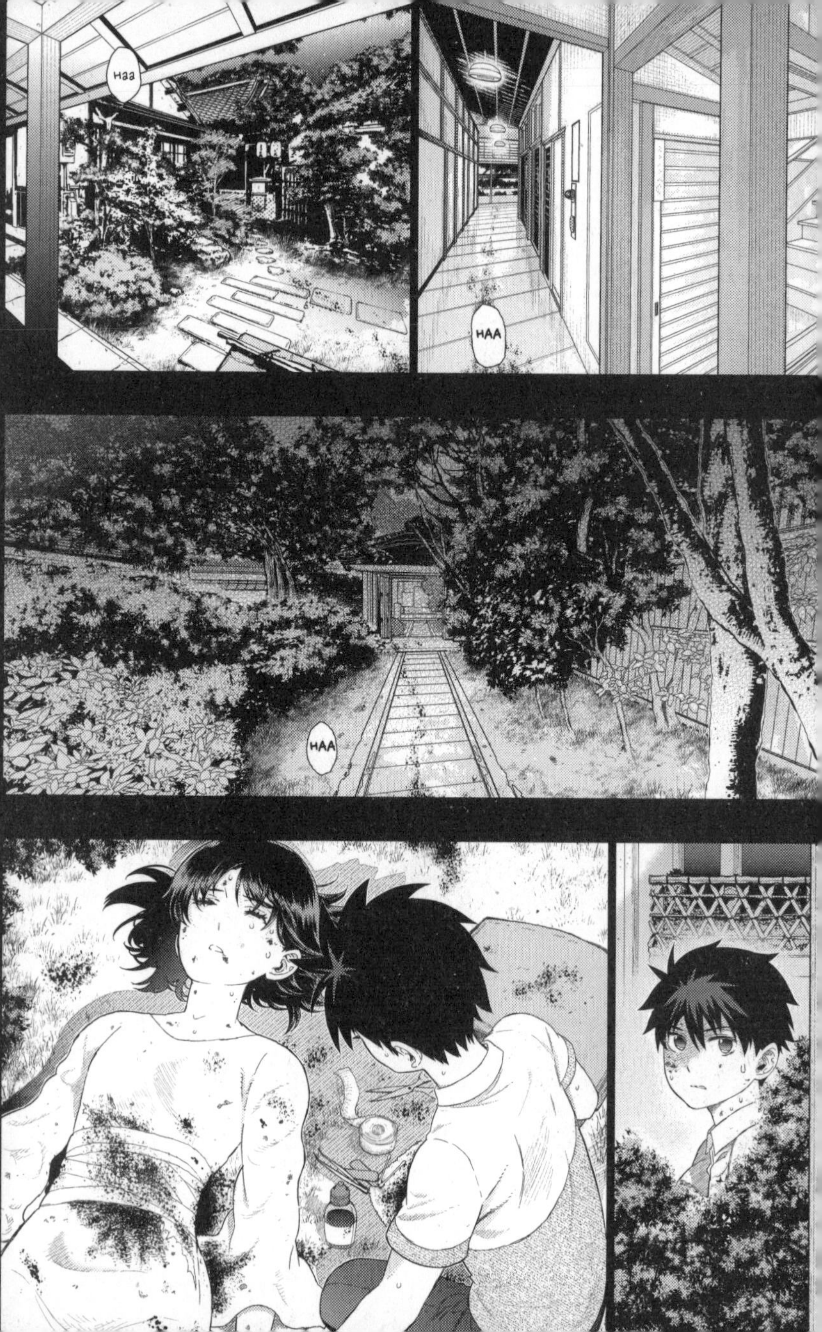
HAA
Haa
HAA

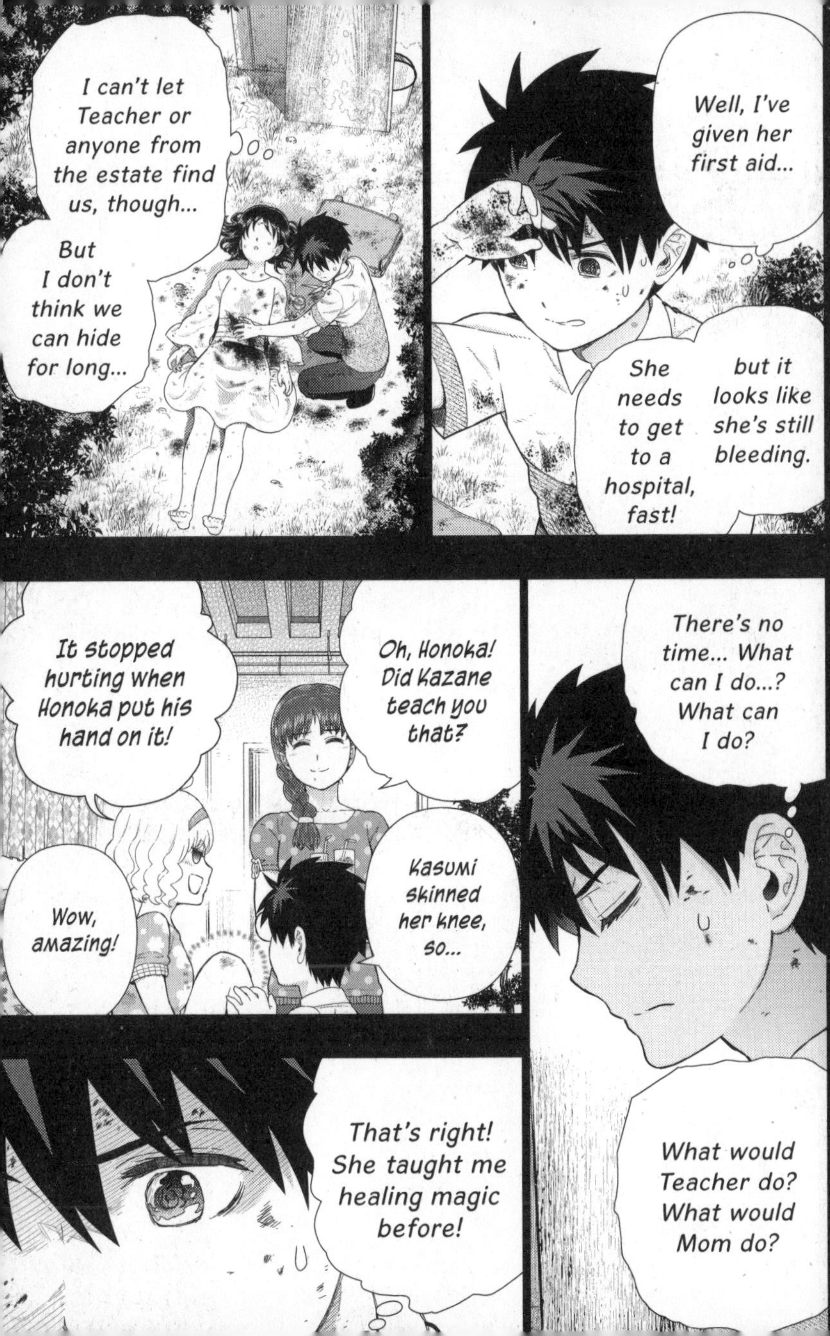
Well, I've given her first aid...
but it looks like she's still bleeding.
She needs to get to a hospital, fast!
I can't let Teacher or anyone from the estate find us, though...
But I don't think we can hide for long...
There's no time... What can I do...? What can I do?
What would Teacher do? What would Mom do?
Oh, Honoka! Did Kazane teach you that?
It stopped hurting when Honoka put his hand on it!
Kasumi skinned her knee, so...
Wow, amazing!
That's right! She taught me healing magic before!

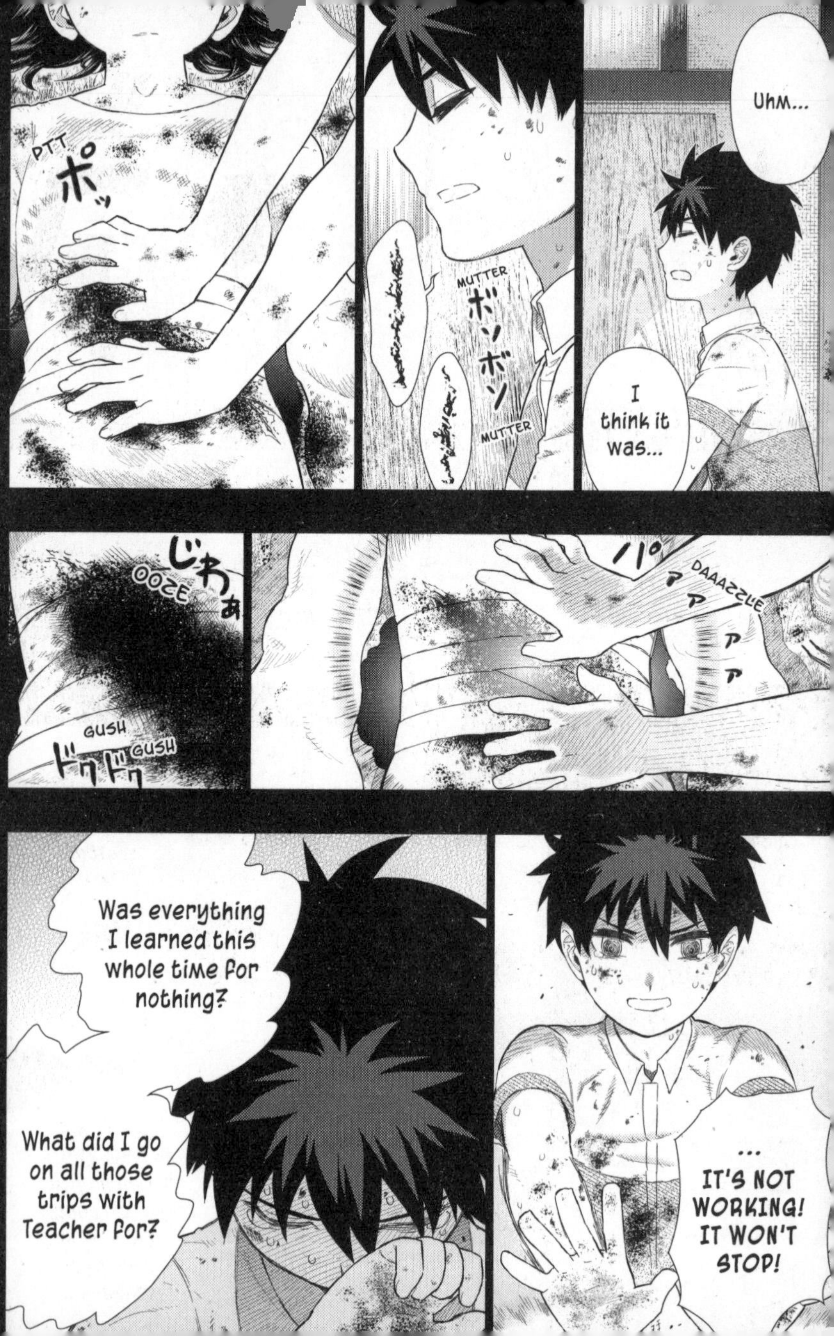
Uhm...
I think it was...
MUTTER
ボソボソ
MUTTER
PTT
ポッ
DAAAZZLE
パアアア
OOZE
じわあ
GUSH
GUSH
ドクドク
... IT'S NOT WORKING! IT WON'T STOP!
Was everything I learned this whole time for nothing?
What did I go on all those trips with Teacher for?

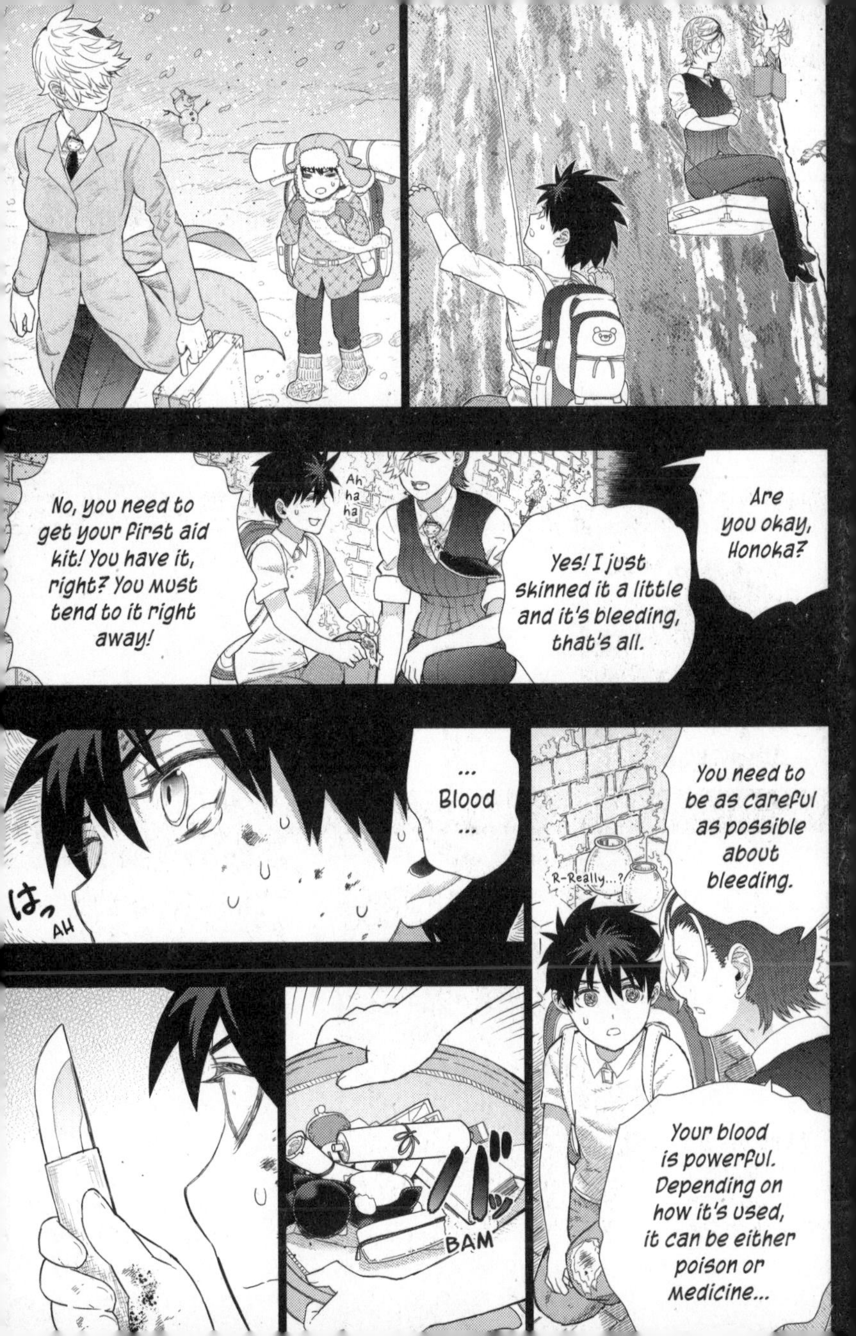
Are you okay, Honoka?
Yes! I just skinned it a little and it's bleeding, that's all.
Ah ha ha
No, you need to get your first aid kit! You have it, right? You must tend to it right away!
You need to be as careful as possible about bleeding.
R-Really...?
Your blood is powerful. Depending on how it's used, it can be either poison or medicine...
... Blood ...
はっ
AH
BAM

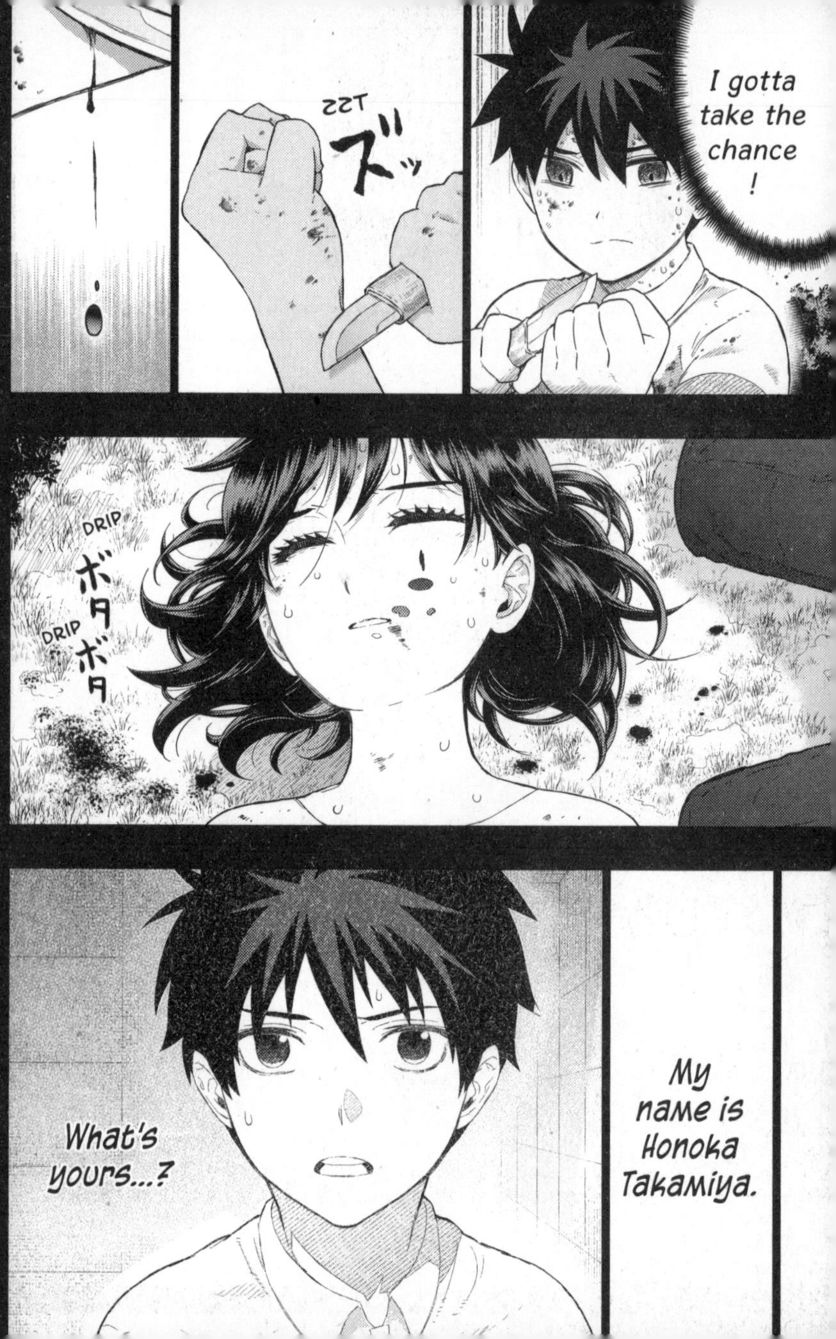
I gotta take the chance!
ZZT
ズッ
DRIP
ボタ
DRIP
ボタ
My name is Honoka Takamiya.
What's yours...?

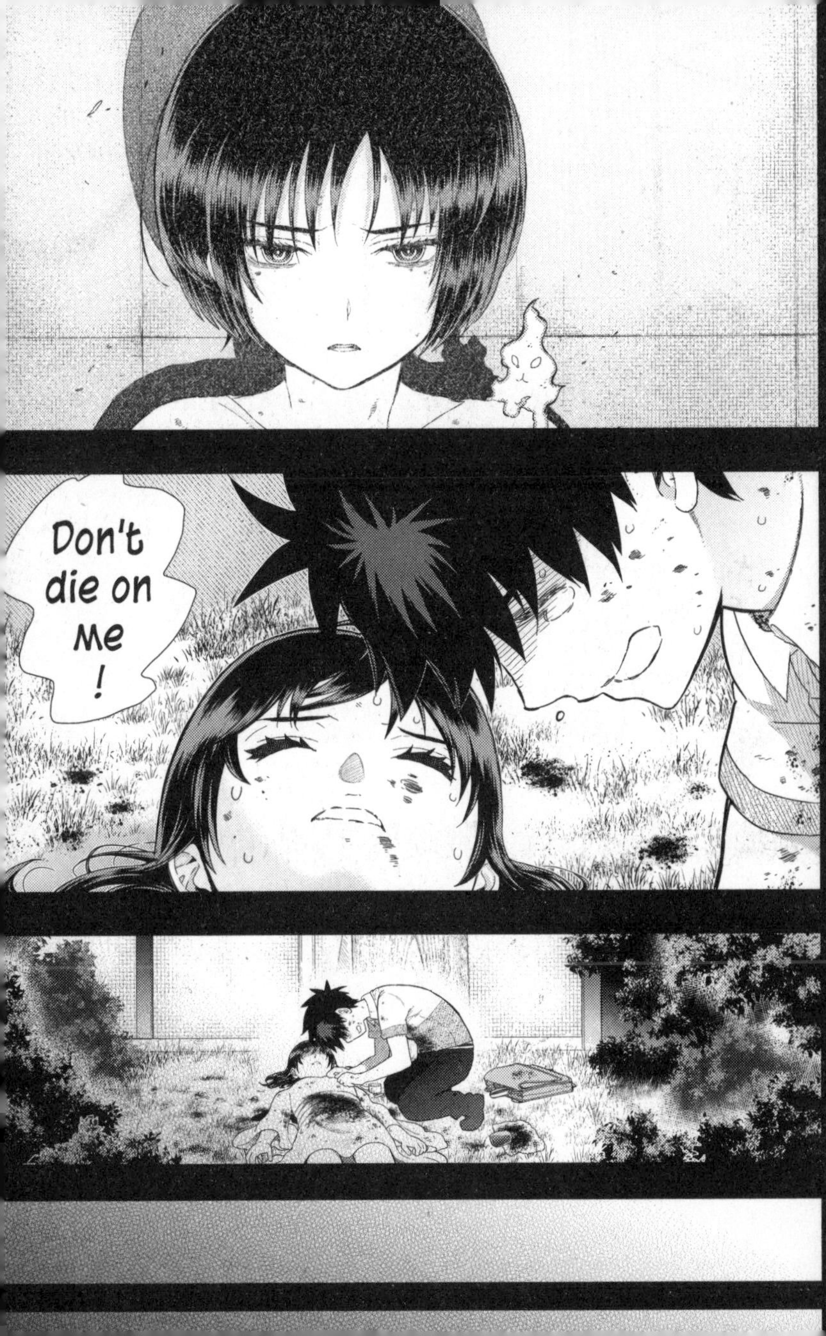
Don't die on Me !

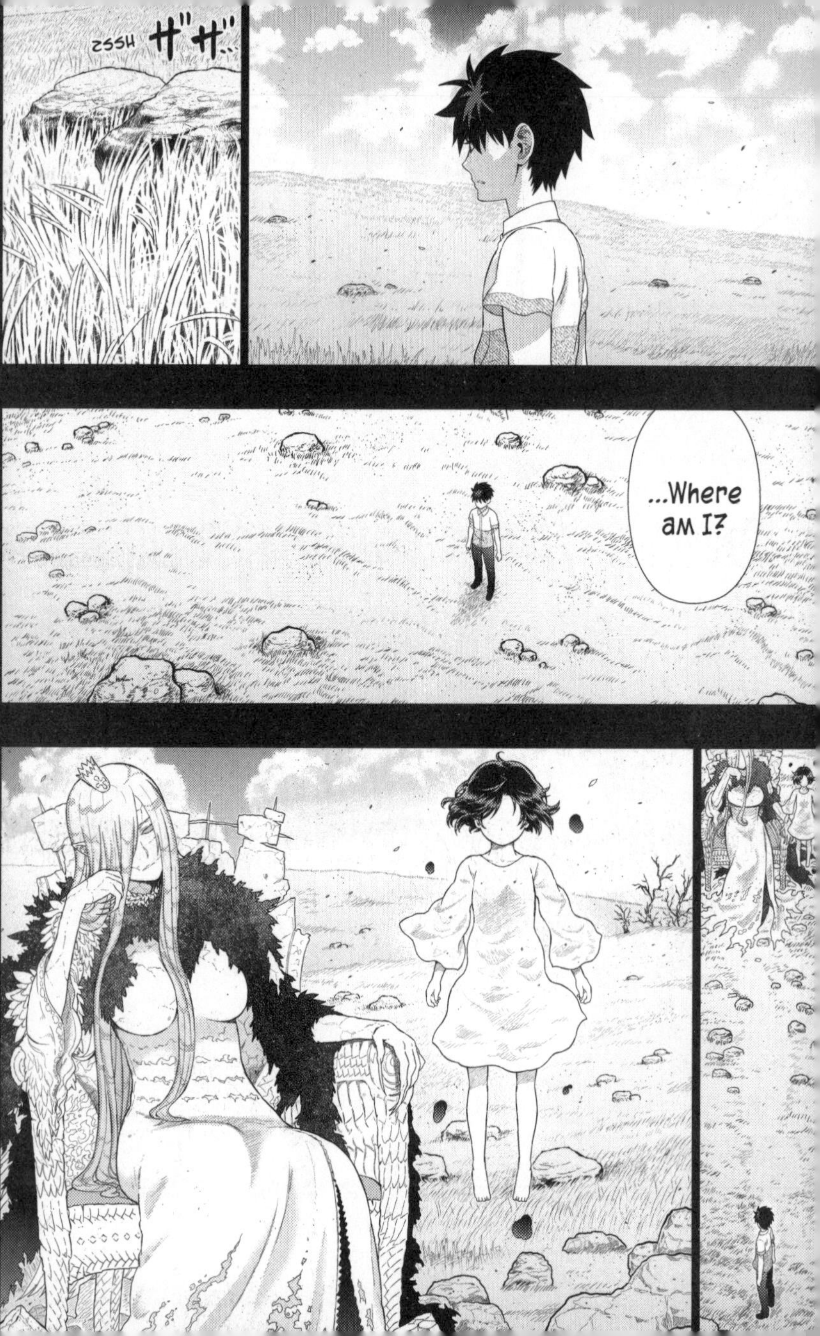
ZSSH
ザザ...
...Where am I?

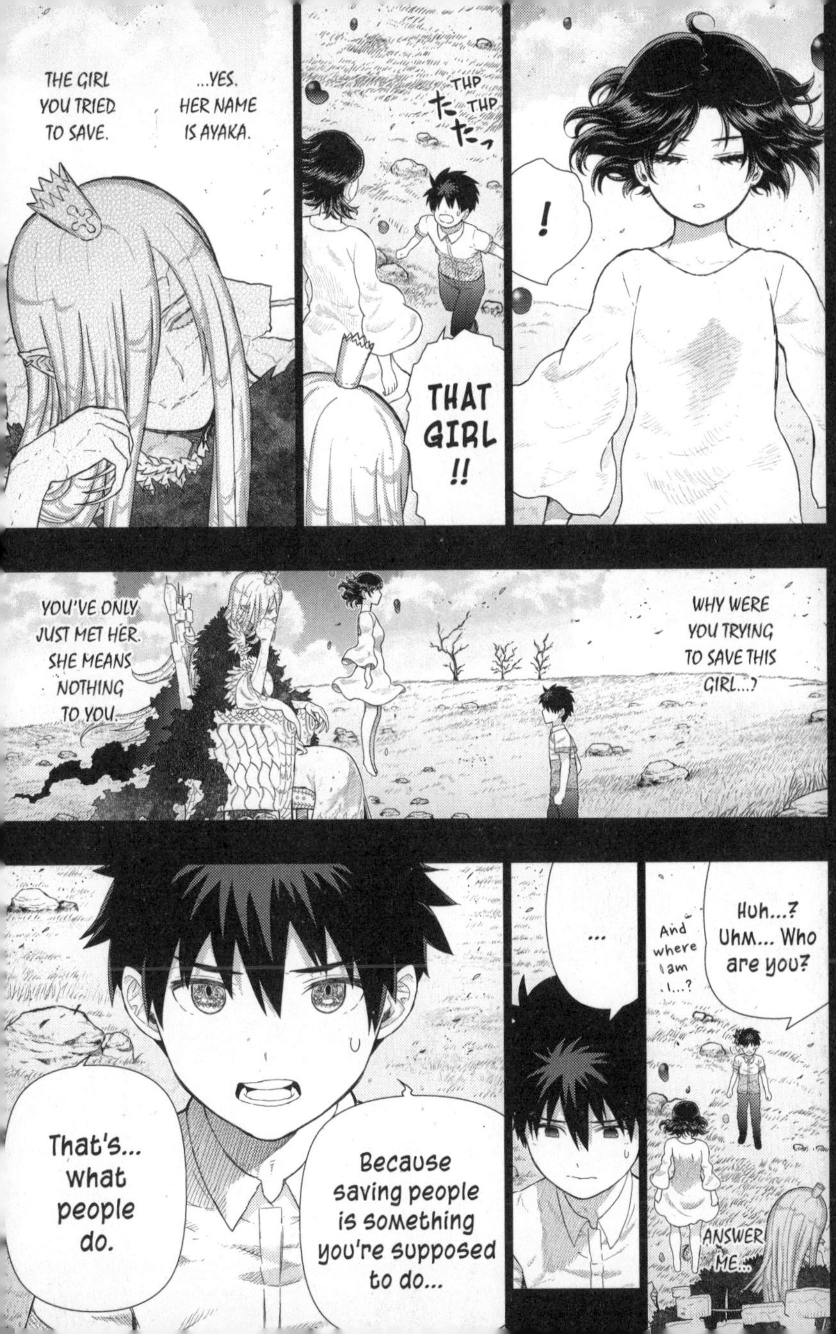
!
THP THP
たったっ
THAT GIRL!!
...YES. HER NAME IS AYAKA.
THE GIRL YOU TRIED TO SAVE.
WHY WERE YOU TRYING TO SAVE THIS GIRL...?
YOU'VE ONLY JUST MET HER. SHE MEANS NOTHING TO YOU.
Huh...? Uhm... Who are you?
And where am I...?
ANSWER ME...
...
Because saving people is something you're supposed to do...
That's... what people do.

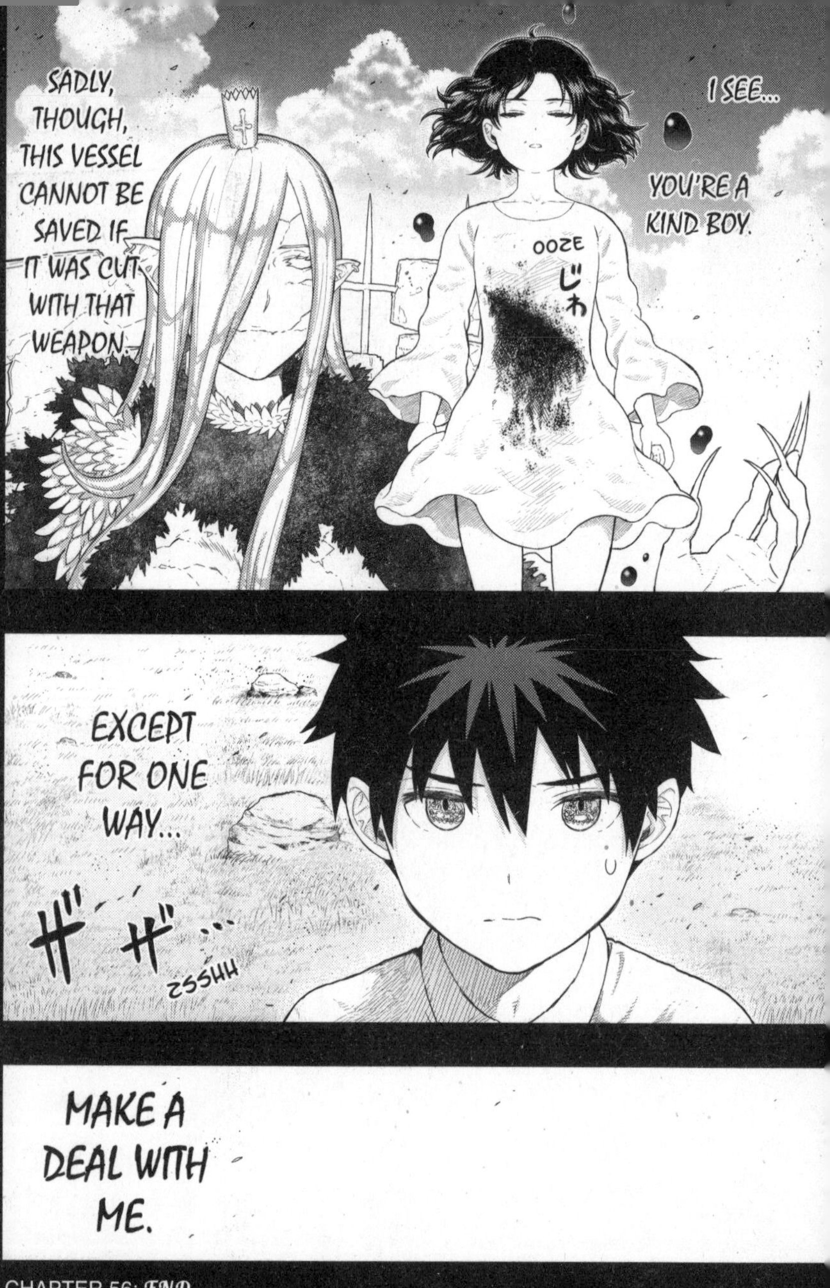
I SEE...
YOU'RE A KIND BOY.
OOZE
じわ
SADLY, THOUGH, THIS VESSEL CANNOT BE SAVED IF IT WAS CUT WITH THAT WEAPON.
EXCEPT FOR ONE WAY...
ザザ…
ZSSHH
MAKE A DEAL WITH ME.

CHAPTER 56: END

Witchcraft Works

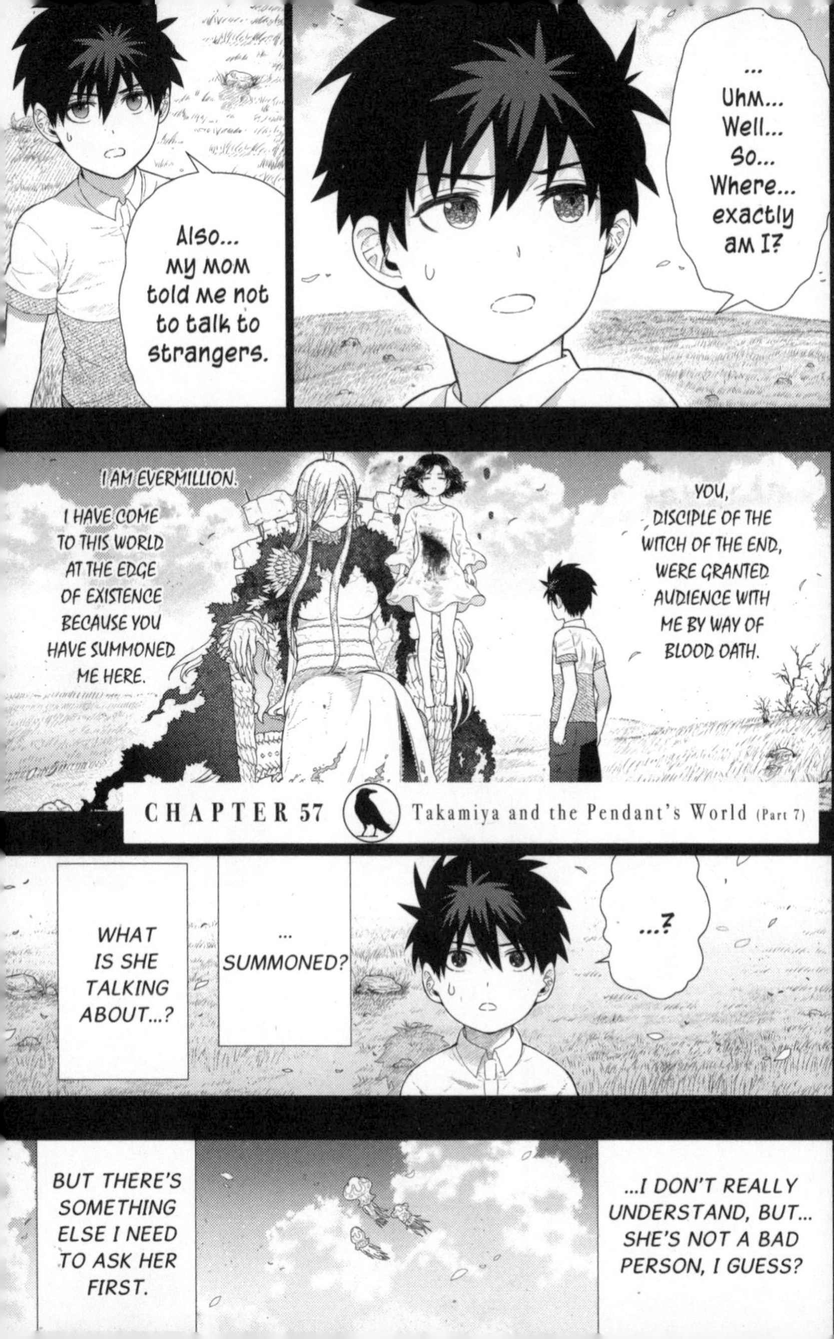
... Uhm... Well... So... Where... exactly am I?
Also... my mom told me not to talk to strangers.
YOU, DISCIPLE OF THE WITCH OF THE END, WERE GRANTED AUDIENCE WITH ME BY WAY OF BLOOD OATH.
I AM EVERMILLION.
I HAVE COME TO THIS WORLD AT THE EDGE OF EXISTENCE BECAUSE YOU HAVE SUMMONED ME HERE.
CHAPTER 57 Takamiya and the Pendant's World (Part 7)
...?
... SUMMONED?
WHAT IS SHE TALKING ABOUT...?
...I DON'T REALLY UNDERSTAND, BUT... SHE'S NOT A BAD PERSON, I GUESS?
BUT THERE'S SOMETHING ELSE I NEED TO ASK HER FIRST.

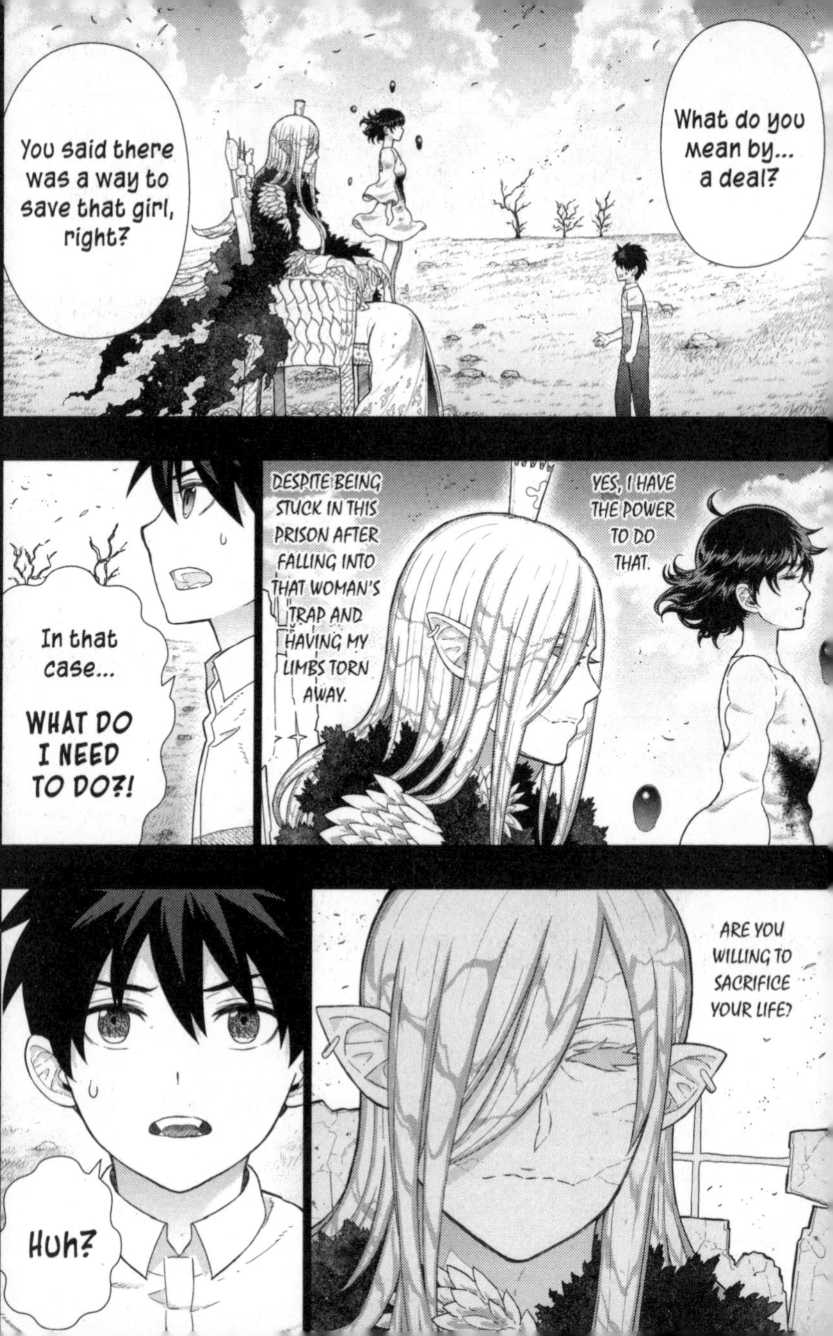
What do you mean by... a deal?
You said there was a way to save that girl, right?
YES, I HAVE THE POWER TO DO THAT.
DESPITE BEING STUCK IN THIS PRISON AFTER FALLING INTO THAT WOMAN'S TRAP AND HAVING MY LIMBS TORN AWAY.
In that case...
WHAT DO I NEED TO DO?!
ARE YOU WILLING TO SACRIFICE YOUR LIFE?
Huh?

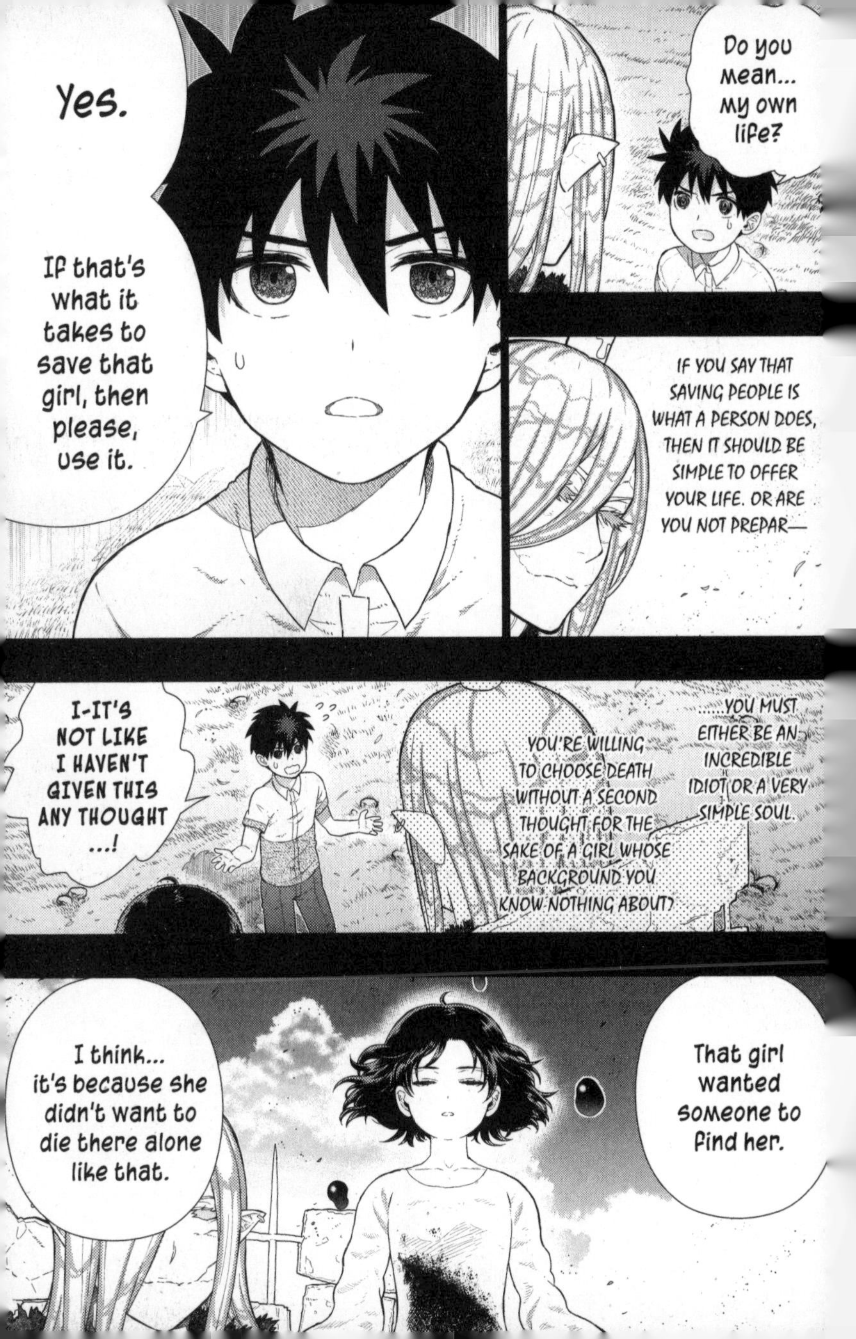
Do you mean... my own life?
IF YOU SAY THAT SAVING PEOPLE IS WHAT A PERSON DOES, THEN IT SHOULD BE SIMPLE TO OFFER YOUR LIFE. OR ARE YOU NOT PREPAR—
Yes.
If that's what it takes to save that girl, then please, use it.
......YOU MUST EITHER BE AN INCREDIBLE IDIOT OR A VERY SIMPLE SOUL.
YOU'RE WILLING TO CHOOSE DEATH WITHOUT A SECOND THOUGHT FOR THE SAKE OF A GIRL WHOSE BACKGROUND YOU KNOW NOTHING ABOUT?
I-IT'S NOT LIKE I HAVEN'T GIVEN THIS ANY THOUGHT ...!
That girl wanted someone to find her.
I think... it's because she didn't want to die there alone like that.

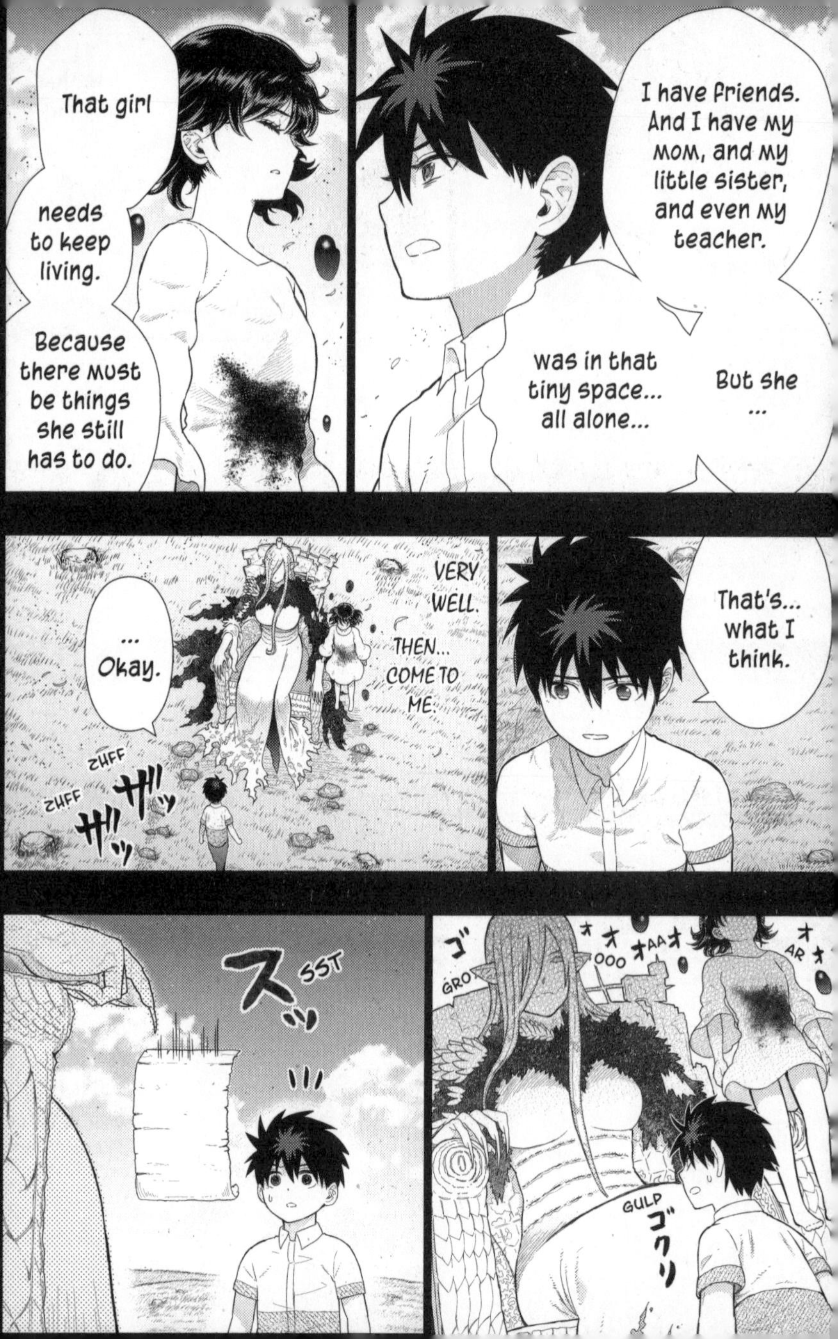

I have friends. And I have my mom, and my little sister, and even my teacher.
But she ...
was in that tiny space... all alone...
That girl
needs to keep living.
Because there must be things she still has to do.
That's... what I think.
VERY WELL. THEN... COME TO ME.
... Okay.
ZHFF
ZHFF
GRO
OOO
AA
AR
GULP
SST

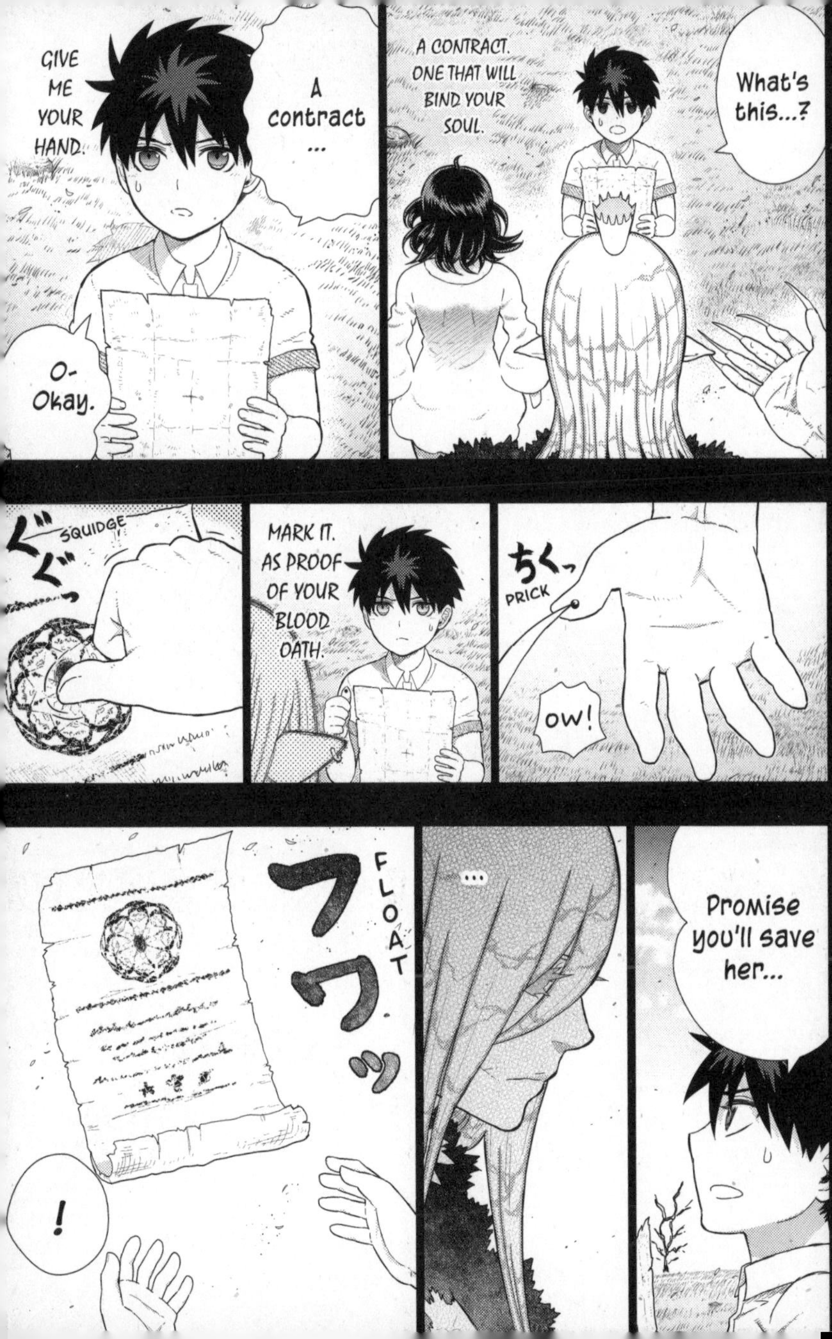
What's this...?
A CONTRACT. ONE THAT WILL BIND YOUR SOUL.
A contract...
GIVE ME YOUR HAND.
O- Okay.
ちくっ
PRICK
OW!
MARK IT. AS PROOF OF YOUR BLOOD OATH.
ぐぐっ
SQUIDGE
Promise you'll save her...
...
フワッ
FLOAT
!

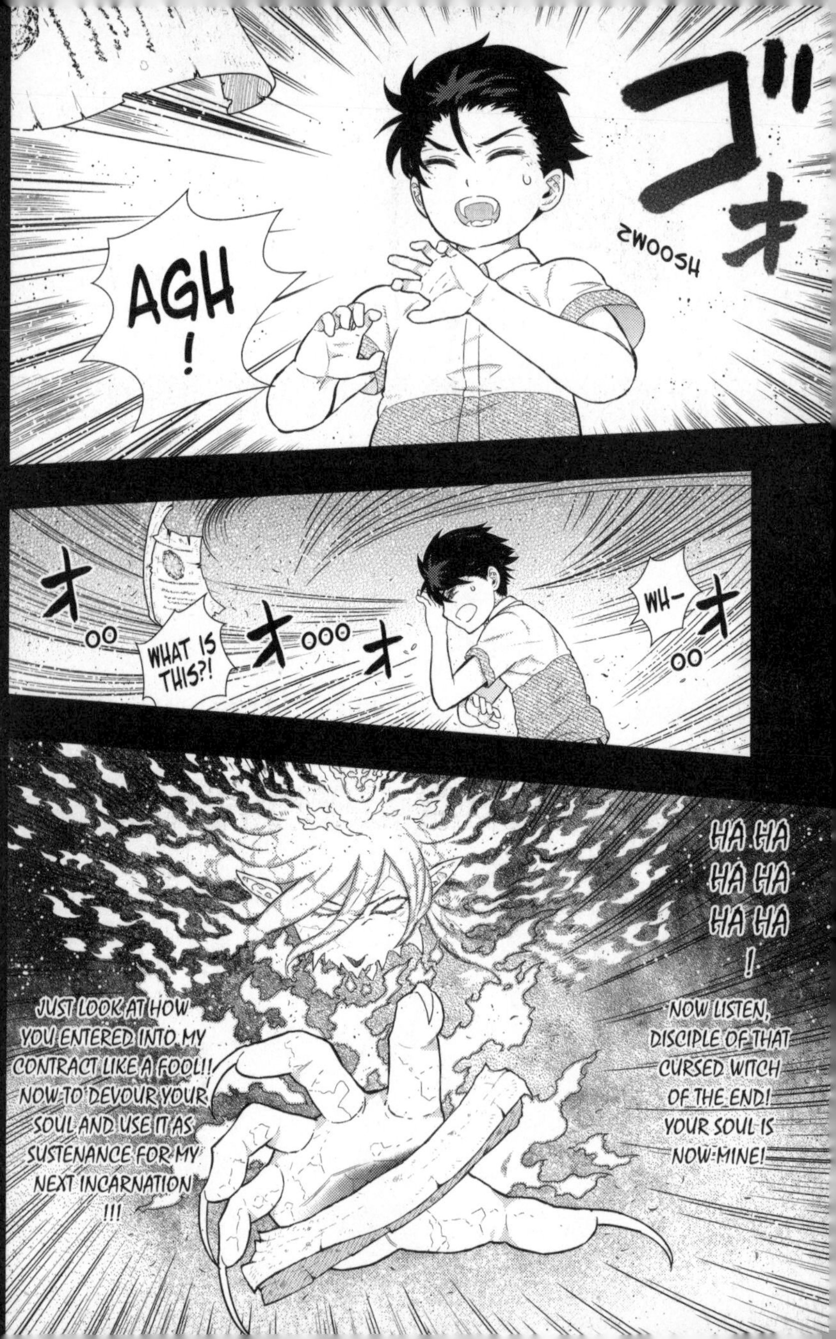
ゴオ
ZWOOSH
AGH!
WH-
オoo
オ
オooo
WHAT IS THIS?!
オoo
HA HA HA HA HA HA!
NOW LISTEN, DISCIPLE OF THAT CURSED WITCH OF THE END! YOUR SOUL IS NOW MINE!
JUST LOOK AT HOW YOU ENTERED INTO MY CONTRACT LIKE A FOOL!! NOW TO DEVOUR YOUR SOUL AND USE IT AS SUSTENANCE FOR MY NEXT INCARNATION!!!

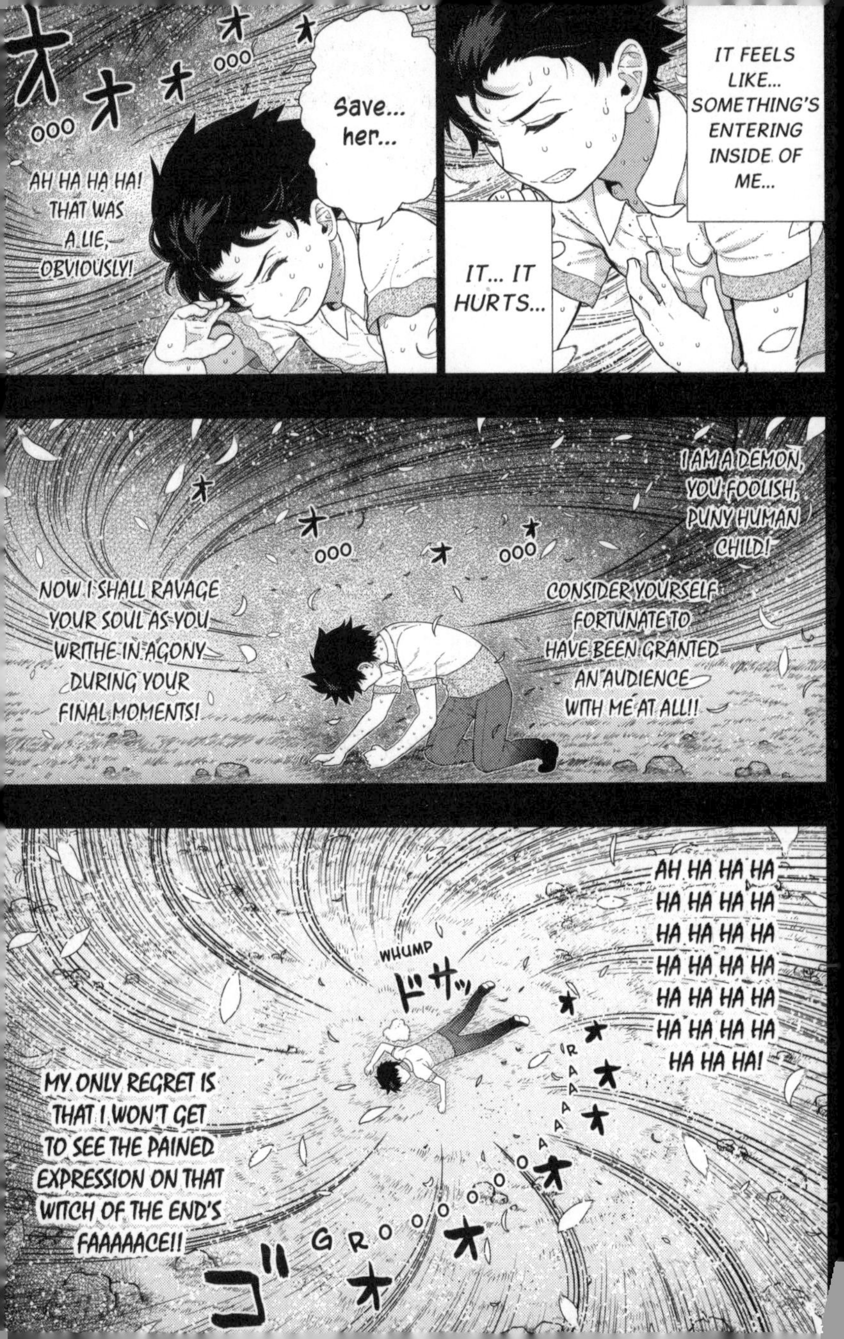
IT FEELS LIKE... SOMETHING'S ENTERING INSIDE OF ME...
IT... IT HURTS...
Save... her...
ooo
ooo
AH HA HA HA! THAT WAS A LIE, OBVIOUSLY!
I AM A DEMON, YOU FOOLISH, PUNY HUMAN CHILD!
CONSIDER YOURSELF FORTUNATE TO HAVE BEEN GRANTED AN AUDIENCE WITH ME AT ALL!!
ooo
ooo
NOW I SHALL RAVAGE YOUR SOUL AS YOU WRITHE IN AGONY DURING YOUR FINAL MOMENTS!
AH HA HA HA HA HA HA HA HA HA HA HA HA HA HA HA HA HA HA HA HA HA HA HA HA HA HA!
WHUMP
MY ONLY REGRET IS THAT I WON'T GET TO SEE THE PAINED EXPRESSION ON THAT WITCH OF THE END'S FAAAAACE!!
GROOOO

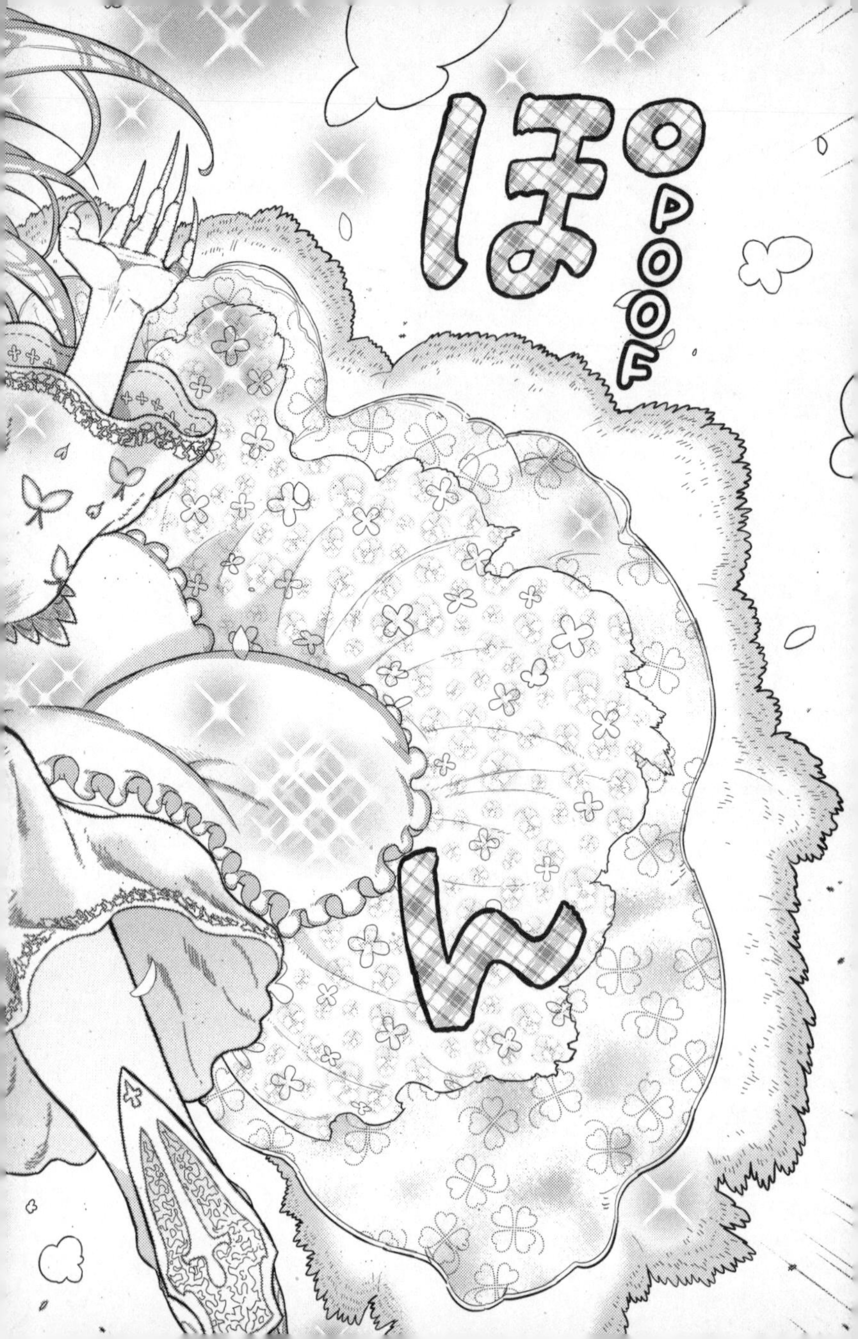
ぽん
POOF

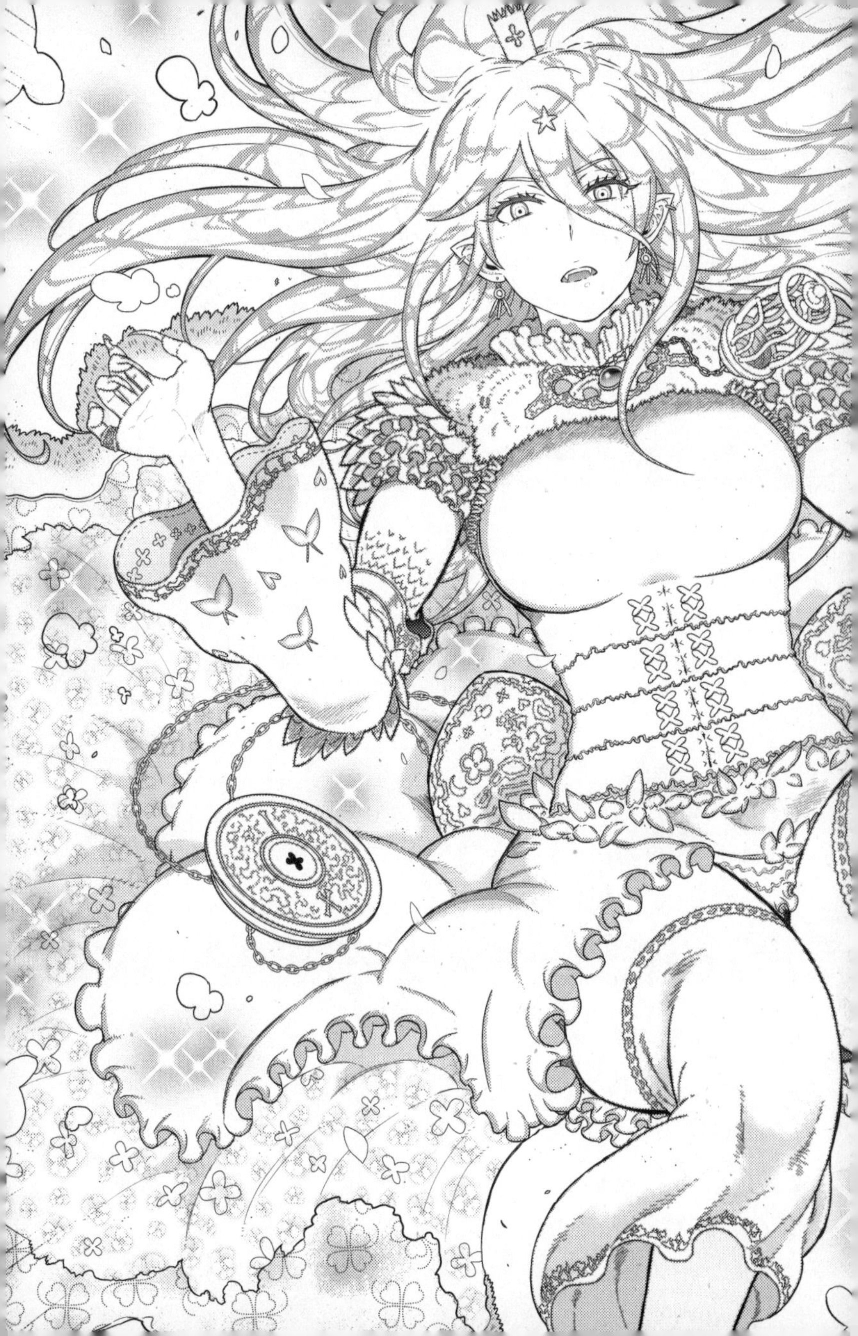

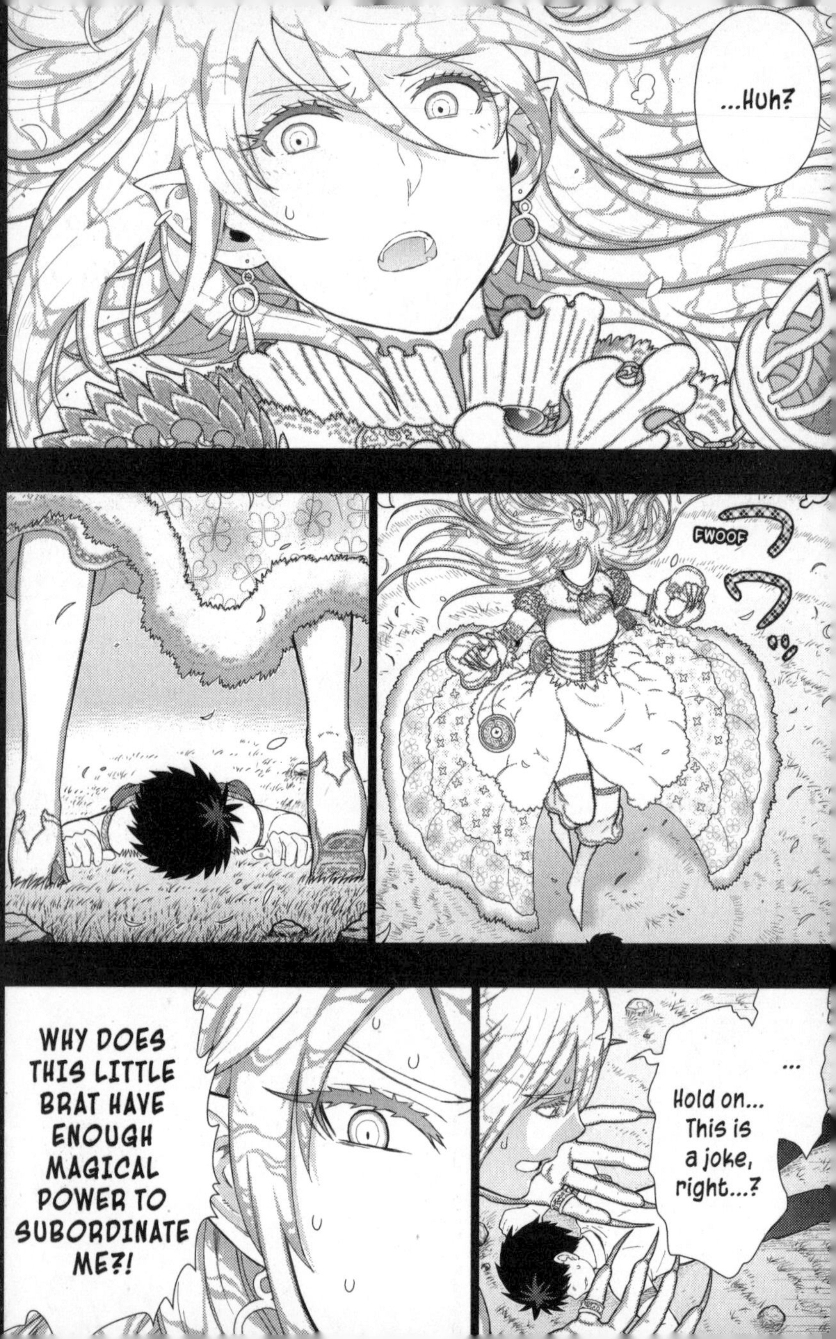
...Huh?
FWOOF
...
Hold on... This is a joke, right...?
WHY DOES THIS LITTLE BRAT HAVE ENOUGH MAGICAL POWER TO SUBORDINATE ME?!

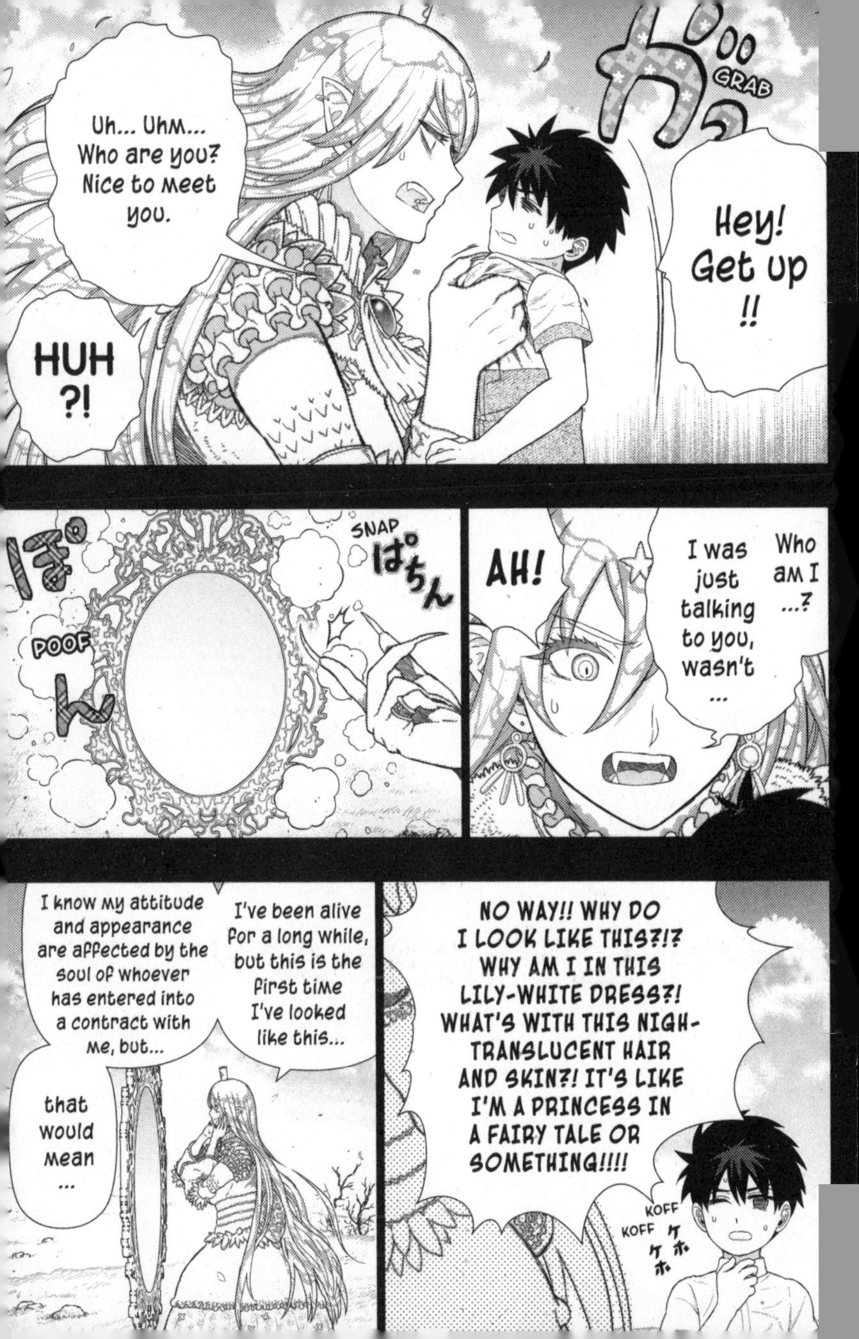
HOO
GRAB
Hey! Get up !!
Uh... Uhm... Who are you? Nice to meet you.
HUH ?!
Who am I ...?
I was just talking to you, wasn't ...
AH!
SNAP
ぱちん
POOF
ぽん
NO WAY!! WHY DO I LOOK LIKE THIS?!? WHY AM I IN THIS LILY-WHITE DRESS?! WHAT'S WITH THIS NIGH-TRANSLUCENT HAIR AND SKIN?! IT'S LIKE I'M A PRINCESS IN A FAIRY TALE OR SOMETHING!!!!
KOFF KOFF
ケホ ケホ
I've been alive for a long while, but this is the first time I've looked like this...
I know my attitude and appearance are affected by the soul of whoever has entered into a contract with me, but...
that would mean ...

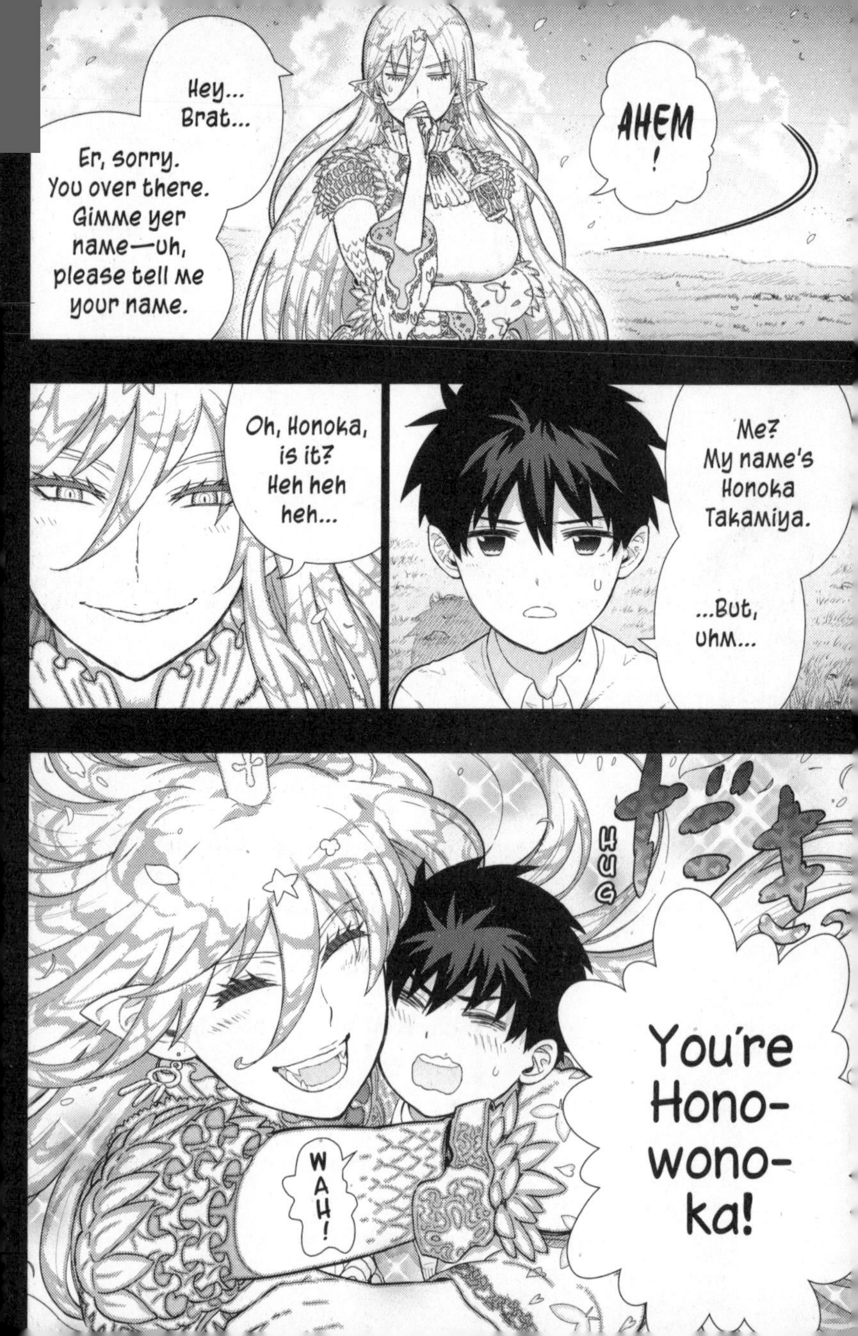
AHEM!
Hey... Brat...
Er, sorry. You over there. Gimme yer name—uh, please tell me your name.
Me? My name's Honoka Takamiya.
...But, uhm...
Oh, Honoka, is it? Heh heh heh...
HUG
You're Hono-wono-ka!
WAH!

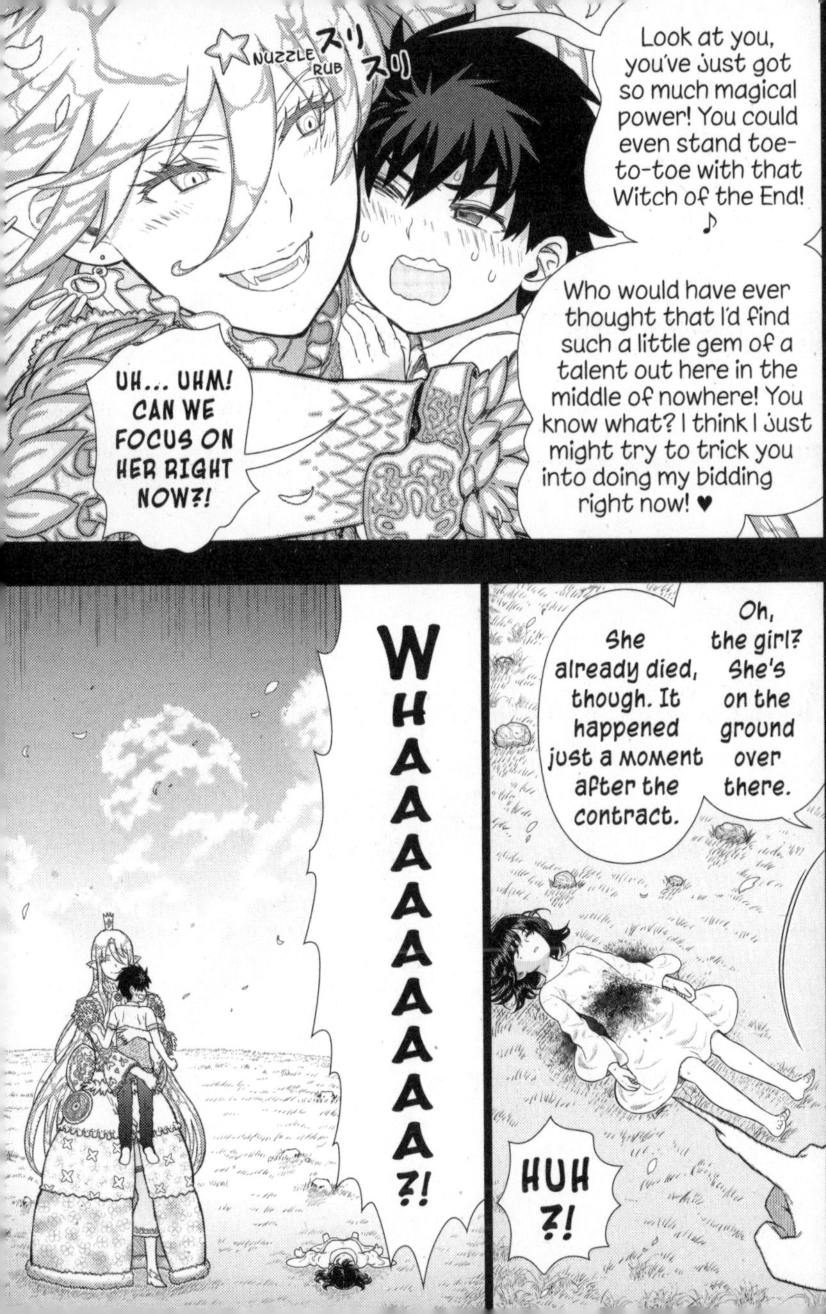
Look at you, you've just got so much magical power! You could even stand toe-to-toe with that Witch of the End! ♪
Who would have ever thought that I'd find such a little gem of a talent out here in the middle of nowhere! You know what? I think I just might try to trick you into doing my bidding right now! ♥
NUZZLE RUB
スリスリ
UH... UHM! CAN WE FOCUS ON HER RIGHT NOW?!
Oh, the girl? She's on the ground over there.
She already died, though. It happened just a moment after the contract.
HUH?!
WHAAAAAAAAA?!

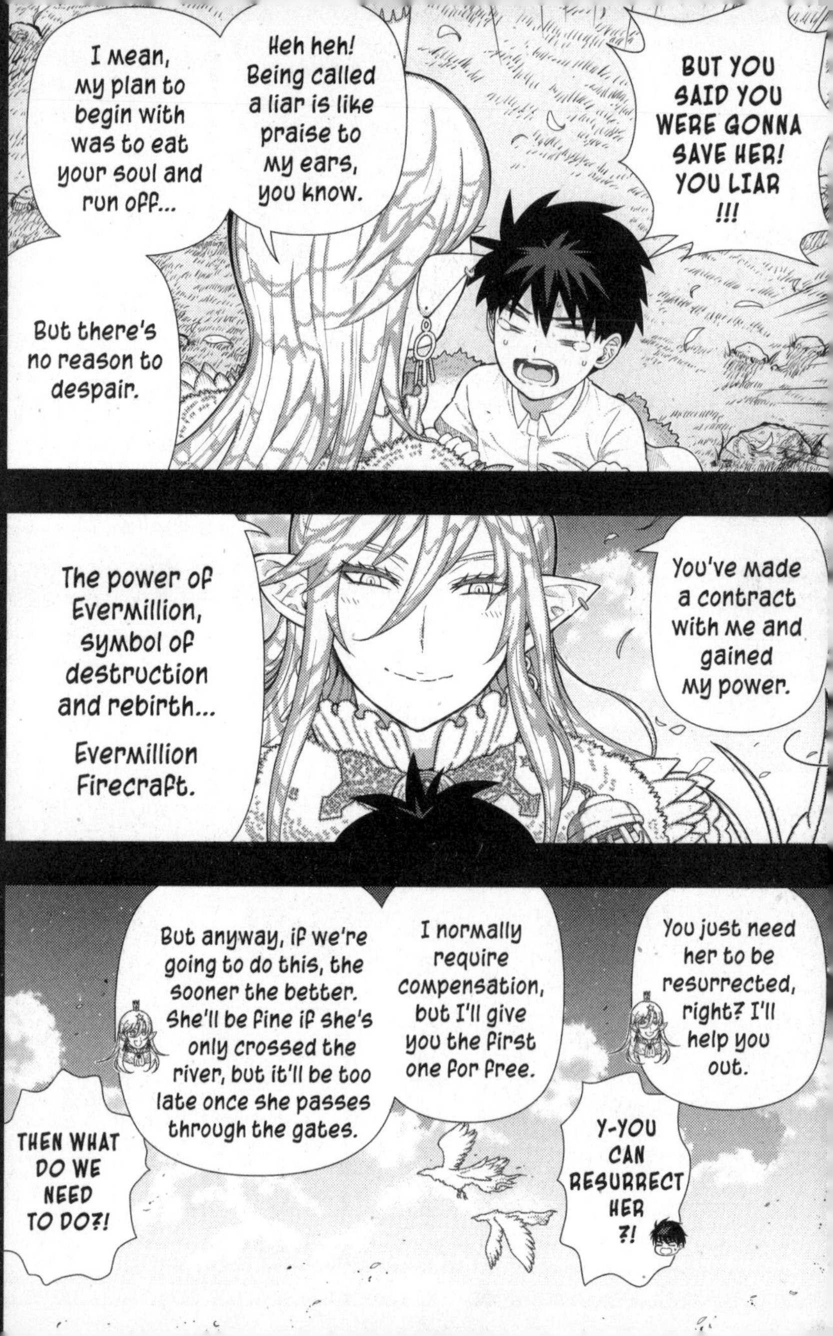
BUT YOU SAID YOU WERE GONNA SAVE HER! YOU LIAR !!!
Heh heh! Being called a liar is like praise to my ears, you know.
I mean, my plan to begin with was to eat your soul and run off...
But there's no reason to despair.
You've made a contract with me and gained my power.
The power of Evermillion, symbol of destruction and rebirth...
Evermillion Firecraft.
You just need her to be resurrected, right? I'll help you out.
Y-YOU CAN RESURRECT HER ?!
I normally require compensation, but I'll give you the first one for free.
But anyway, if we're going to do this, the sooner the better. She'll be fine if she's only crossed the river, but it'll be too late once she passes through the gates.
THEN WHAT DO WE NEED TO DO?!

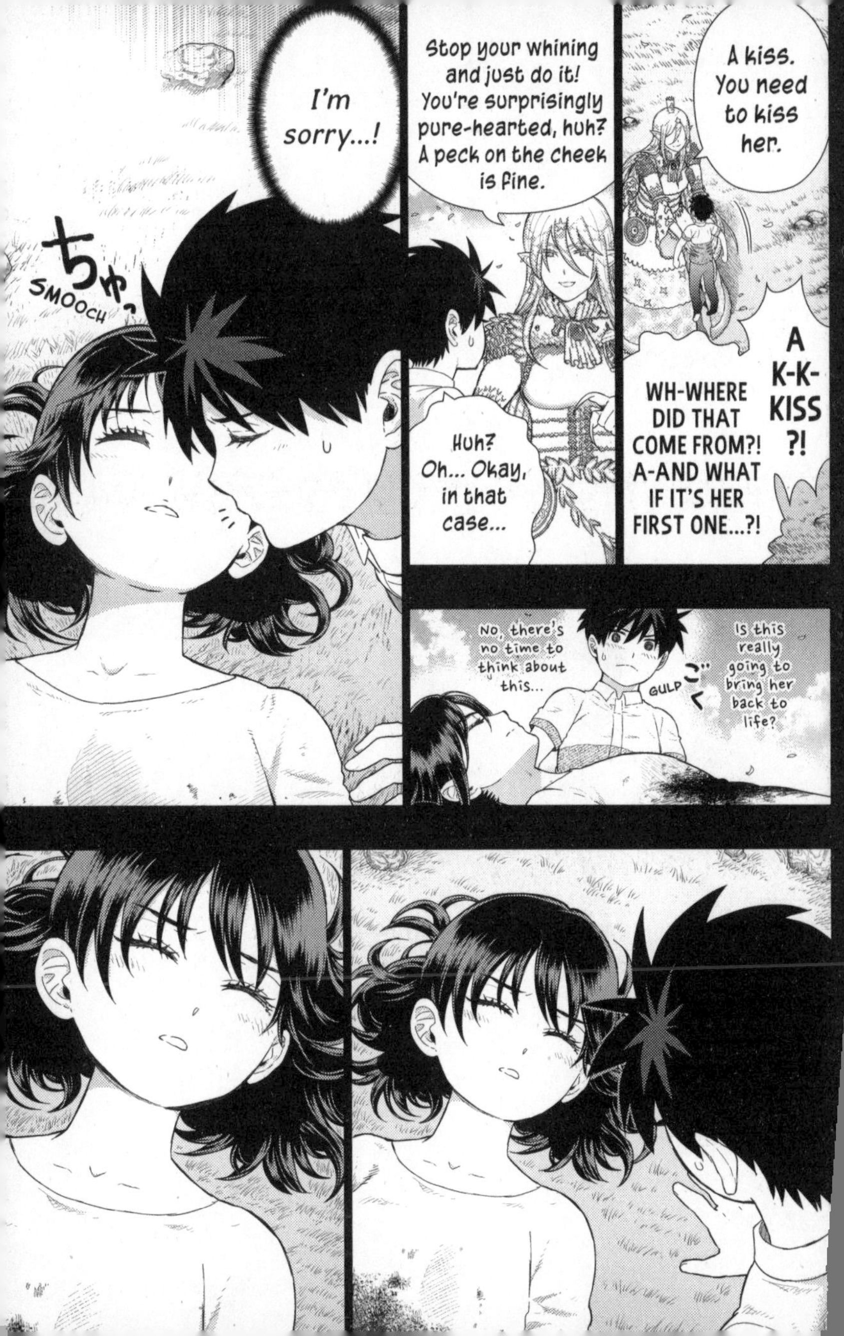
A kiss. You need to kiss her.
A K-K-KISS?!
WH-WHERE DID THAT COME FROM?! A-AND WHAT IF IT'S HER FIRST ONE...?!
Stop your whining and just do it! You're surprisingly pure-hearted, huh? A peck on the cheek is fine.
Huh? Oh... Okay, in that case...
Is this really going to bring her back to life?
ごく GULP
No, there's no time to think about this...
I'm sorry...!
ちゅっ SMOOCH

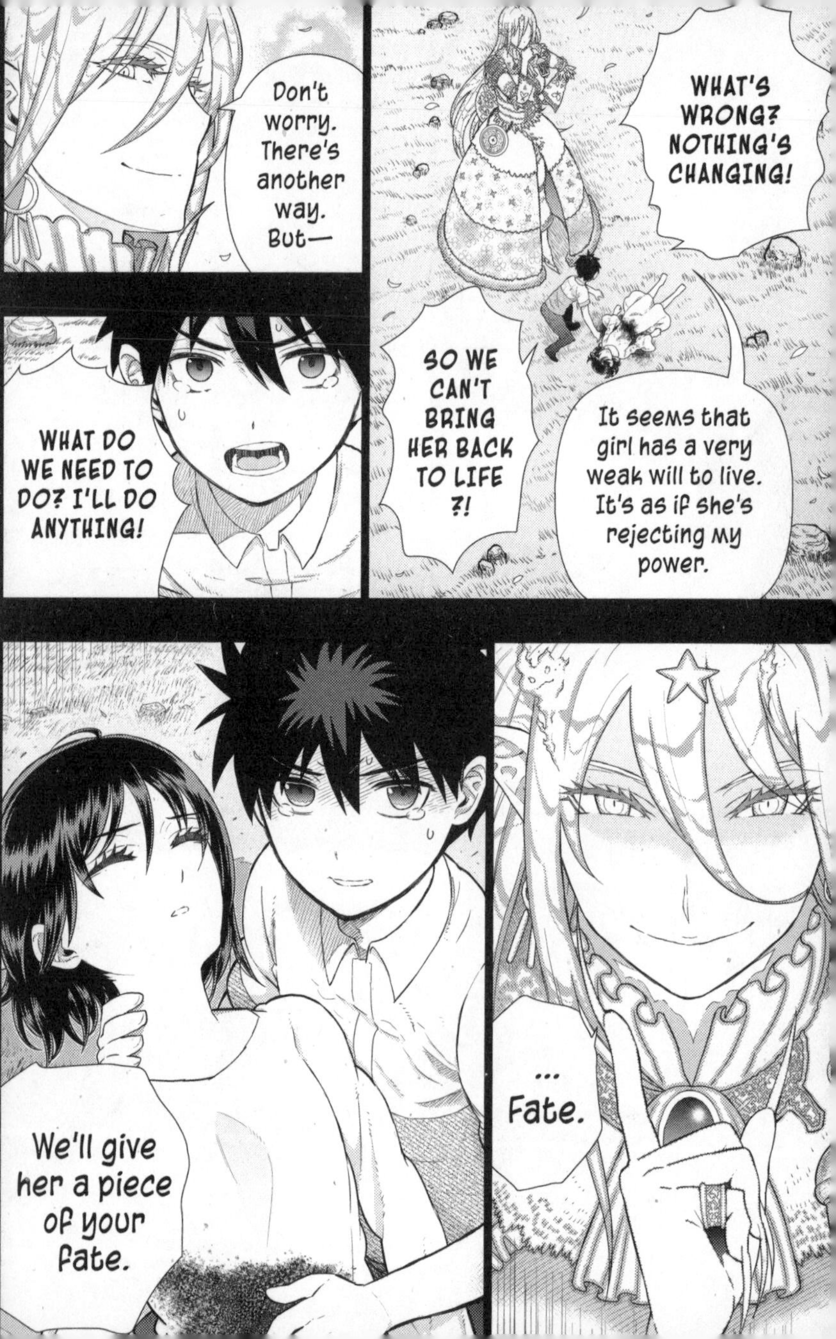
WHAT'S WRONG? NOTHING'S CHANGING!
It seems that girl has a very weak will to live. It's as if she's rejecting my power.
SO WE CAN'T BRING HER BACK TO LIFE ?!
Don't worry. There's another way. But—
WHAT DO WE NEED TO DO? I'LL DO ANYTHING!
... Fate.
We'll give her a piece of your fate.

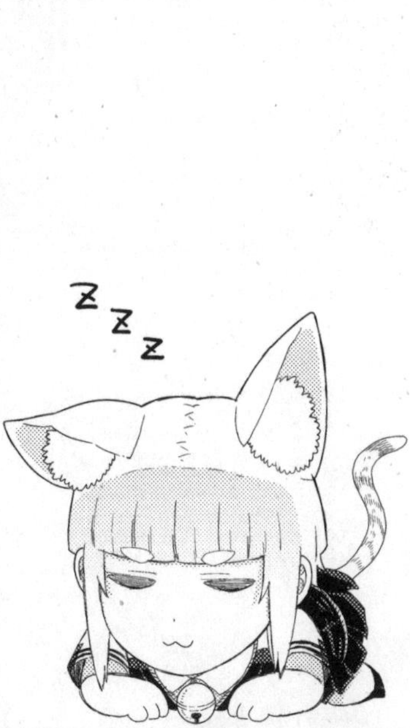
Z Z Z

Witchcraft Works

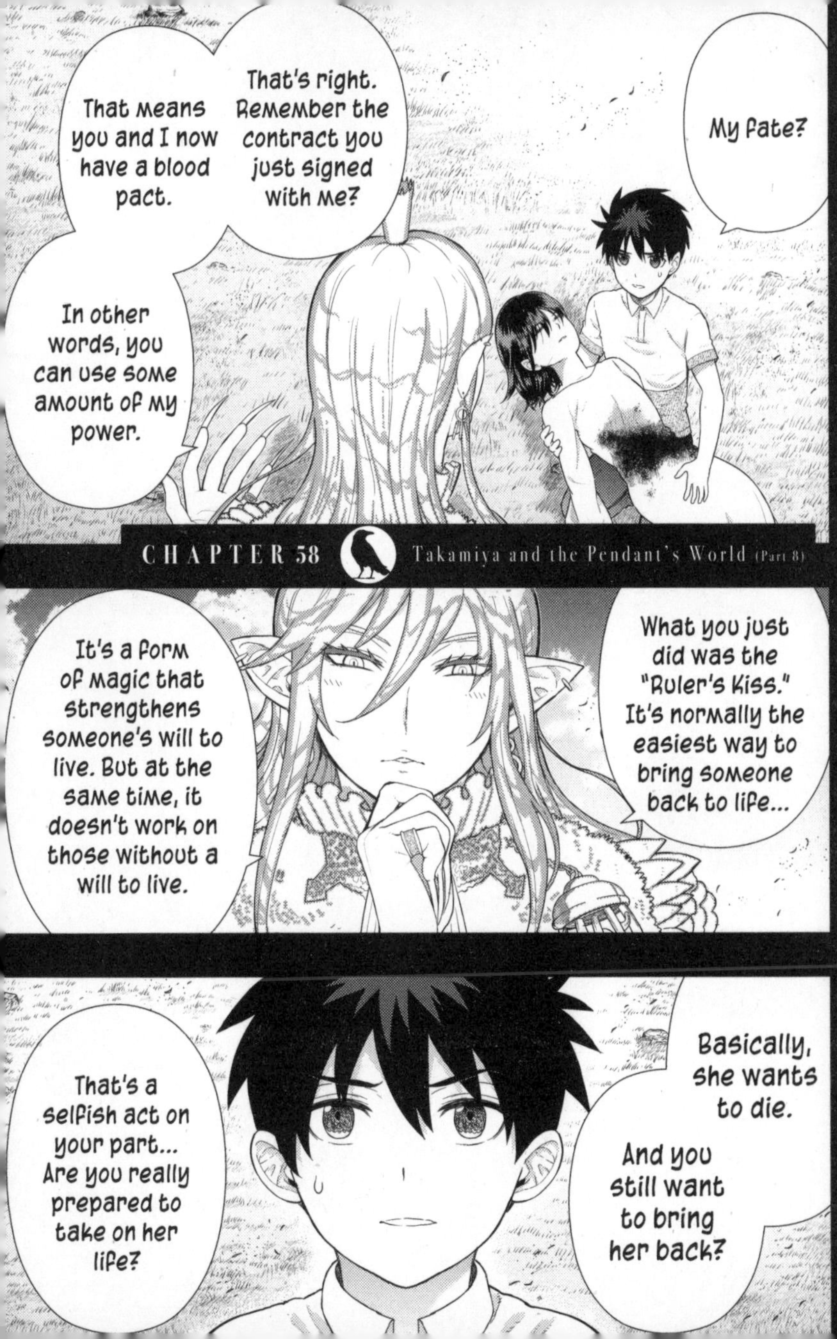
My fate?
That's right. Remember the contract you just signed with me?
That means you and I now have a blood pact.
In other words, you can use some amount of my power.
CHAPTER 58 Takamiya and the Pendant's World (Part 8)
What you just did was the "Ruler's Kiss." It's normally the easiest way to bring someone back to life...
It's a form of magic that strengthens someone's will to live. But at the same time, it doesn't work on those without a will to live.
Basically, she wants to die.
And you still want to bring her back?
That's a selfish act on your part... Are you really prepared to take on her life?

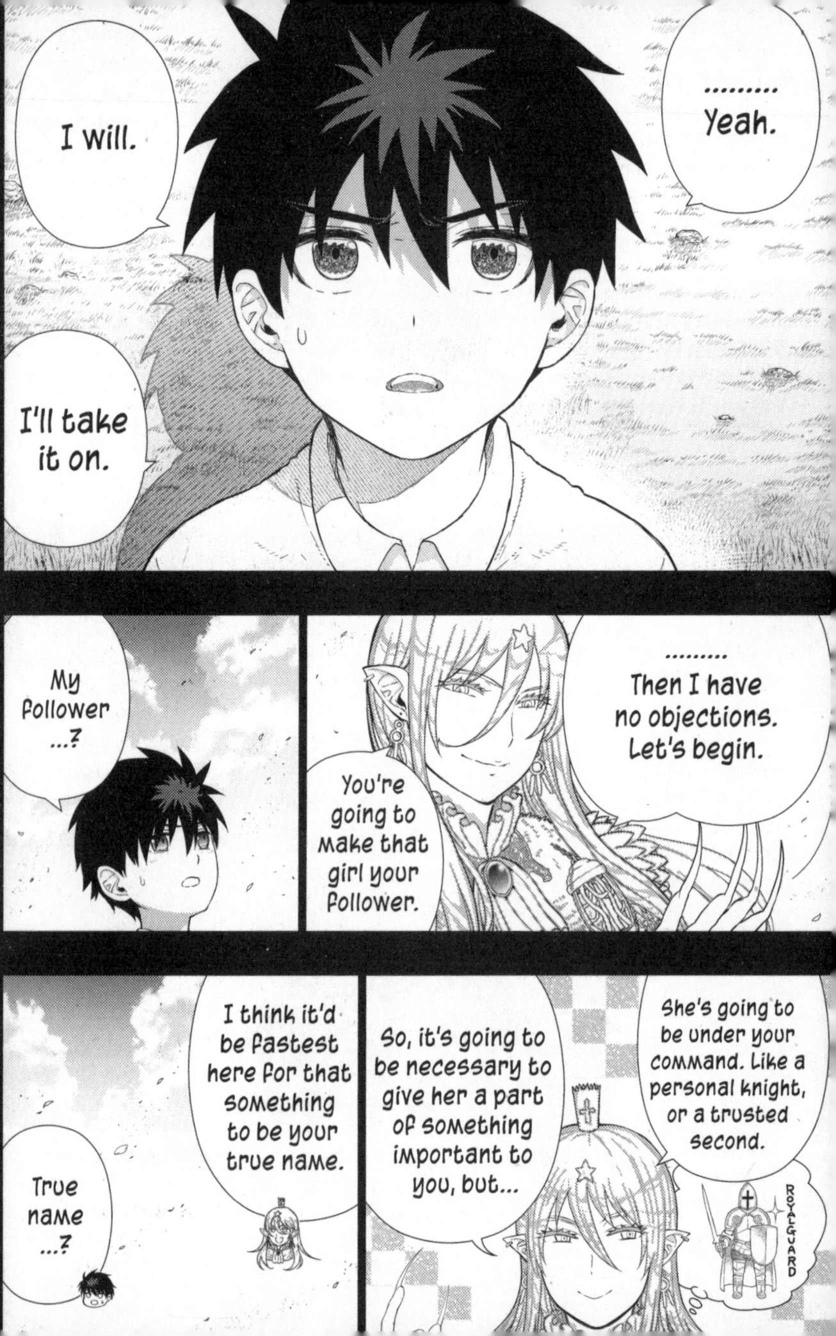
.... Yeah.
I will.
I'll take it on.
.... Then I have no objections. Let's begin.
You're going to make that girl your follower.
My follower ...?
She's going to be under your command. Like a personal knight, or a trusted second.
ROYAL GUARD
So, it's going to be necessary to give her a part of something important to you, but...
I think it'd be fastest here for that something to be your true name.
True name ...?

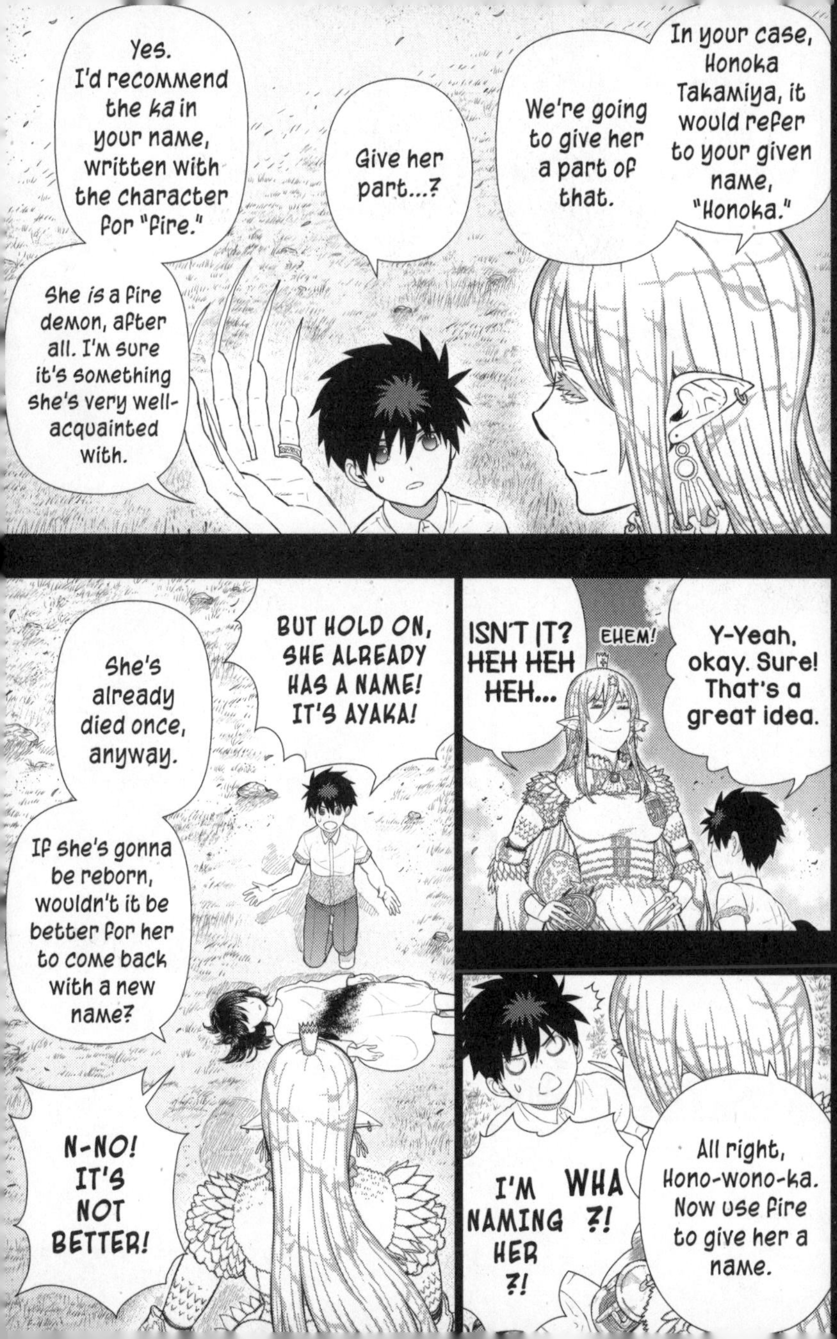
In your case, Honoka Takamiya, it would refer to your given name, "Honoka."
We're going to give her a part of that.
Give her part...?
Yes. I'd recommend the *ka* in your name, written with the character for "fire."
She *is* a fire demon, after all. I'm sure it's something she's very well-acquainted with.
Y-Yeah, okay. Sure! That's a great idea.
EHEM!
ISN'T IT? HEH HEH HEH...
All right, Hono-wono-ka. Now use fire to give her a name.
WHA ?!
I'M NAMING HER ?!
BUT HOLD ON, SHE ALREADY HAS A NAME! IT'S AYAKA!
She's already died once, anyway.
If she's gonna be reborn, wouldn't it be better for her to come back with a new name?
N-NO! IT'S NOT BETTER!

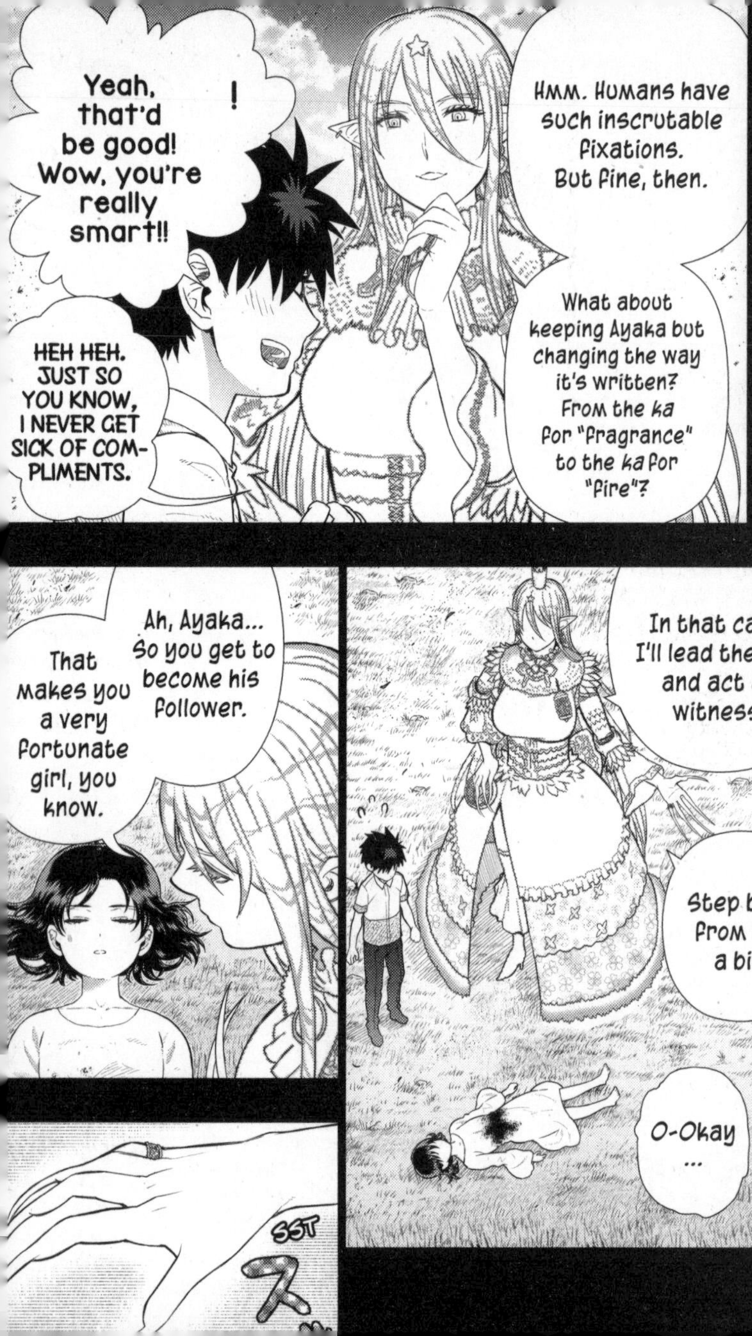
HMM. Humans have such inscrutable fixations. But fine, then.
What about keeping Ayaka but changing the way it's written? From the ka for "fragrance" to the ka for "fire"?
!
Yeah, that'd be good! Wow, you're really smart!!
HEH HEH. JUST SO YOU KNOW, I NEVER GET SICK OF COM-PLIMENTS.
In that case, I'll lead the rite and act as witness.
Step back from her a bit.
O-Okay ...
Ah, Ayaka... So you get to become his follower.
That makes you a very fortunate girl, you know.
SST

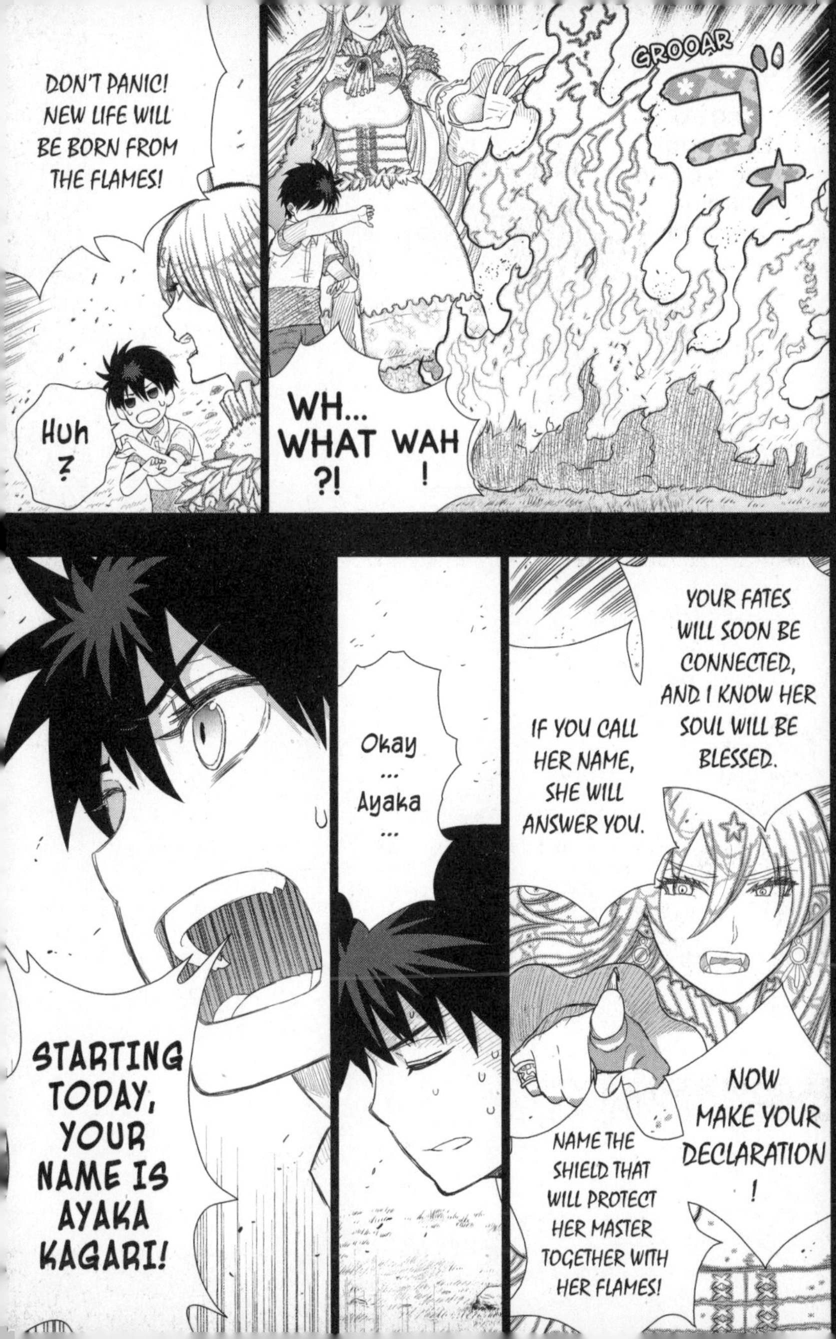
GROOAR
WAH !
WH... WHAT ?!
DON'T PANIC! NEW LIFE WILL BE BORN FROM THE FLAMES!
Huh ?
YOUR FATES WILL SOON BE CONNECTED, AND I KNOW HER SOUL WILL BE BLESSED.
IF YOU CALL HER NAME, SHE WILL ANSWER YOU.
NOW MAKE YOUR DECLARATION !
NAME THE SHIELD THAT WILL PROTECT HER MASTER TOGETHER WITH HER FLAMES!
Okay ... Ayaka ...
STARTING TODAY, YOUR NAME IS AYAKA KAGARI!

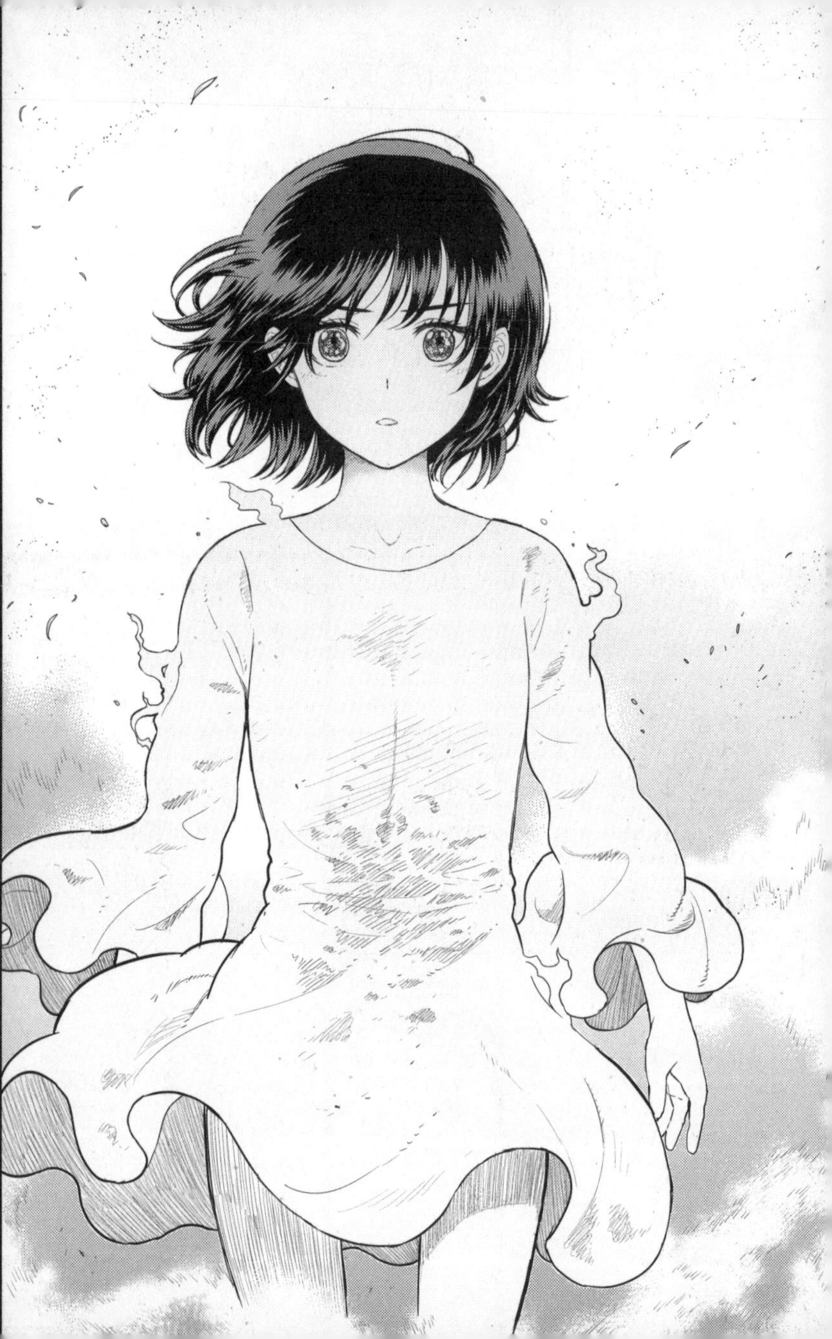

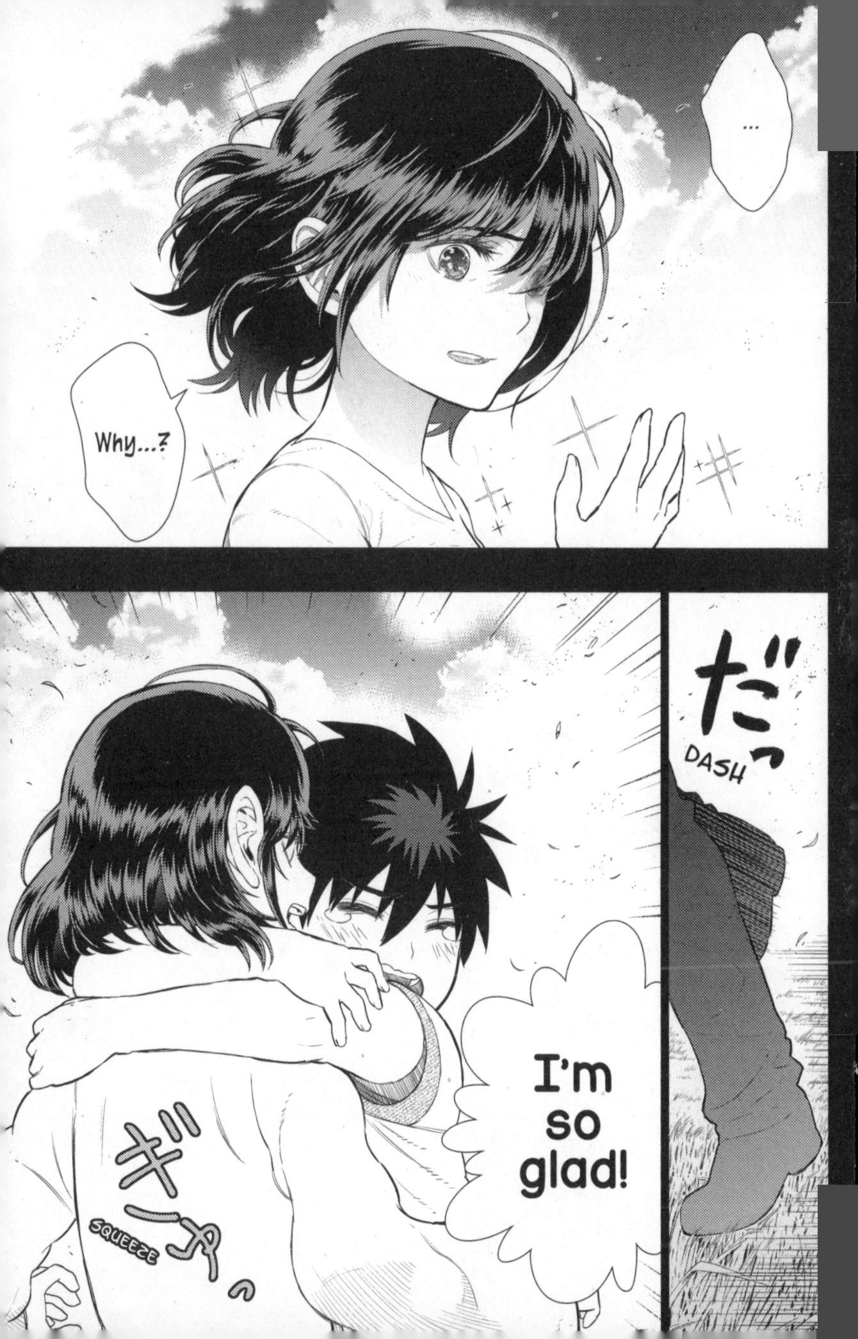
...
Why...?
だっ
DASH
I'm so glad!
SQUEEZE

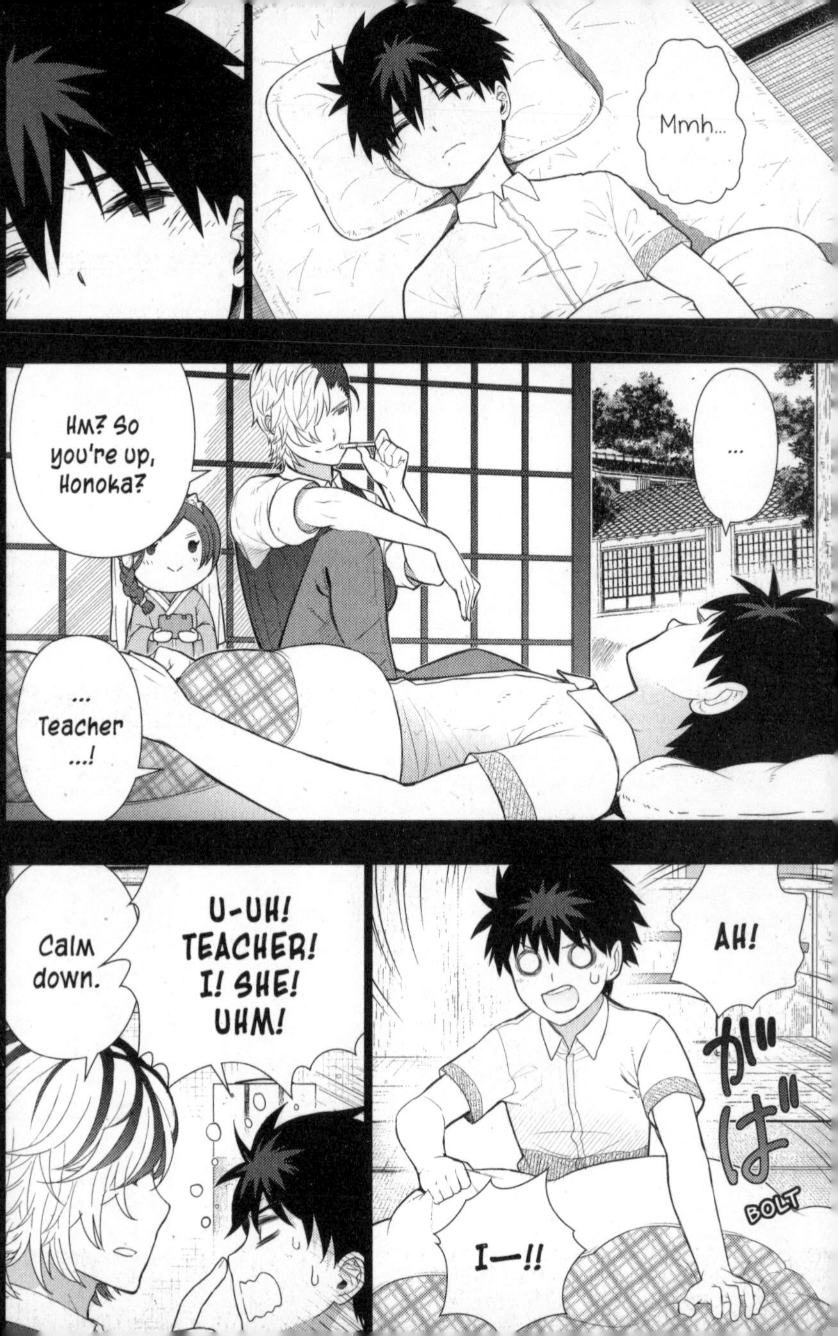

Mmh...
...
Hm? So you're up, Honoka?
... Teacher ...!
AH!
がば
BOLT
I—!!
U-UH! TEACHER! I! SHE! UHM!
Calm down.

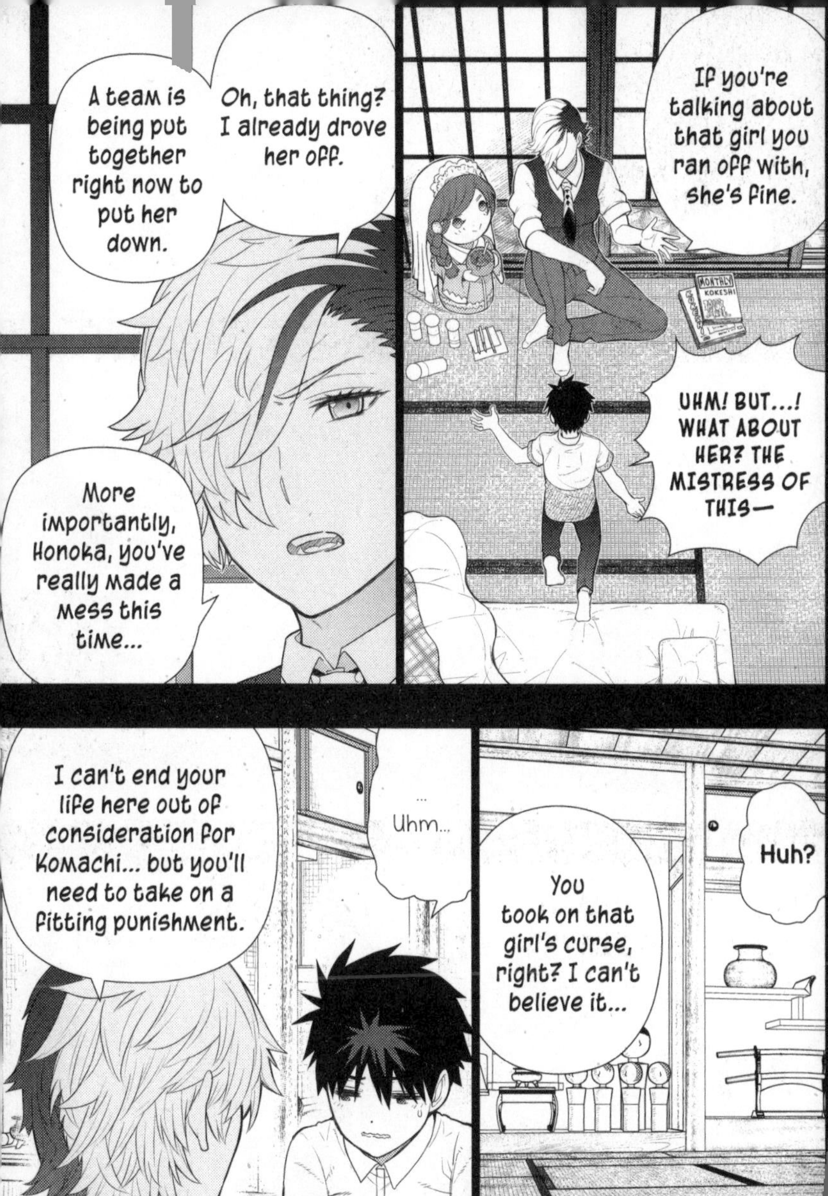
If you're talking about that girl you ran off with, she's fine.
MONTHLY KOKESHI
UHM! BUT...! WHAT ABOUT HER? THE MISTRESS OF THIS—
Oh, that thing? I already drove her off.
A team is being put together right now to put her down.
More importantly, Honoka, you've really made a mess this time...
Huh?
You took on that girl's curse, right? I can't believe it...
... Uhm...
I can't end your life here out of consideration for Komachi... but you'll need to take on a fitting punishment.

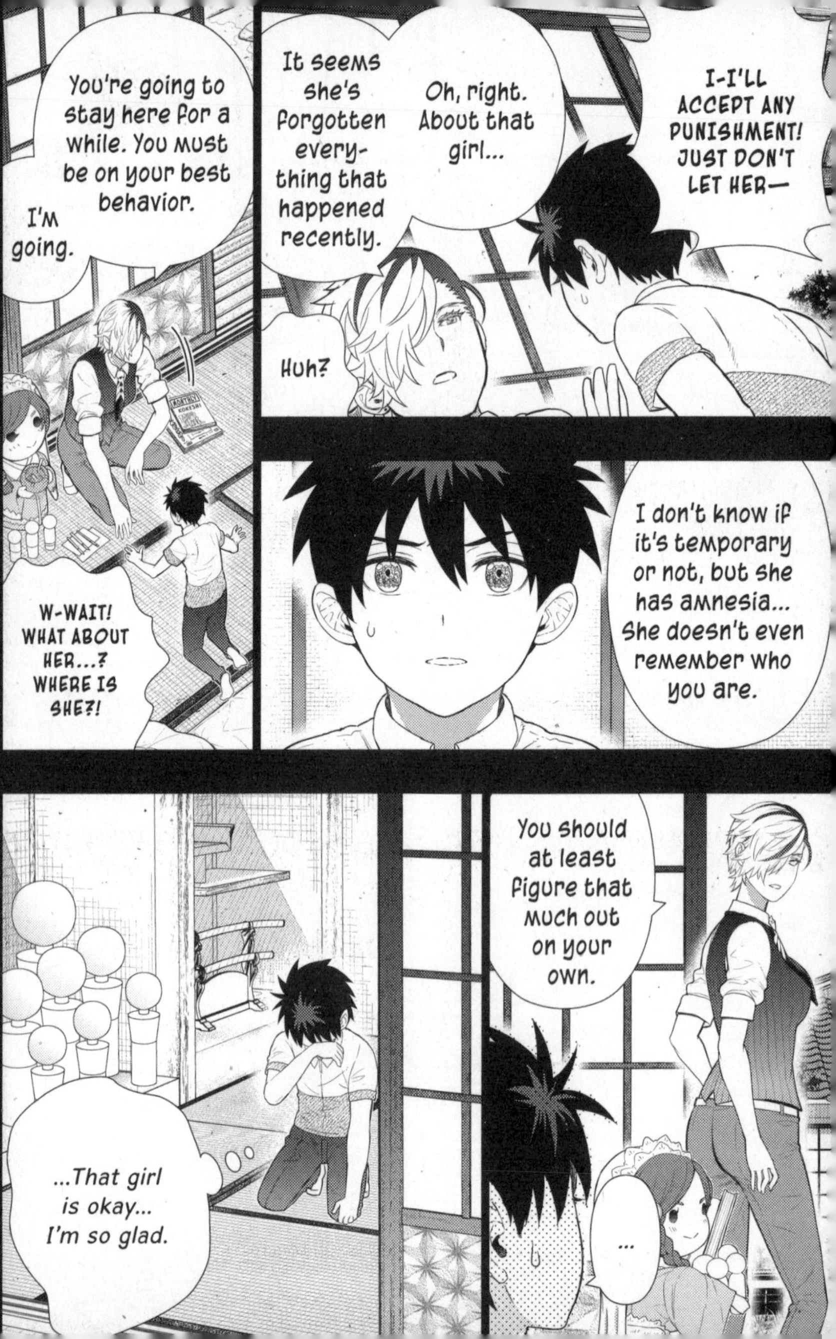
I-I'LL ACCEPT ANY PUNISHMENT! JUST DON'T LET HER—
Oh, right. About that girl...
It seems she's forgotten everything that happened recently.
Huh?
I don't know if it's temporary or not, but she has amnesia... She doesn't even remember who you are.
You're going to stay here for a while. You must be on your best behavior.
I'm going.
W-WAIT! WHAT ABOUT HER...? WHERE IS SHE?!
You should at least figure that much out on your own.
...
...That girl is okay... I'm so glad.

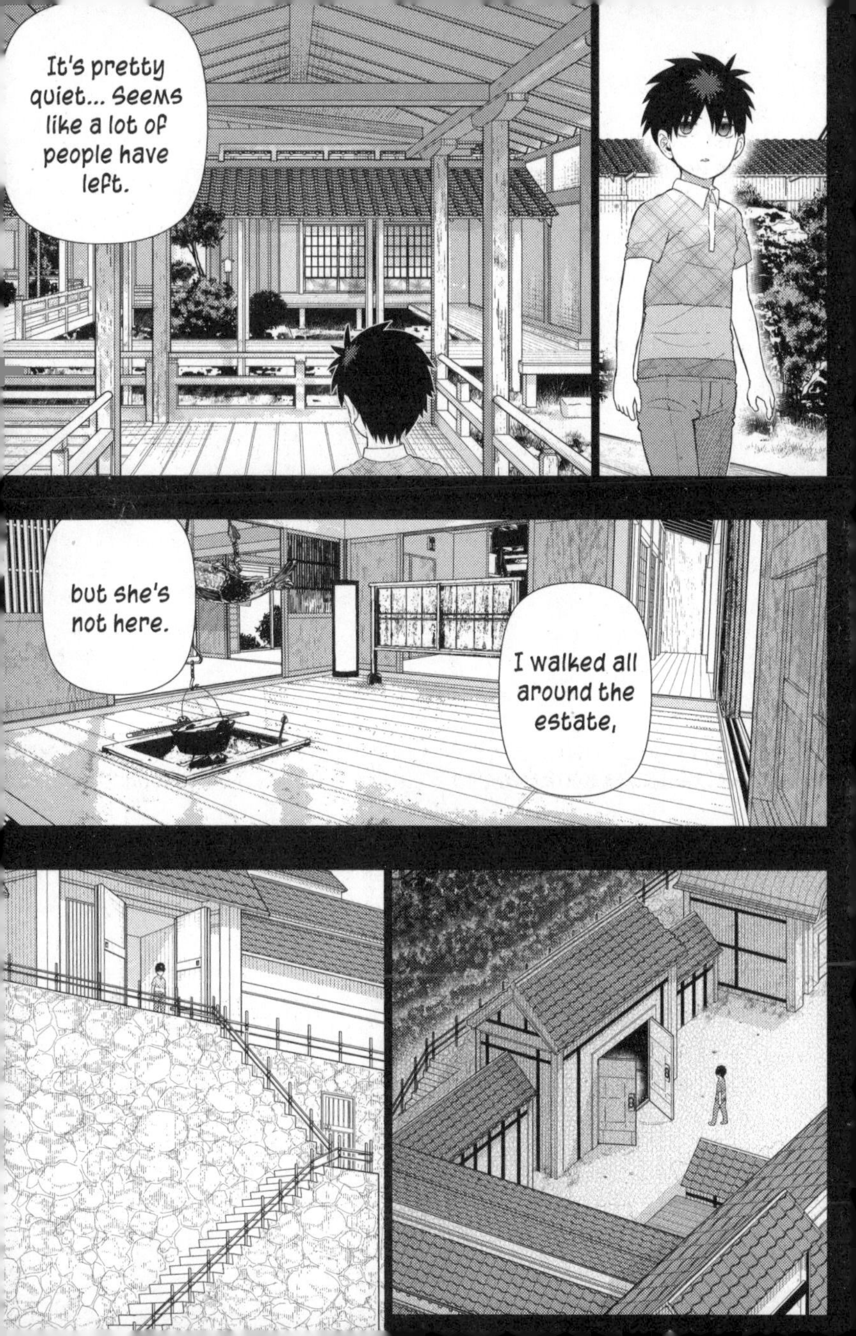
It's pretty quiet... Seems like a lot of people have left.
I walked all around the estate,
but she's not here.

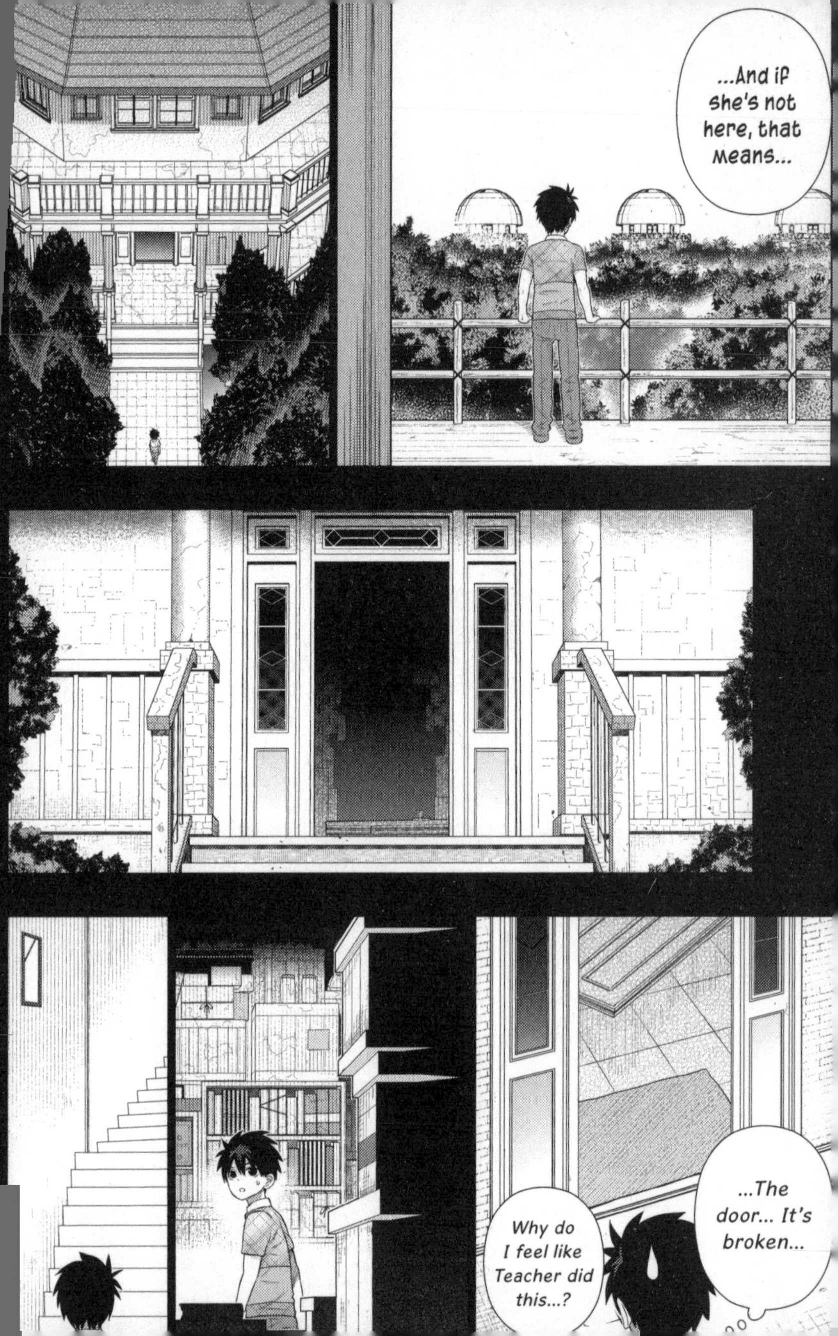
...And if she's not here, that means...
...The door... It's broken...
Why do I feel like Teacher did this...?

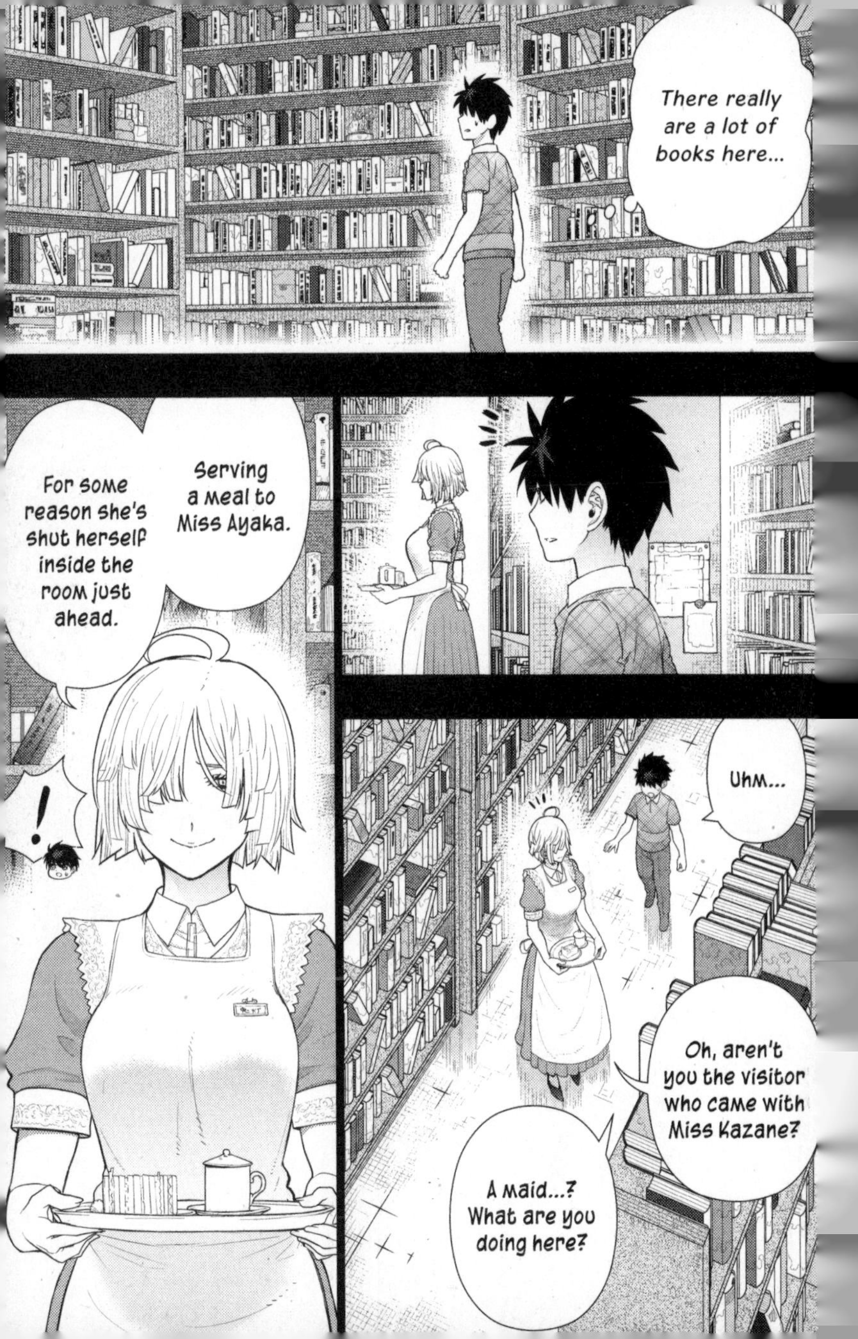
There really are a lot of books here...
Uhm...
Oh, aren't you the visitor who came with Miss Kazane?
A maid...? What are you doing here?
Serving a meal to Miss Ayaka.
For some reason she's shut herself inside the room just ahead.
!

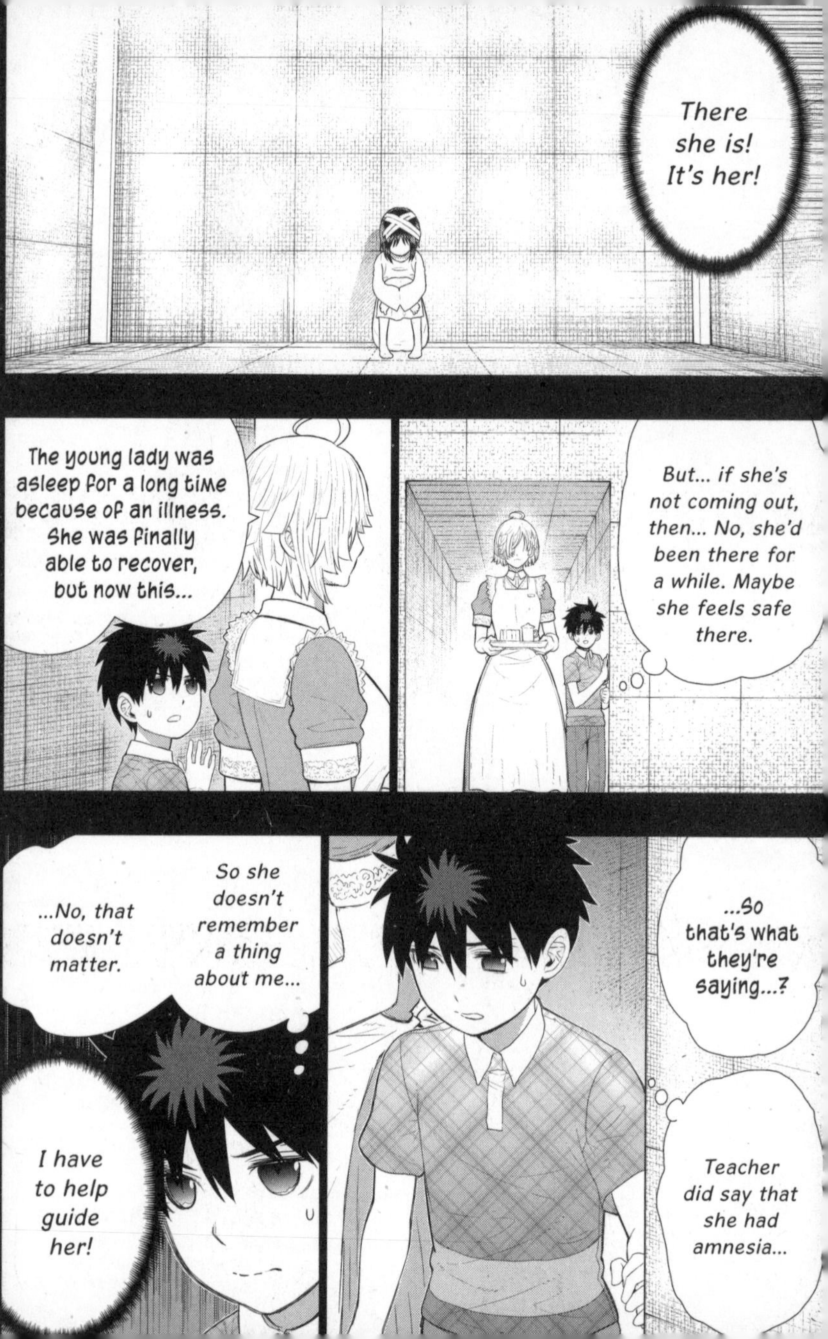
There she is! It's her!
But... if she's not coming out, then... No, she'd been there for a while. Maybe she feels safe there.
The young lady was asleep for a long time because of an illness. She was finally able to recover, but now this...
...So that's what they're saying...?
Teacher did say that she had amnesia...
So she doesn't remember a thing about me...
...No, that doesn't matter.
I have to help guide her!

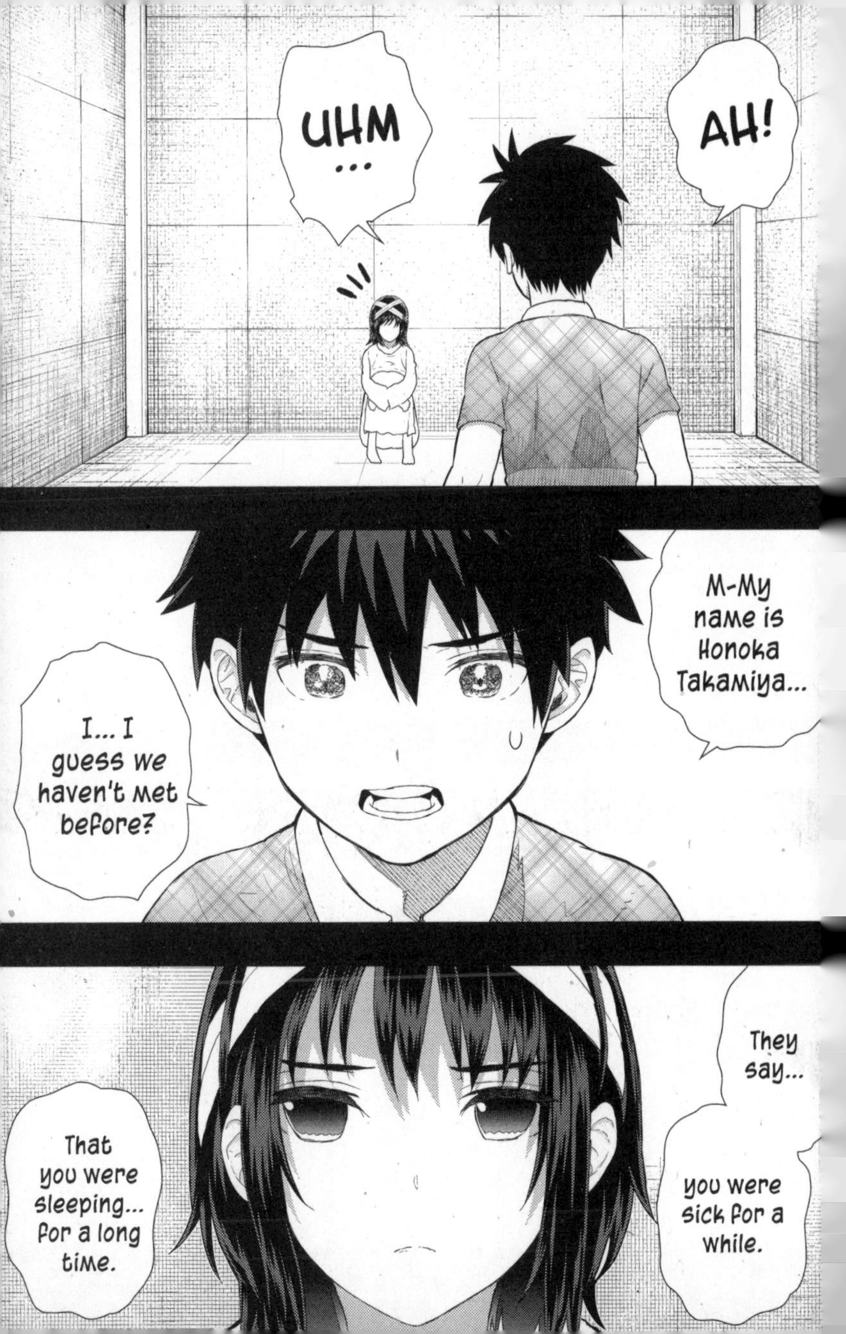
AH!
UHM ...
M-My name is Honoka Takamiya...
I... I guess we haven't met before?
They say...
you were sick for a while.
That you were sleeping... for a long time.

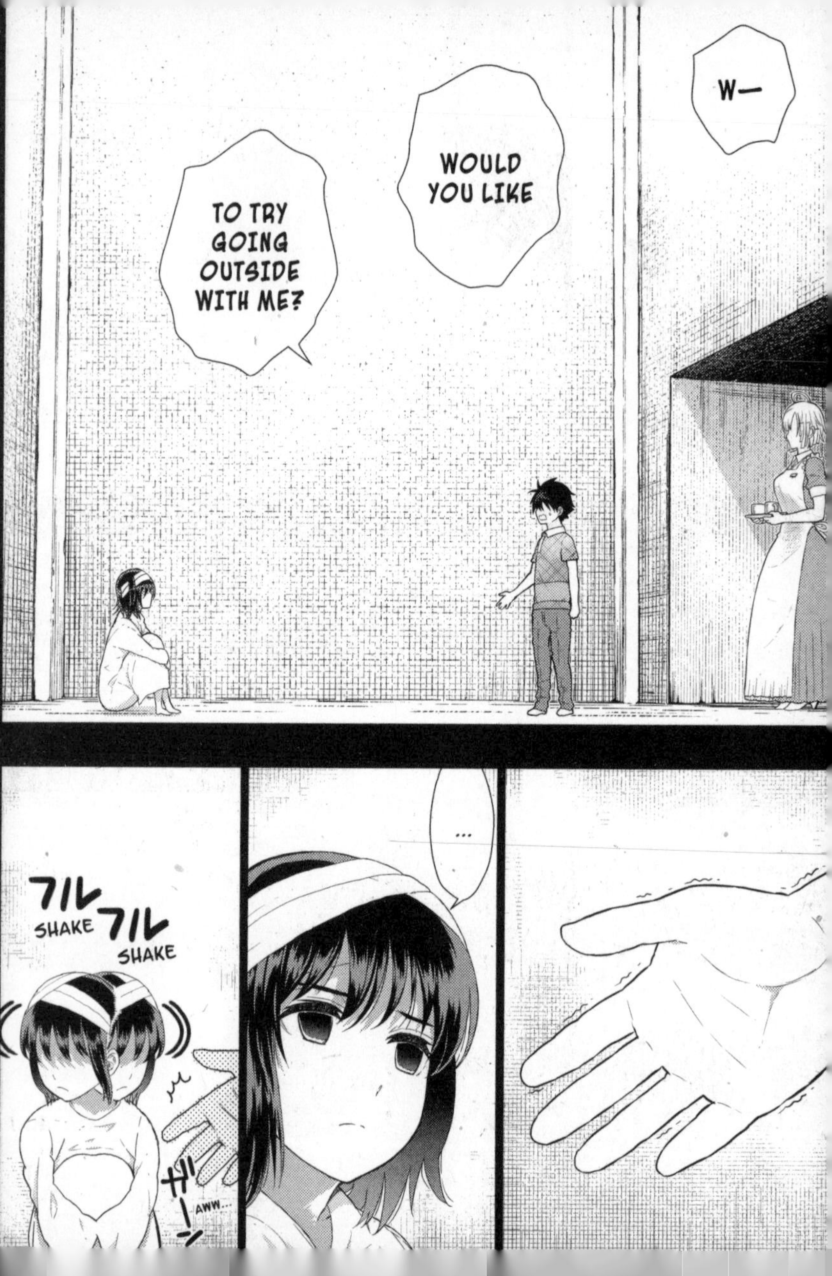
W—
WOULD YOU LIKE
TO TRY GOING OUTSIDE WITH ME?
...
フル SHAKE フル SHAKE
ガーン AWW...

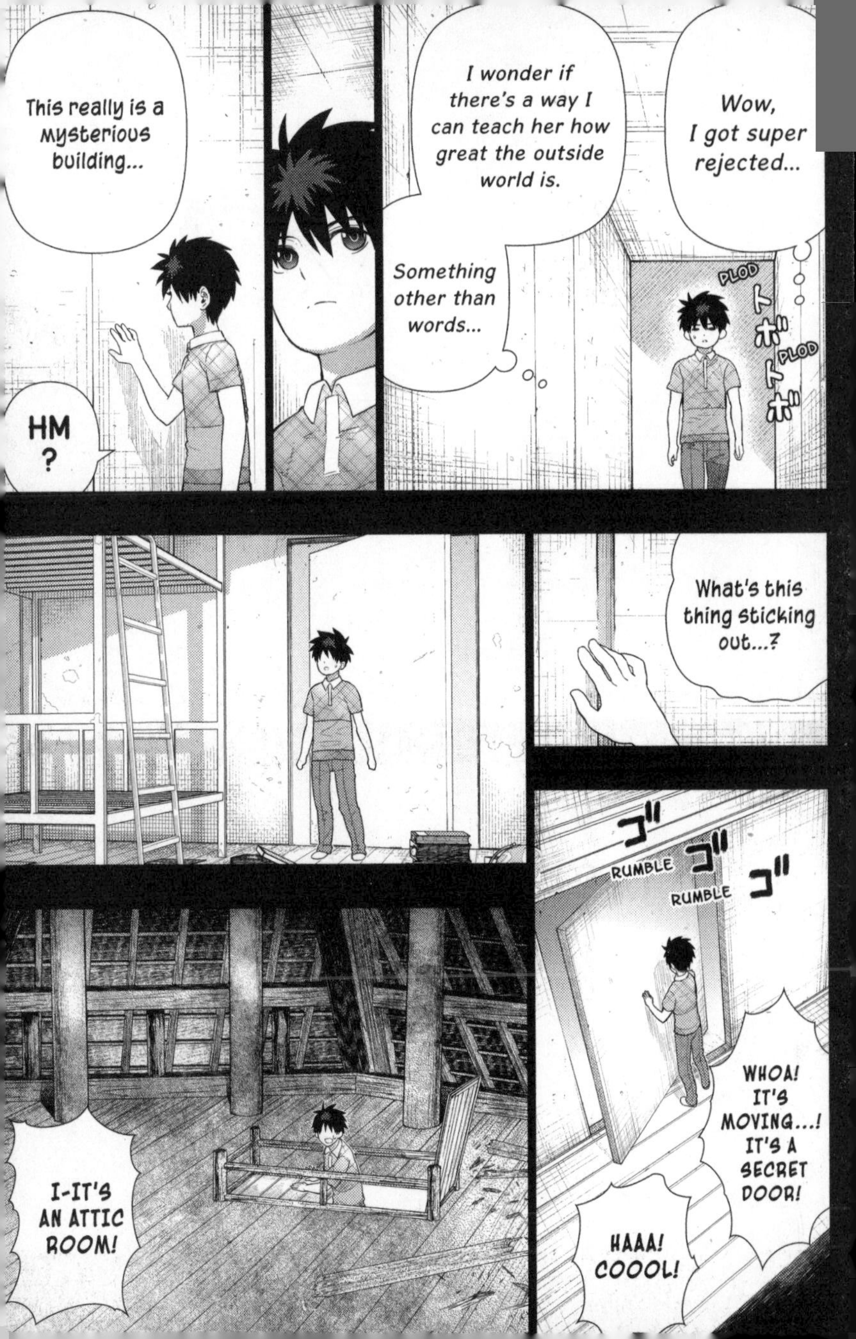
Wow, I got super rejected...
PLOD
トボ
PLOD
トボ
I wonder if there's a way I can teach her how great the outside world is.
Something other than words...
This really is a mysterious building...
HM?
What's this thing sticking out...?
ゴ
RUMBLE
ゴ
RUMBLE
ゴ
WHOA! IT'S MOVING...! IT'S A SECRET DOOR!
HAAA! COOOL!
I-IT'S AN ATTIC ROOM!

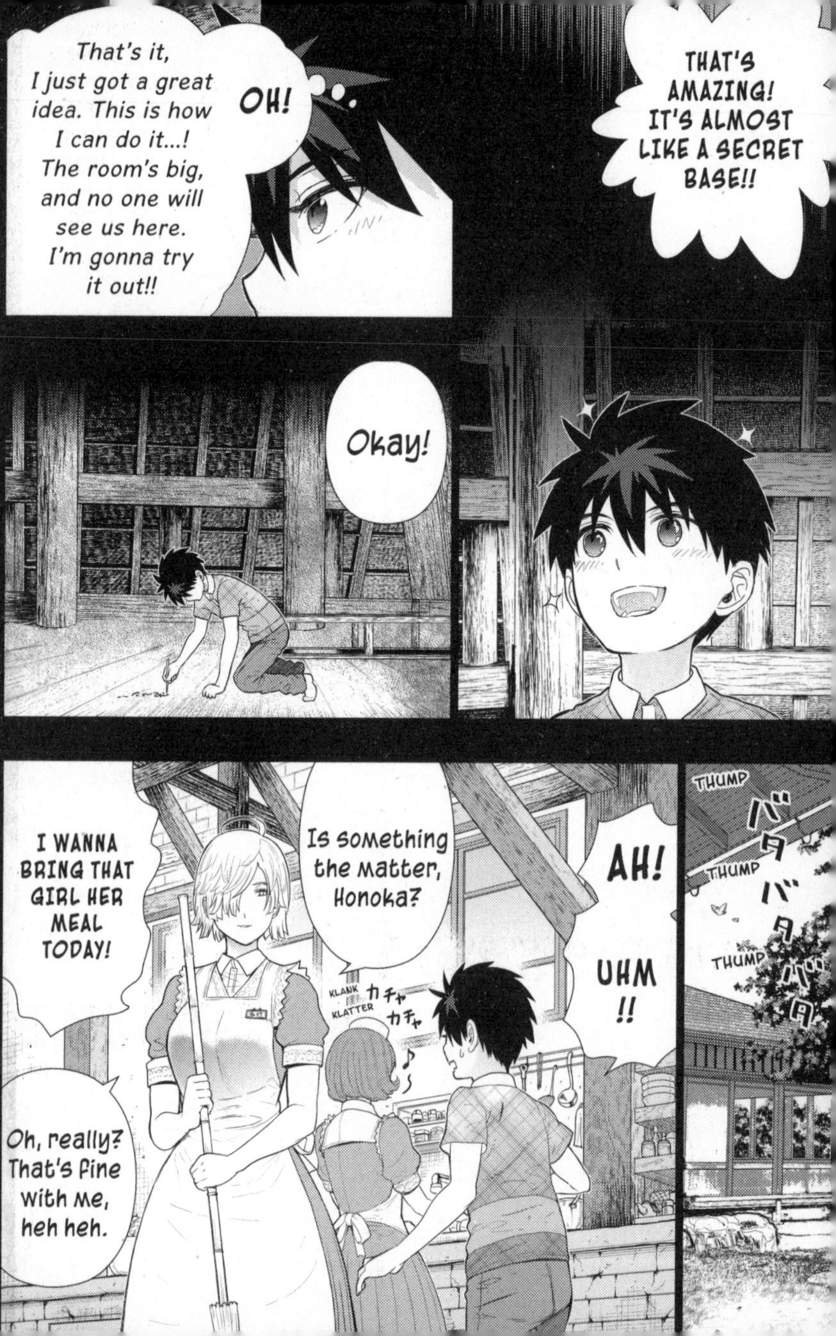
THAT'S AMAZING! IT'S ALMOST LIKE A SECRET BASE!!
OH!
That's it, I just got a great idea. This is how I can do it...! The room's big, and no one will see us here. I'm gonna try it out!!
Okay!
THUMP
バタ
THUMP
バタ
THUMP
バタ
AH!
UHM !!
Is something the matter, Honoka?
KLANK KLATTER
カチャ カチャ
I WANNA BRING THAT GIRL HER MEAL TODAY!
Oh, really? That's fine with me, heh heh.

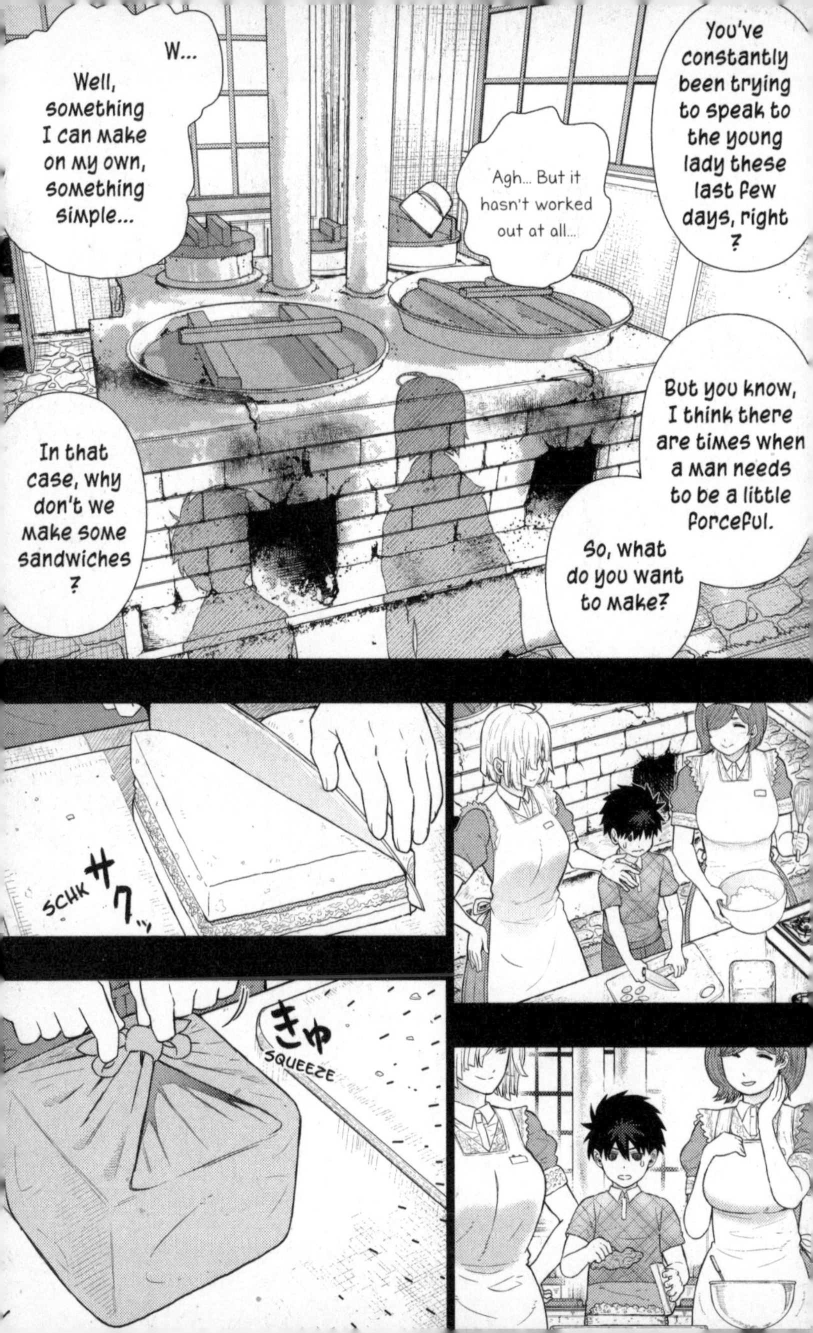
You've constantly been trying to speak to the young lady these last few days, right?
Agh... But it hasn't worked out at all...
But you know, I think there are times when a man needs to be a little forceful.
So, what do you want to make?
W...
Well, something I can make on my own, something simple...
In that case, why don't we make some sandwiches?
サク
SCHK
きゅ
SQUEEZE

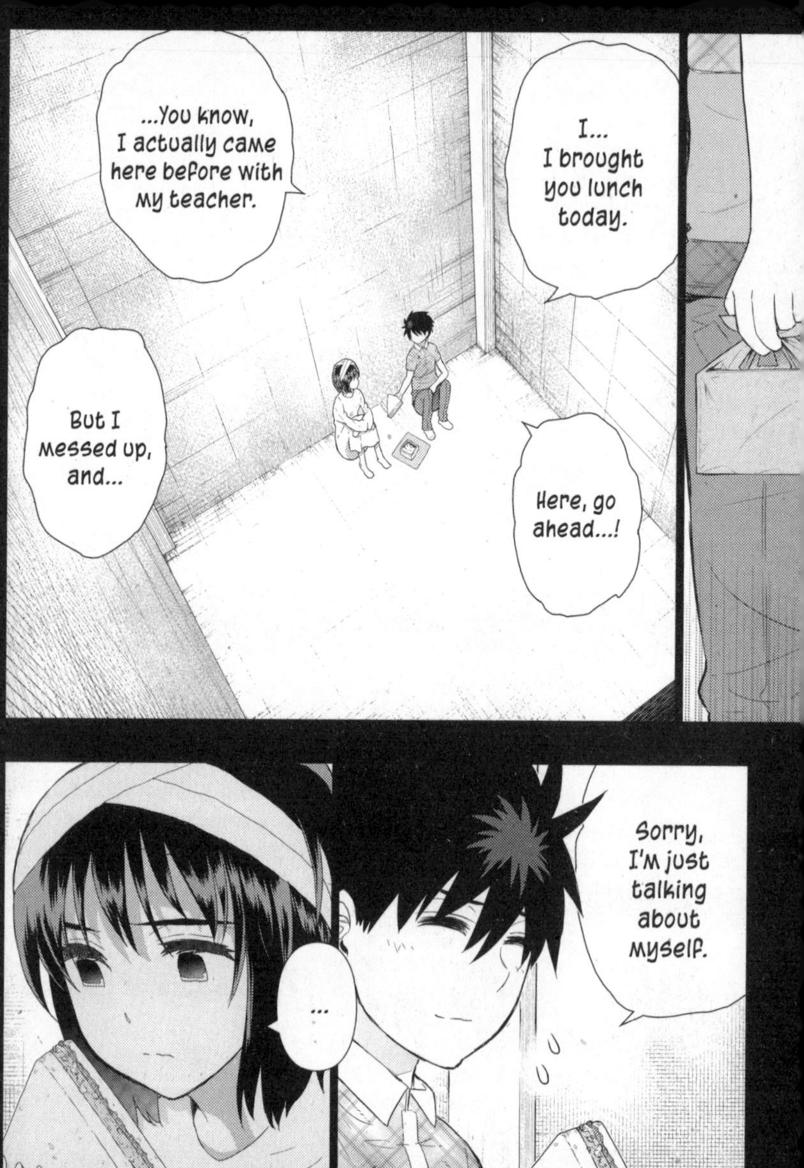
I... I brought you lunch today.
Here, go ahead...!
...You know, I actually came here before with my teacher.
But I messed up, and...
Sorry, I'm just talking about myself.
...

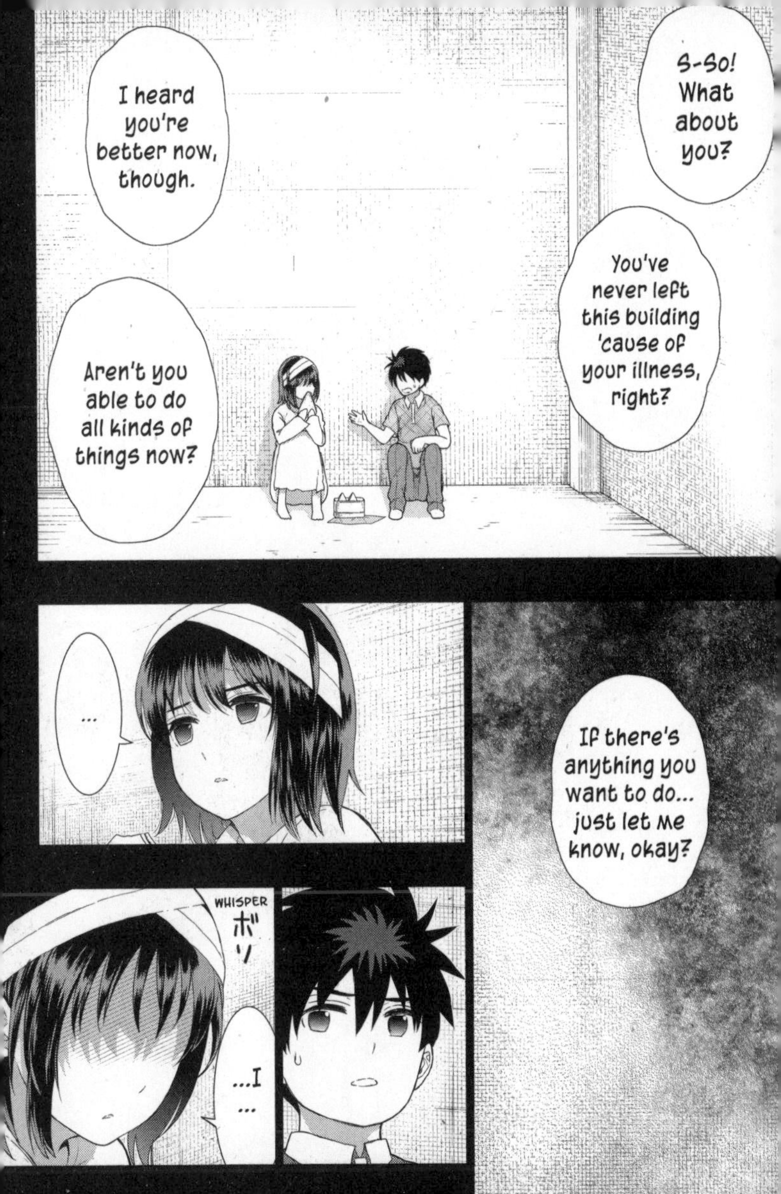
S-So! What about you?
You've never left this building 'cause of your illness, right?
I heard you're better now, though.
Aren't you able to do all kinds of things now?
If there's anything you want to do... just let me know, okay?
...
WHISPER
ボソ
...I ...

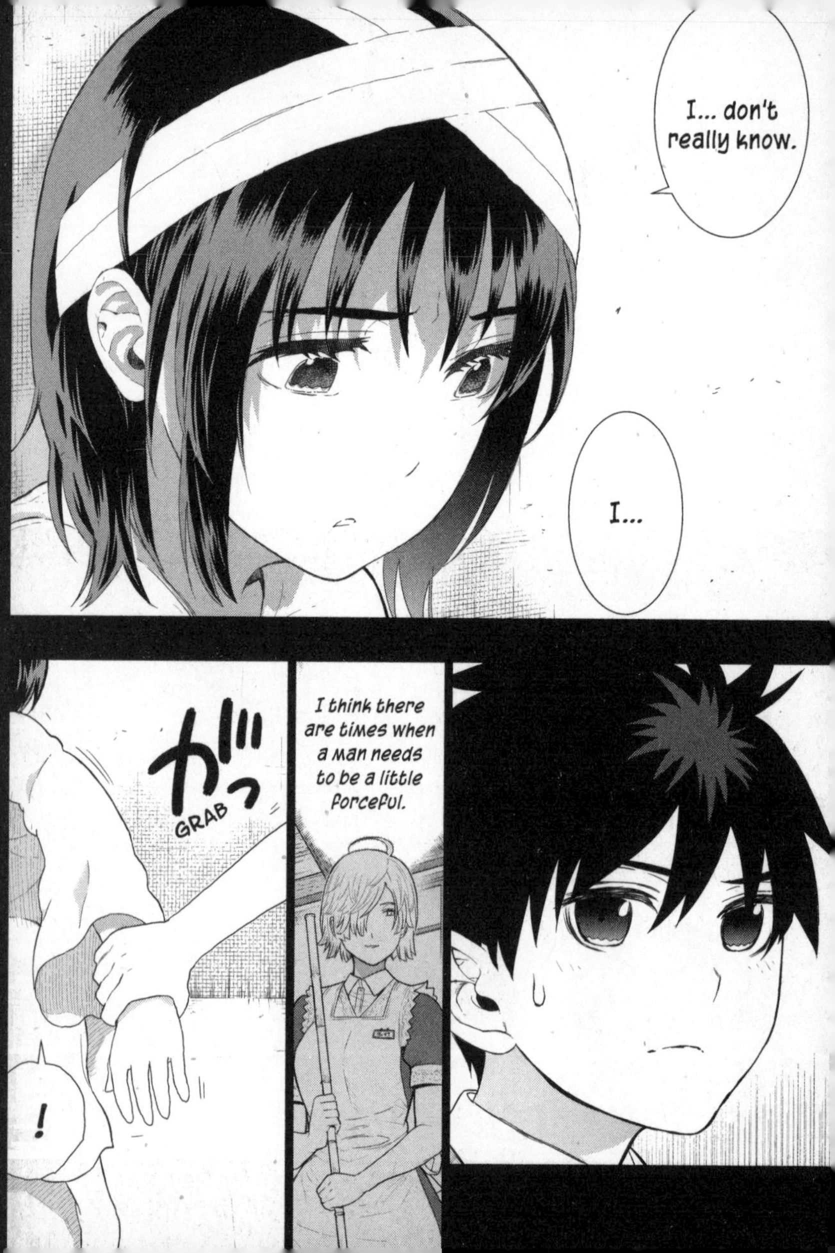
I... don't really know.
I...
I think there are times when a man needs to be a little forceful.
がっ
GRAB
!

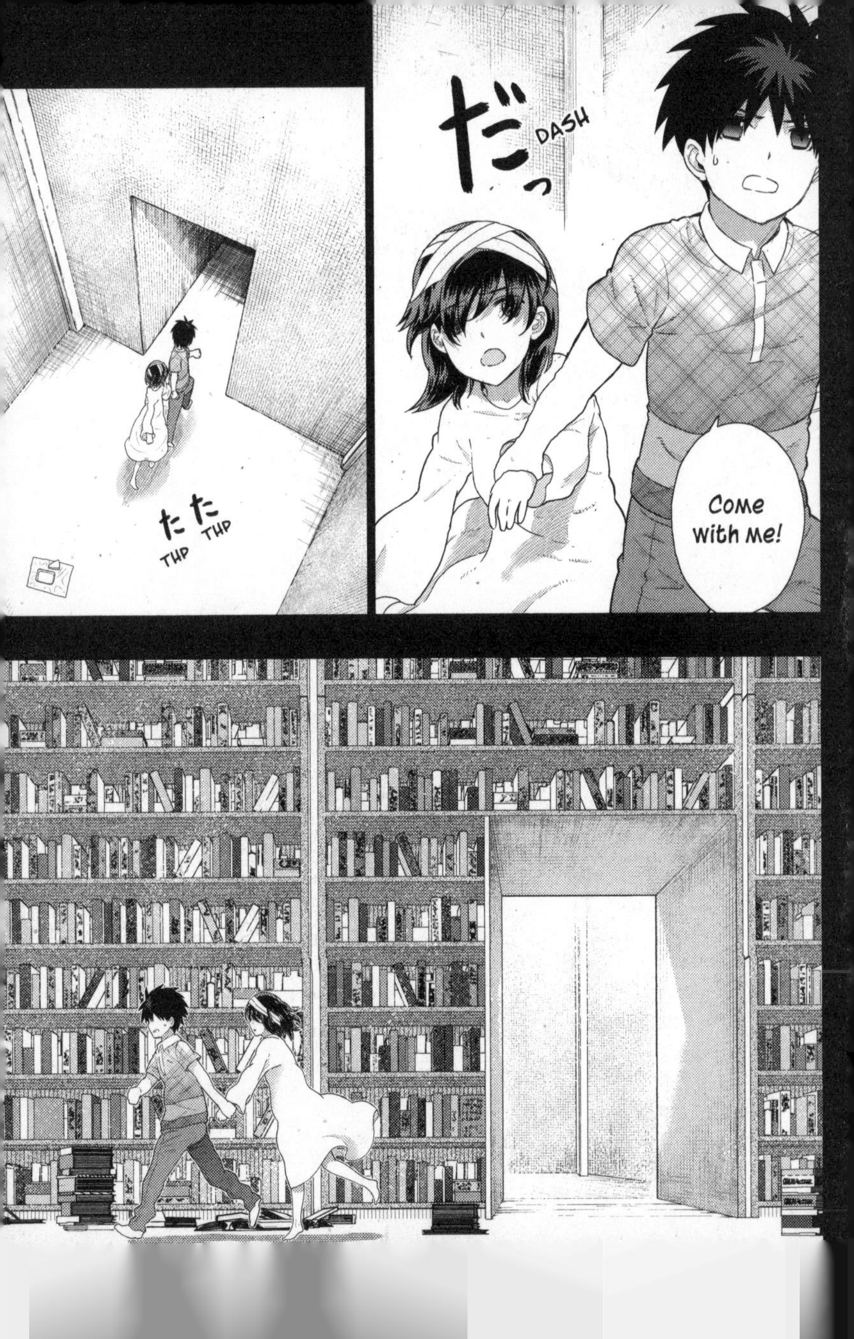
だっ
DASH
Come with me!
たた
THP THP

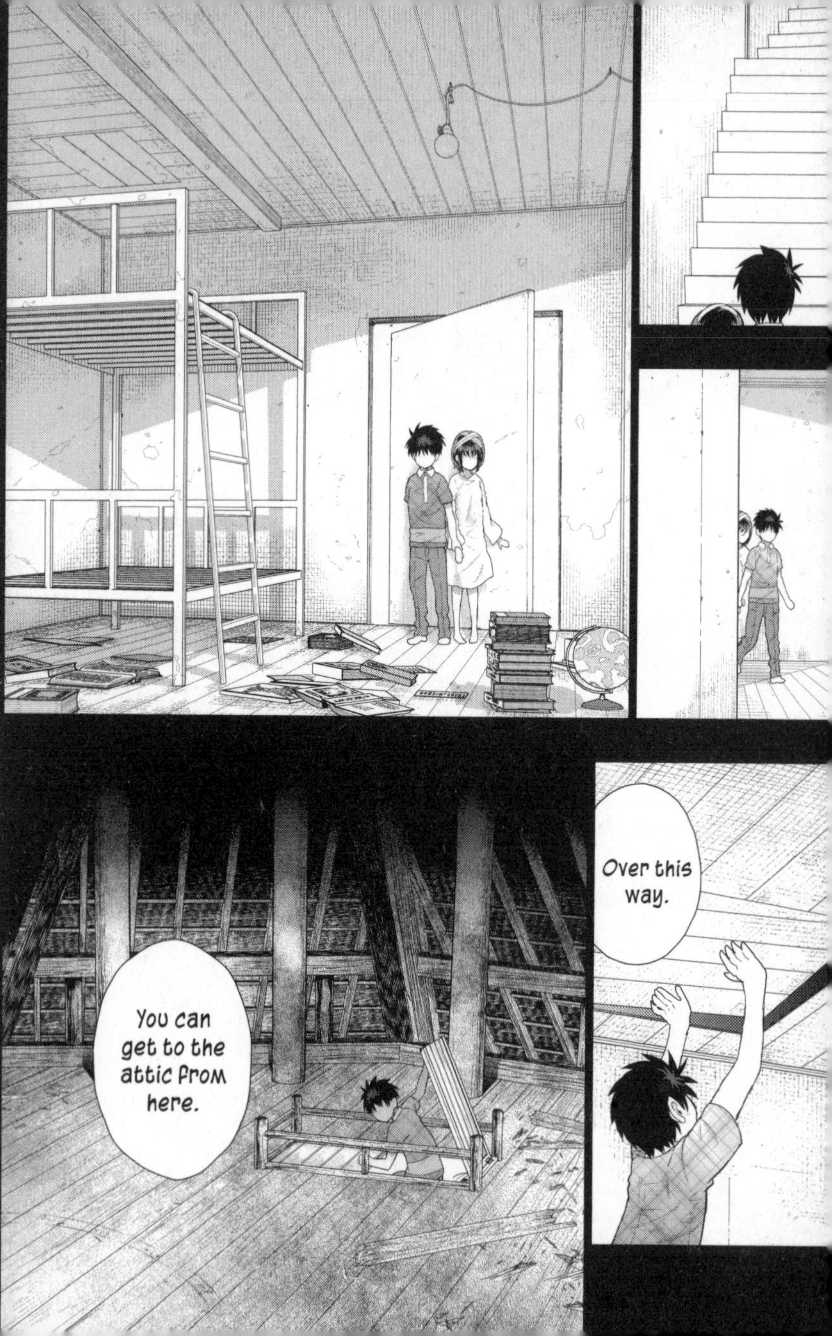
Over this way.
You can get to the attic from here.

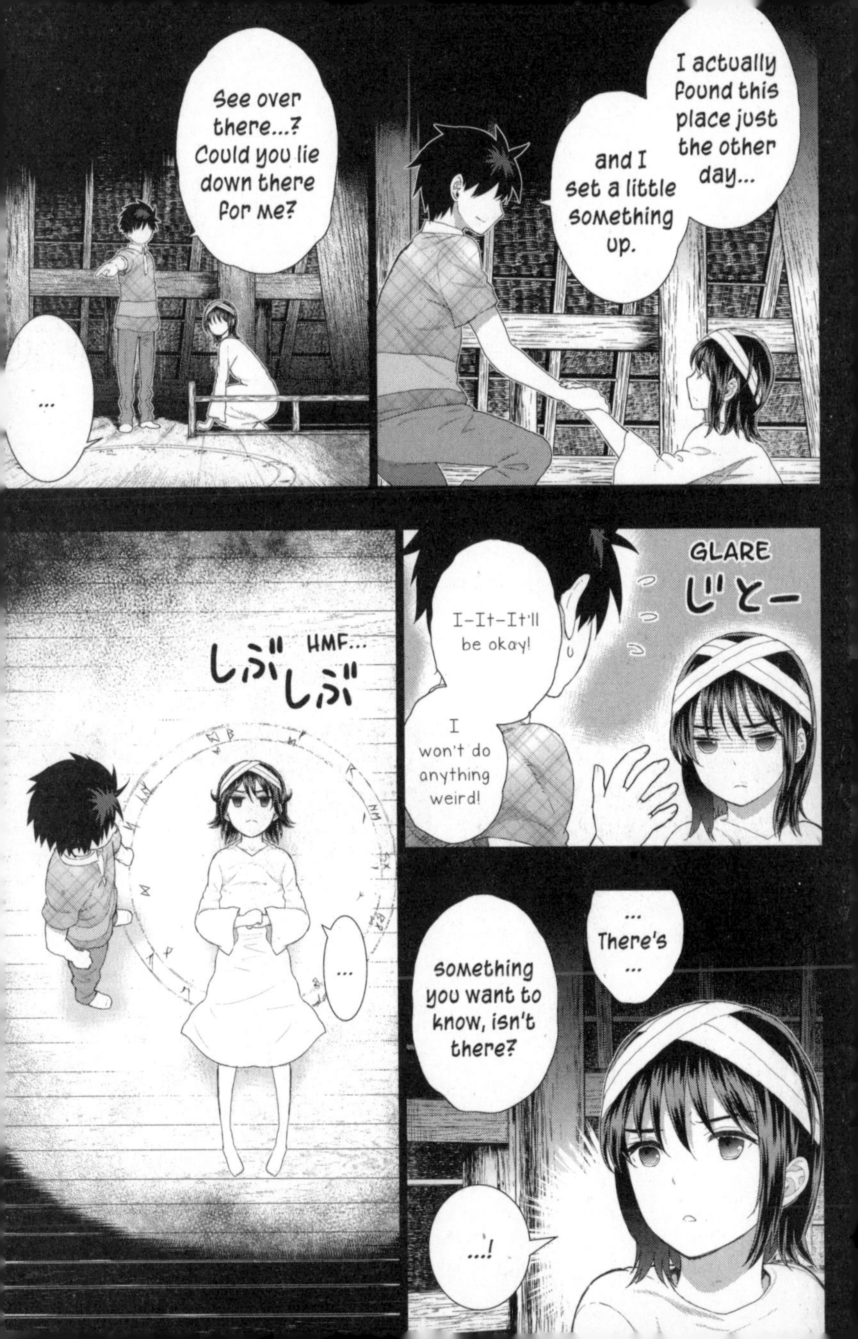
I actually found this place just the other day...
and I set a little something up.
See over there...? Could you lie down there for me?
...
GLARE
じとー
I-It-It'll be okay!
I won't do anything weird!
... There's ...
something you want to know, isn't there?
...!
しぶしぶ
HMF...
...

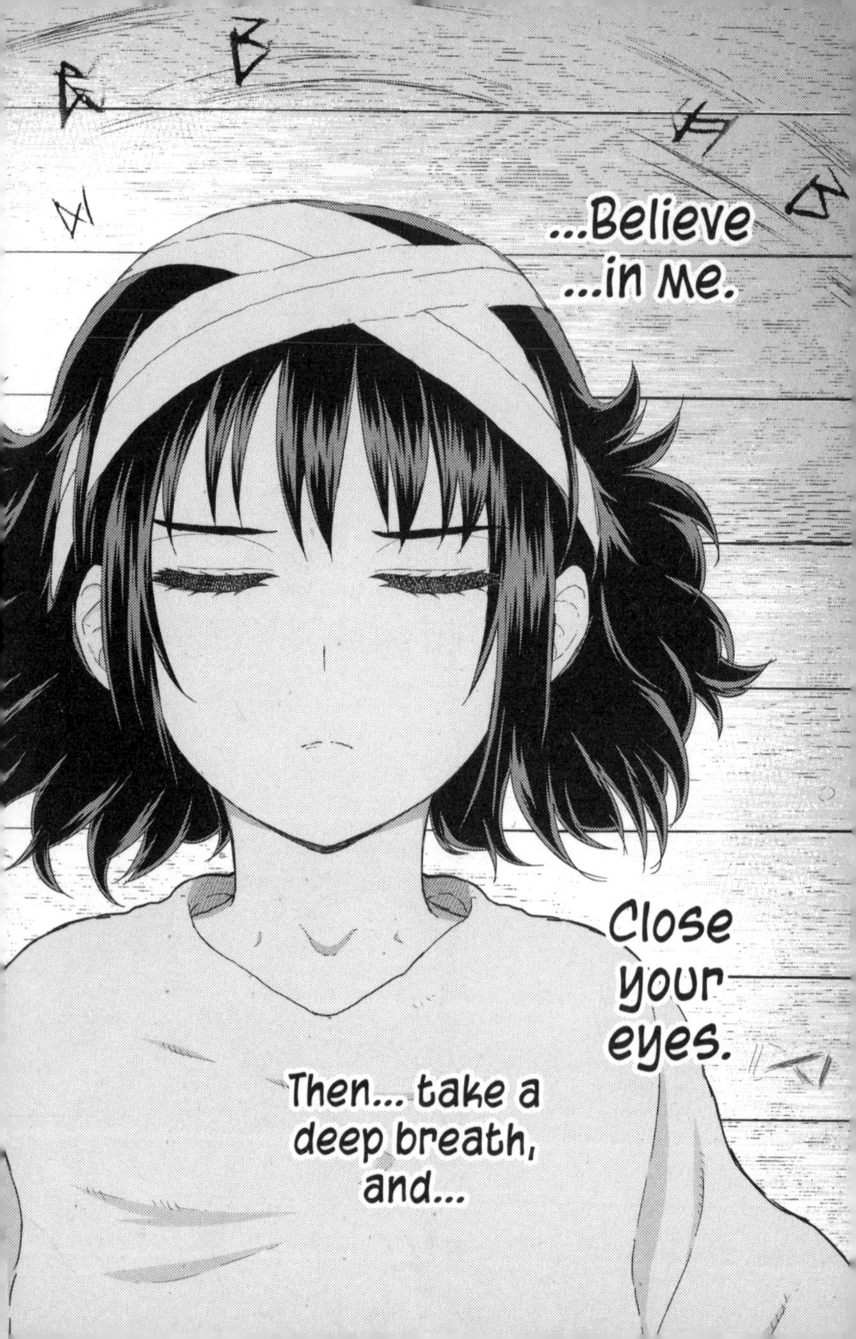
...Believe ...in me.
Close your eyes.
Then... take a deep breath, and...

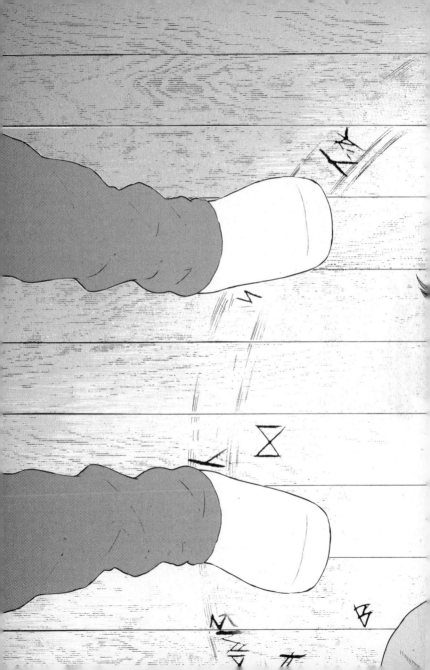

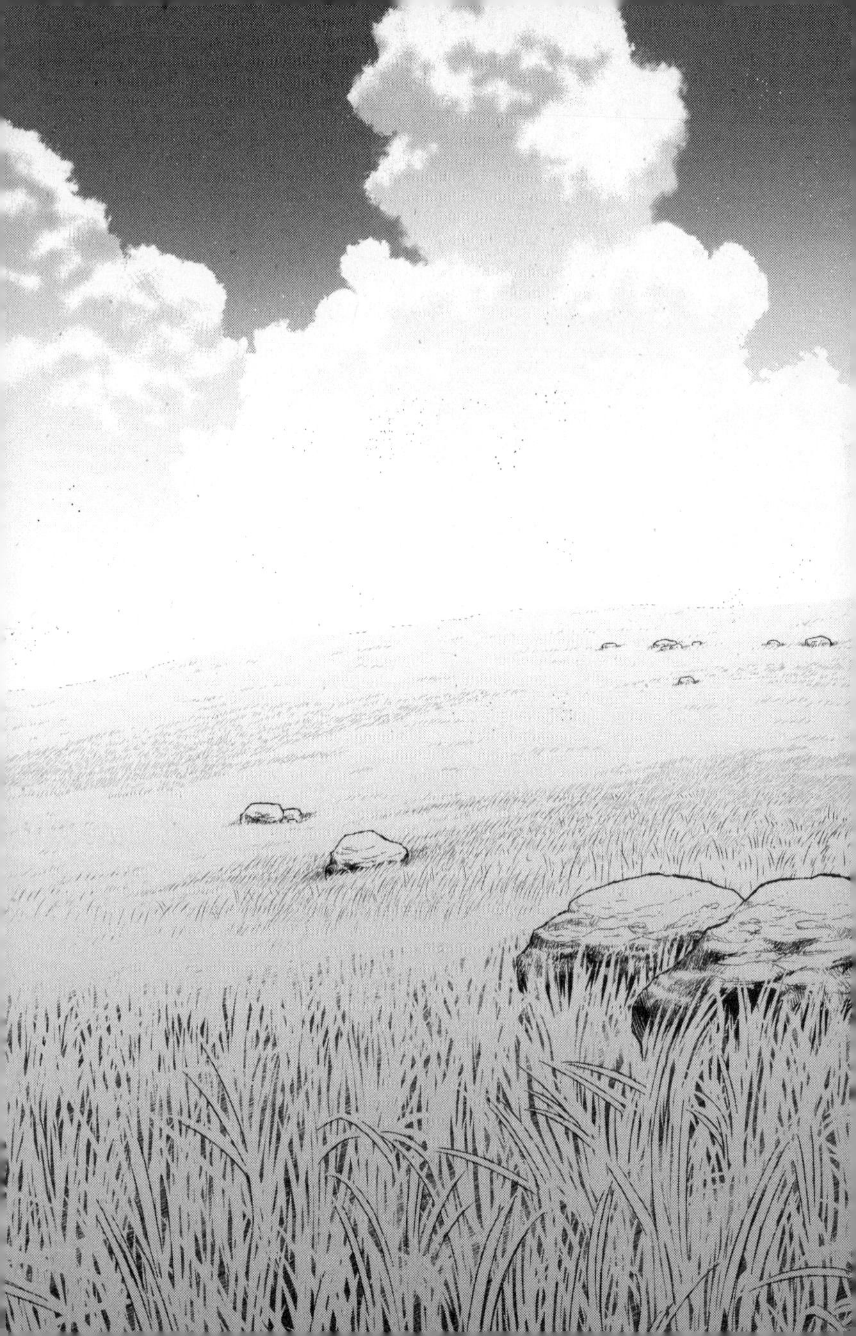

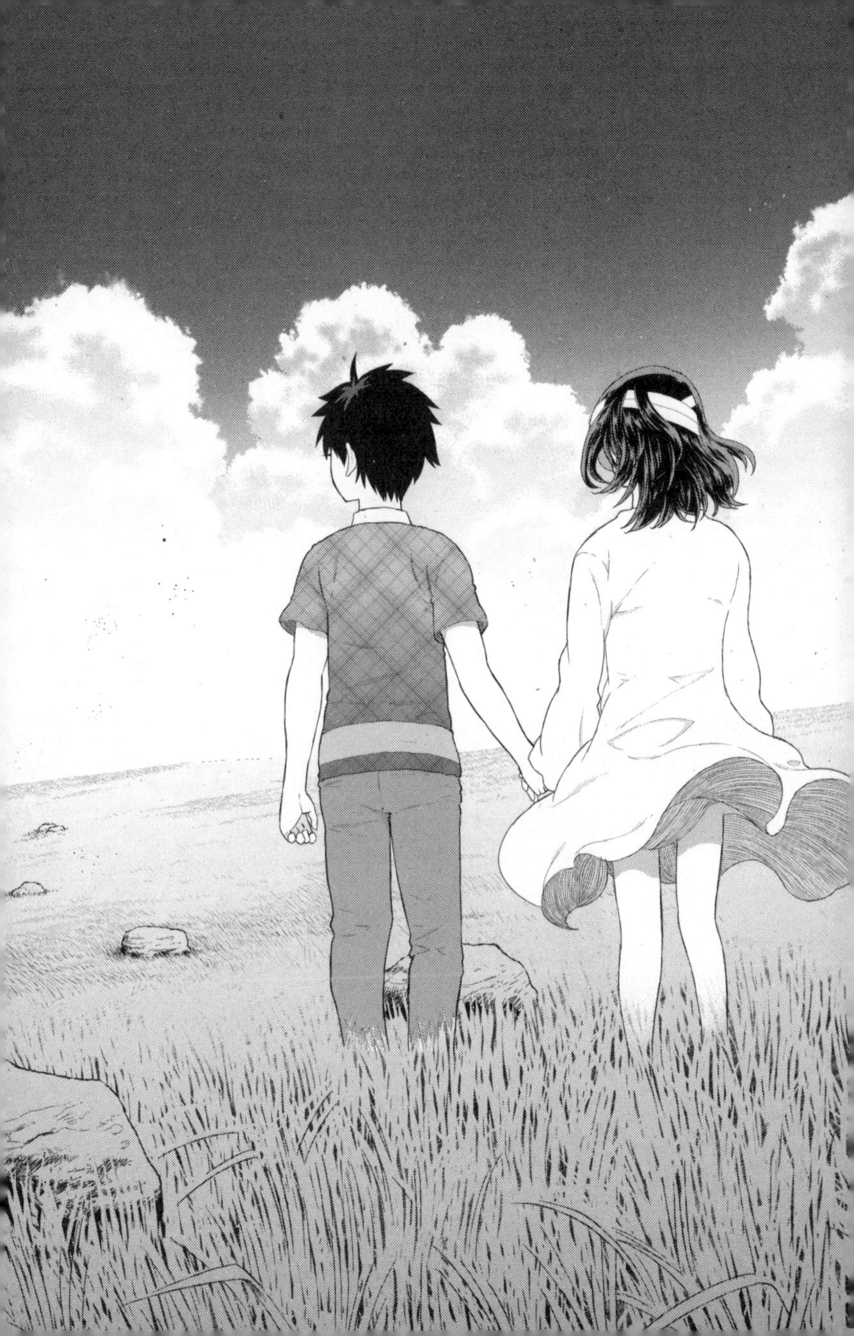

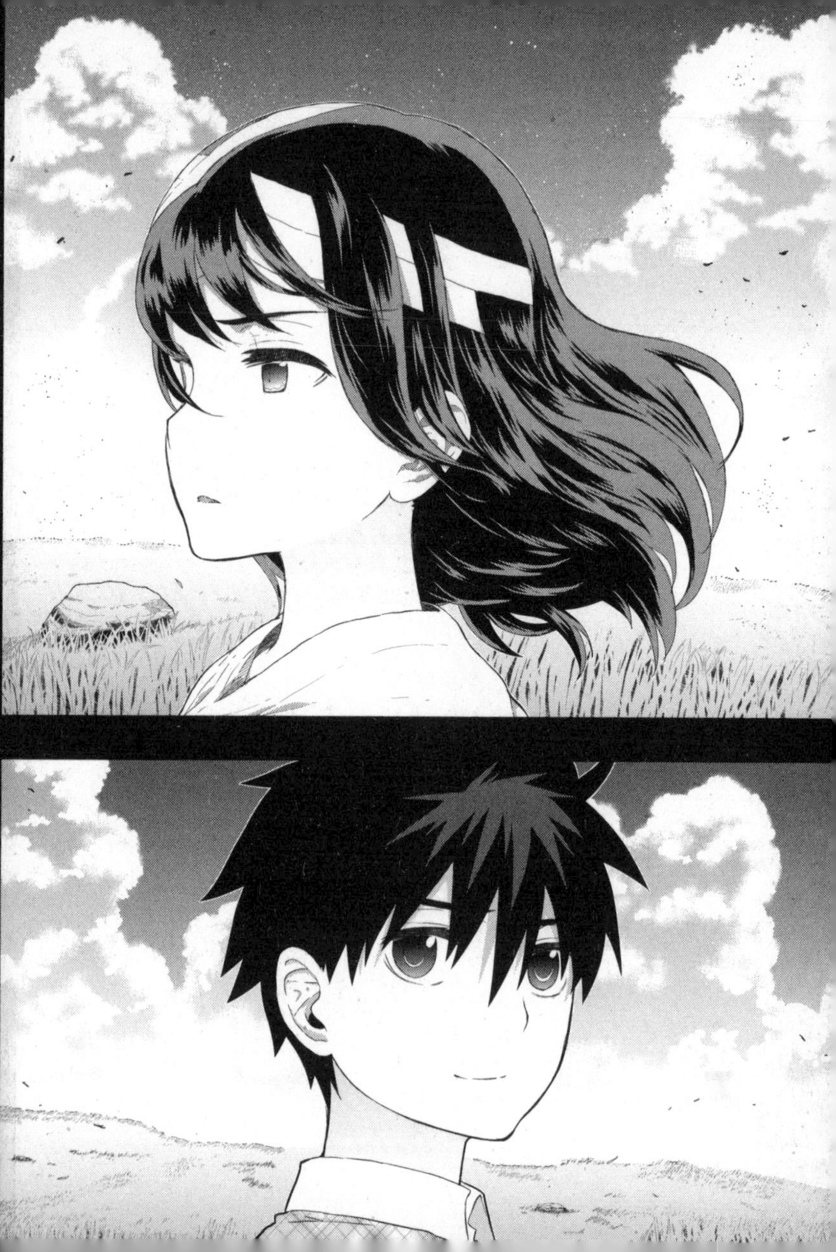

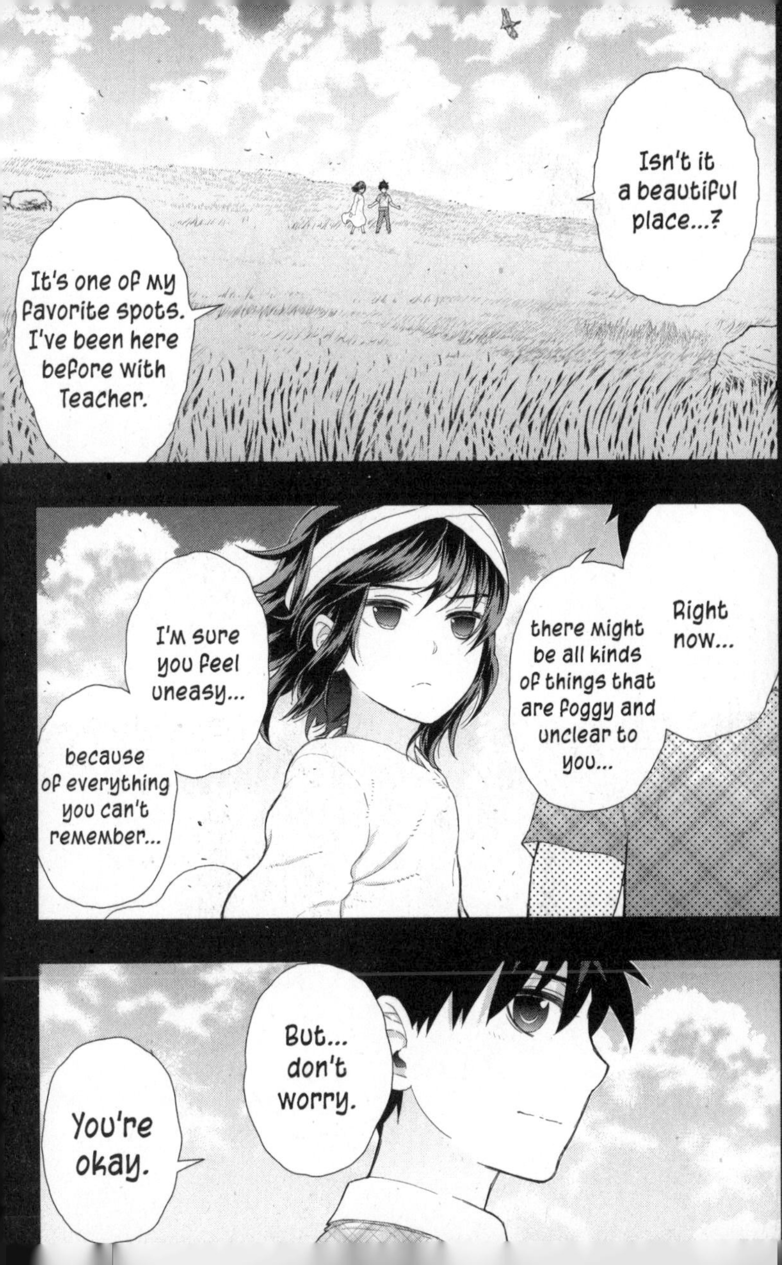
Isn't it a beautiful place...?
It's one of my favorite spots. I've been here before with Teacher.
Right now...
there might be all kinds of things that are foggy and unclear to you...
I'm sure you feel uneasy...
because of everything you can't remember...
But... don't worry.
You're okay.

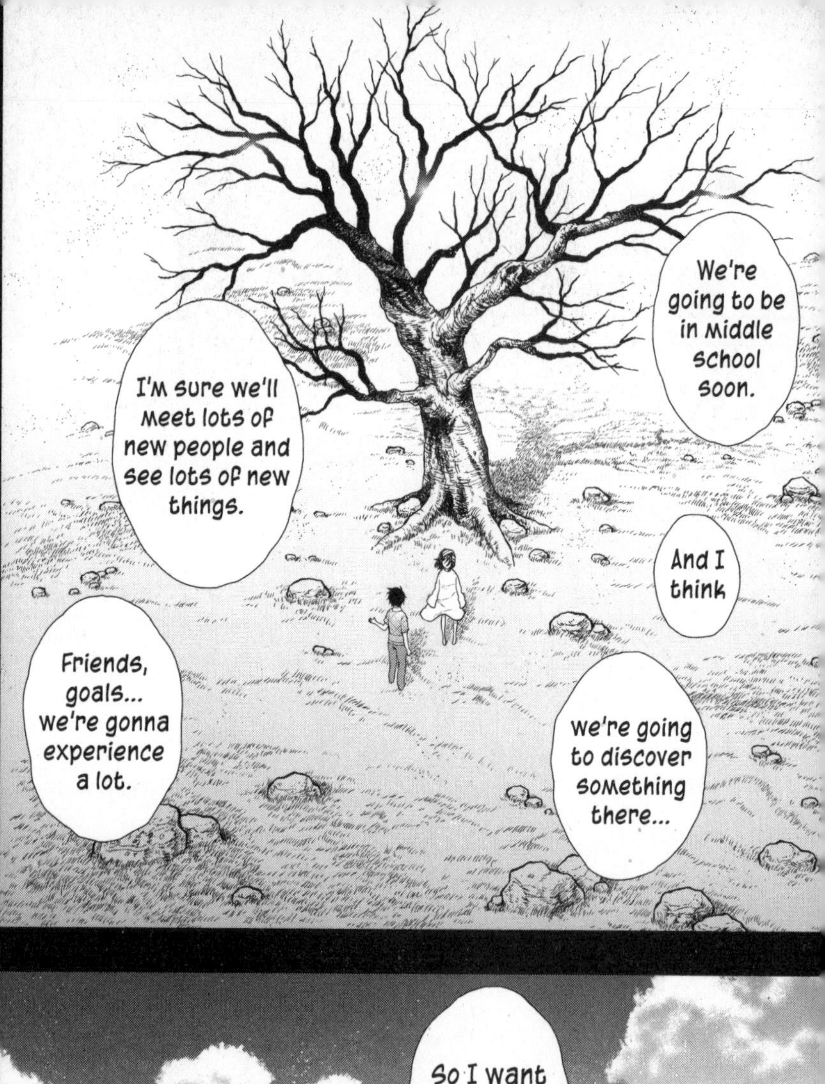
We're going to be in middle school soon.
I'm sure we'll meet lots of new people and see lots of new things.
Friends, goals... we're gonna experience a lot.
And I think
we're going to discover something there...
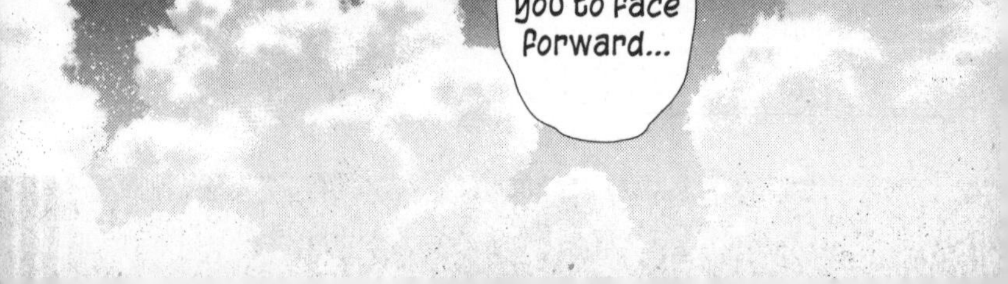
So I want you to face forward...

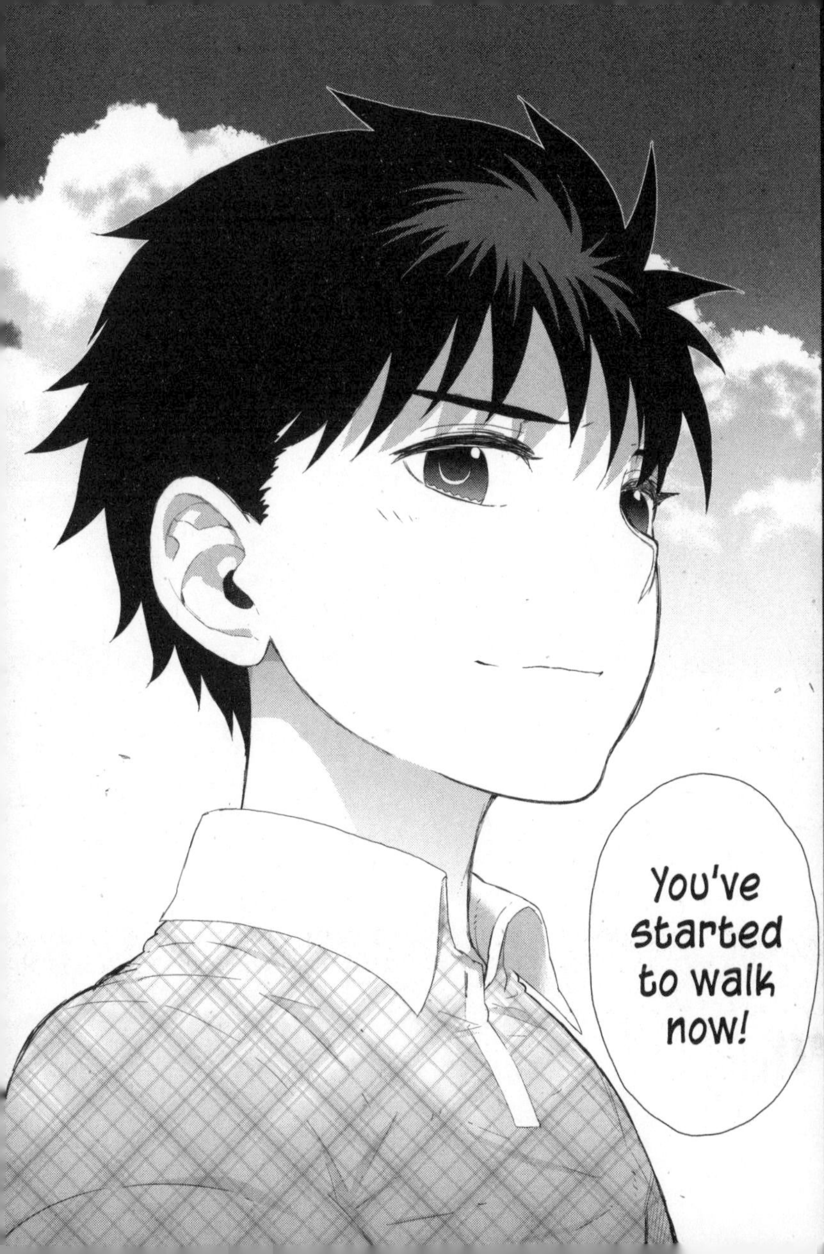
You've started to walk now!

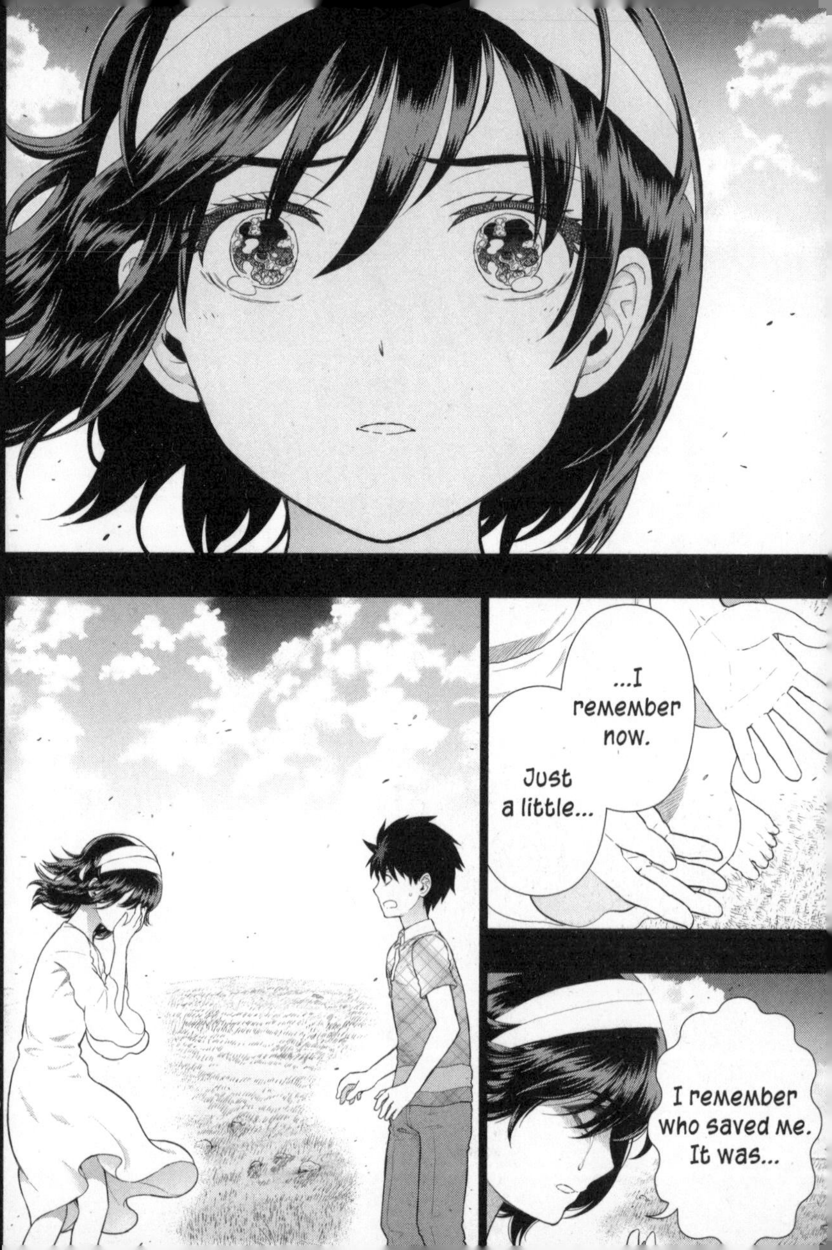
...I remember now.
Just a little...
I remember who saved me. It was...

CHAPTER 8 END

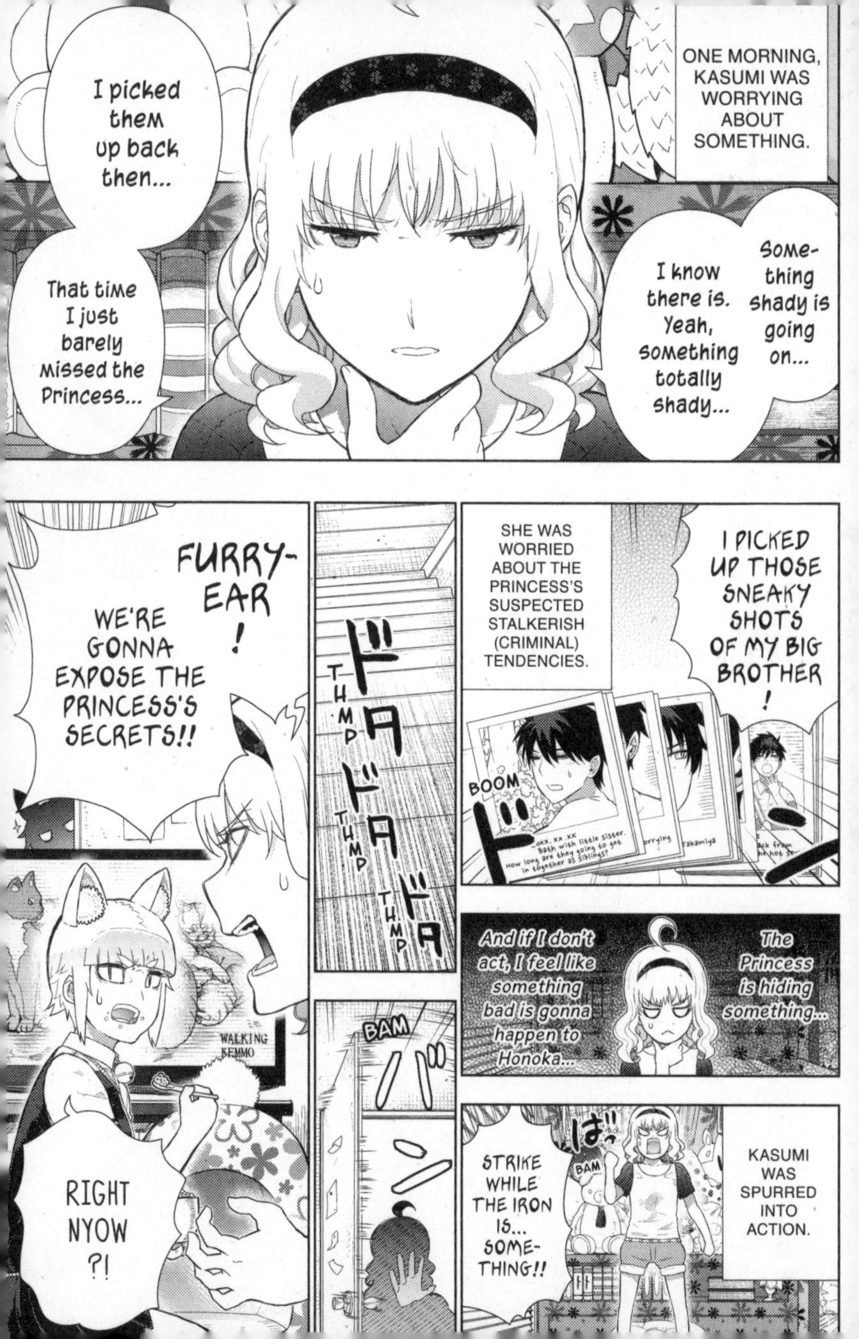

ONE MORNING, KASUMI WAS WORRYING ABOUT SOMETHING.
Something shady is going on...
I know there is. Yeah, something totally shady...
I picked them up back then...
That time I just barely missed the Princess...
I PICKED UP THOSE SNEAKY SHOTS OF MY BIG BROTHER!
SHE WAS WORRIED ABOUT THE PRINCESS'S SUSPECTED STALKERISH (CRIMINAL) TENDENCIES.
BOOM
Bath with little sister. How long are they going to get in together as siblings?
The Princess is hiding something...
And if I don't act, I feel like something bad is gonna happen to Honoka...
KASUMI WAS SPURRED INTO ACTION.
BAM
STRIKE WHILE THE IRON IS... SOMETHING!!
THUMP
THUMP
THUMP
BAM
FURRY-EAR!
WE'RE GONNA EXPOSE THE PRINCESS'S SECRETS!!
WALKING KEMMO
RIGHT NYOW?!

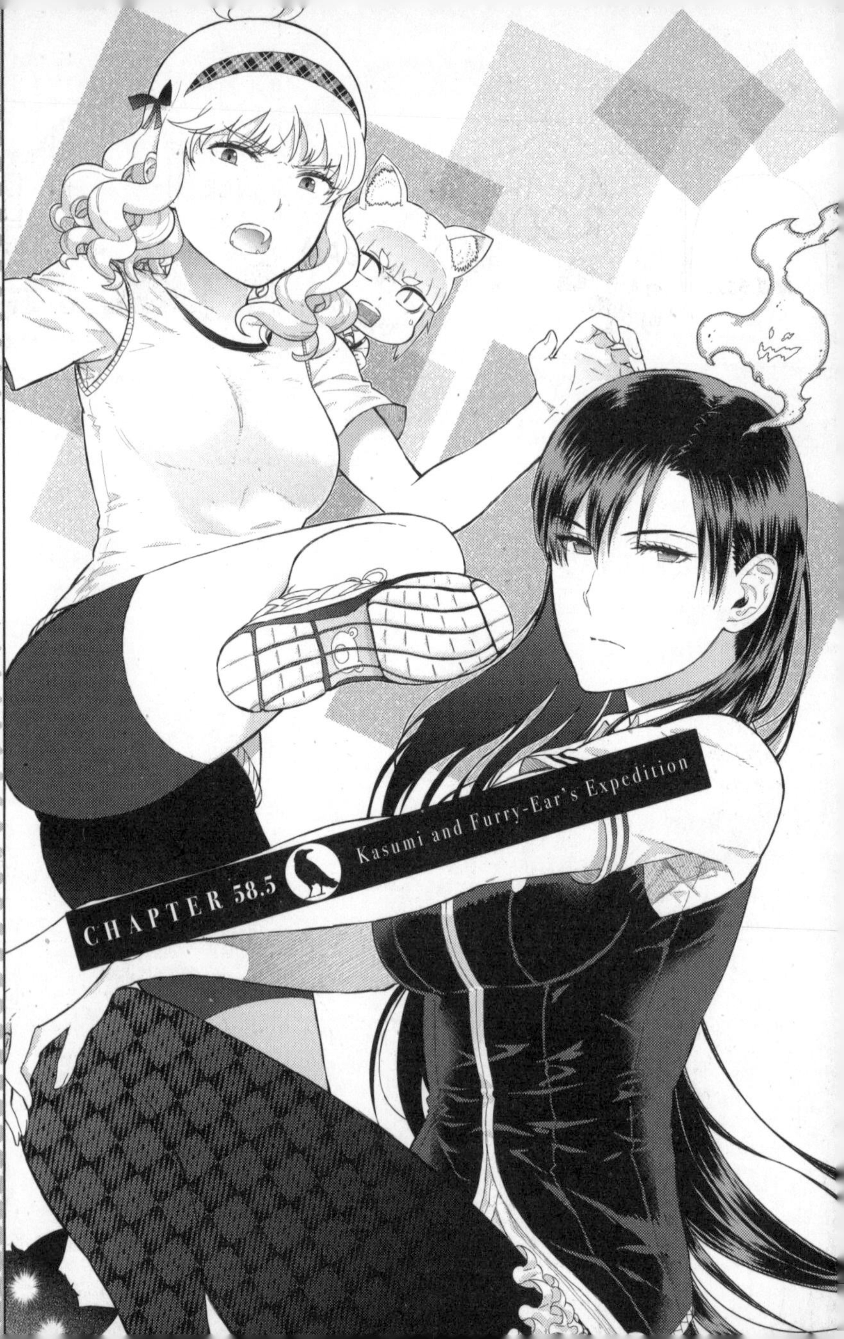
CHAPTER 58.5
Kasumi and Furry-Ear's Expedition

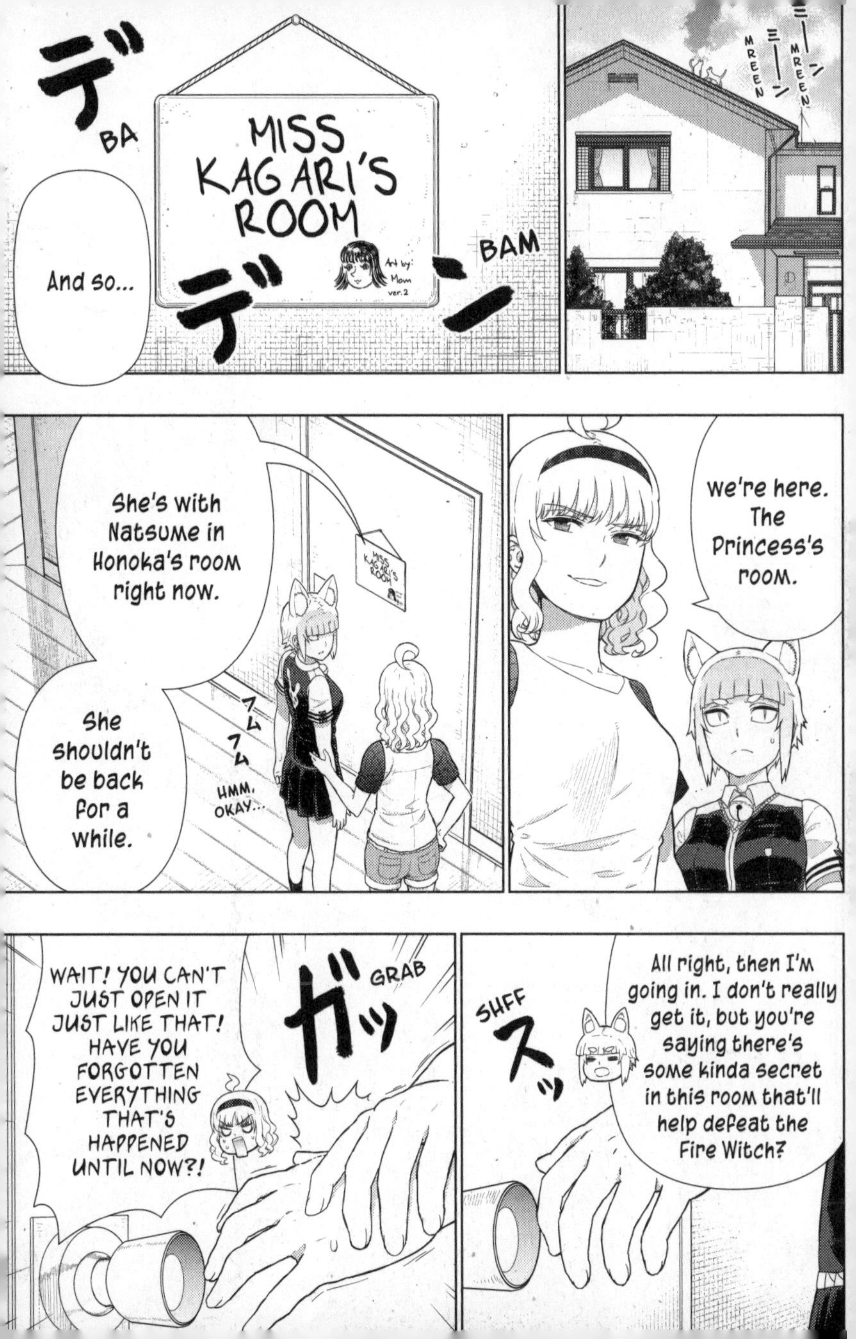
ミーン ミーン
MREEN MREEN
デデーン
BA BAM
MISS KAGARI'S ROOM
Art by: Mom ver.2
And so...
We're here. The Princess's room.
She's with Natsume in Honoka's room right now.
She shouldn't be back for a while.
フムフム
HMM, OKAY...
スッ
SHFF
All right, then I'm going in. I don't really get it, but you're saying there's some kinda secret in this room that'll help defeat the Fire Witch?
ガッ
GRAB
WAIT! YOU CAN'T JUST OPEN IT JUST LIKE THAT! HAVE YOU FORGOTTEN EVERYTHING THAT'S HAPPENED UNTIL NOW?!

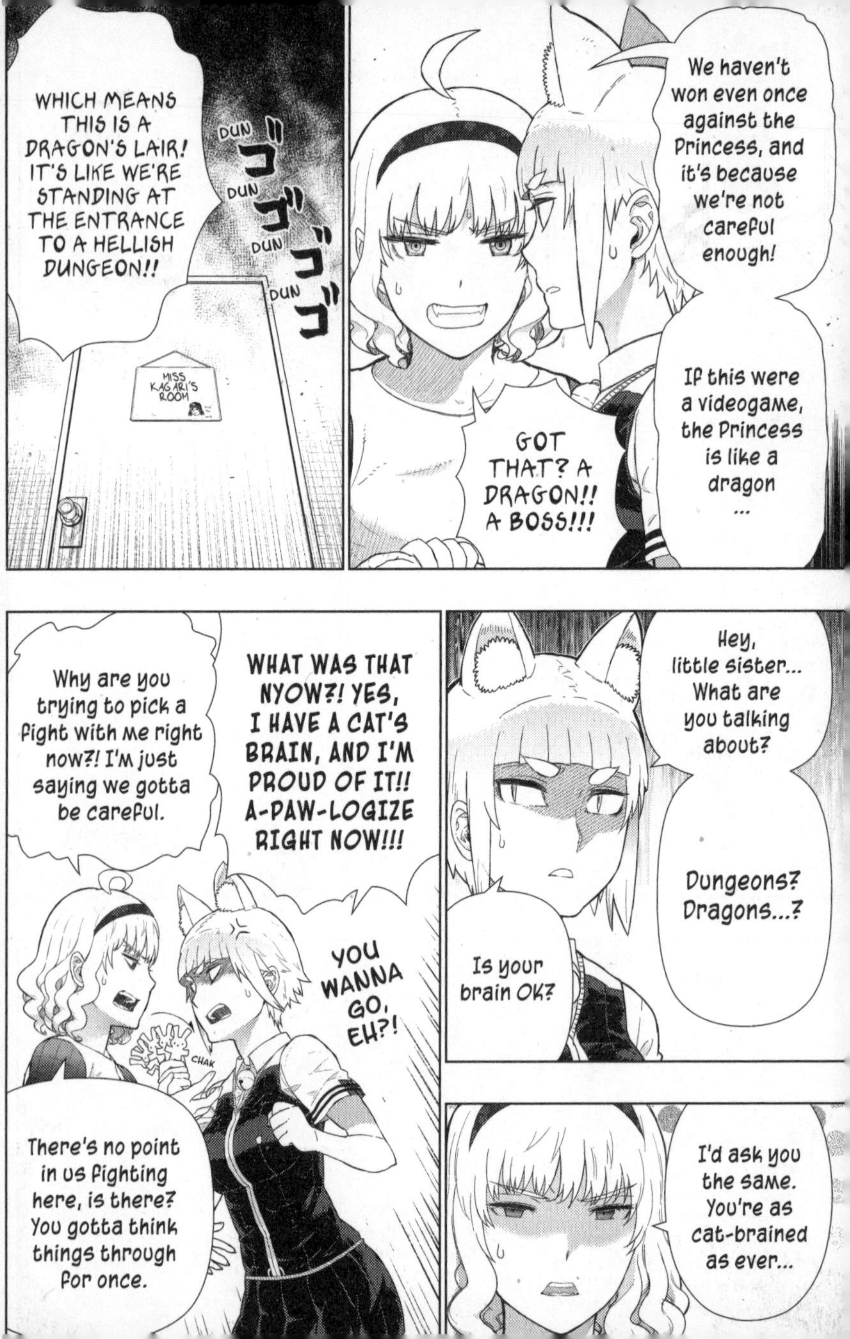

We haven't won even once against the Princess, and it's because we're not careful enough!
If this were a videogame, the Princess is like a dragon ...
GOT THAT? A DRAGON!! A BOSS!!!
WHICH MEANS THIS IS A DRAGON'S LAIR! IT'S LIKE WE'RE STANDING AT THE ENTRANCE TO A HELLISH DUNGEON!!
DUN
DUN
DUN
DUN
MISS KAGARI'S ROOM
Hey, little sister... What are you talking about?
Dungeons? Dragons...?
Is your brain OK?
I'd ask you the same. You're as cat-brained as ever...
WHAT WAS THAT NYOW?! YES, I HAVE A CAT'S BRAIN, AND I'M PROUD OF IT!! A-PAW-LOGIZE RIGHT NOW!!!
Why are you trying to pick a fight with me right now?! I'm just saying we gotta be careful.
YOU WANNA GO, EH?!
CHAK
There's no point in us fighting here, is there? You gotta think things through for once.

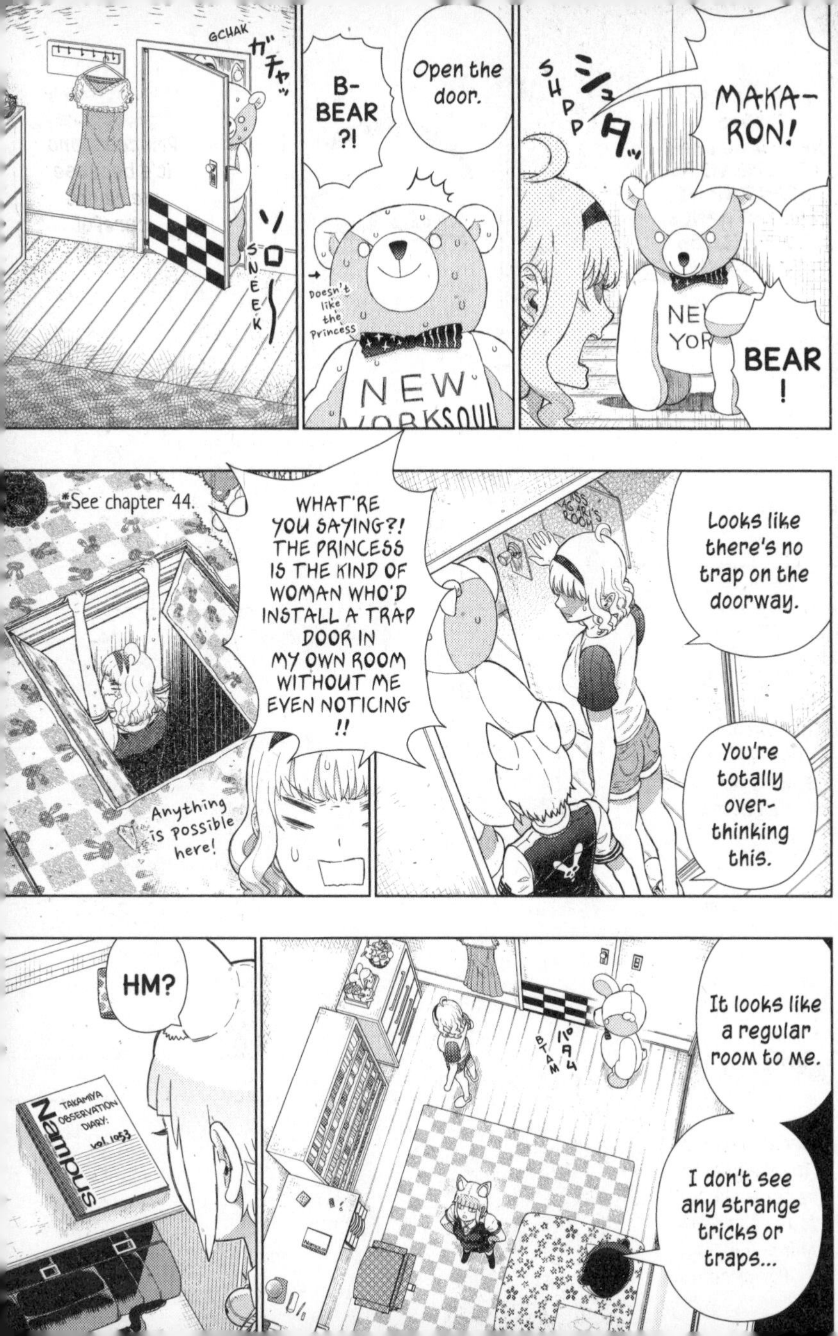MAKA-RON!
シュタッ
SHPP
BEAR!
Open the door.
B-BEAR?!
Doesn't like the Princess
ガチャッ
GCHAK
ソロ〜
SNEEK
Looks like there's no trap on the doorway.
You're totally over-thinking this.
WHAT'RE YOU SAYING?! THE PRINCESS IS THE KIND OF WOMAN WHO'D INSTALL A TRAP DOOR IN MY OWN ROOM WITHOUT ME EVEN NOTICING!!
*See chapter 44.
Anything is possible here!
It looks like a regular room to me.
I don't see any strange tricks or traps...
パタム
BTAM
HM?
TAKAMIYA OBSERVATION DIARY: vol. 1053
Nampus

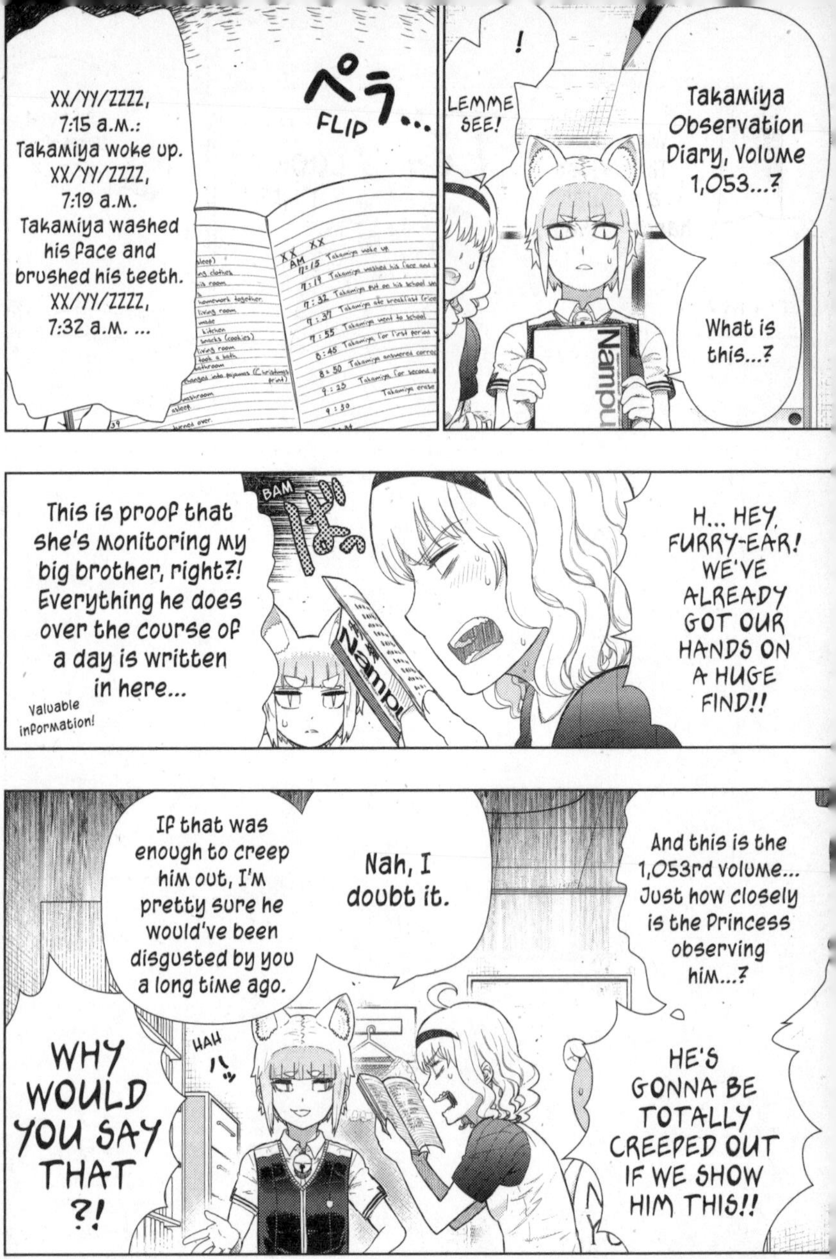
Takamiya Observation Diary, Volume 1,053...?
What is this...?
!
LEMME SEE!
FLIP
XX/YY/ZZZZ, 7:15 a.m.: Takamiya woke up. XX/YY/ZZZZ, 7:19 a.m. Takamiya washed his face and brushed his teeth. XX/YY/ZZZZ, 7:32 a.m. ...
H... HEY, FURRY-EAR! WE'VE ALREADY GOT OUR HANDS ON A HUGE FIND!!
BAM
This is proof that she's monitoring my big brother, right?! Everything he does over the course of a day is written in here...
Valuable information!
And this is the 1,053rd volume... Just how closely is the Princess observing him...?
HE'S GONNA BE TOTALLY CREEPED OUT IF WE SHOW HIM THIS!!
Nah, I doubt it.
If that was enough to creep him out, I'm pretty sure he would've been disgusted by you a long time ago.
HAH
WHY WOULD YOU SAY THAT?!

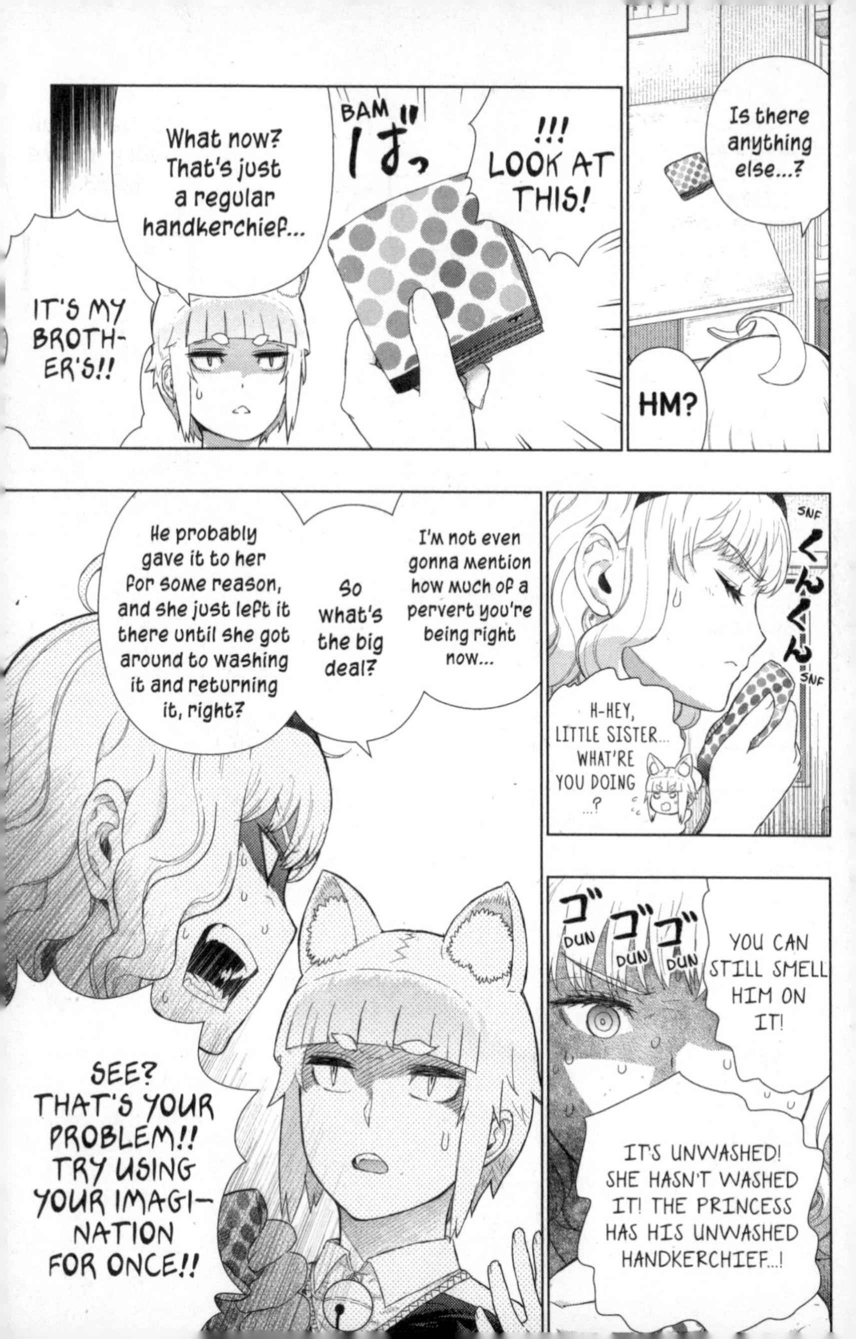
Is there anything else...?
HM?
!!! LOOK AT THIS!
BAM
ばっ
What now? That's just a regular handkerchief...
IT'S MY BROTHER'S!!
SNF
くんくん
SNF
H-HEY, LITTLE SISTER... WHAT'RE YOU DOING ...?
ゴ DUN ゴ DUN ゴ DUN
YOU CAN STILL SMELL HIM ON IT!
IT'S UNWASHED! SHE HASN'T WASHED IT! THE PRINCESS HAS HIS UNWASHED HANDKERCHIEF...!
I'm not even gonna mention how much of a pervert you're being right now...
So what's the big deal?
He probably gave it to her for some reason, and she just left it there until she got around to washing it and returning it, right?
SEE? THAT'S YOUR PROBLEM!! TRY USING YOUR IMAGINATION FOR ONCE!!

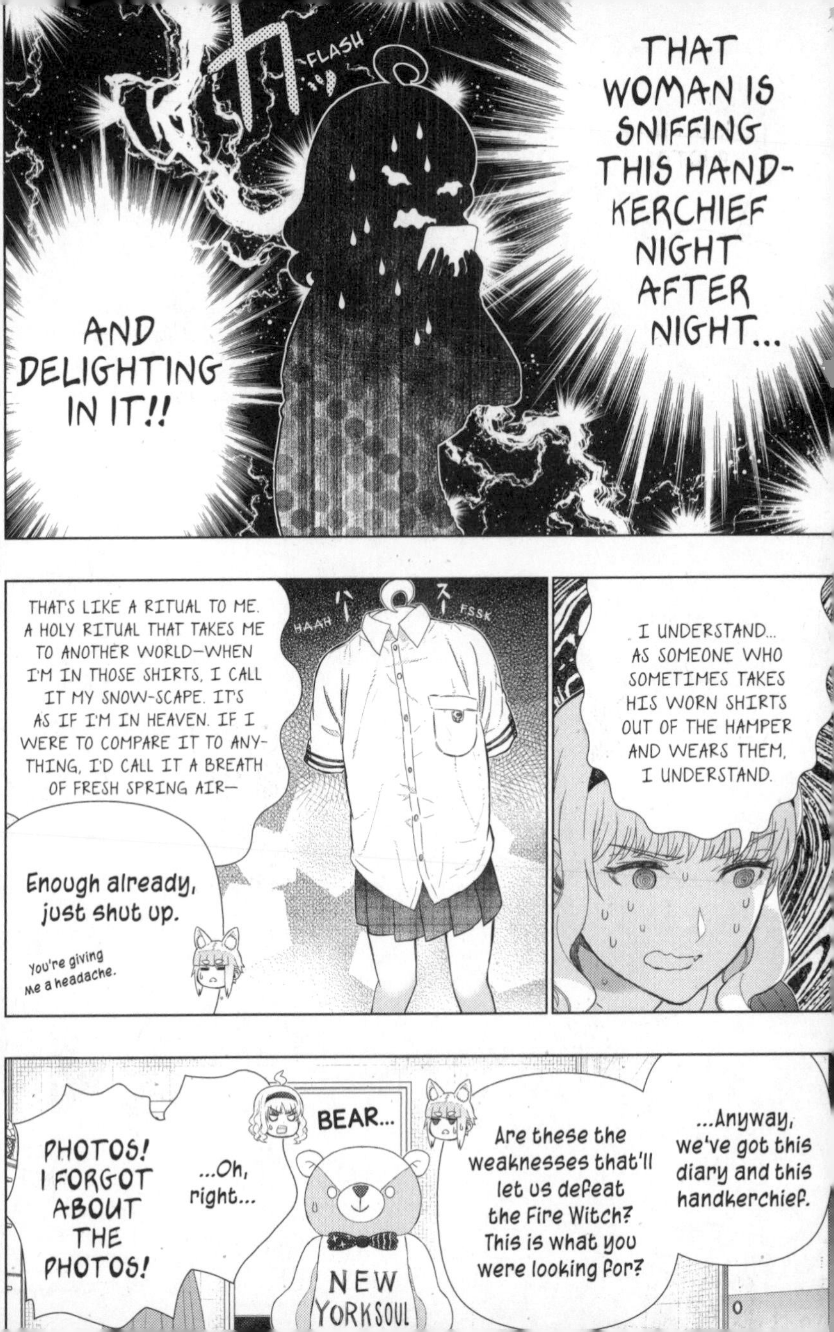
FLASH
THAT WOMAN IS SNIFFING THIS HAND-KERCHIEF NIGHT AFTER NIGHT...
AND DELIGHTING IN IT!!
I UNDERSTAND... AS SOMEONE WHO SOMETIMES TAKES HIS WORN SHIRTS OUT OF THE HAMPER AND WEARS THEM, I UNDERSTAND.
HAAH
FSSK
THAT'S LIKE A RITUAL TO ME. A HOLY RITUAL THAT TAKES ME TO ANOTHER WORLD—WHEN I'M IN THOSE SHIRTS, I CALL IT MY SNOW-SCAPE. IT'S AS IF I'M IN HEAVEN. IF I WERE TO COMPARE IT TO ANY-THING, I'D CALL IT A BREATH OF FRESH SPRING AIR—
Enough already, just shut up.
You're giving me a headache.
...Anyway, we've got this diary and this handkerchief.
Are these the weaknesses that'll let us defeat the Fire Witch? This is what you were looking for?
BEAR...
NEW YORKSOUL
...Oh, right...
PHOTOS! I FORGOT ABOUT THE PHOTOS!

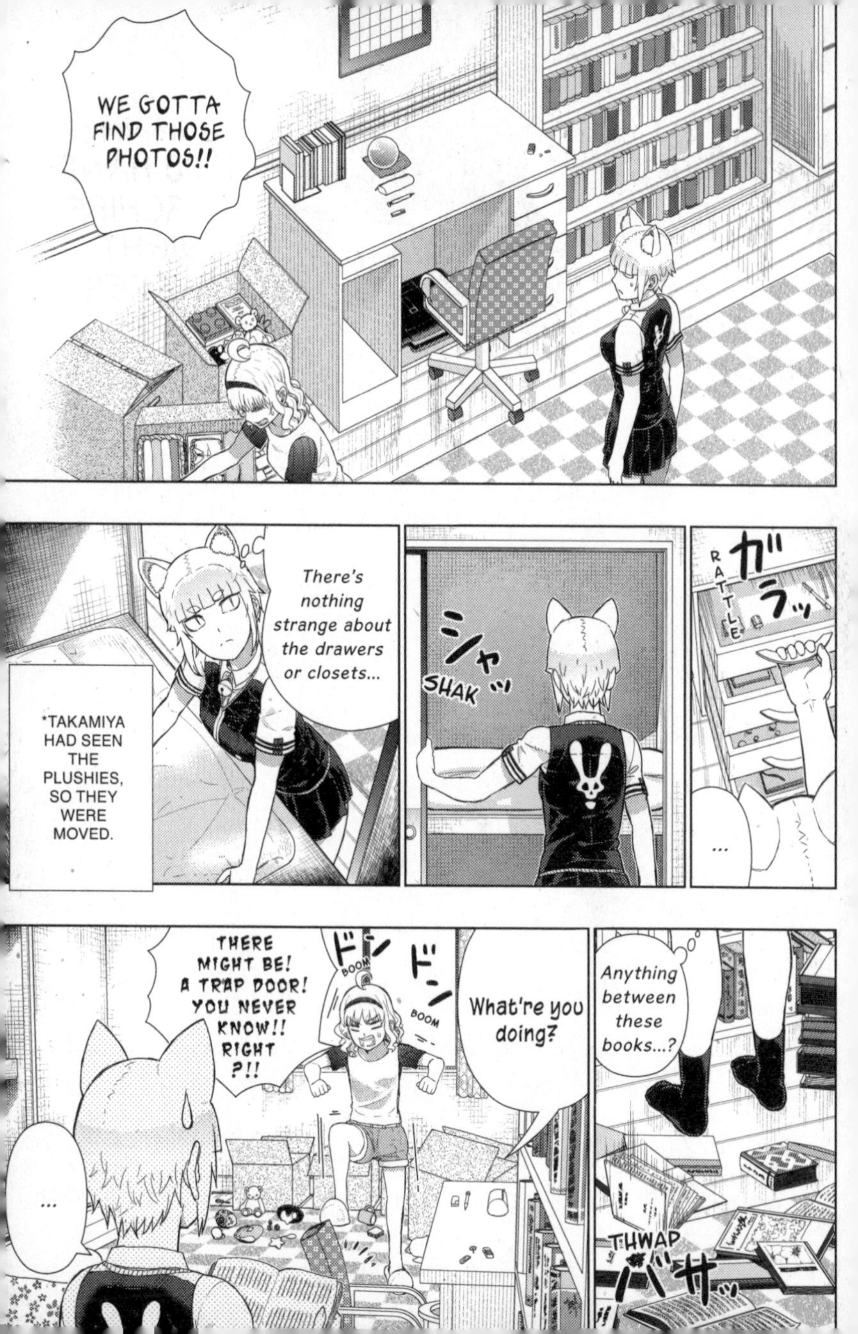

WE GOTTA FIND THOSE PHOTOS!!
ガラッ
RATTLE
...
シャッ
SHAK
There's nothing strange about the drawers or closets...
*TAKAMIYA HAD SEEN THE PLUSHIES, SO THEY WERE MOVED.
Anything between these books...?
バサッ
THWAP
What're you doing?
ドン
BOOM
ドン
BOOM
THERE MIGHT BE! A TRAP DOOR! YOU NEVER KNOW!! RIGHT?!!
...

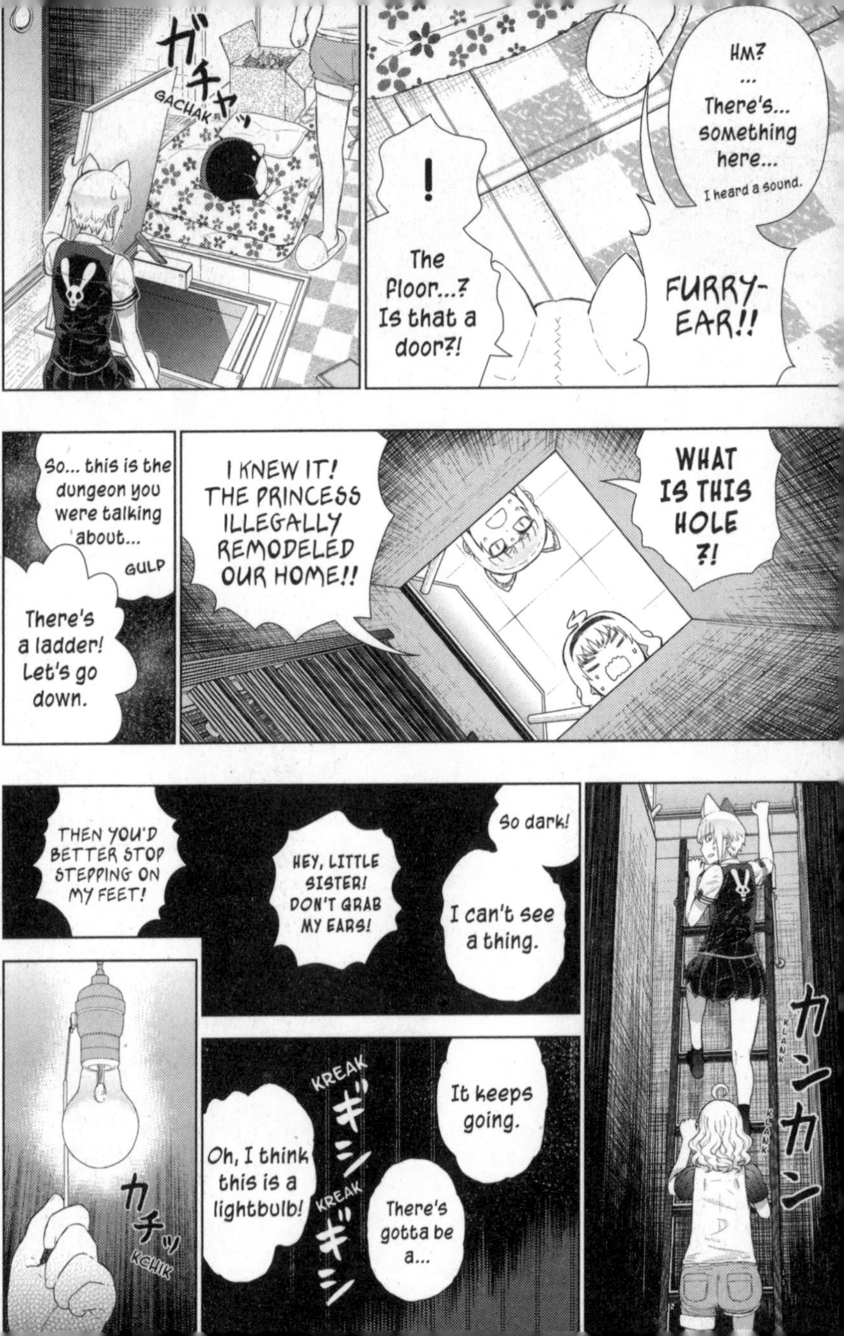
Hm?
...
There's... something here...
I heard a sound.
FURRY-EAR!!
!
The floor...? Is that a door?!
ガチャッ
GACHAK
WHAT IS THIS HOLE?!
I KNEW IT! THE PRINCESS ILLEGALLY REMODELED OUR HOME!!
So... this is the dungeon you were talking about...
GULP
There's a ladder! Let's go down.
カンカン
KLANK
KLANK
So dark!
I can't see a thing.
HEY, LITTLE SISTER! DON'T GRAB MY EARS!
THEN YOU'D BETTER STOP STEPPING ON MY FEET!
It keeps going.
There's gotta be a...
KREAK
ギシ
KREAK
ギシ
Oh, I think this is a lightbulb!
カチッ
KCHIK

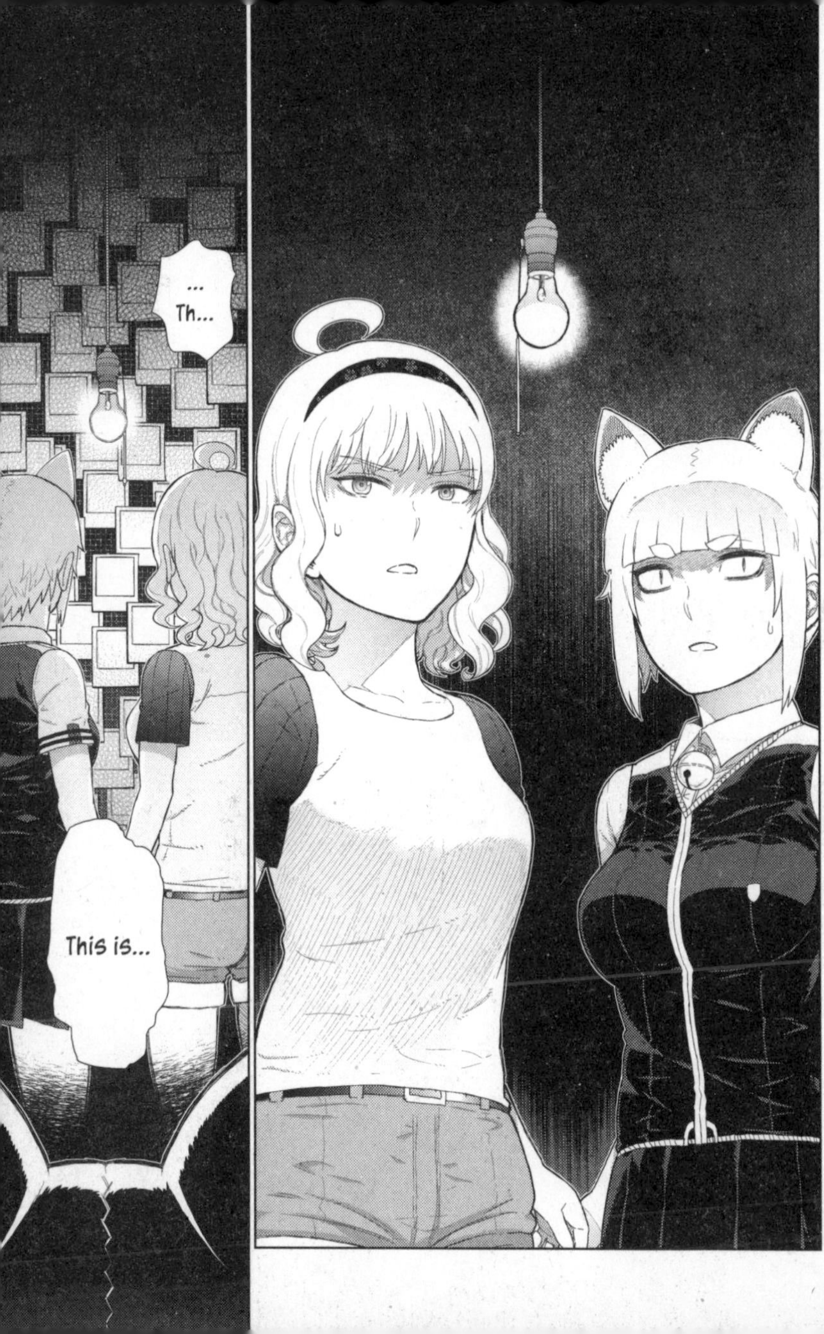
... Th...
This is...

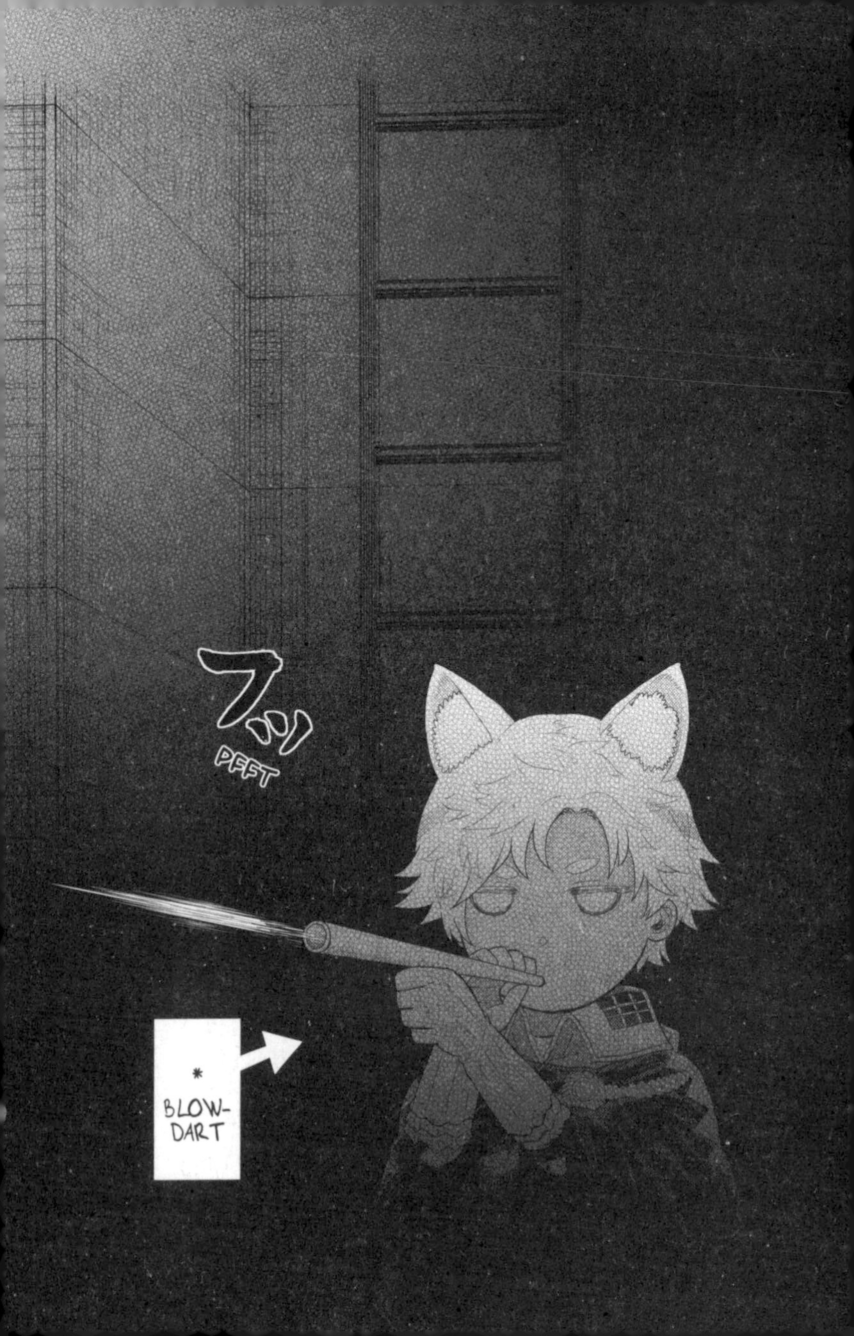
フッ
PFFT
* BLOW-DART

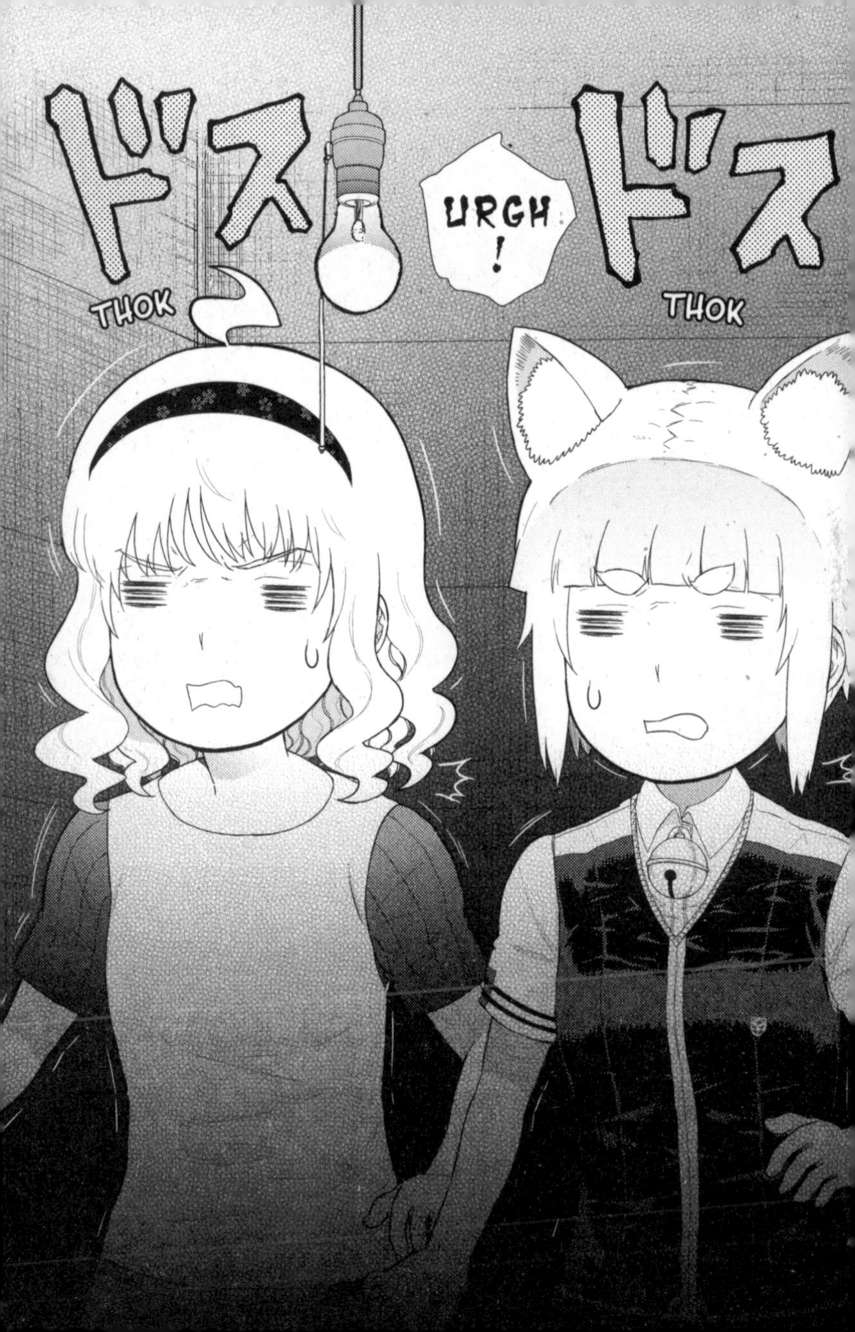
ドス
THOK
URGH!
ドス
THOK

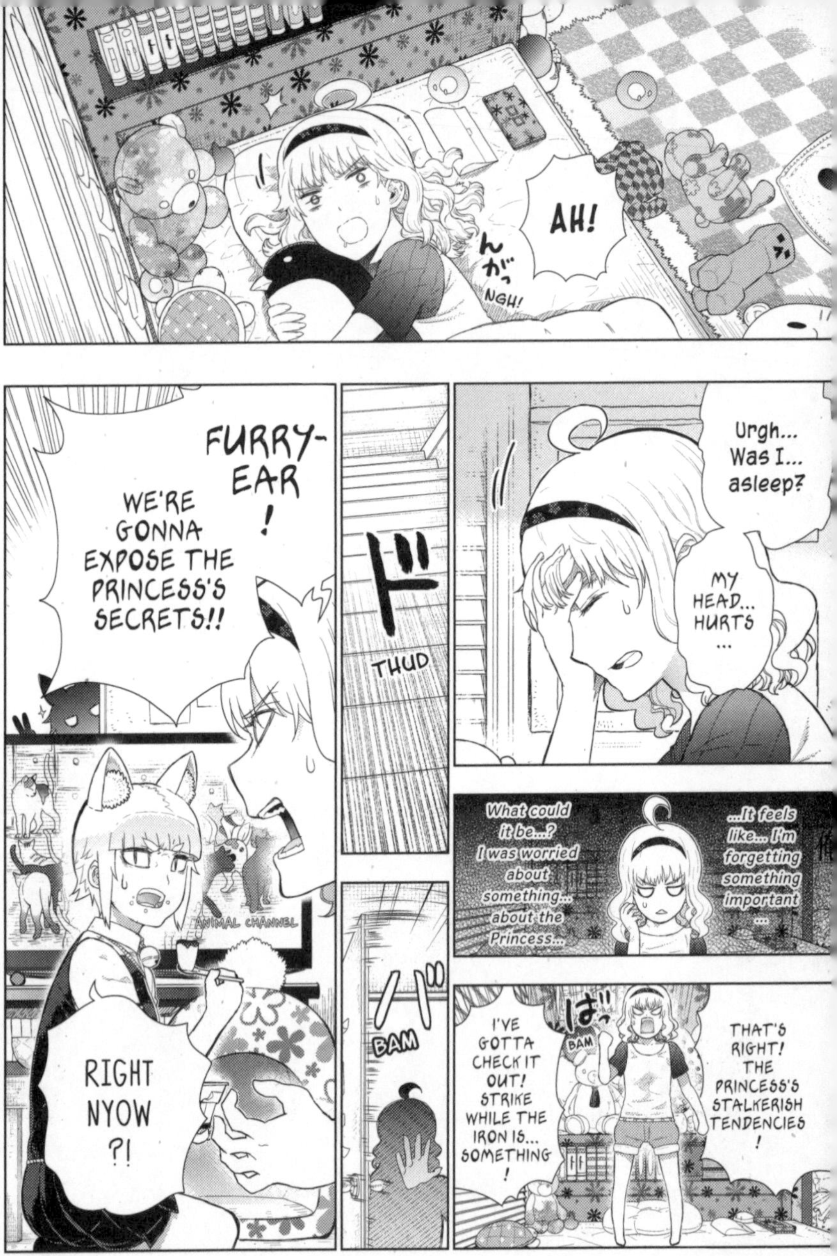
AH!
んがっ
NGH!
Urgh... Was I... asleep?
MY HEAD... HURTS...
...It feels like... I'm forgetting something important...
What could it be...? I was worried about something... about the Princess...
THAT'S RIGHT! THE PRINCESS'S STALKERISH TENDENCIES!
はっ
BAM
I'VE GOTTA CHECK IT OUT! STRIKE WHILE THE IRON IS... SOMETHING!
ド
THUD
バ
BAM
FURRY-EAR!
WE'RE GONNA EXPOSE THE PRINCESS'S SECRETS!!
ANIMAL CHANNEL
RIGHT NYOW?!

Witchcraft Works

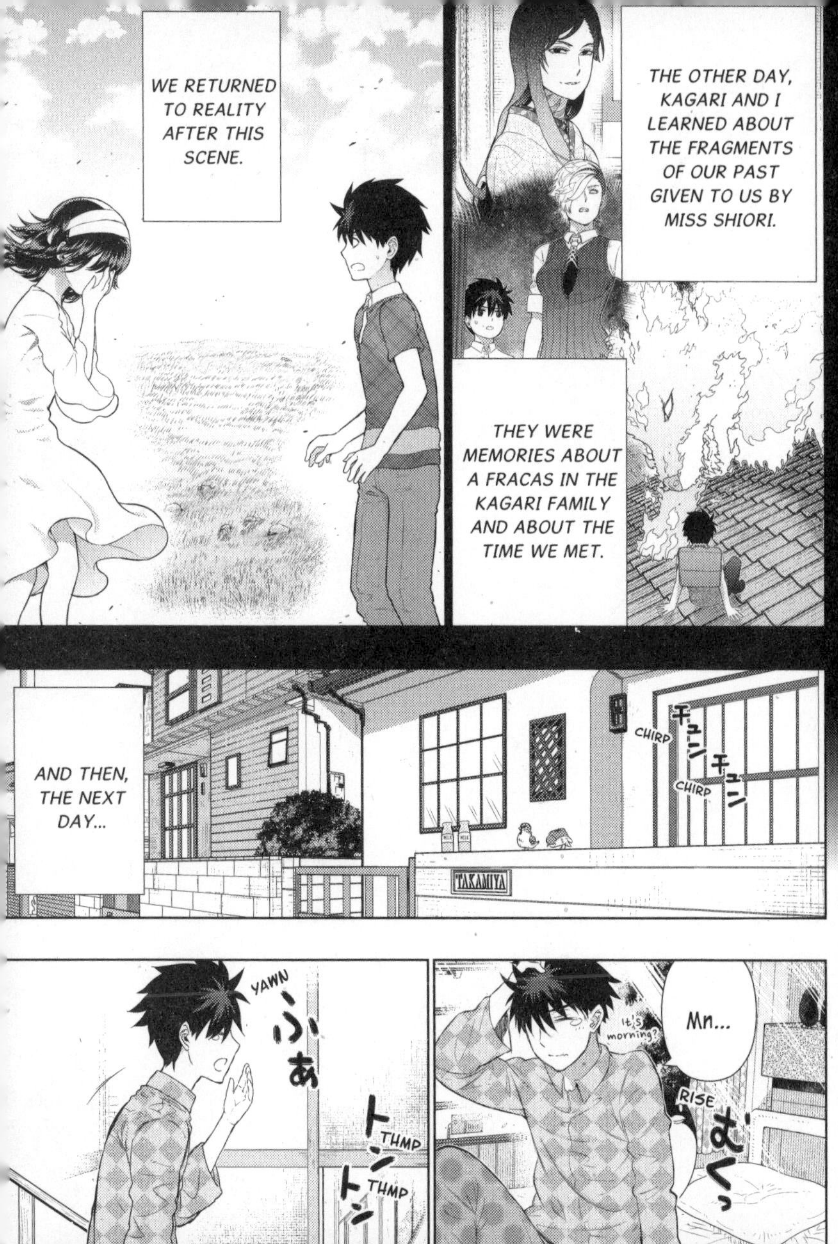
THE OTHER DAY, KAGARI AND I LEARNED ABOUT THE FRAGMENTS OF OUR PAST GIVEN TO US BY MISS SHIORI.
THEY WERE MEMORIES ABOUT A FRACAS IN THE KAGARI FAMILY AND ABOUT THE TIME WE MET.
WE RETURNED TO REALITY AFTER THIS SCENE.
AND THEN, THE NEXT DAY...
チュン
CHIRP
チュン
CHIRP
TAKAMIYA
Mn...
It's morning?
むくっ
RISE
ふあ
YAWN
トン
THMP
トン
THMP

CHAPTER 59 Takamiya and the Pendant's World (The Aftermath)

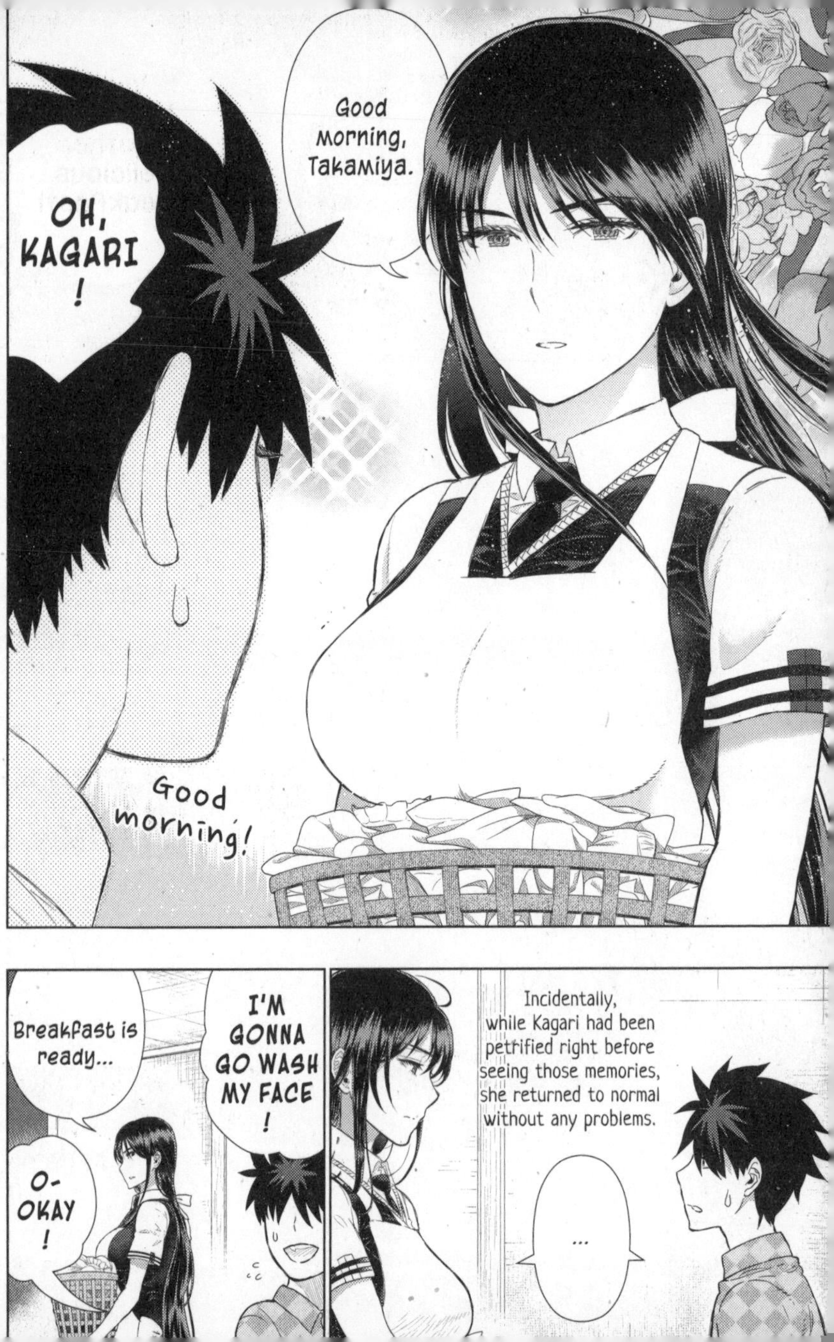

Good morning, Takamiya.
OH, KAGARI!
Good morning!
Incidentally, while Kagari had been petrified right before seeing those memories, she returned to normal without any problems.
...
Breakfast is ready...
O-OKAY!
I'M GONNA GO WASH MY FACE!

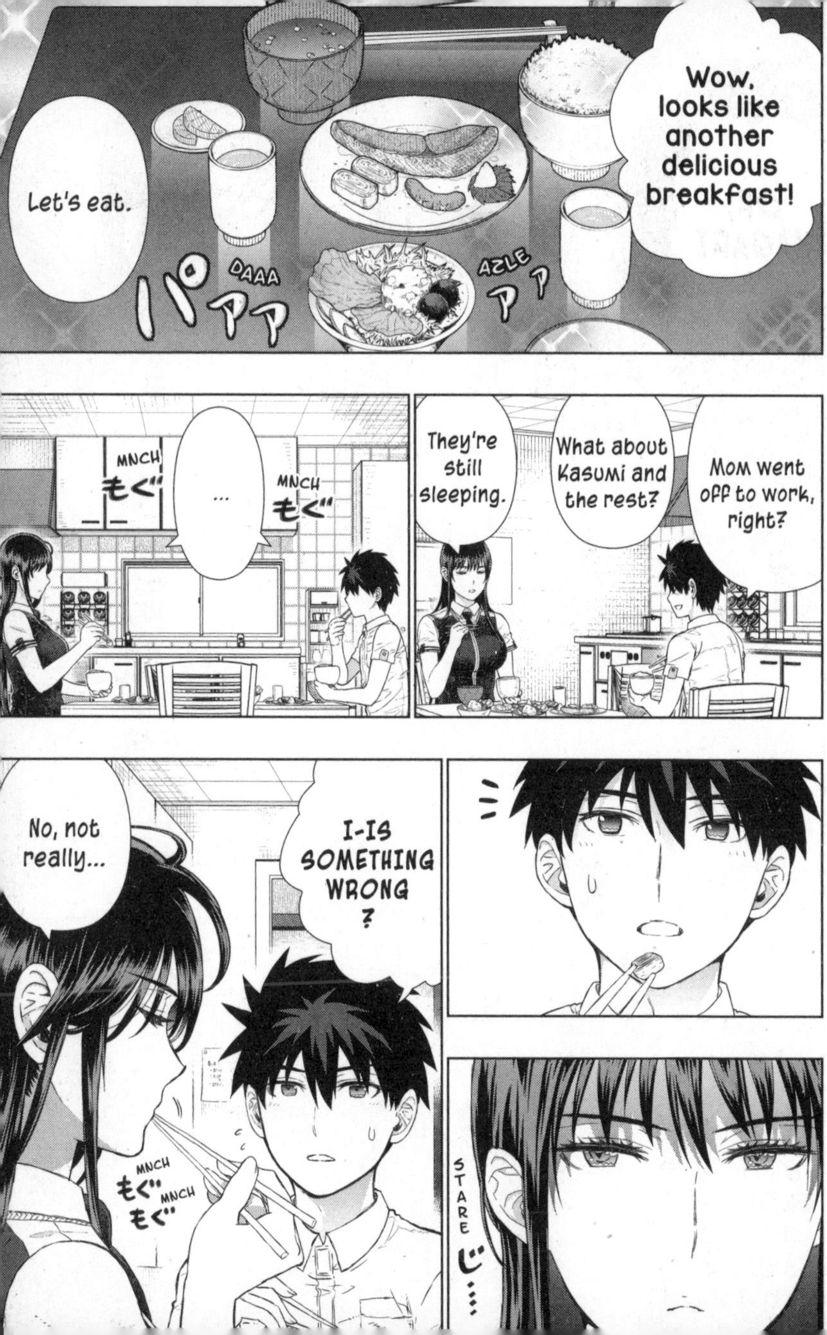
Wow, looks like another delicious breakfast!
Let's eat.
パァァ DAAA
アァ AZLE
Mom went off to work, right?
What about Kasumi and the rest?
They're still sleeping.
MNCH もぐ
...
MNCH もぐ
STARE じ…
I-IS SOMETHING WRONG?
No, not really...
MNCH もぐ MNCH もぐ

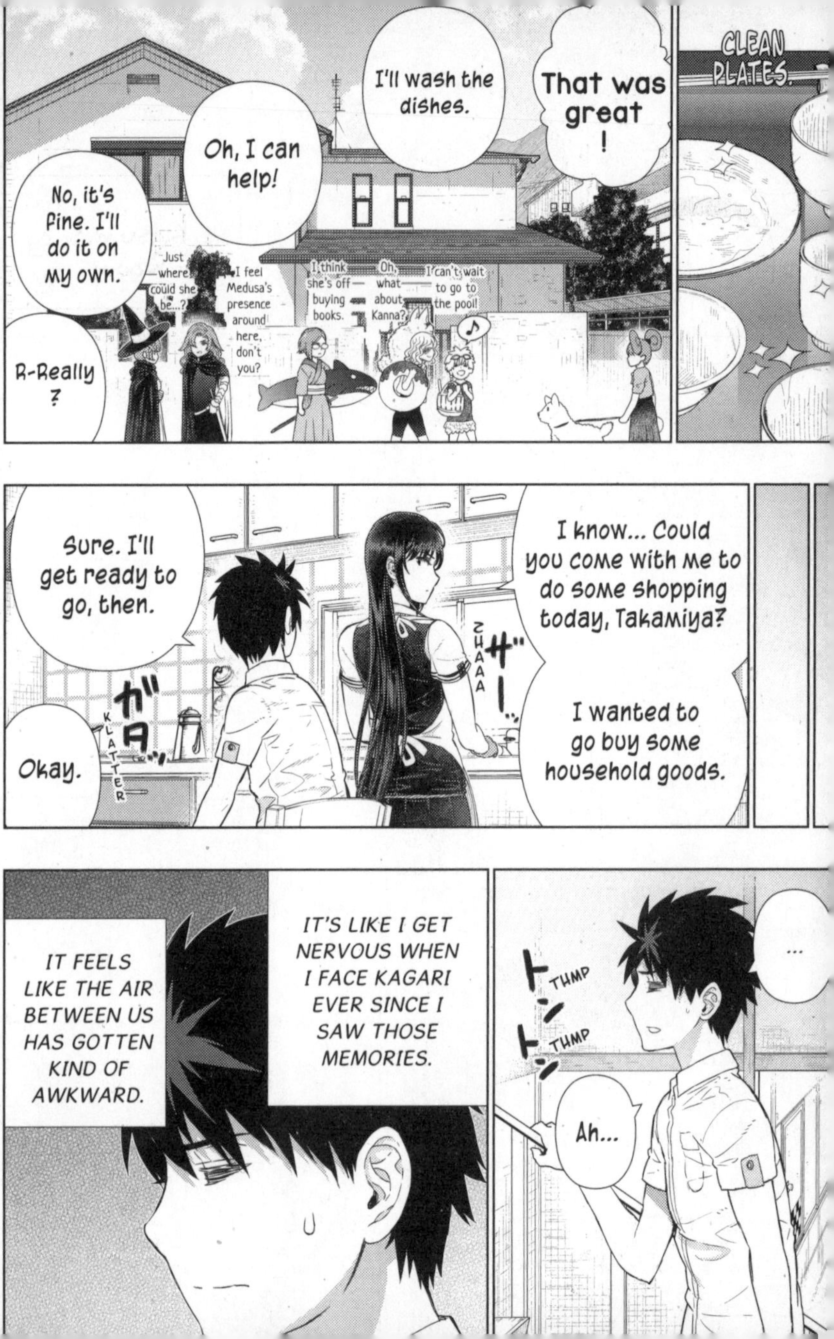

CLEAN PLATES.
That was great!
I'll wash the dishes.
Oh, I can help!
No, it's fine. I'll do it on my own.
I can't wait to go to the pool!
Oh, what about Kanna?
I think she's off buying books.
I feel Medusa's presence around here, don't you?
Just where could she be...?
R-Really?
I know... Could you come with me to do some shopping today, Takamiya?
ZHAAAA
I wanted to go buy some household goods.
Sure. I'll get ready to go, then.
KLATTER
Okay.
...
THUMP
THUMP
Ah...
IT'S LIKE I GET NERVOUS WHEN I FACE KAGARI EVER SINCE I SAW THOSE MEMORIES.
IT FEELS LIKE THE AIR BETWEEN US HAS GOTTEN KIND OF AWKWARD.

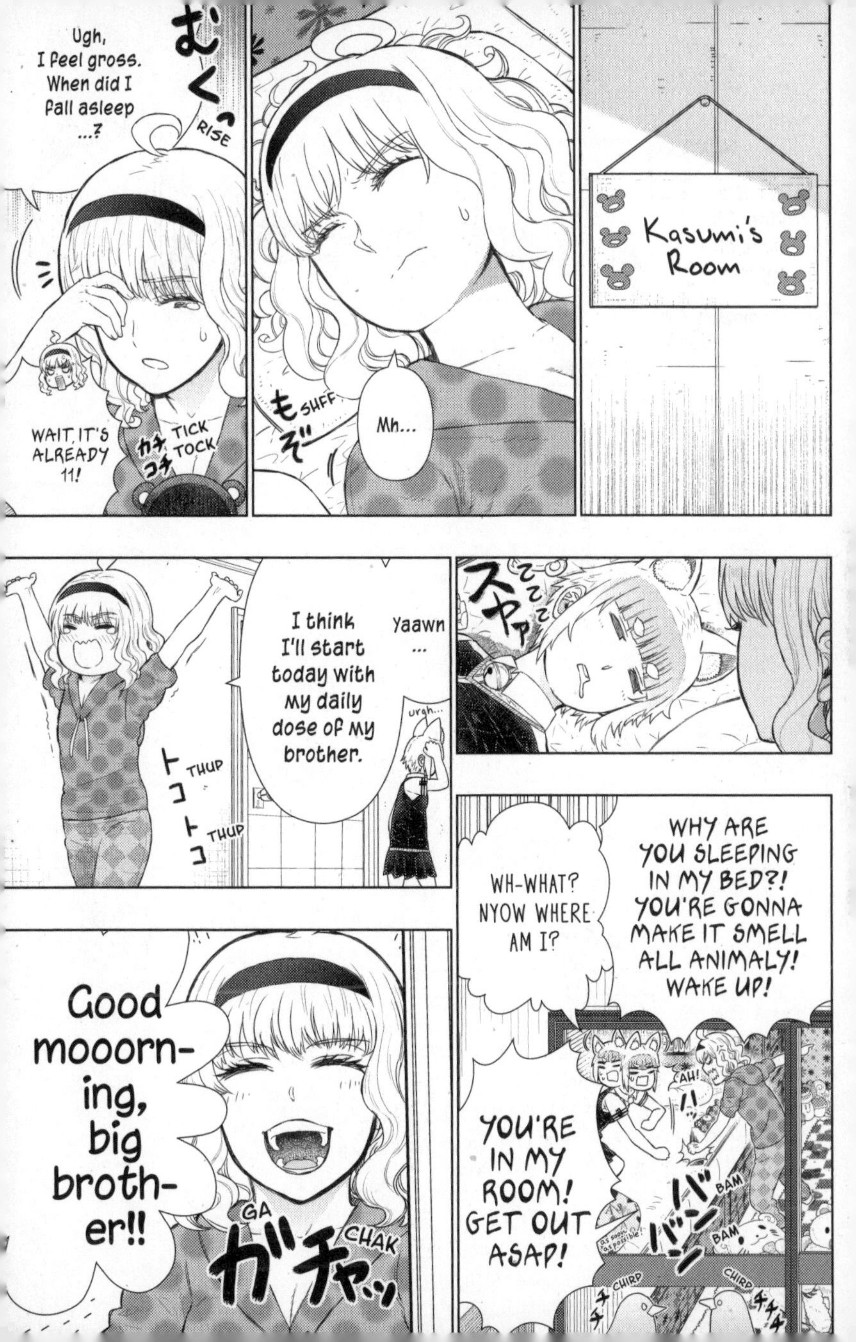
Kasumi's Room
もぞ SHFF
Mh...
むく RISE
Ugh, I feel gross. When did I fall asleep ...?
WAIT, IT'S ALREADY 11!
カチ TICK
コチ TOCK
Yaawn ...
I think I'll start today with my daily dose of my brother.
urgh...
トコ THUP
トコ THUP
Good mooorn-ing, big broth-er!!
ガチャッ GA CHAK
スヤァ
WHY ARE YOU SLEEPING IN MY BED?! YOU'RE GONNA MAKE IT SMELL ALL ANIMALY! WAKE UP!
WH-WHAT? NYOW WHERE AM I?
AH!
YOU'RE IN MY ROOM! GET OUT ASAP!
as soon as possible!
バン BAM
バン BAM
チチ CHIRP
チチチ CHIRP

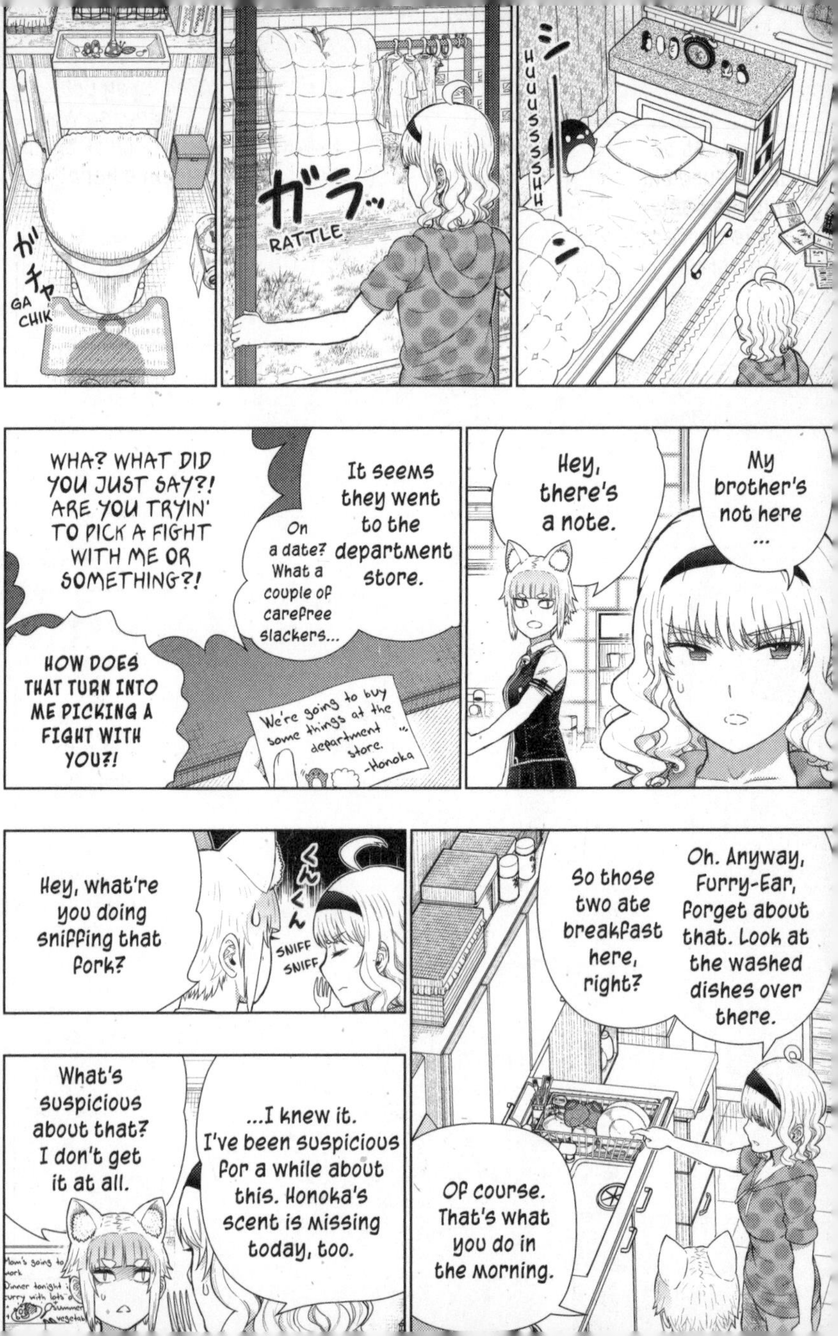
シーン
HUUUSSSSHH
ガラッ
RATTLE
ガチャ
GA CHIK
My brother's not here ...
Hey, there's a note.
It seems they went to the department store.
On a date? What a couple of carefree slackers...
WHA? WHAT DID YOU JUST SAY?! ARE YOU TRYIN' TO PICK A FIGHT WITH ME OR SOMETHING?!
HOW DOES THAT TURN INTO ME PICKING A FIGHT WITH YOU?!
We're going to buy some things at the department store. -Honoka
Oh. Anyway, Furry-Ear, forget about that. Look at the washed dishes over there.
So those two ate breakfast here, right?
Of course. That's what you do in the morning.
Hey, what're you doing sniffing that fork?
くんくん
SNIFF SNIFF
...I knew it. I've been suspicious for a while about this. Honoka's scent is missing today, too.
What's suspicious about that? I don't get it at all.

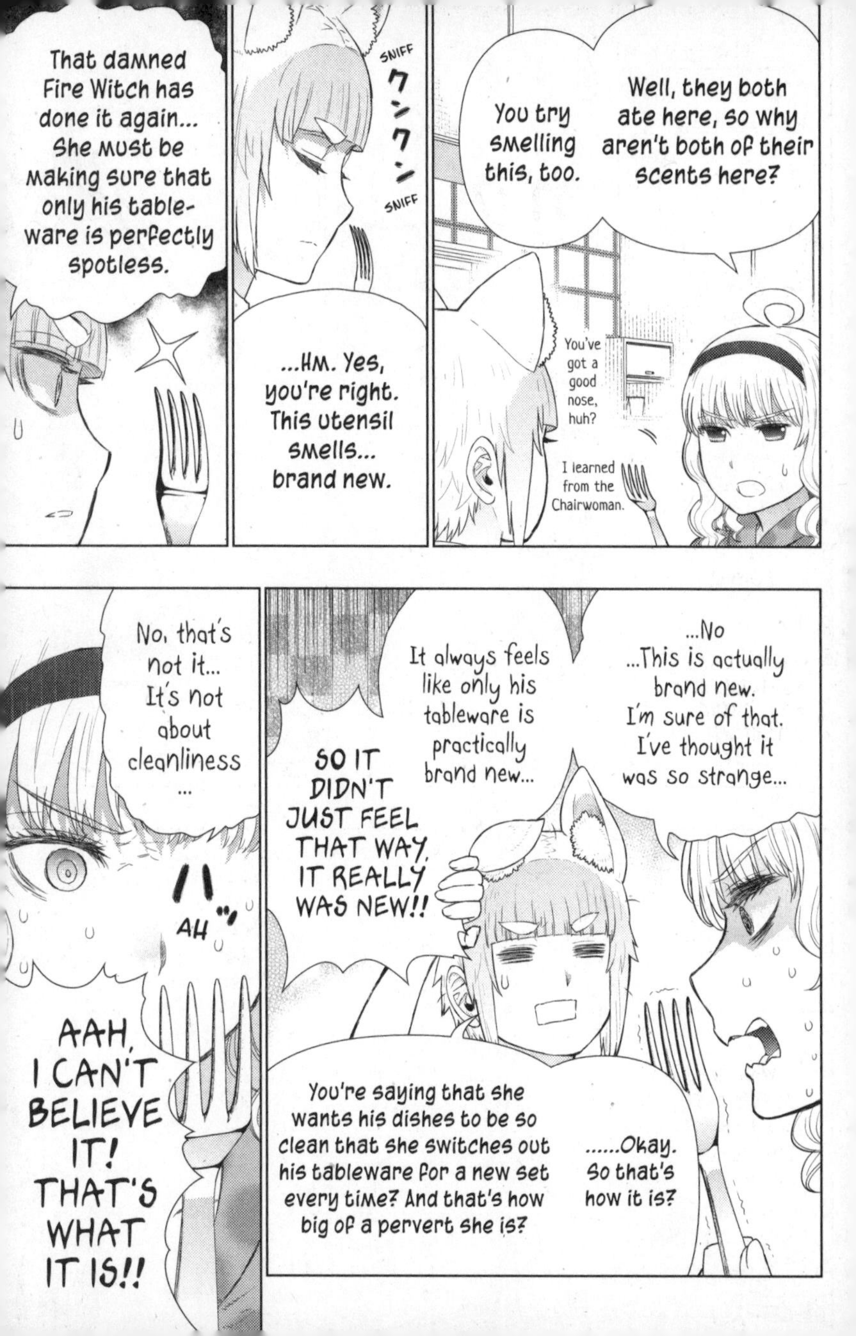
Well, they both ate here, so why aren't both of their scents here?
You try smelling this, too.
You've got a good nose, huh?
I learned from the Chairwoman.
SNIFF
クンクン
SNIFF
...HM. Yes, you're right. This utensil smells... brand new.
That damned Fire Witch has done it again... She must be making sure that only his tableware is perfectly spotless.
...No ...This is actually brand new. I'm sure of that. I've thought it was so strange...
It always feels like only his tableware is practically brand new...
SO IT DIDN'T JUST FEEL THAT WAY, IT REALLY WAS NEW!!
......Okay. So that's how it is?
You're saying that she wants his dishes to be so clean that she switches out his tableware for a new set every time? And that's how big of a pervert she is?
No, that's not it... It's not about cleanliness ...
AH
AAH, I CAN'T BELIEVE IT! THAT'S WHAT IT IS!!

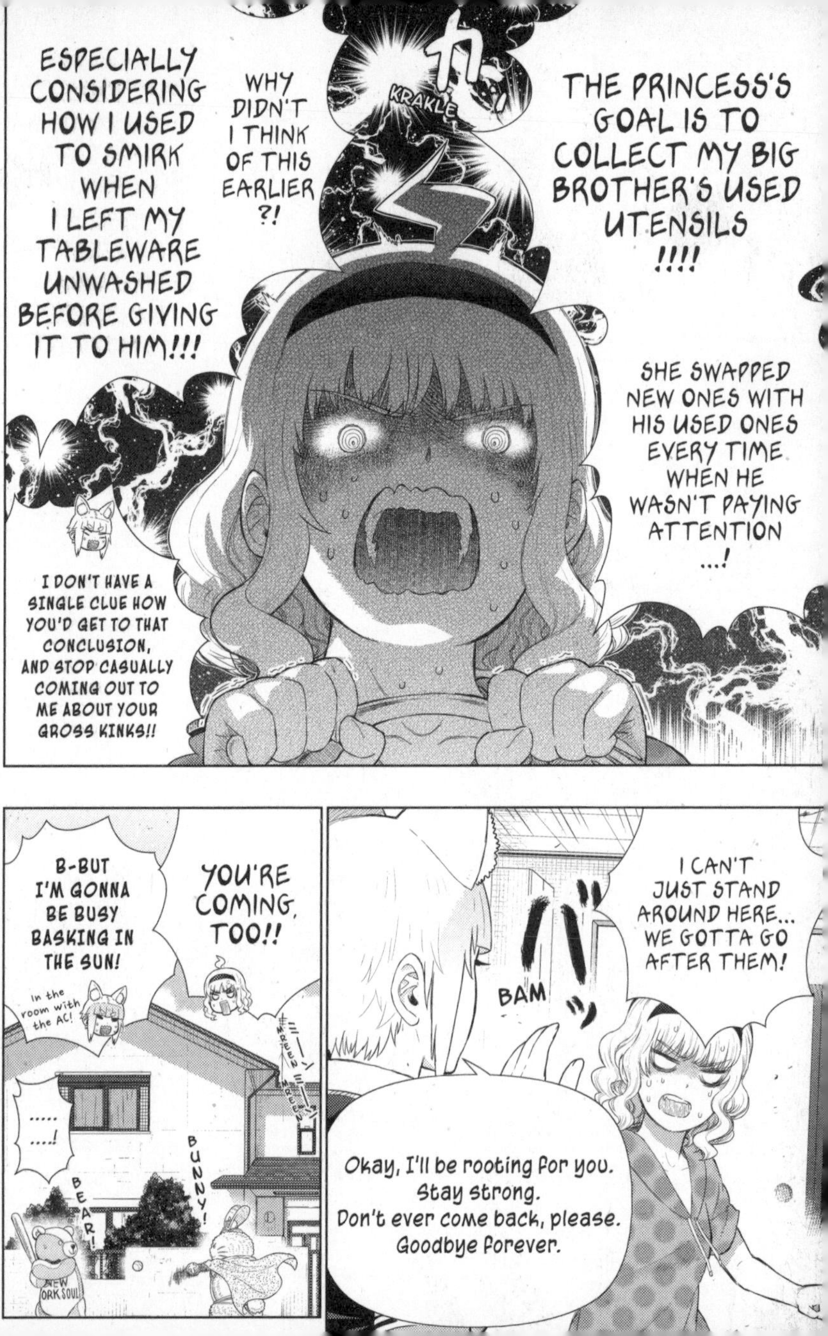
THE PRINCESS'S GOAL IS TO COLLECT MY BIG BROTHER'S USED UTENSILS !!!!
KRAKLE
WHY DIDN'T I THINK OF THIS EARLIER ?!
ESPECIALLY CONSIDERING HOW I USED TO SMIRK WHEN I LEFT MY TABLEWARE UNWASHED BEFORE GIVING IT TO HIM!!!
SHE SWAPPED NEW ONES WITH HIS USED ONES EVERY TIME WHEN HE WASN'T PAYING ATTENTION ...!
I DON'T HAVE A SINGLE CLUE HOW YOU'D GET TO THAT CONCLUSION, AND STOP CASUALLY COMING OUT TO ME ABOUT YOUR GROSS KINKS!!
I CAN'T JUST STAND AROUND HERE... WE GOTTA GO AFTER THEM!
BAM
Okay, I'll be rooting for you. Stay strong. Don't ever come back, please. Goodbye forever.
YOU'RE COMING, TOO!!
B-BUT I'M GONNA BE BUSY BASKING IN THE SUN!
In the room with the AC!
MREEN
MREEN
....!
BUNNY!
BEAR!
NEW ORK SOUL

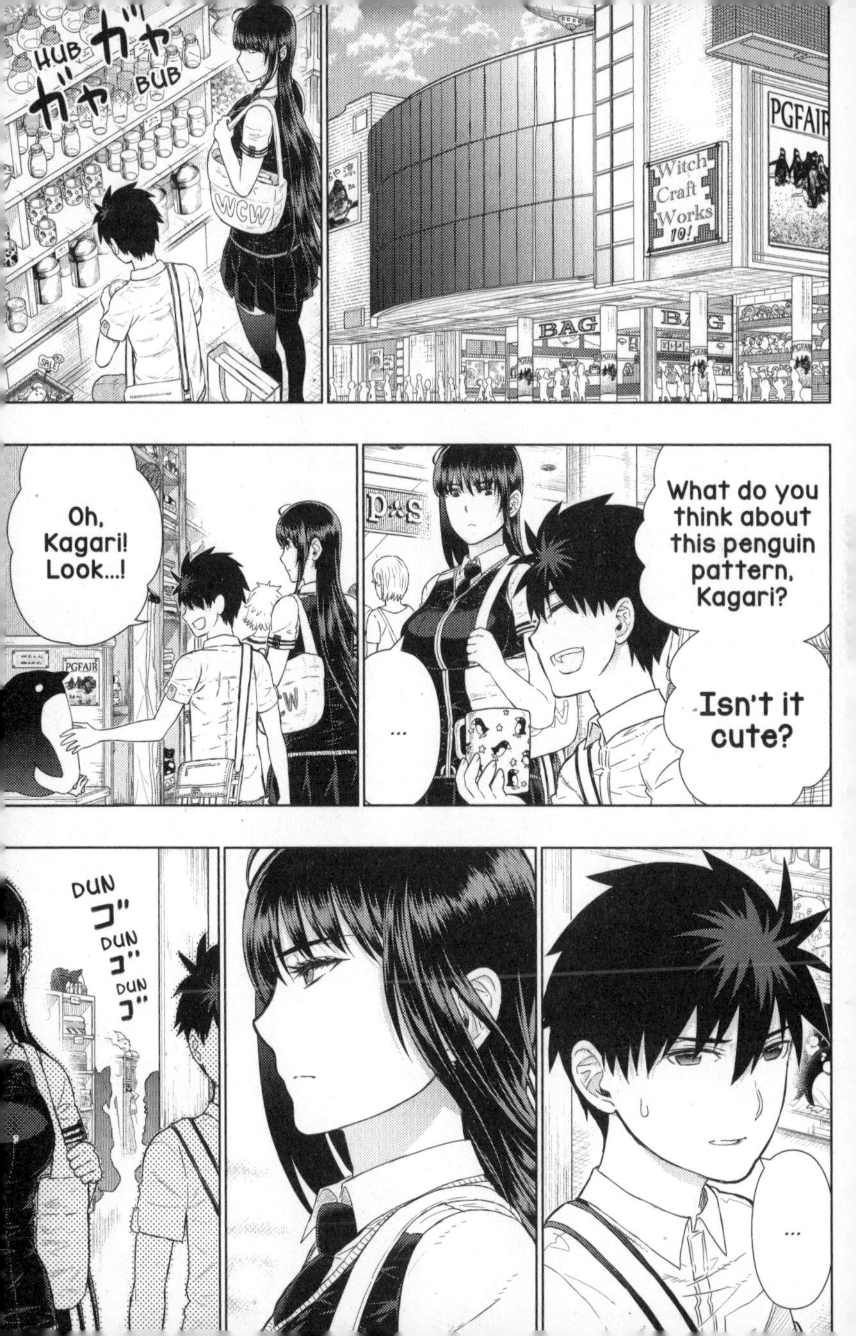

PGFAIR
Witch Craft Works 10!
BAG
BAG
HUB ガヤ
BUB ガヤ
WCW
What do you think about this penguin pattern, Kagari?
Isn't it cute?
...
Oh, Kagari! Look...!
PGFAIR
...
DUN ゴ"
DUN ゴ"
DUN ゴ"

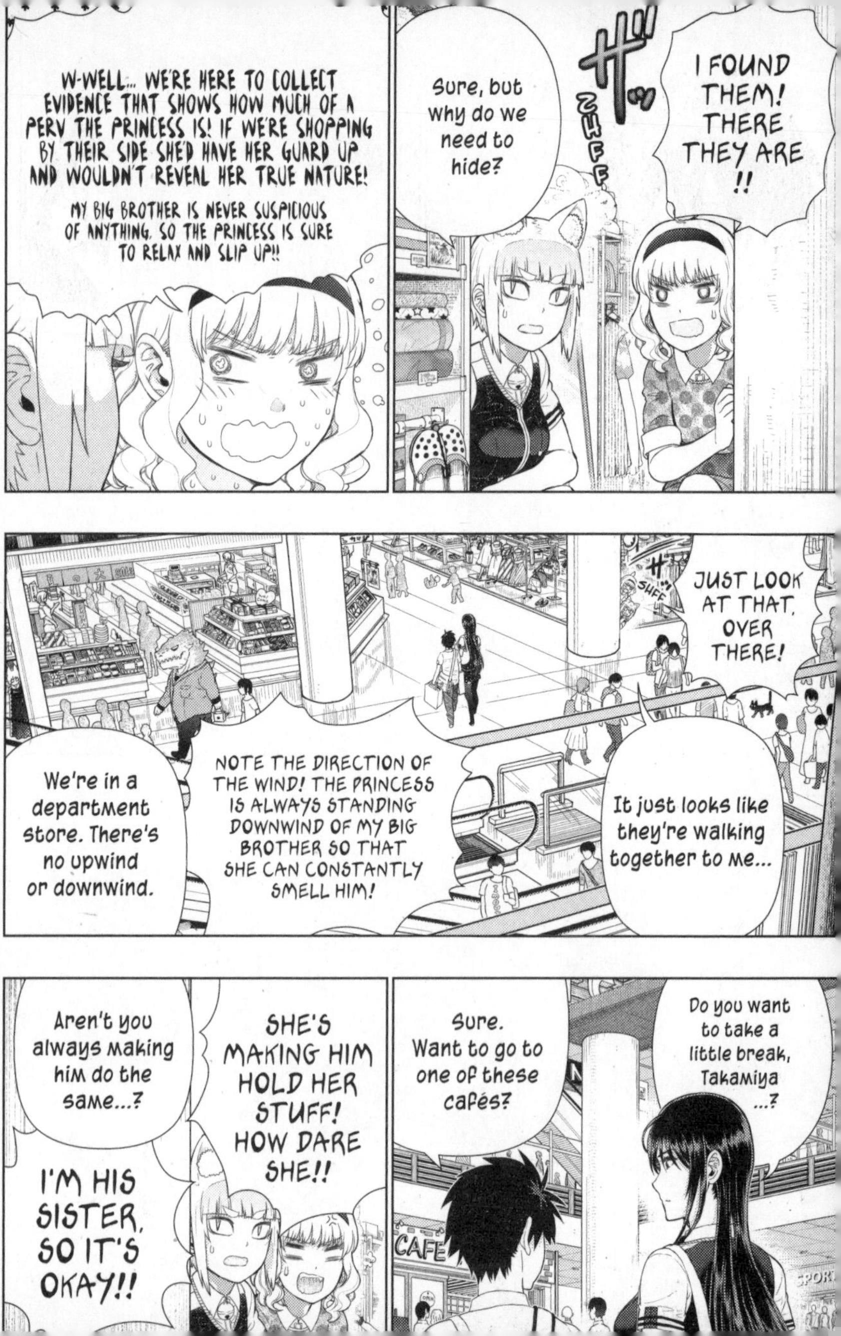

I FOUND THEM! THERE THEY ARE!!
SHFF
Sure, but why do we need to hide?
W-WELL... WE'RE HERE TO COLLECT EVIDENCE THAT SHOWS HOW MUCH OF A PERV THE PRINCESS IS! IF WE'RE SHOPPING BY THEIR SIDE SHE'D HAVE HER GUARD UP AND WOULDN'T REVEAL HER TRUE NATURE!
MY BIG BROTHER IS NEVER SUSPICIOUS OF ANYTHING, SO THE PRINCESS IS SURE TO RELAX AND SLIP UP!!
JUST LOOK AT THAT, OVER THERE!
SHUFF
It just looks like they're walking together to me...
NOTE THE DIRECTION OF THE WIND! THE PRINCESS IS ALWAYS STANDING DOWNWIND OF MY BIG BROTHER SO THAT SHE CAN CONSTANTLY SMELL HIM!
We're in a department store. There's no upwind or downwind.
Do you want to take a little break, Takamiya ...?
Sure. Want to go to one of these cafés?
CAFE
SHE'S MAKING HIM HOLD HER STUFF! HOW DARE SHE!!
Aren't you always making him do the same...?
I'M HIS SISTER, SO IT'S OKAY!!

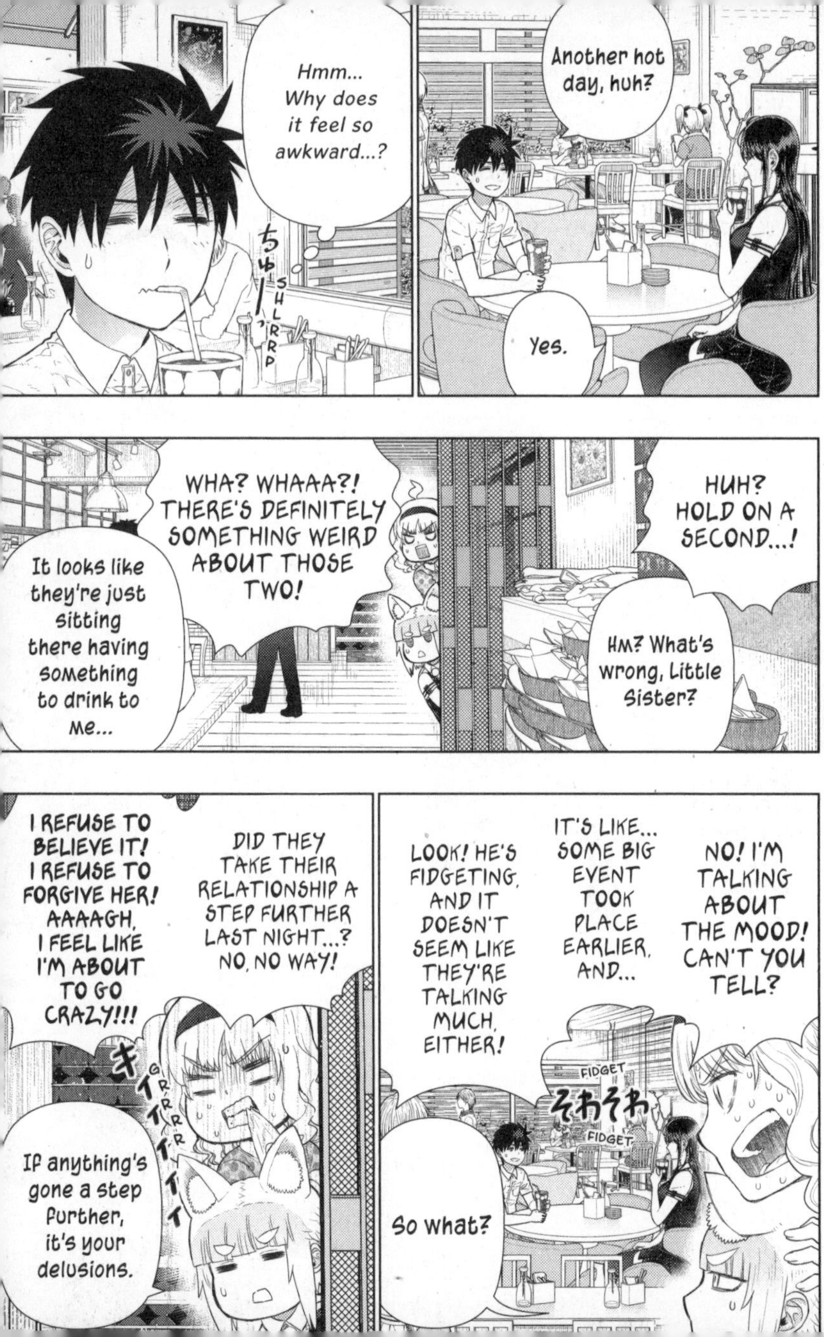
Another hot day, huh?
Yes.
Hmm... Why does it feel so awkward...?
ちゅーっ
SHLRRP
HUH? HOLD ON A SECOND...!
HM? What's wrong, Little Sister?
WHA? WHAAA?! THERE'S DEFINITELY SOMETHING WEIRD ABOUT THOSE TWO!
It looks like they're just sitting there having something to drink to me...
NO! I'M TALKING ABOUT THE MOOD! CAN'T YOU TELL?
IT'S LIKE... SOME BIG EVENT TOOK PLACE EARLIER, AND...
LOOK! HE'S FIDGETING, AND IT DOESN'T SEEM LIKE THEY'RE TALKING MUCH, EITHER!
FIDGET
そわそわ
FIDGET
So what?
DID THEY TAKE THEIR RELATIONSHIP A STEP FURTHER LAST NIGHT...? NO, NO WAY!
I REFUSE TO BELIEVE IT! I REFUSE TO FORGIVE HER! AAAAGH, I FEEL LIKE I'M ABOUT TO GO CRAZY!!!
キイイイイイ
GRRRRR
If anything's gone a step further, it's your delusions.

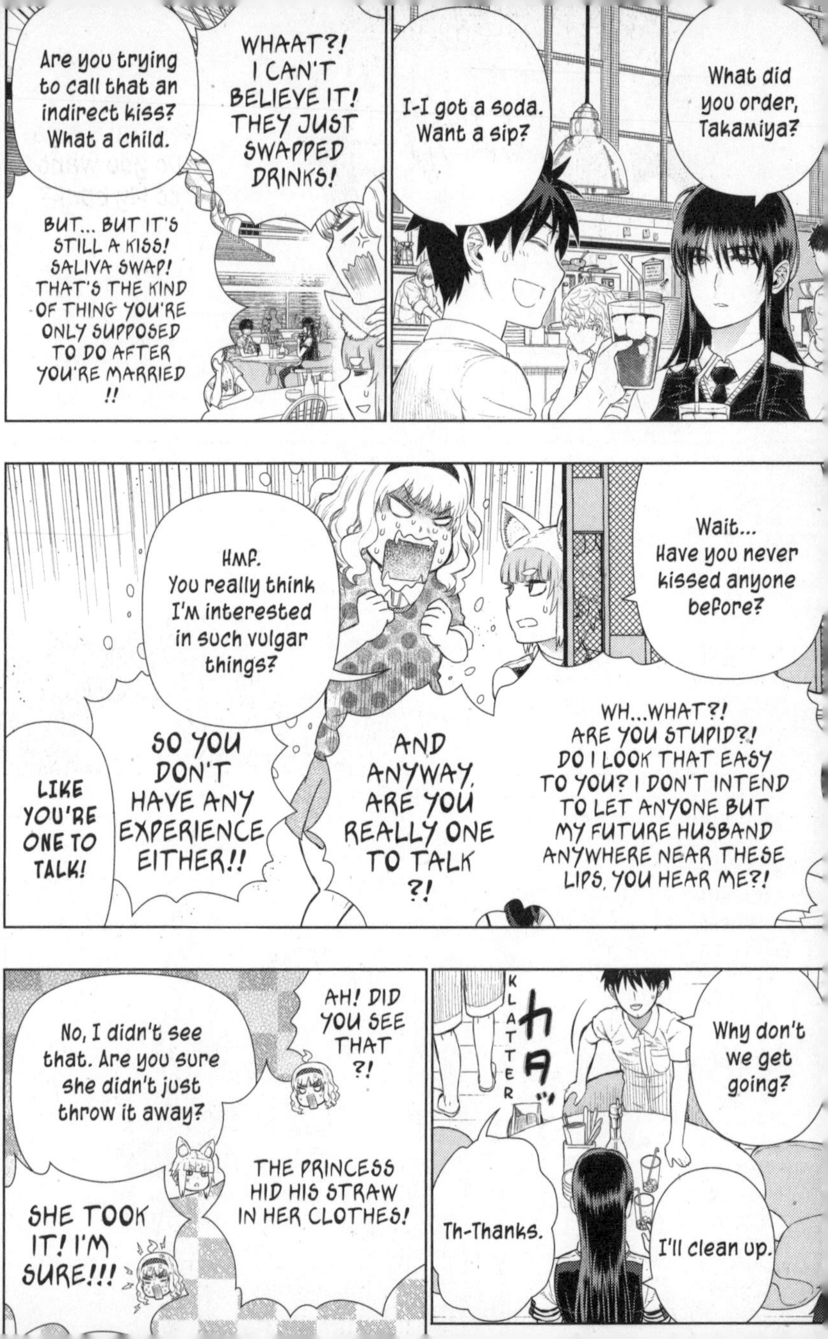
What did you order, Takamiya?
I-I got a soda. Want a sip?
WHAAT?! I CAN'T BELIEVE IT! THEY JUST SWAPPED DRINKS!
Are you trying to call that an indirect kiss? What a child.
BUT... BUT IT'S STILL A KISS! SALIVA SWAP! THAT'S THE KIND OF THING YOU'RE ONLY SUPPOSED TO DO AFTER YOU'RE MARRIED!!
Wait... Have you never kissed anyone before?
WH...WHAT?! ARE YOU STUPID?! DO I LOOK THAT EASY TO YOU? I DON'T INTEND TO LET ANYONE BUT MY FUTURE HUSBAND ANYWHERE NEAR THESE LIPS, YOU HEAR ME?!
AND ANYWAY, ARE YOU REALLY ONE TO TALK?!
HMF. You really think I'm interested in such vulgar things?
SO YOU DON'T HAVE ANY EXPERIENCE EITHER!!
LIKE YOU'RE ONE TO TALK!
Why don't we get going?
KLATTER
I'll clean up.
Th-Thanks.
AH! DID YOU SEE THAT?!
No, I didn't see that. Are you sure she didn't just throw it away?
THE PRINCESS HID HIS STRAW IN HER CLOTHES!
SHE TOOK IT! I'M SURE!!!

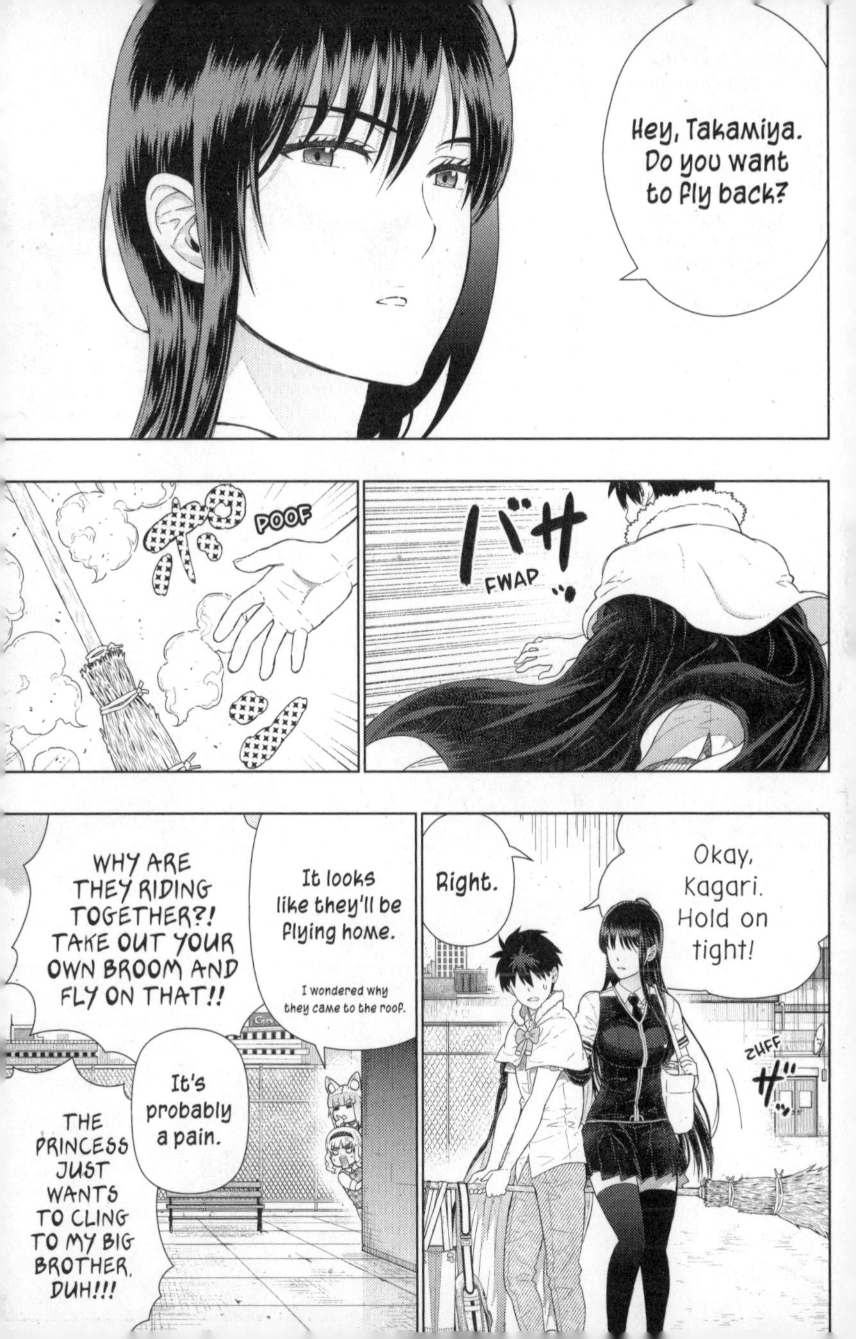
Hey, Takamiya. Do you want to fly back?
バサ
FWAP
POOF
Okay, Kagari. Hold on tight!
Right.
ザッ
ZUFF
It looks like they'll be flying home.
I wondered why they came to the roof.
WHY ARE THEY RIDING TOGETHER?! TAKE OUT YOUR OWN BROOM AND FLY ON THAT!!
It's probably a pain.
THE PRINCESS JUST WANTS TO CLING TO MY BIG BROTHER, DUH!!!

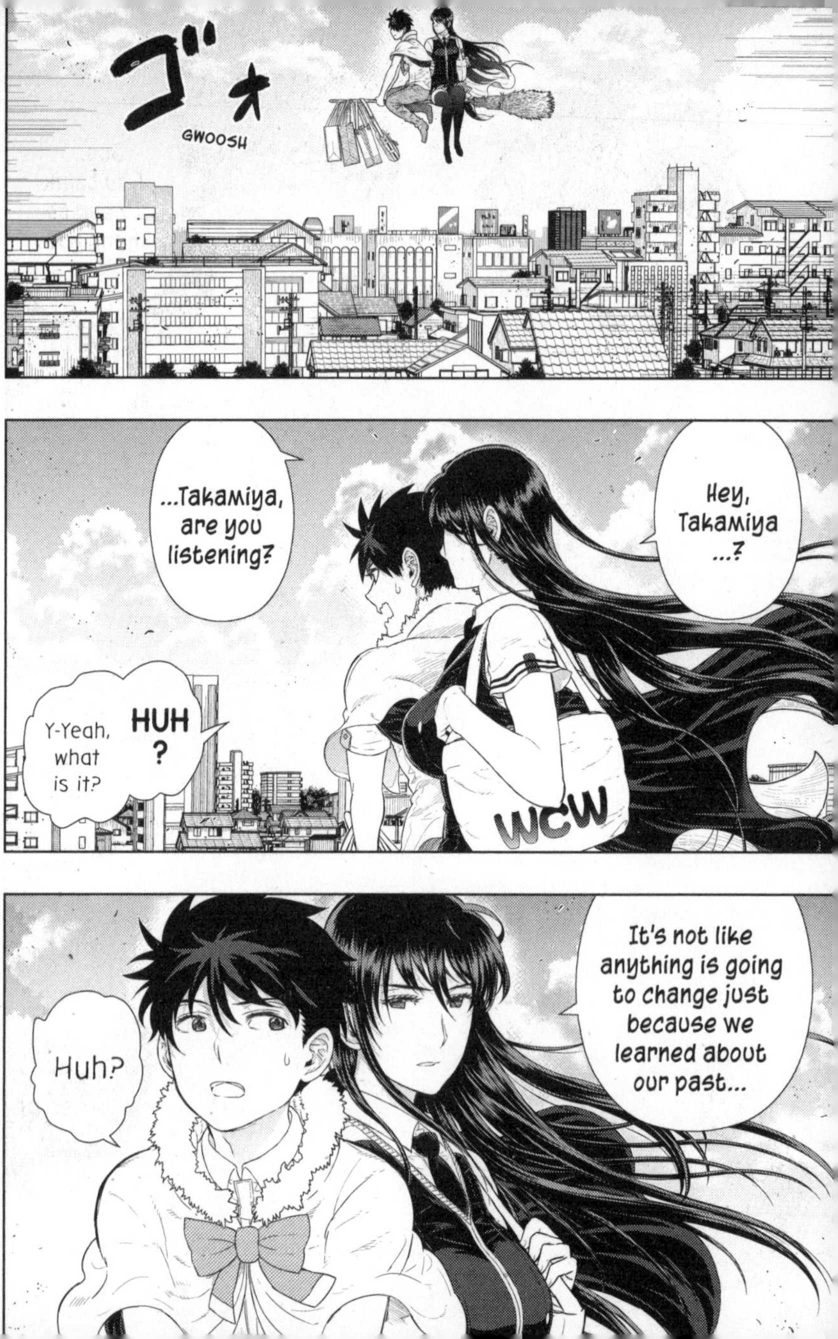
ゴォ
GWOOSH
Hey, Takamiya ...?
...Takamiya, are you listening?
HUH ?
Y-Yeah, what is it?
WCW
It's not like anything is going to change just because we learned about our past...
Huh?

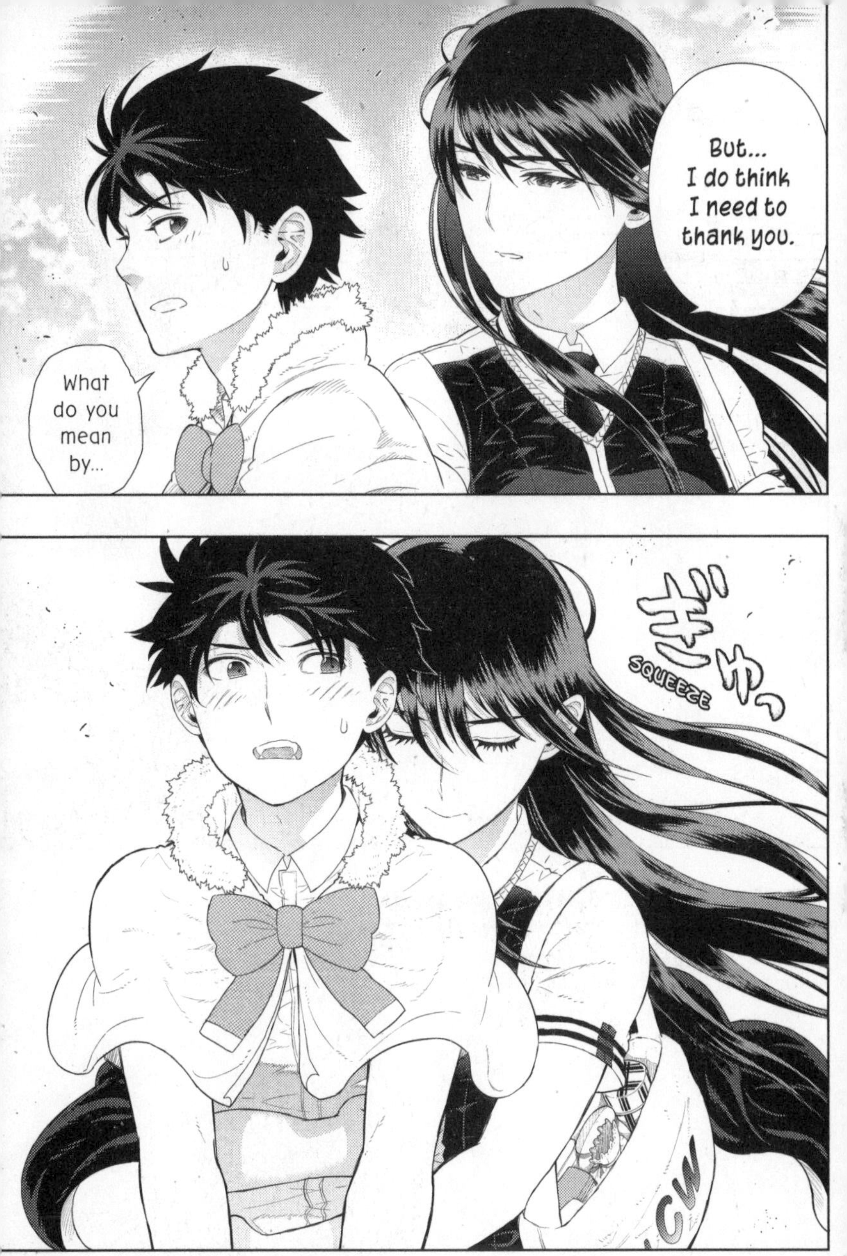
But...
I do think
I need to
thank you.
What
do you
mean
by...
ぎゅっ
SQUEEZE

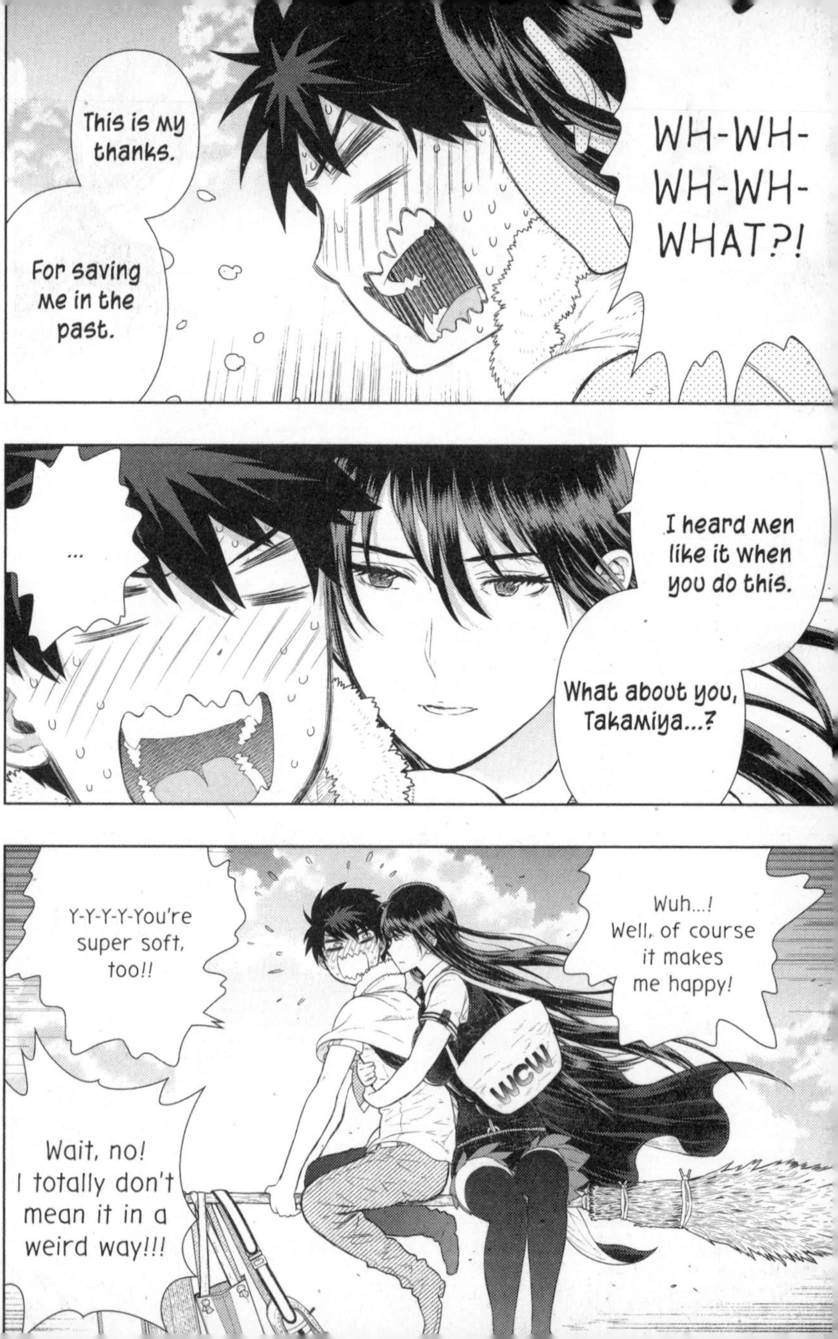
WH-WH-WH-WH-WHAT?!
This is my thanks.
For saving me in the past.
I heard men like it when you do this.
What about you, Takamiya...?
...
Wuh...! Well, of course it makes me happy!
Y-Y-Y-Y-You're super soft, too!!
Wait, no! I totally don't mean it in a weird way!!!

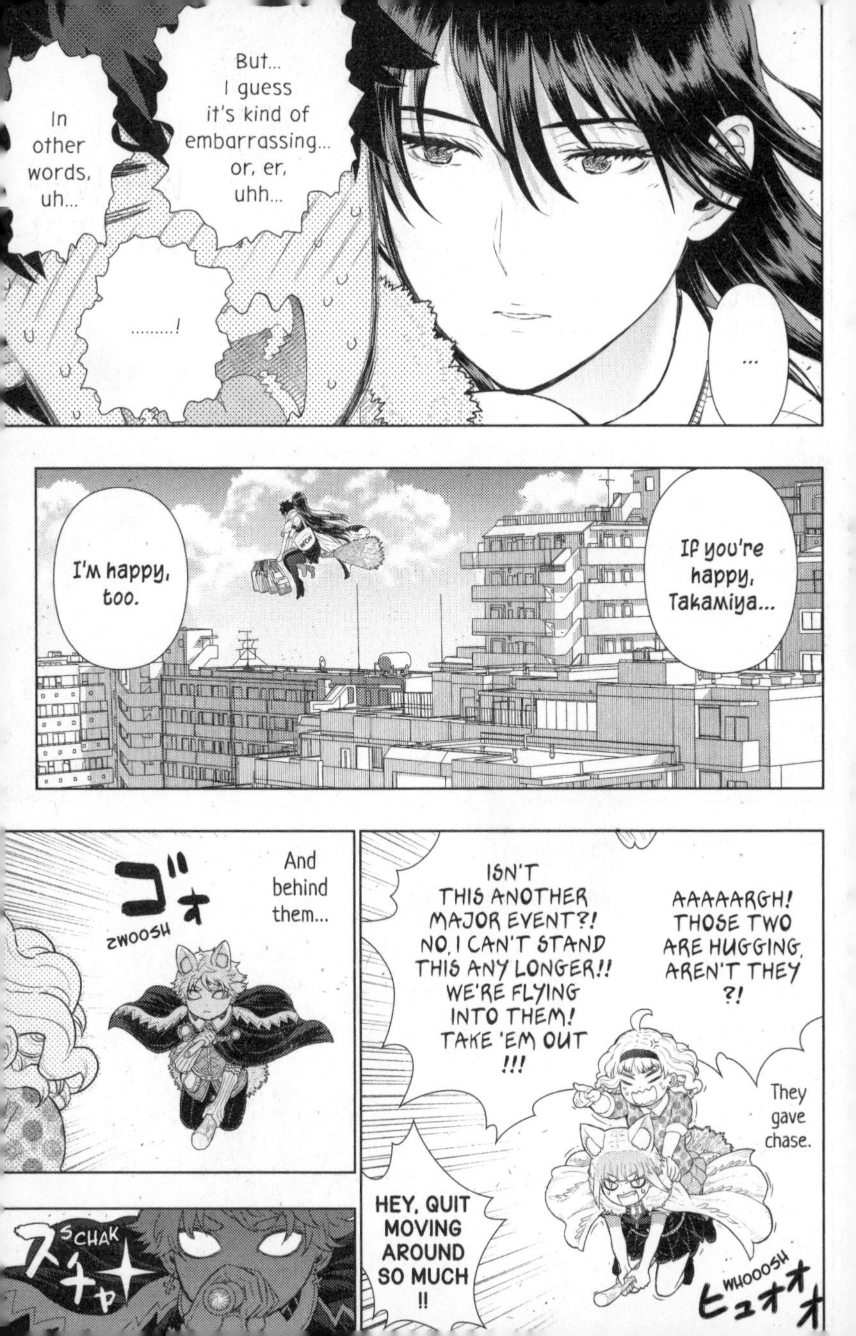
But... I guess it's kind of embarrassing... or, er, uhh...
In other words, uh...
.........!
...
If you're happy, Takamiya...
I'm happy, too.
AAAAARGH! THOSE TWO ARE HUGGING, AREN'T THEY?!
ISN'T THIS ANOTHER MAJOR EVENT?! NO, I CAN'T STAND THIS ANY LONGER!! WE'RE FLYING INTO THEM! TAKE 'EM OUT!!!
They gave chase.
HEY, QUIT MOVING AROUND SO MUCH!!
ヒュオオオ WHOOOSH
And behind them...
ゴォ ZWOOSH
スチャ SCHAK

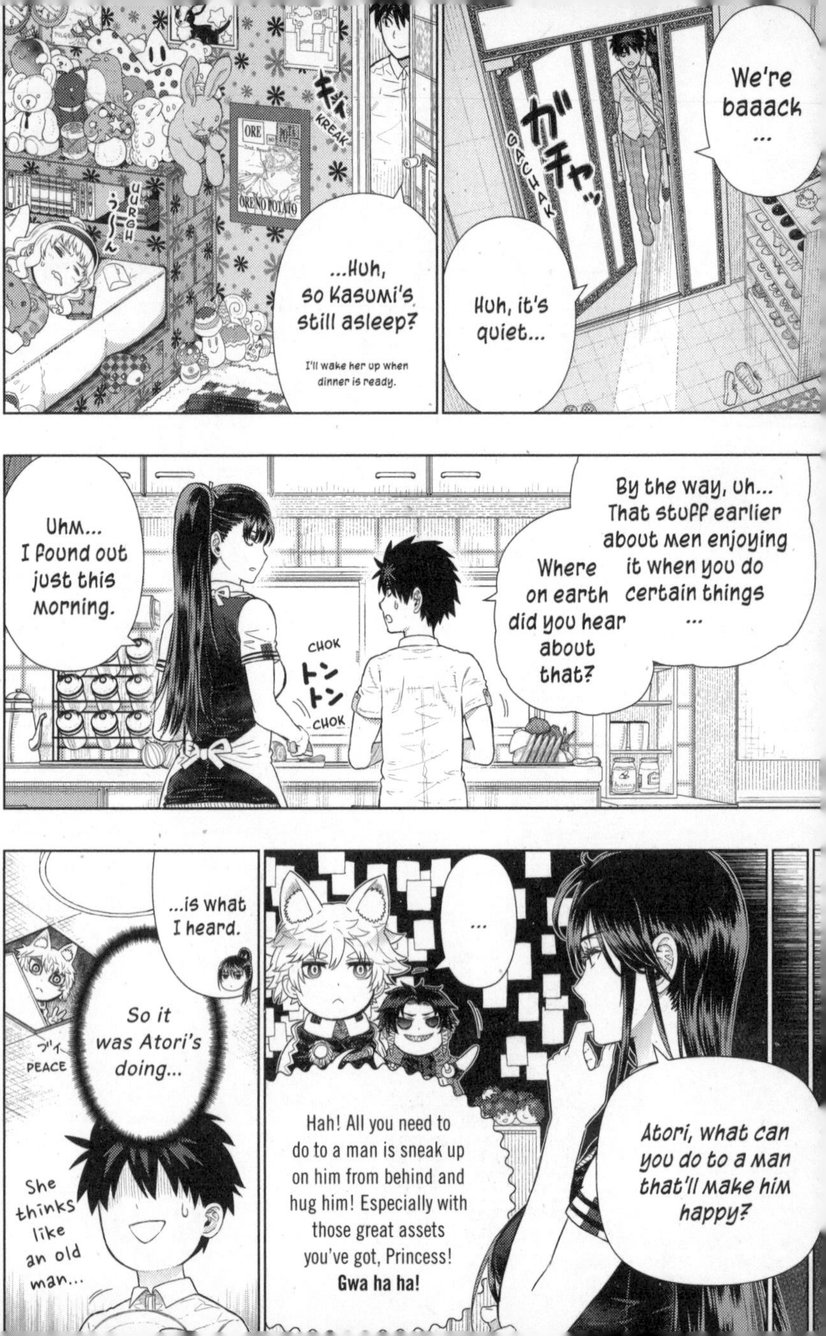
We're baaack ...
ガチャッ GACHAK
Huh, it's quiet...
キィ KREAK
...Huh, so Kasumi's still asleep?
I'll wake her up when dinner is ready.
うーん URGH
By the way, uh... That stuff earlier about men enjoying it when you do certain things ...
Where on earth did you hear about that?
トントン CHOK CHOK
Uhm... I found out just this morning.
Atori, what can you do to a man that'll make him happy?
...
Hah! All you need to do to a man is sneak up on him from behind and hug him! Especially with those great assets you've got, Princess! **Gwa ha ha!**
...is what I heard.
So it was Atori's doing...
ブイ PEACE
She thinks like an old man...

CHAPTER 59 END

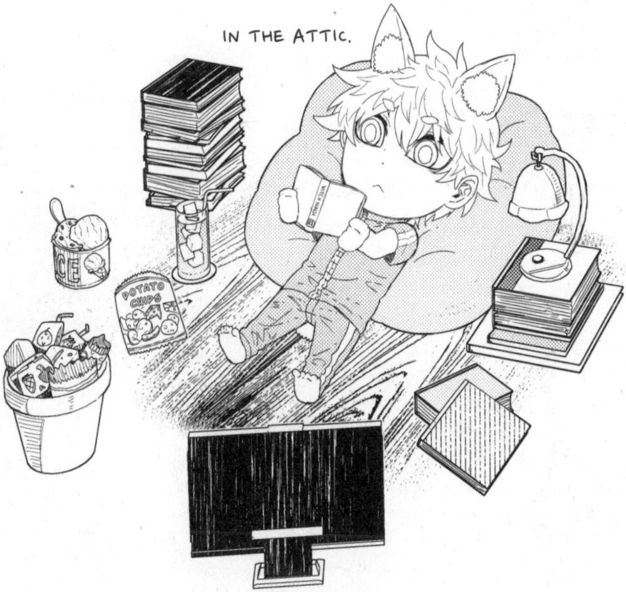
IN THE ATTIC.
POTATO CHIPS

Witchcraft Works

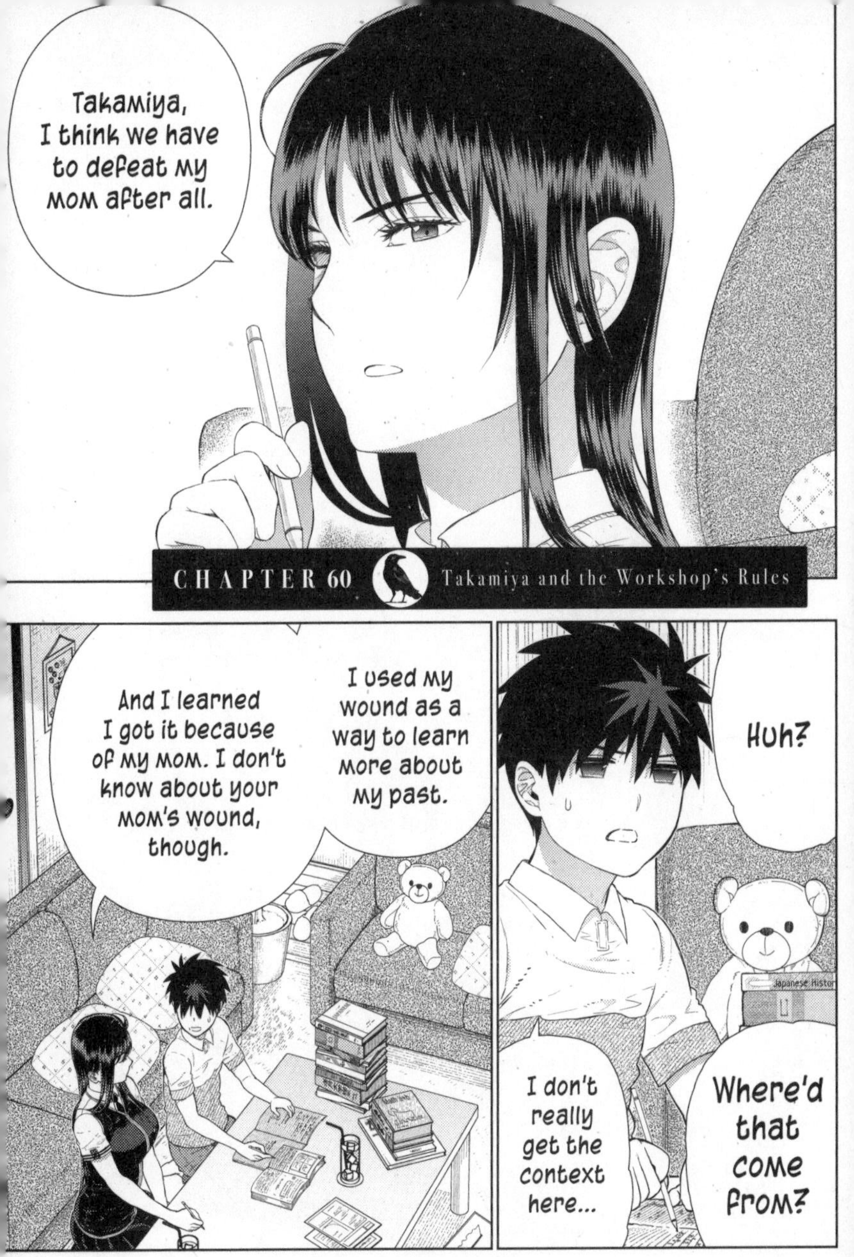
Takamiya, I think we have to defeat my mom after all.
CHAPTER 60 Takamiya and the Workshop's Rules
Huh?
Where'd that come from?
I don't really get the context here...
I used my wound as a way to learn more about my past.
And I learned I got it because of my mom. I don't know about your mom's wound, though.

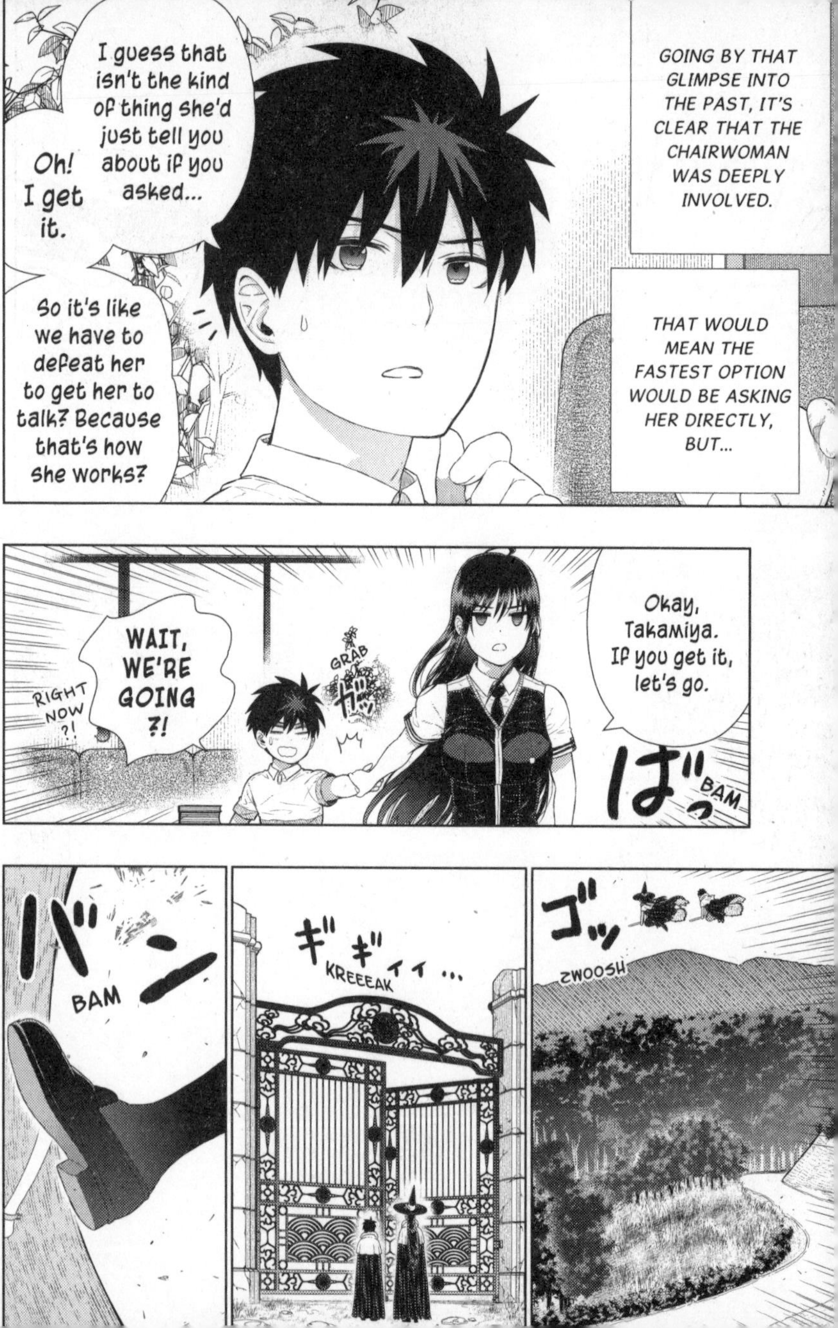
GOING BY THAT GLIMPSE INTO THE PAST, IT'S CLEAR THAT THE CHAIRWOMAN WAS DEEPLY INVOLVED.
THAT WOULD MEAN THE FASTEST OPTION WOULD BE ASKING HER DIRECTLY, BUT...
I guess that isn't the kind of thing she'd just tell you about if you asked...
Oh! I get it.
So it's like we have to defeat her to get her to talk? Because that's how she works?
Okay, Takamiya. If you get it, let's go.
ばっ
BAM
ガッ
GRAB
WAIT, WE'RE GOING ?!
RIGHT NOW ?!
ゴッ
ZWOOSH
ギギィイ...
KREEEAK
バーン
BAM

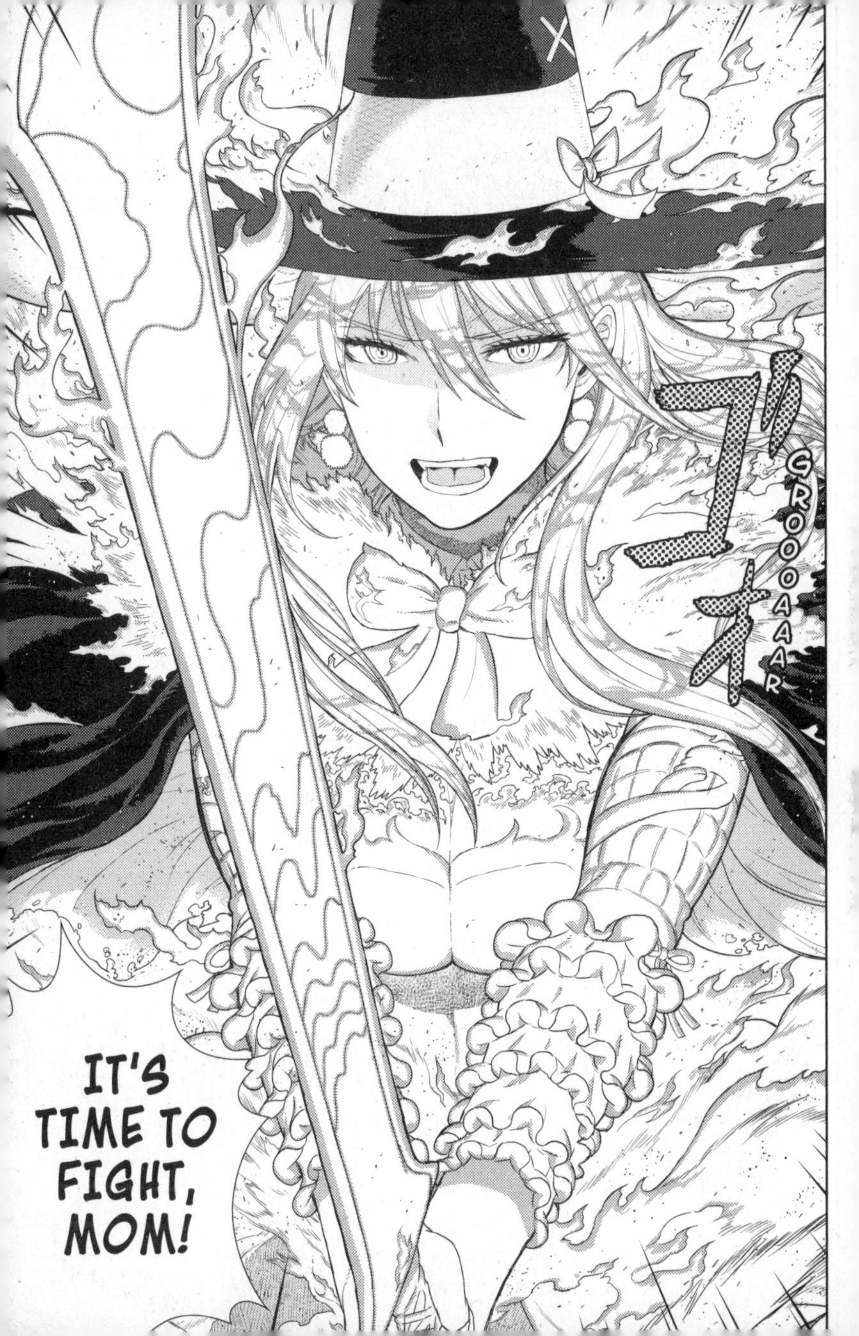
ゴオ
GROOOAAAR
IT'S TIME TO FIGHT, MOM!

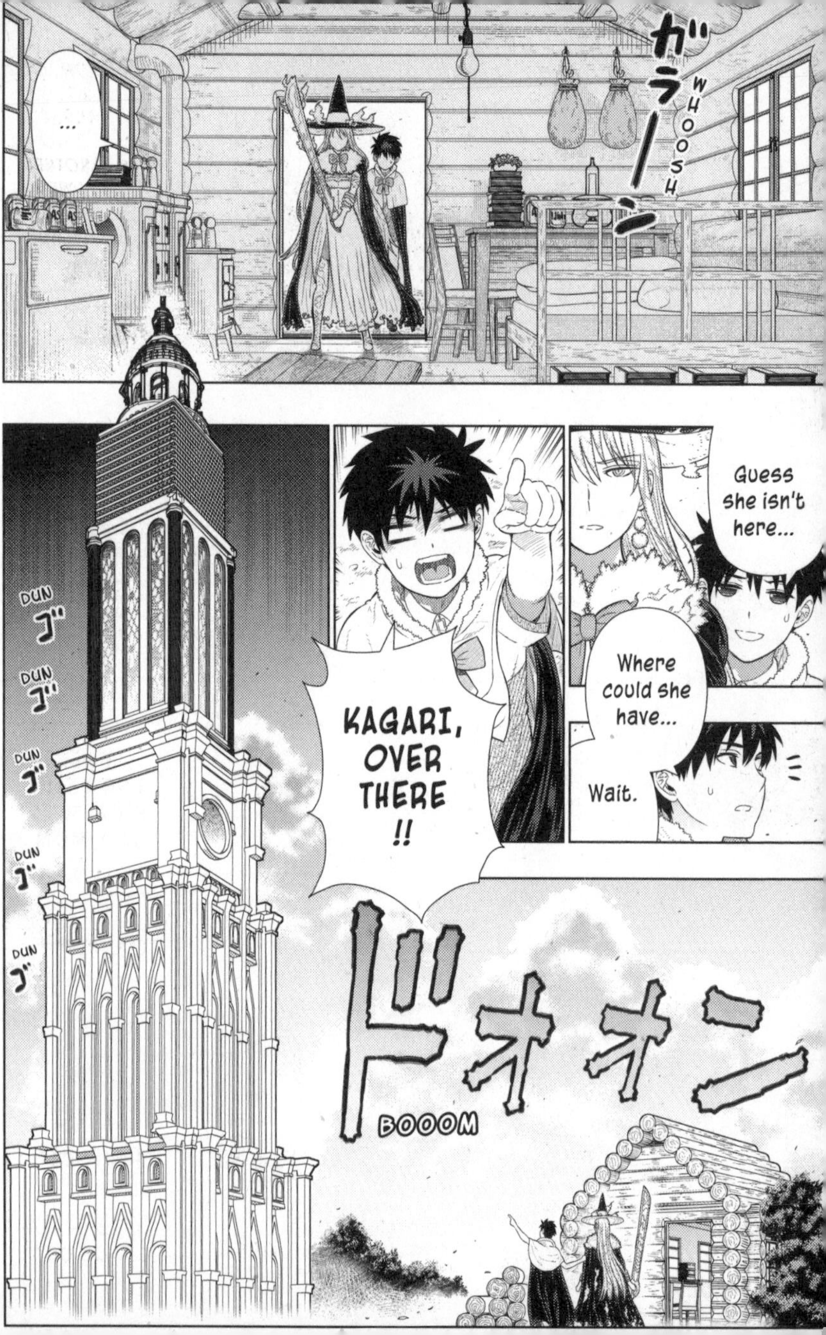

...
ガラーン
WHOOSH
Guess she isn't here...
Where could she have...
Wait.
KAGARI, OVER THERE !!
DUN ゴ
DUN ゴ
DUN ゴ
DUN ゴ
DUN ゴ
ドオン
BOOOM

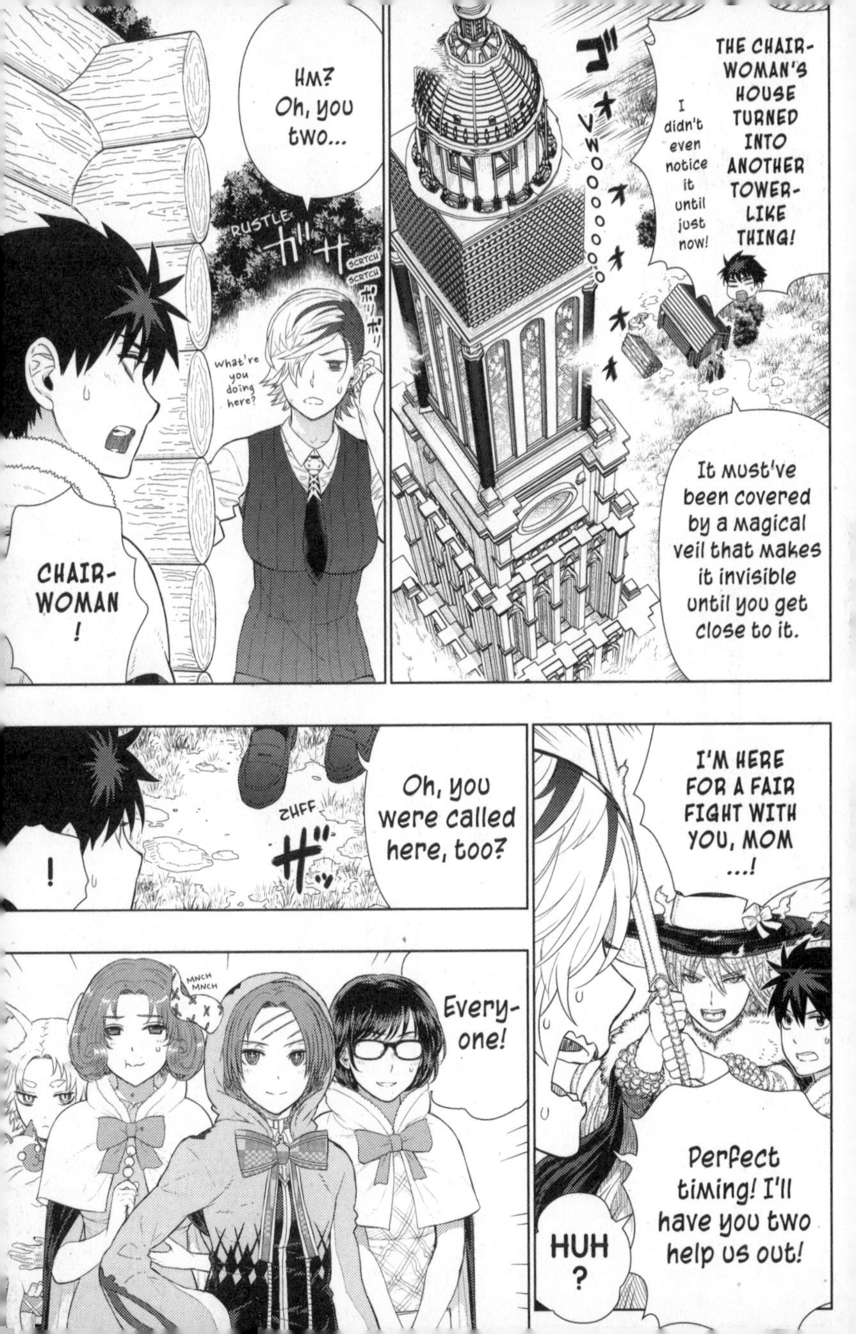

VWOOOOOOOO
THE CHAIR-WOMAN'S HOUSE TURNED INTO ANOTHER TOWER-LIKE THING!
I didn't even notice it until just now!
It must've been covered by a magical veil that makes it invisible until you get close to it.
HM? Oh, you two...
RUSTLE
SCRTCH SCRTCH
What're you doing here?
CHAIR-WOMAN!
I'M HERE FOR A FAIR FIGHT WITH YOU, MOM ...!
Perfect timing! I'll have you two help us out!
HUH?
Oh, you were called here, too?
ZHFF
!
Every-one!
MNCH MNCH

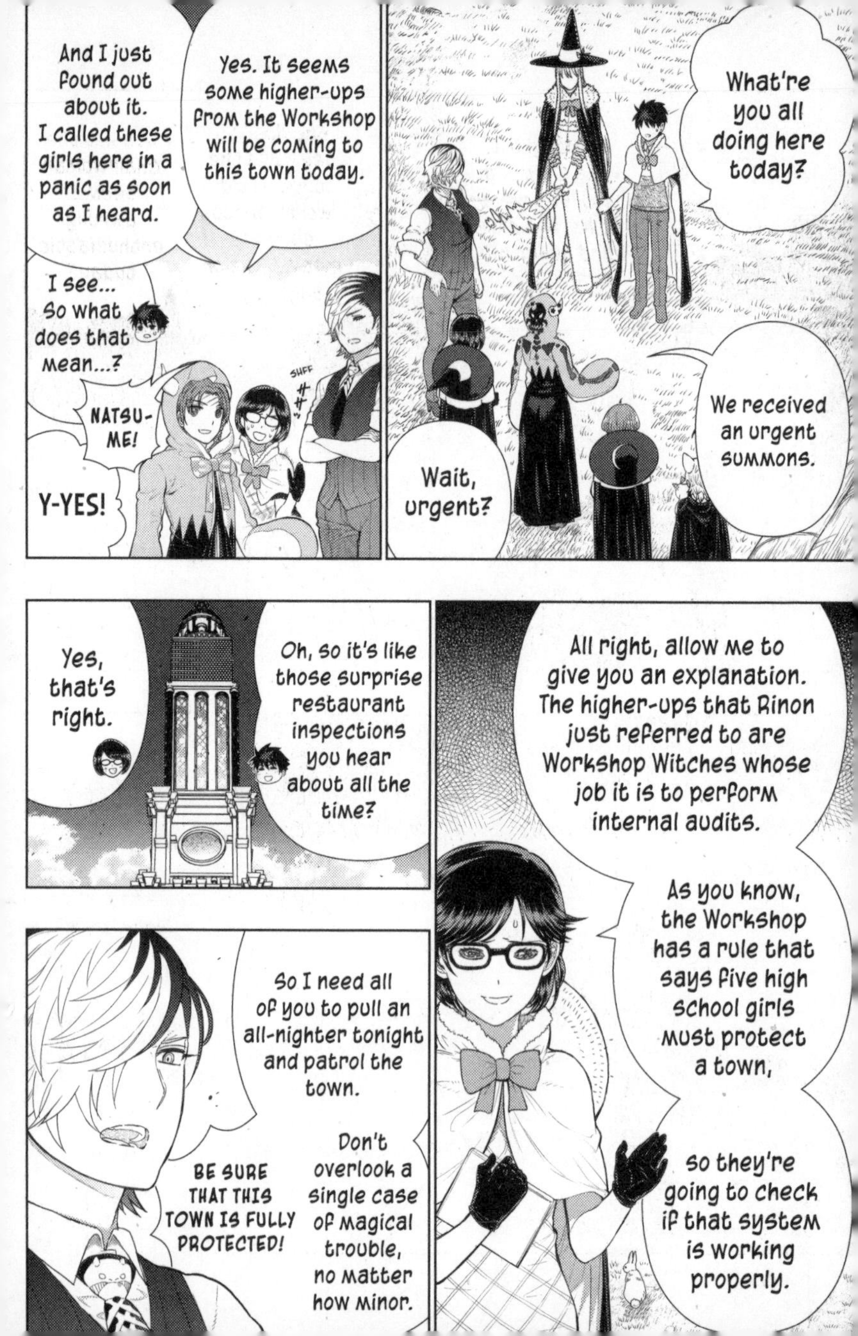
What're you all doing here today?
We received an urgent summons.
Wait, urgent?
Yes. It seems some higher-ups from the Workshop will be coming to this town today.
And I just found out about it. I called these girls here in a panic as soon as I heard.
I see... So what does that mean...?
SHFF
NATSUME!
Y-YES!
All right, allow me to give you an explanation. The higher-ups that Rinon just referred to are Workshop Witches whose job it is to perform internal audits.
As you know, the Workshop has a rule that says five high school girls must protect a town,
so they're going to check if that system is working properly.
Oh, so it's like those surprise restaurant inspections you hear about all the time?
Yes, that's right.
So I need all of you to pull an all-nighter tonight and patrol the town.
Don't overlook a single case of magical trouble, no matter how minor.
BE SURE THAT THIS TOWN IS FULLY PROTECTED!

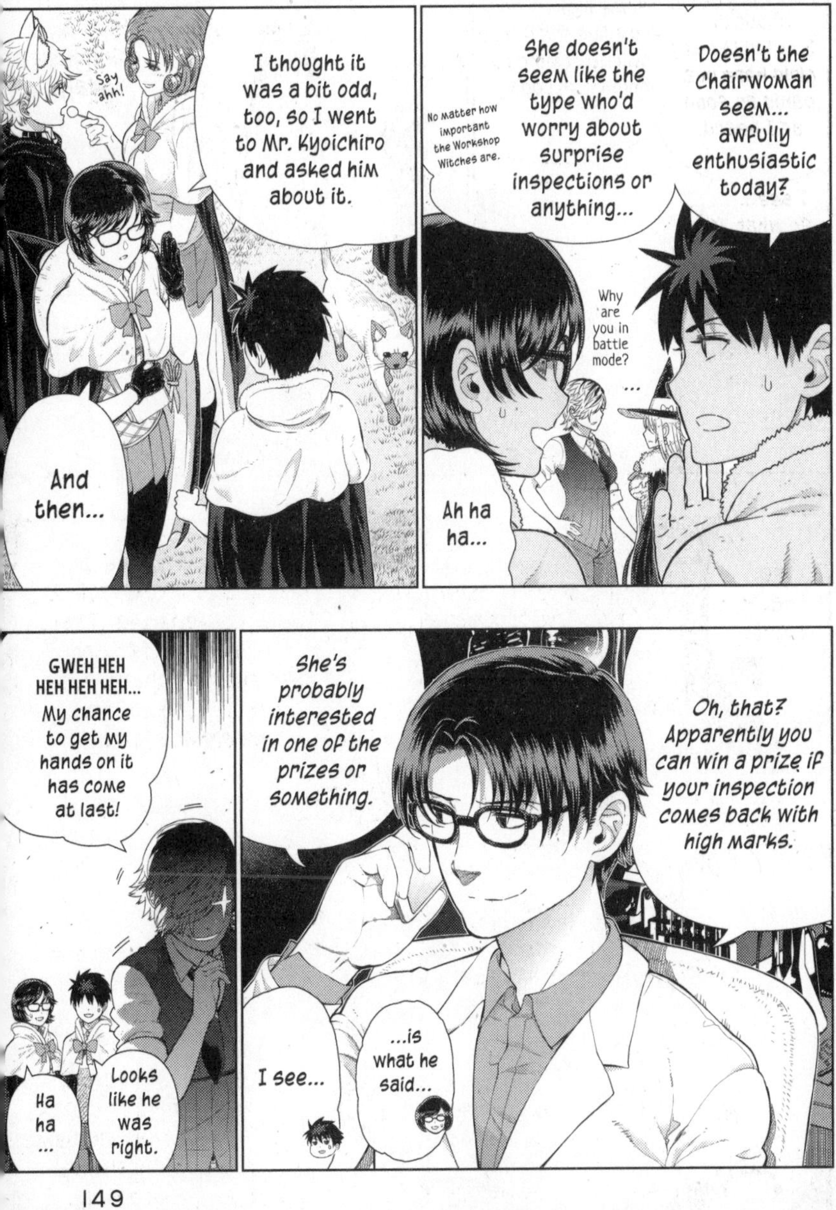
Doesn't the Chairwoman seem... awfully enthusiastic today?
She doesn't seem like the type who'd worry about surprise inspections or anything...
No matter how important the Workshop Witches are.
Why are you in battle mode?
...
Ah ha ha...
I thought it was a bit odd, too, so I went to Mr. Kyoichiro and asked him about it.
Say ahh!
And then...
Oh, that? Apparently you can win a prize if your inspection comes back with high marks.
She's probably interested in one of the prizes or something.
...is what he said...
I see...
GWEH HEH HEH HEH HEH... My chance to get my hands on it has come at last!
Looks like he was right.
Ha ha ...

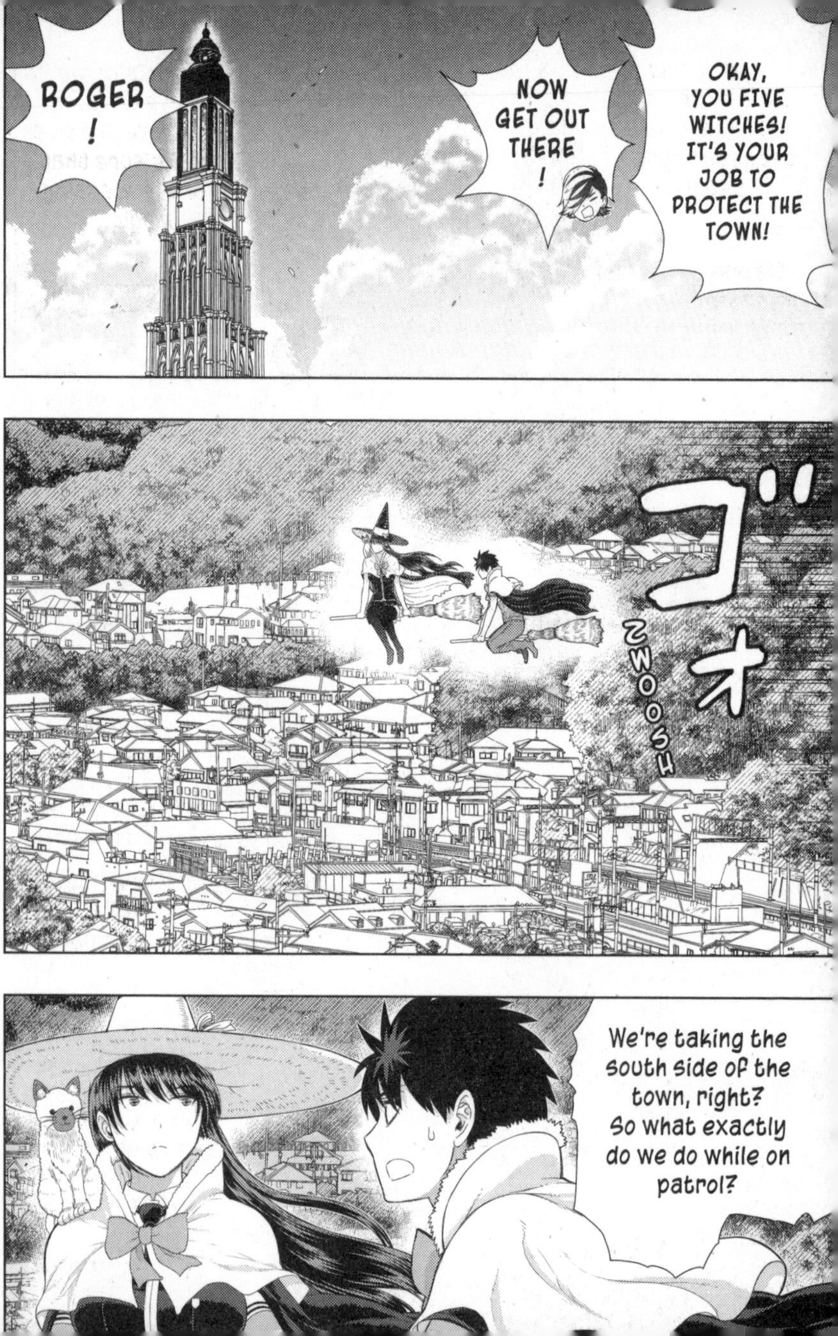
OKAY, YOU FIVE WITCHES! IT'S YOUR JOB TO PROTECT THE TOWN!
NOW GET OUT THERE!
ROGER!
ゴオ
ZWOOSH
We're taking the south side of the town, right? So what exactly do we do while on patrol?

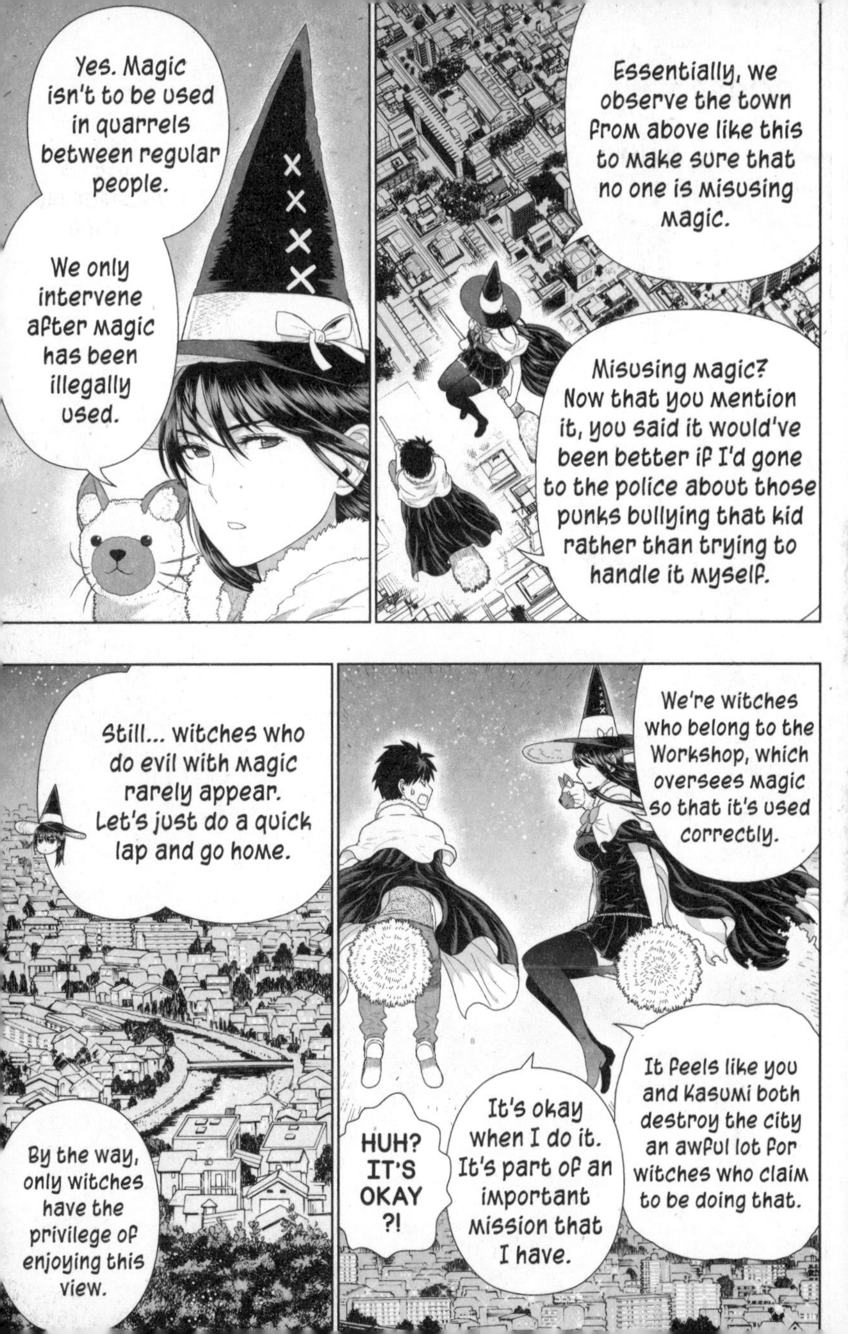
Essentially, we observe the town from above like this to make sure that no one is misusing magic.
Misusing magic? Now that you mention it, you said it would've been better if I'd gone to the police about those punks bullying that kid rather than trying to handle it myself.
Yes. Magic isn't to be used in quarrels between regular people.
We only intervene after magic has been illegally used.
We're witches who belong to the Workshop, which oversees magic so that it's used correctly.
It feels like you and Kasumi both destroy the city an awful lot for witches who claim to be doing that.
It's okay when I do it. It's part of an important mission that I have.
HUH? IT'S OKAY ?!
Still... witches who do evil with magic rarely appear. Let's just do a quick lap and go home.
By the way, only witches have the privilege of enjoying this view.

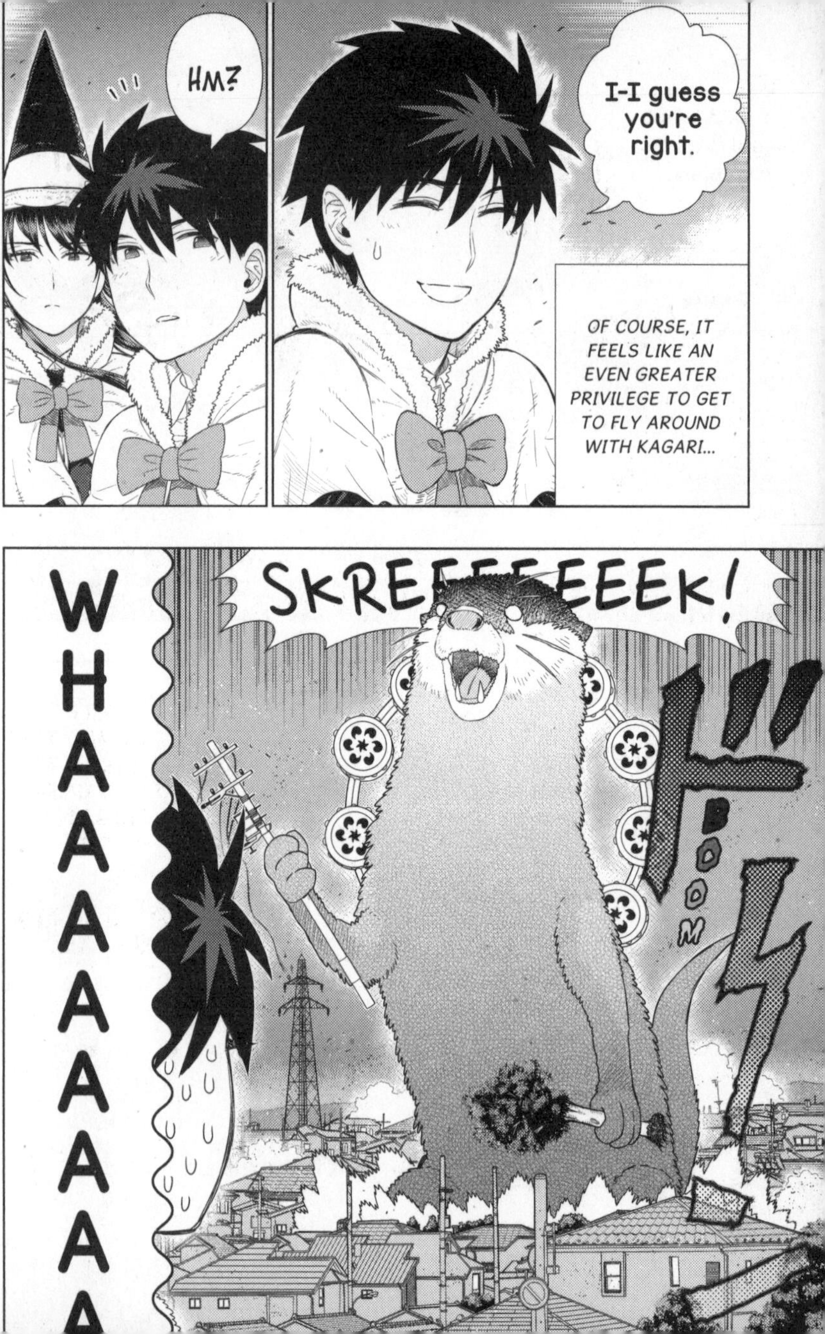
I-I guess you're right.
OF COURSE, IT FEELS LIKE AN EVEN GREATER PRIVILEGE TO GET TO FLY AROUND WITH KAGARI...
HM?
SKREEEEEEEK!
BOOM
WHAAAAAAAA

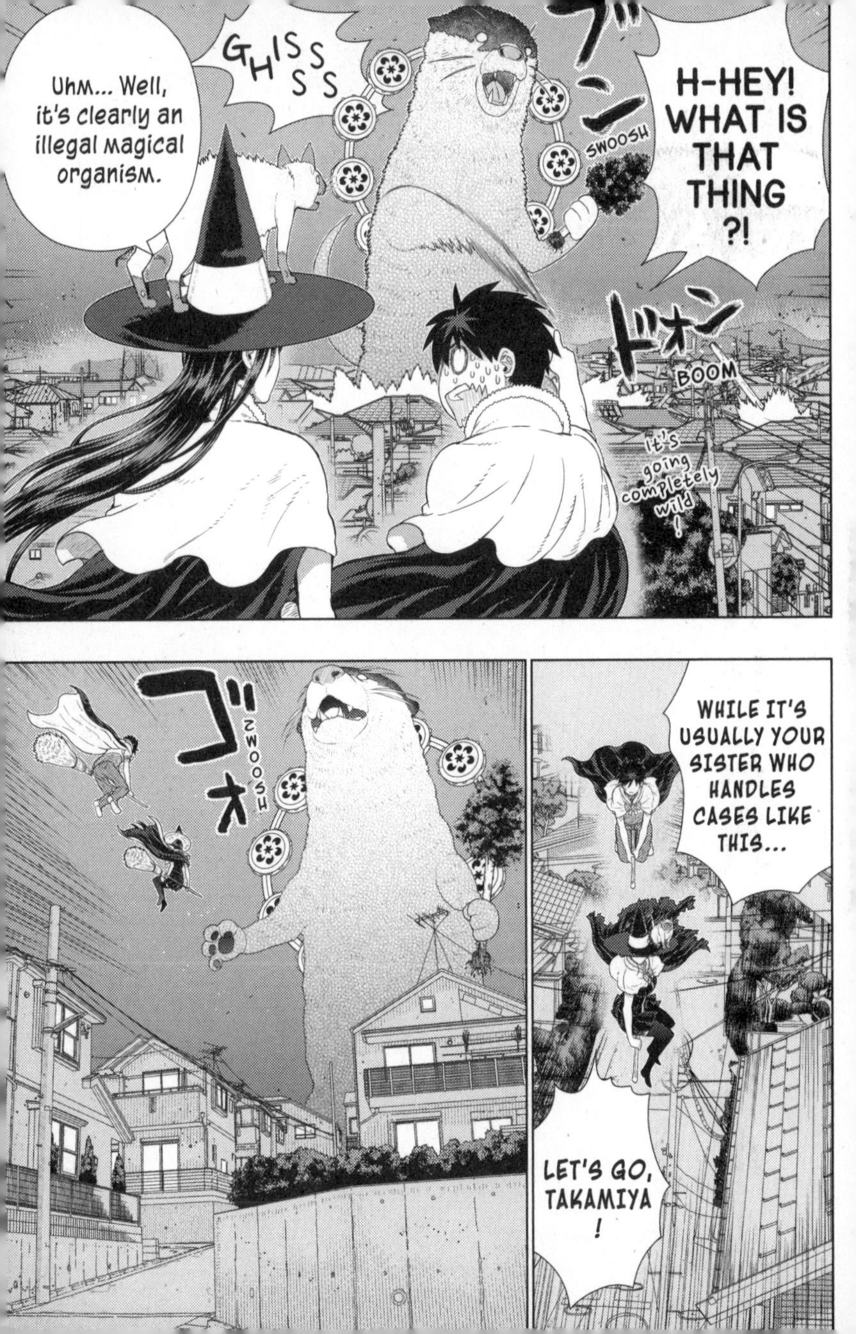
H-HEY! WHAT IS THAT THING?!
SWOOSH
GHISSSS
Uhm... Well, it's clearly an illegal magical organism.
BOOM
It's going completely wild!
WHILE IT'S USUALLY YOUR SISTER WHO HANDLES CASES LIKE THIS...
LET'S GO, TAKAMIYA!
ZWOOSH

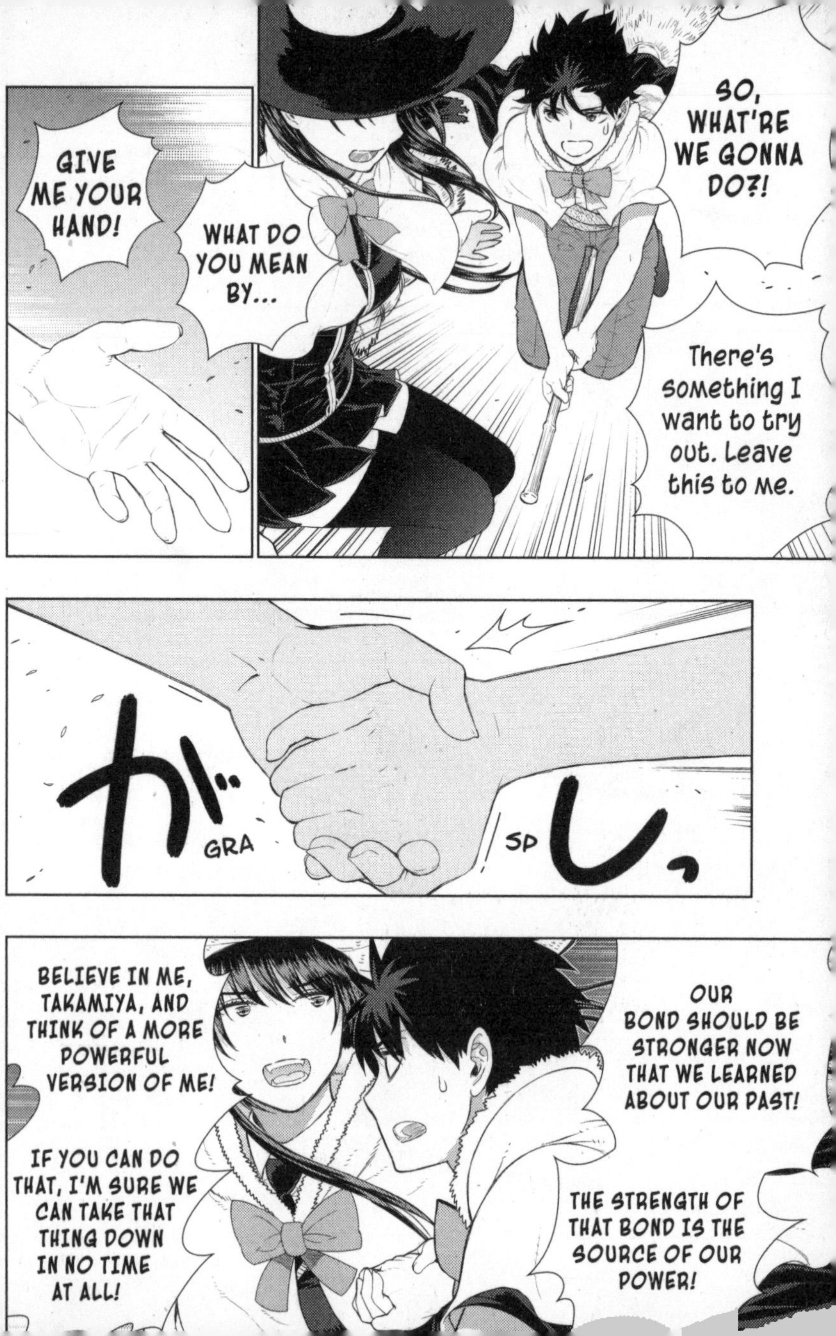
SO, WHAT'RE WE GONNA DO?!
There's something I want to try out. Leave this to me.
WHAT DO YOU MEAN BY...
GIVE ME YOUR HAND!
がし
GRA
SP
OUR BOND SHOULD BE STRONGER NOW THAT WE LEARNED ABOUT OUR PAST!
THE STRENGTH OF THAT BOND IS THE SOURCE OF OUR POWER!
BELIEVE IN ME, TAKAMIYA, AND THINK OF A MORE POWERFUL VERSION OF ME!
IF YOU CAN DO THAT, I'M SURE WE CAN TAKE THAT THING DOWN IN NO TIME AT ALL!

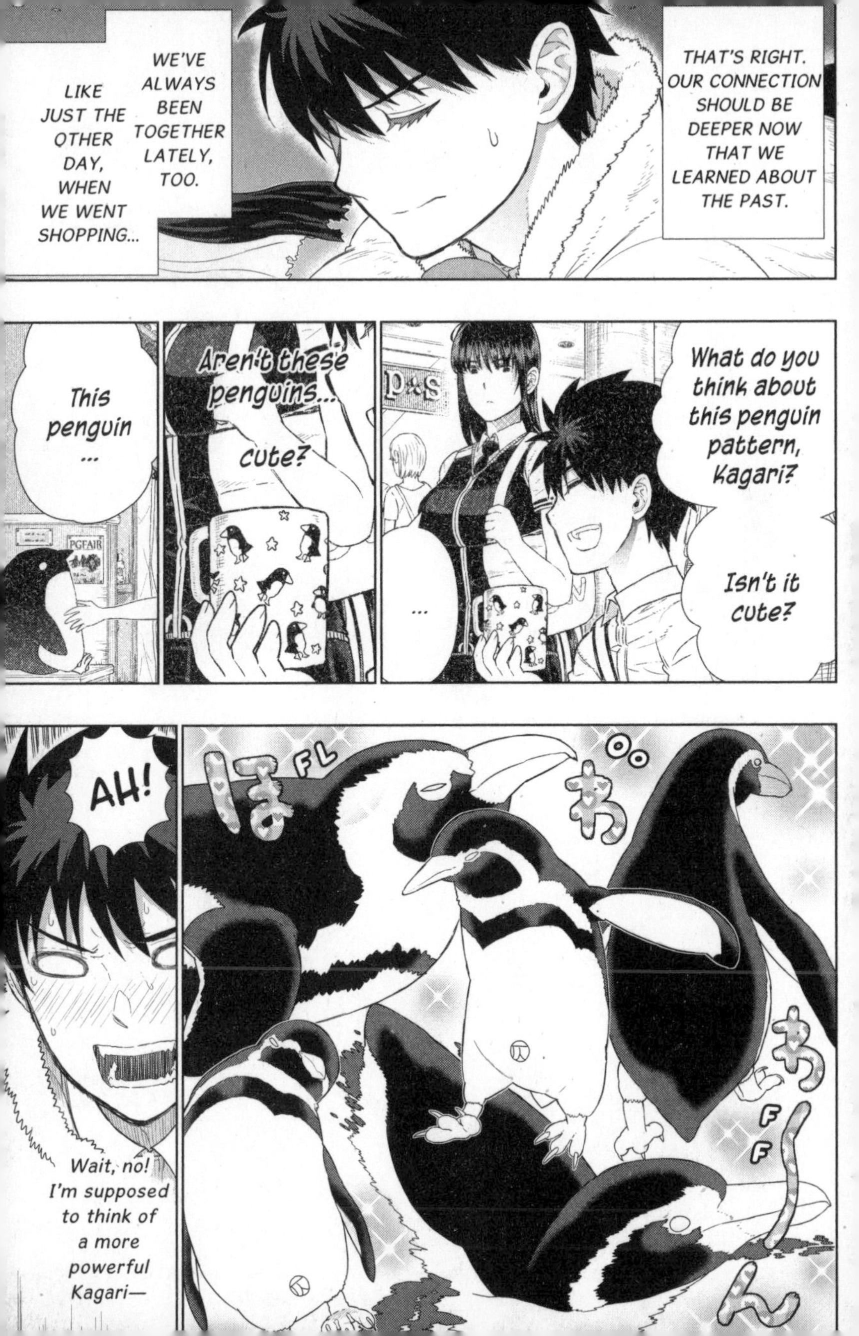
THAT'S RIGHT. OUR CONNECTION SHOULD BE DEEPER NOW THAT WE LEARNED ABOUT THE PAST.
WE'VE ALWAYS BEEN TOGETHER LATELY, TOO.
LIKE JUST THE OTHER DAY, WHEN WE WENT SHOPPING...
What do you think about this penguin pattern, Kagari?
Isn't it cute?
...
Aren't these penguins...
cute?
This penguin ...
FL
FF
AH!
Wait, no! I'm supposed to think of a more powerful Kagari—

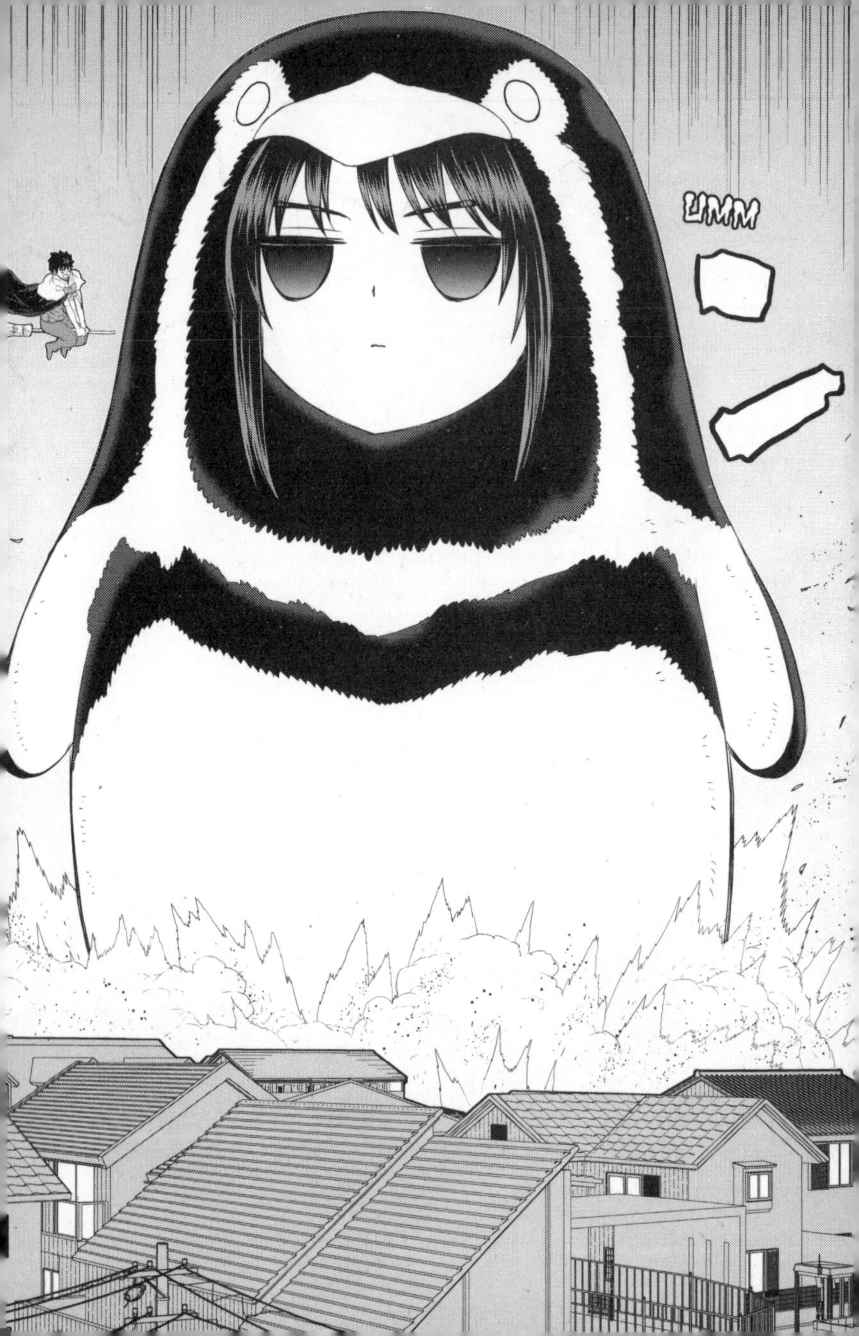
UMM

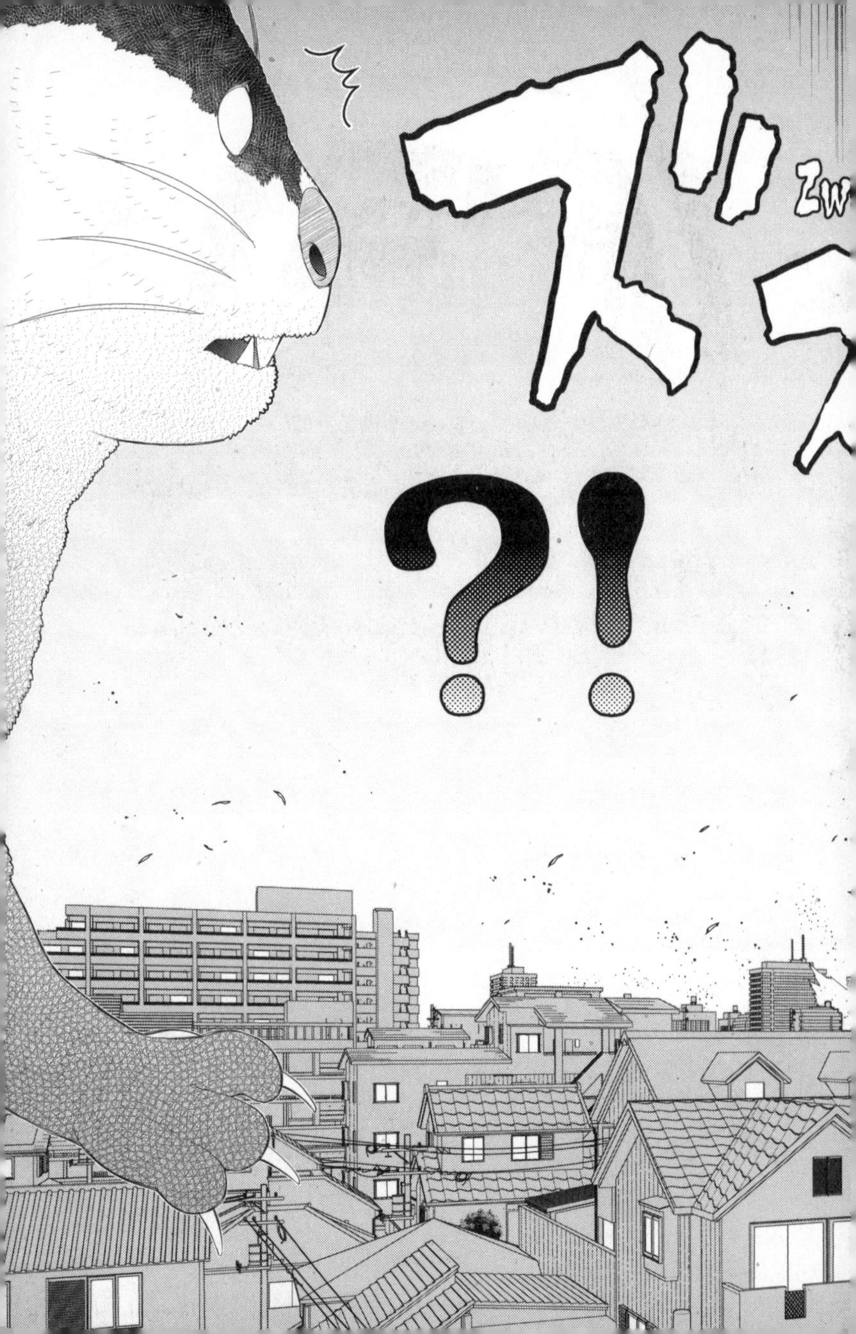
ズ
?!

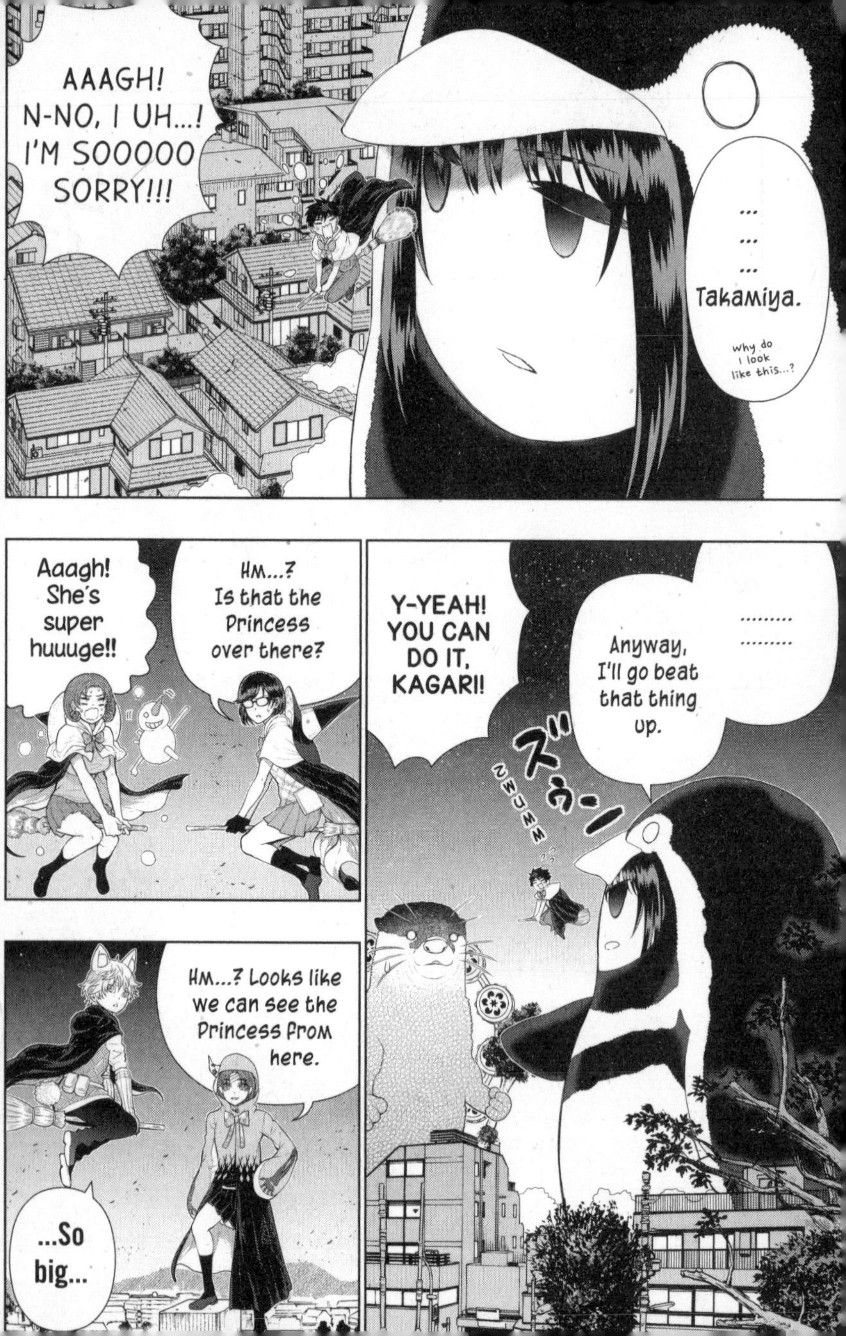

... ... Takamiya.
why do I look like this...?
AAAGH! N-NO, I UH...! I'M SOOOOO SORRY!!!
....
Anyway, I'll go beat that thing up.
ズゥーー
ZWUMM
Y-YEAH! YOU CAN DO IT, KAGARI!
Hm...? Is that the Princess over there?
Aaagh! She's super huuuge!!
Hm...? Looks like we can see the Princess from here.
...So big...

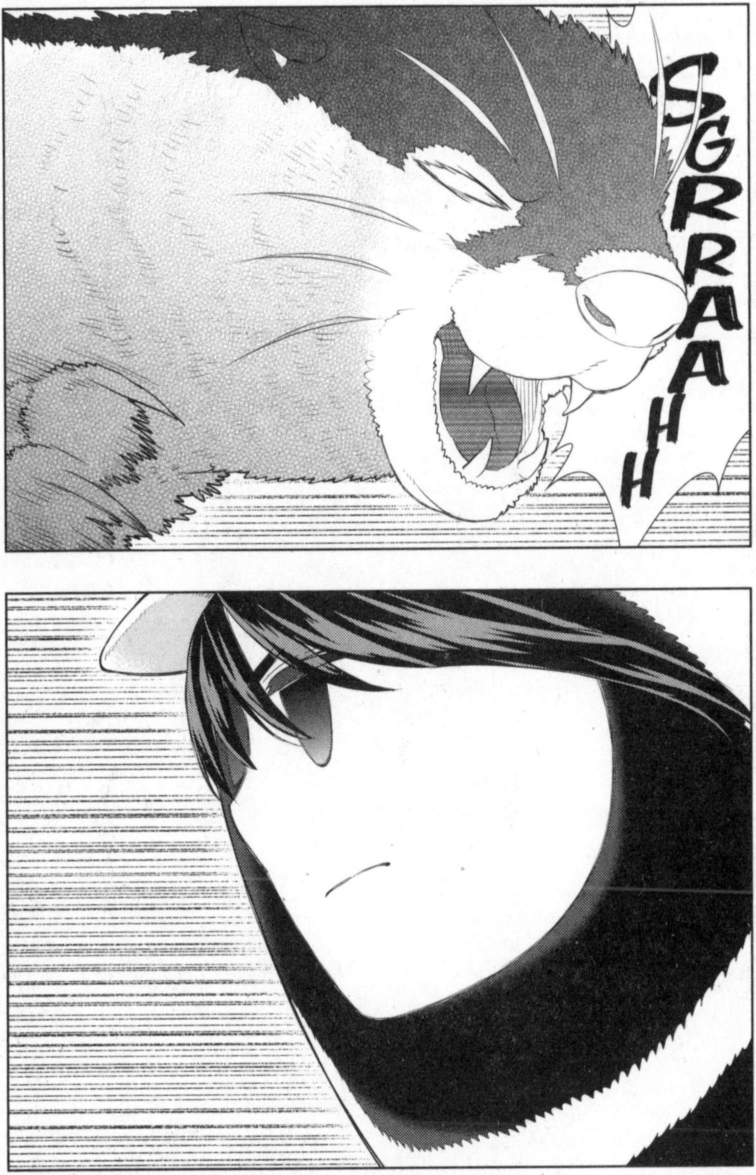
SGRRAAHHH

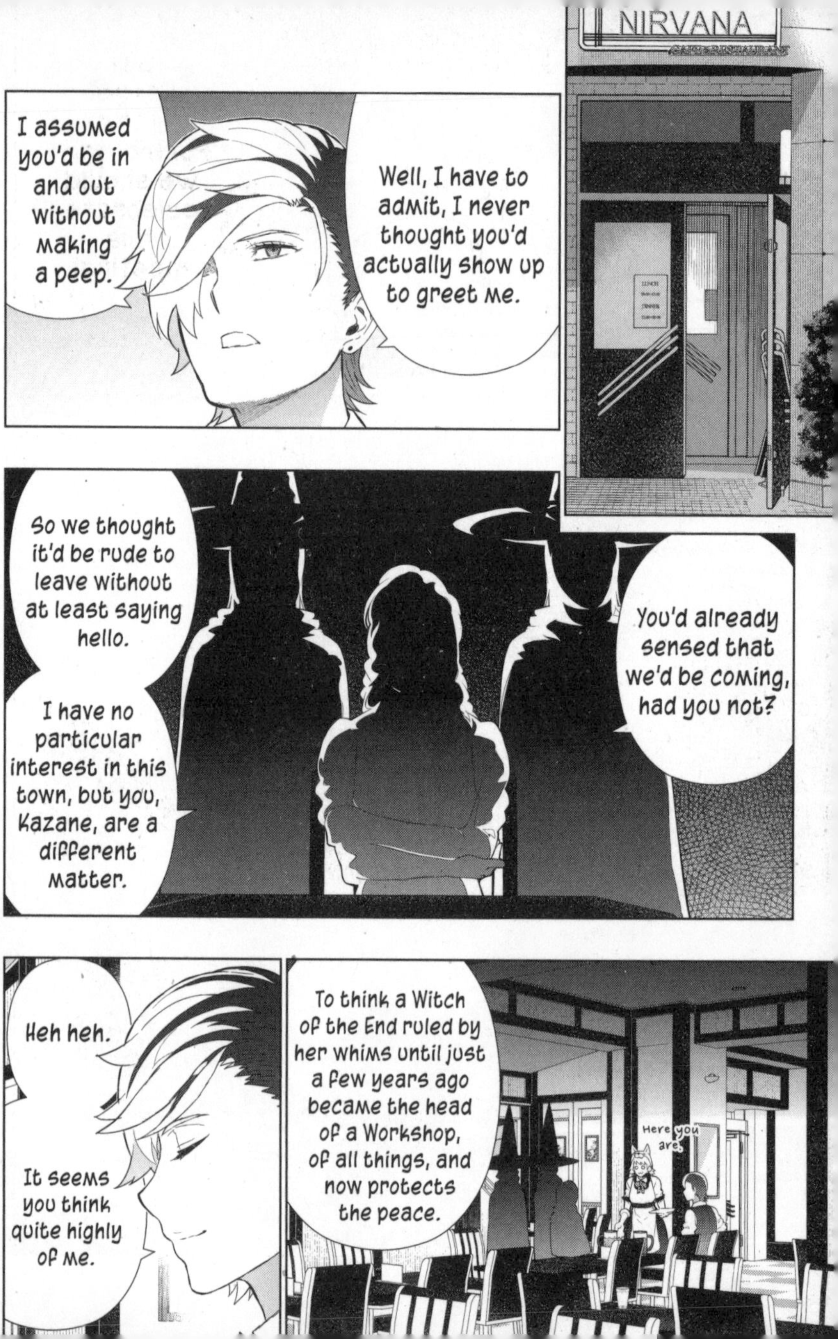
NIRVANA
Well, I have to admit, I never thought you'd actually show up to greet me.
I assumed you'd be in and out without making a peep.
You'd already sensed that we'd be coming, had you not?
So we thought it'd be rude to leave without at least saying hello.
I have no particular interest in this town, but you, Kazane, are a different matter.
To think a Witch of the End ruled by her whims until just a few years ago became the head of a Workshop, of all things, and now protects the peace.
Here you are.
Heh heh.
It seems you think quite highly of me.

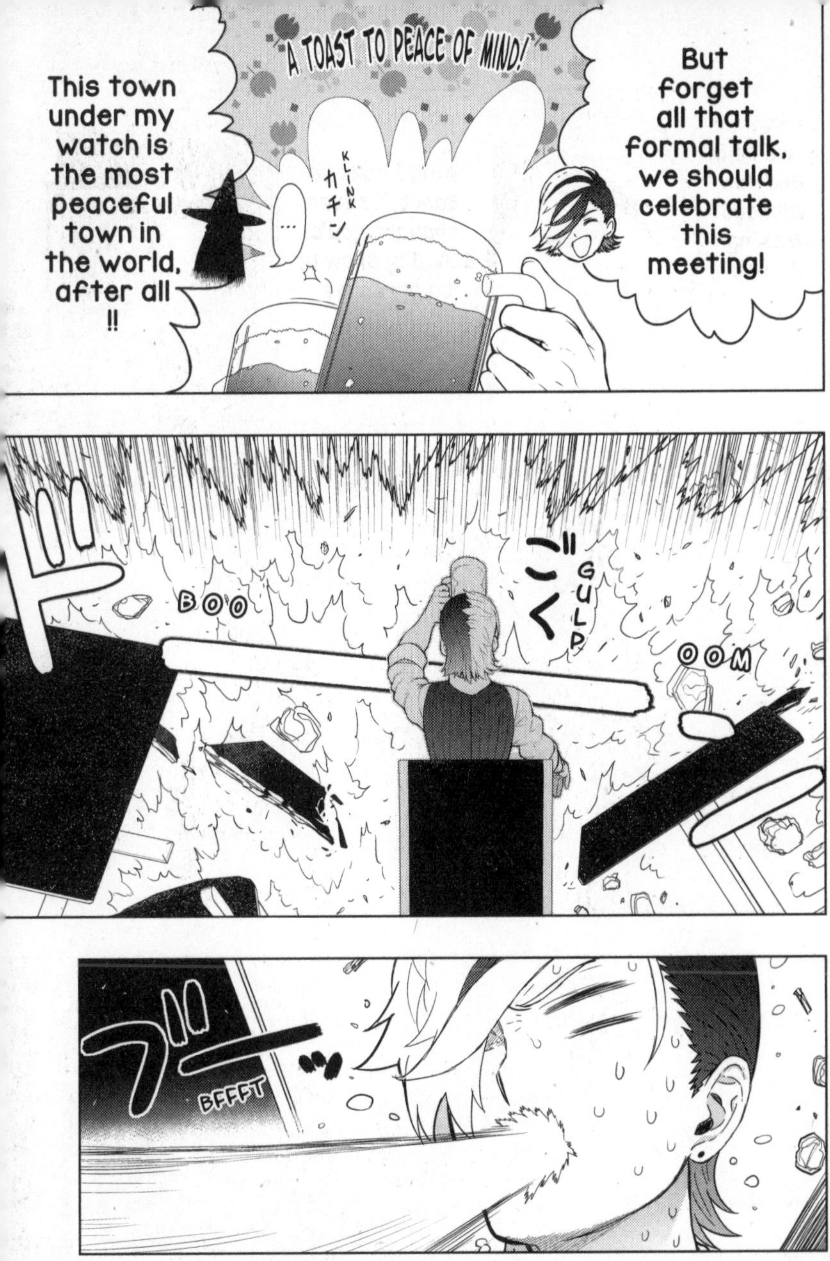
But forget all that formal talk, we should celebrate this meeting!
A TOAST TO PEACE OF MIND!
KLINK
カチン
...
This town under my watch is the most peaceful town in the world, after all !!
ごく
GULP
BOO
OOM
BFFFT

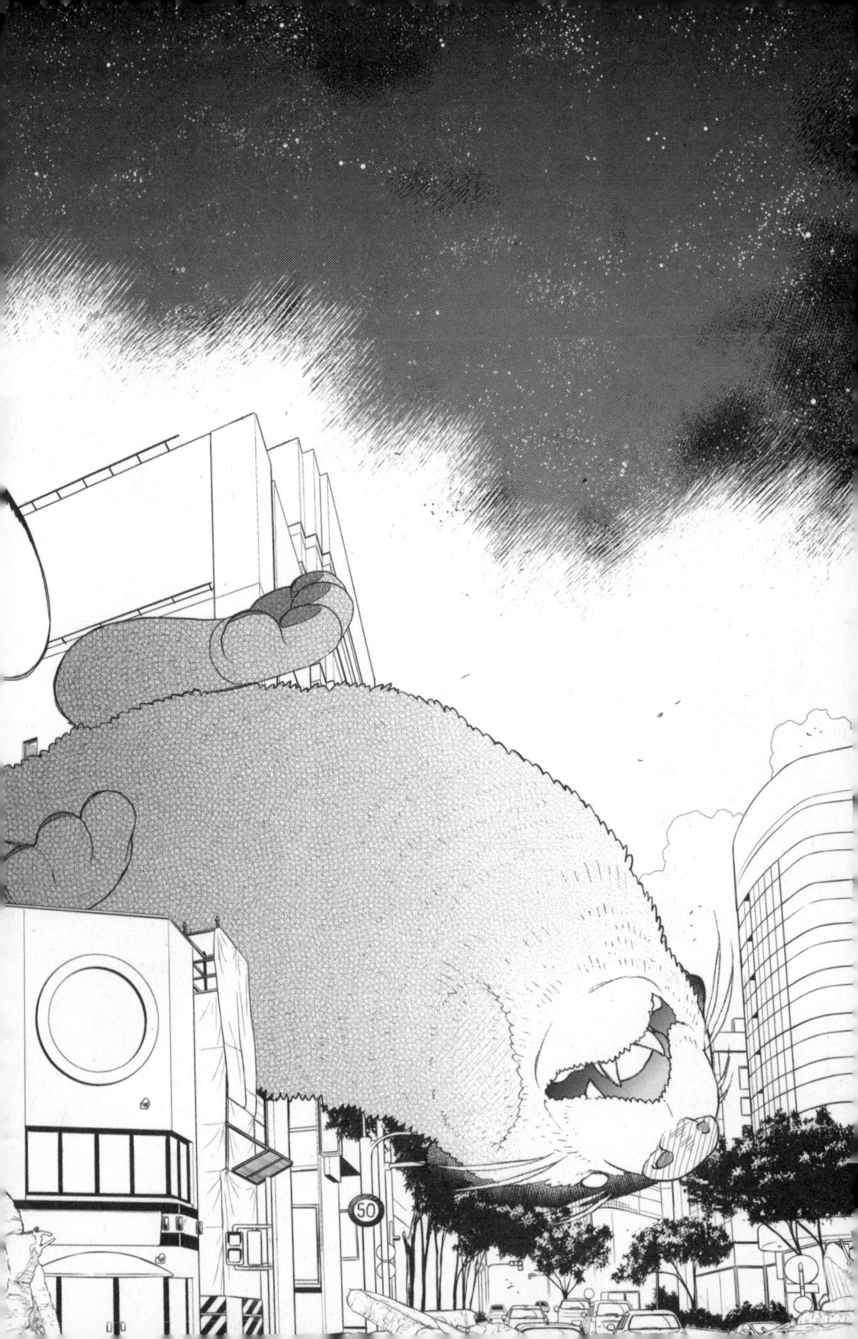
50

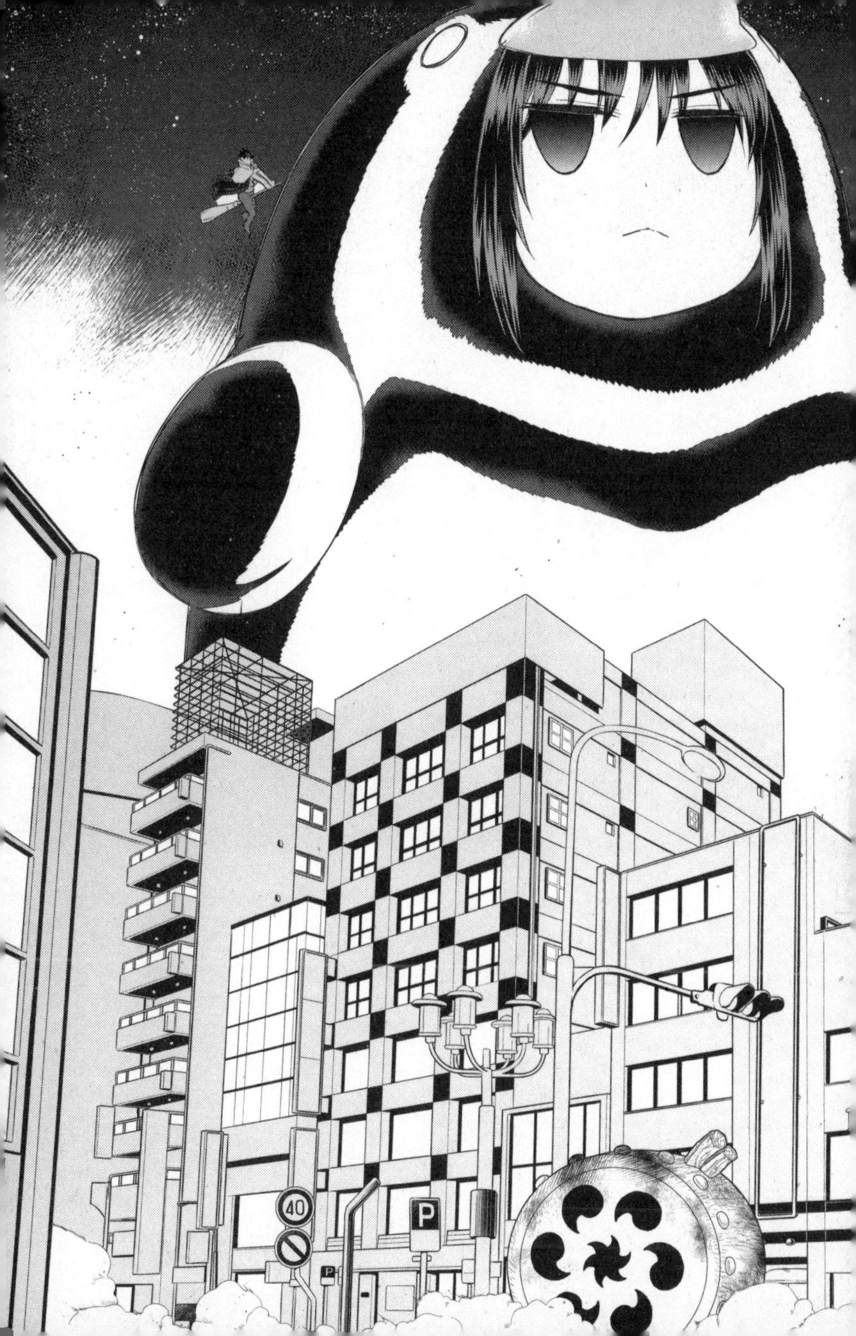
40
P
P

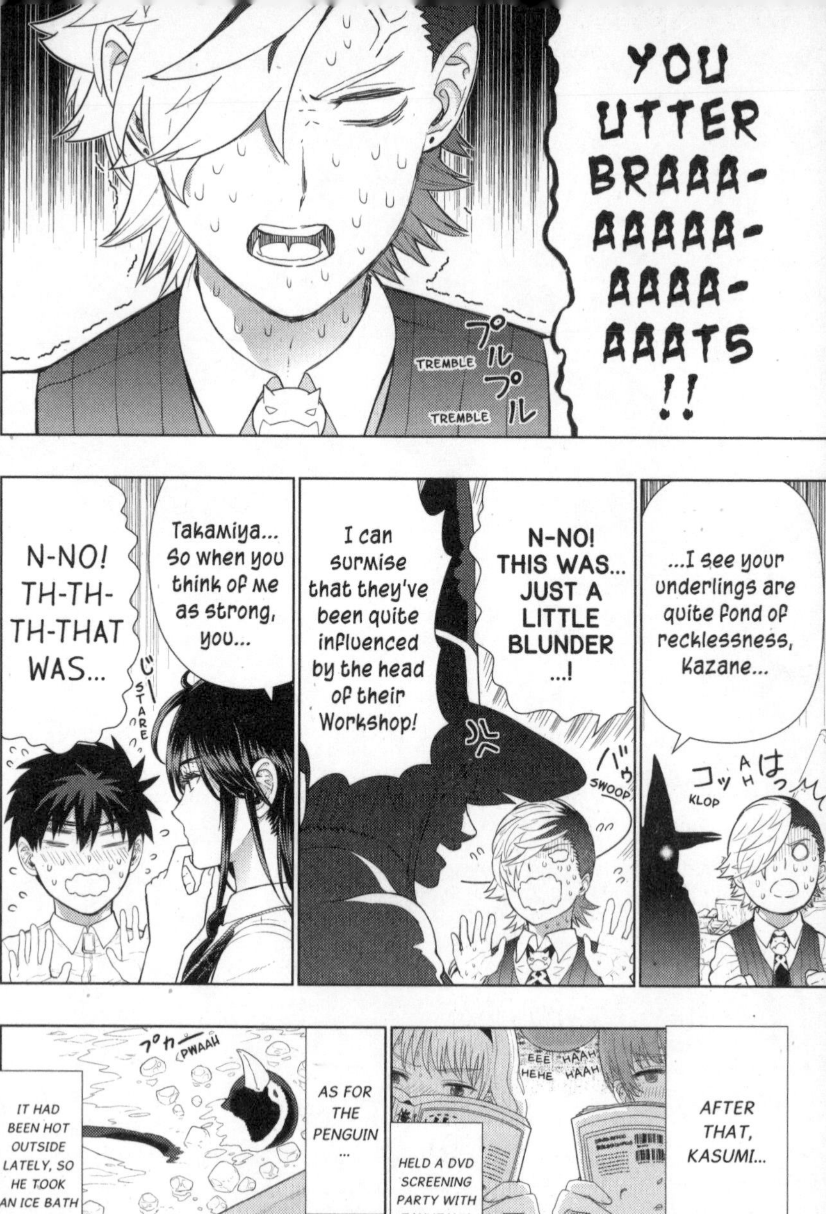
YOU UTTER BRAAA-AAAAA-AAAA-AAATS!!
プルプル
TREMBLE
TREMBLE
...I see your underlings are quite fond of recklessness, Kazane...
はっ
AH
コッ
KLOP
N-NO! THIS WAS... JUST A LITTLE BLUNDER ...!
バッ
SWOOP
I can surmise that they've been quite influenced by the head of their Workshop!
Takamiya... So when you think of me as strong, you...
N-NO! TH-TH-TH-THAT WAS...
じー
STARE
AFTER THAT, KASUMI...
EEE HEHE
HAAH HAAH
HELD A DVD SCREENING PARTY WITH TANUTANU.
AS FOR THE PENGUIN...
プカー
PWAAH
IT HAD BEEN HOT OUTSIDE LATELY, SO HE TOOK AN ICE BATH ALL DAY.

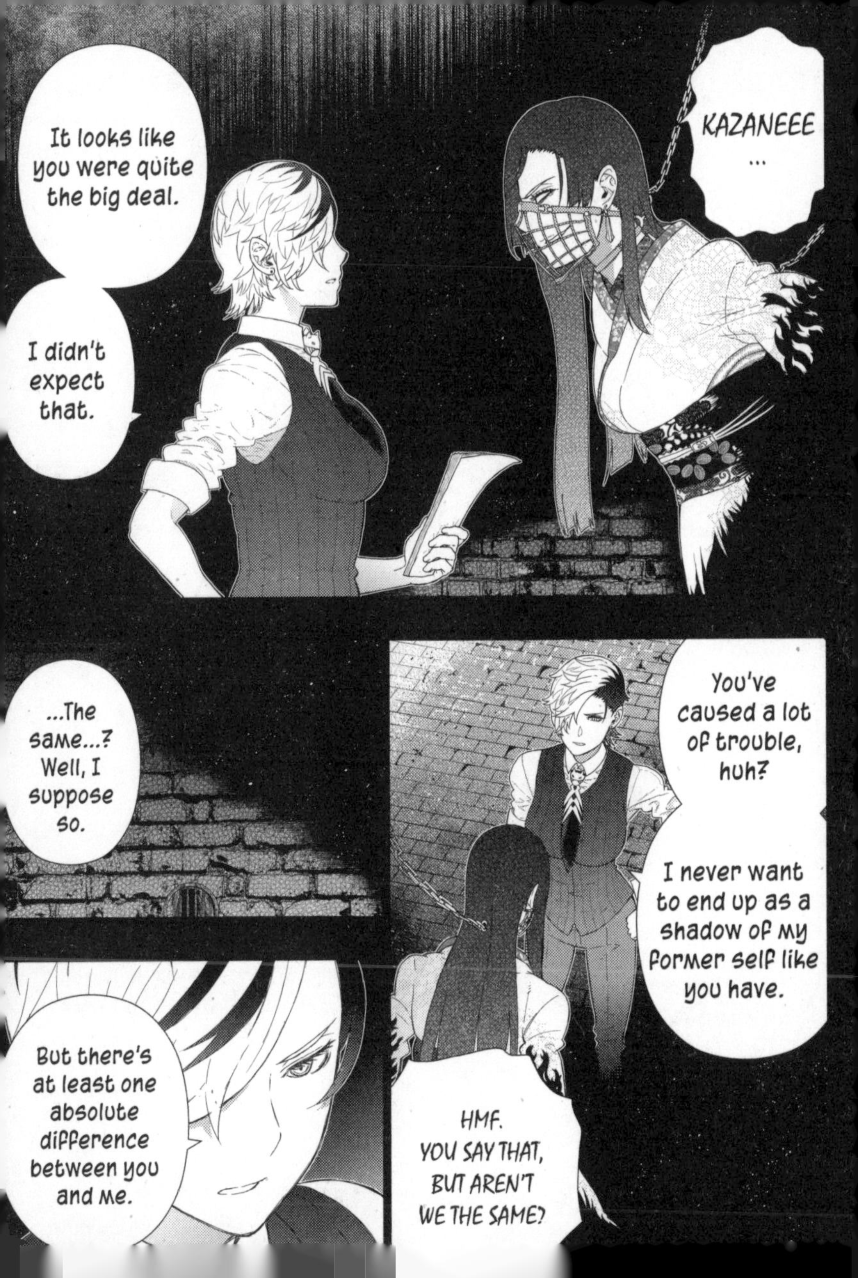
KAZANEEE ...
It looks like you were quite the big deal.
I didn't expect that.
You've caused a lot of trouble, huh?
I never want to end up as a shadow of my former self like you have.
HMF. YOU SAY THAT, BUT AREN'T WE THE SAME?
...The same...? Well, I suppose so.
But there's at least one absolute difference between you and me.

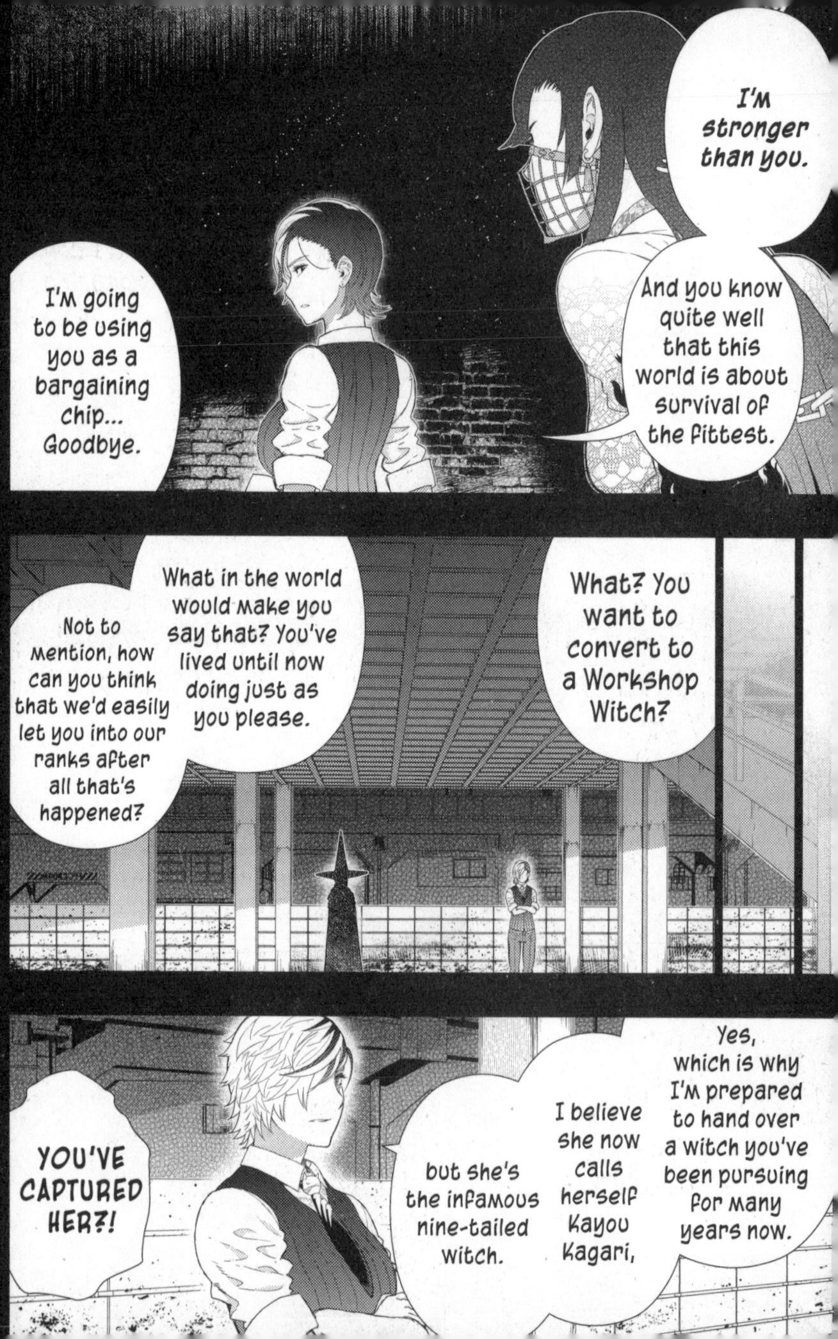
I'm stronger than you.
And you know quite well that this world is about survival of the fittest.
I'm going to be using you as a bargaining chip... Goodbye.
What? You want to convert to a Workshop Witch?
What in the world would make you say that? You've lived until now doing just as you please.
Not to mention, how can you think that we'd easily let you into our ranks after all that's happened?
Yes, which is why I'm prepared to hand over a witch you've been pursuing for many years now.
I believe she now calls herself Kayou Kagari,
but she's the infamous nine-tailed witch.
YOU'VE CAPTURED HER?!

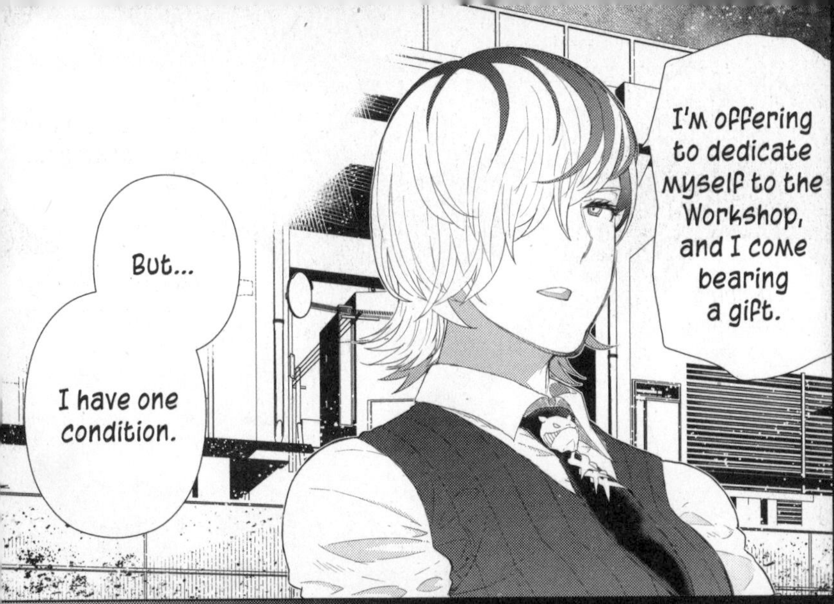
I'm offering to dedicate myself to the Workshop, and I come bearing a gift.
But...
I have one condition.

CHAPTER 61 Takamiya and the Chairwoman's Melancholy

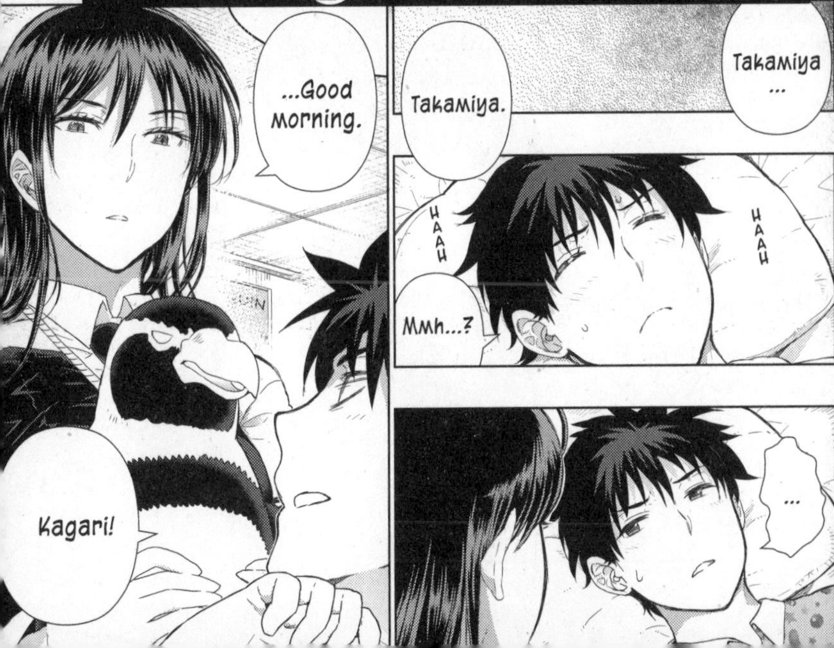
Takamiya...
Takamiya.
HAAH
HAAH
Mmh...?
...
...Good morning.
Kagari!

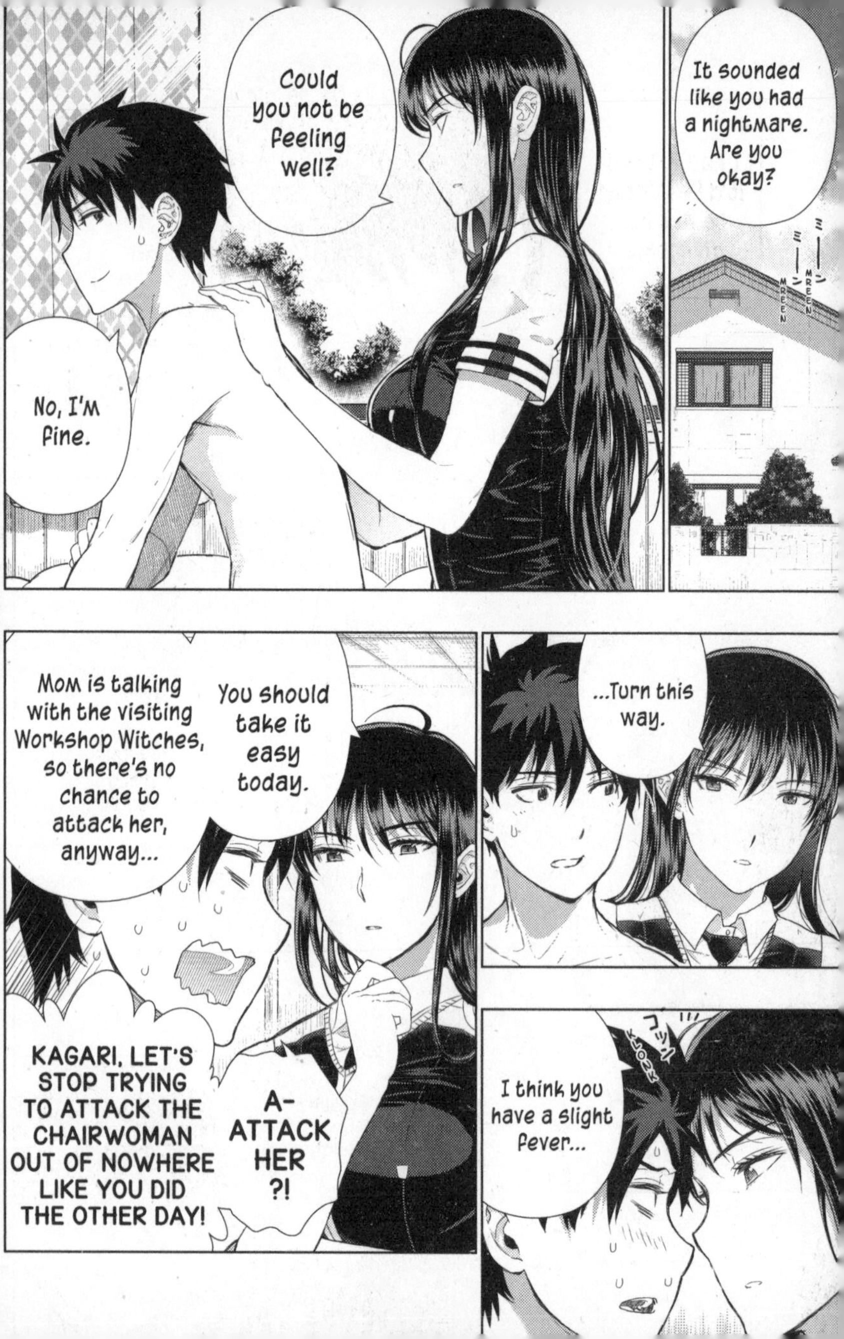
It sounded like you had a nightmare. Are you okay?
ミーン ミーン
MREEN MREEN
Could you not be feeling well?
No, I'm fine.
...Turn this way.
コツッ
KLONK
I think you have a slight fever...
You should take it easy today.
Mom is talking with the visiting Workshop Witches, so there's no chance to attack her, anyway...
KAGARI, LET'S STOP TRYING TO ATTACK THE CHAIRWOMAN OUT OF NOWHERE LIKE YOU DID THE OTHER DAY!
A- ATTACK HER?!

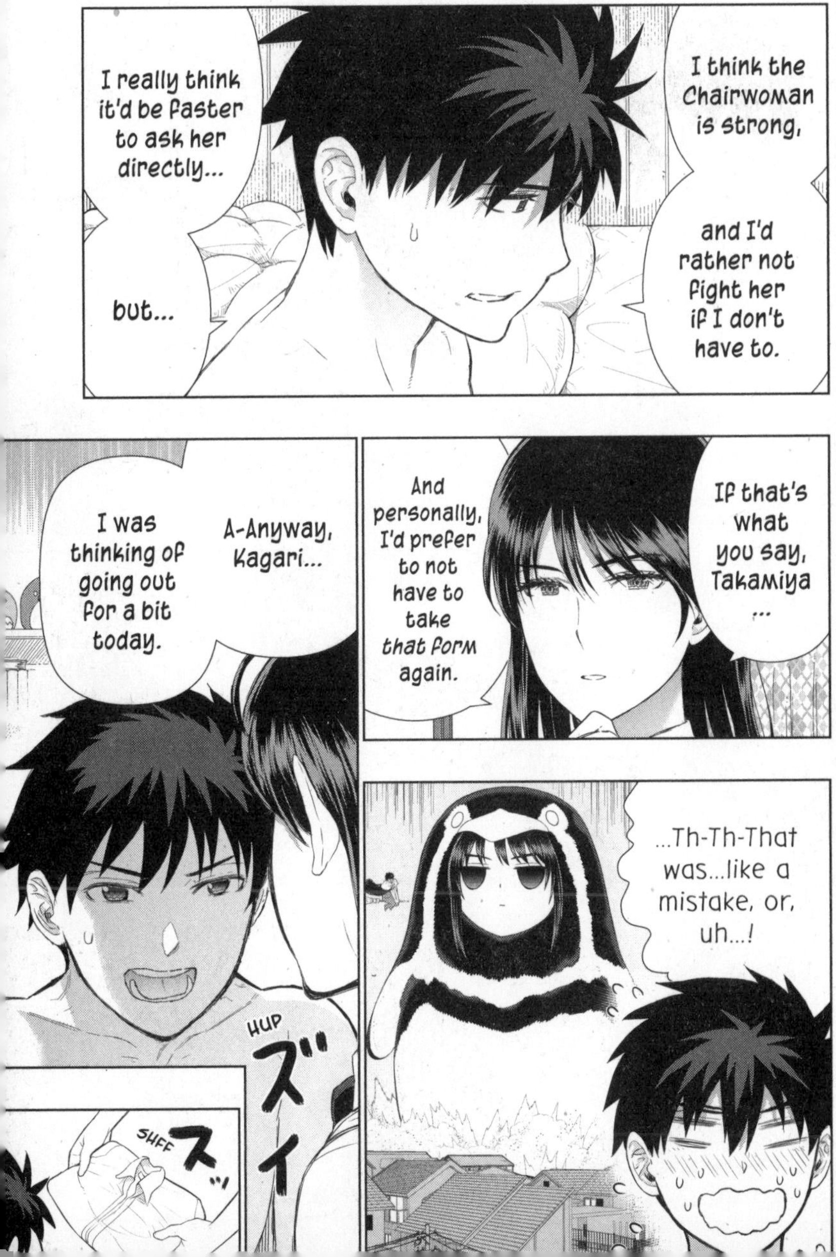
I think the Chairwoman is strong,
and I'd rather not fight her if I don't have to.
I really think it'd be faster to ask her directly...
but...
If that's what you say, Takamiya...
And personally, I'd prefer to not have to take *that form* again.
...Th-Th-That was...like a mistake, or, uh...!
A-Anyway, Kagari...
I was thinking of going out for a bit today.
HUP
ズイ
SHFF
スッ

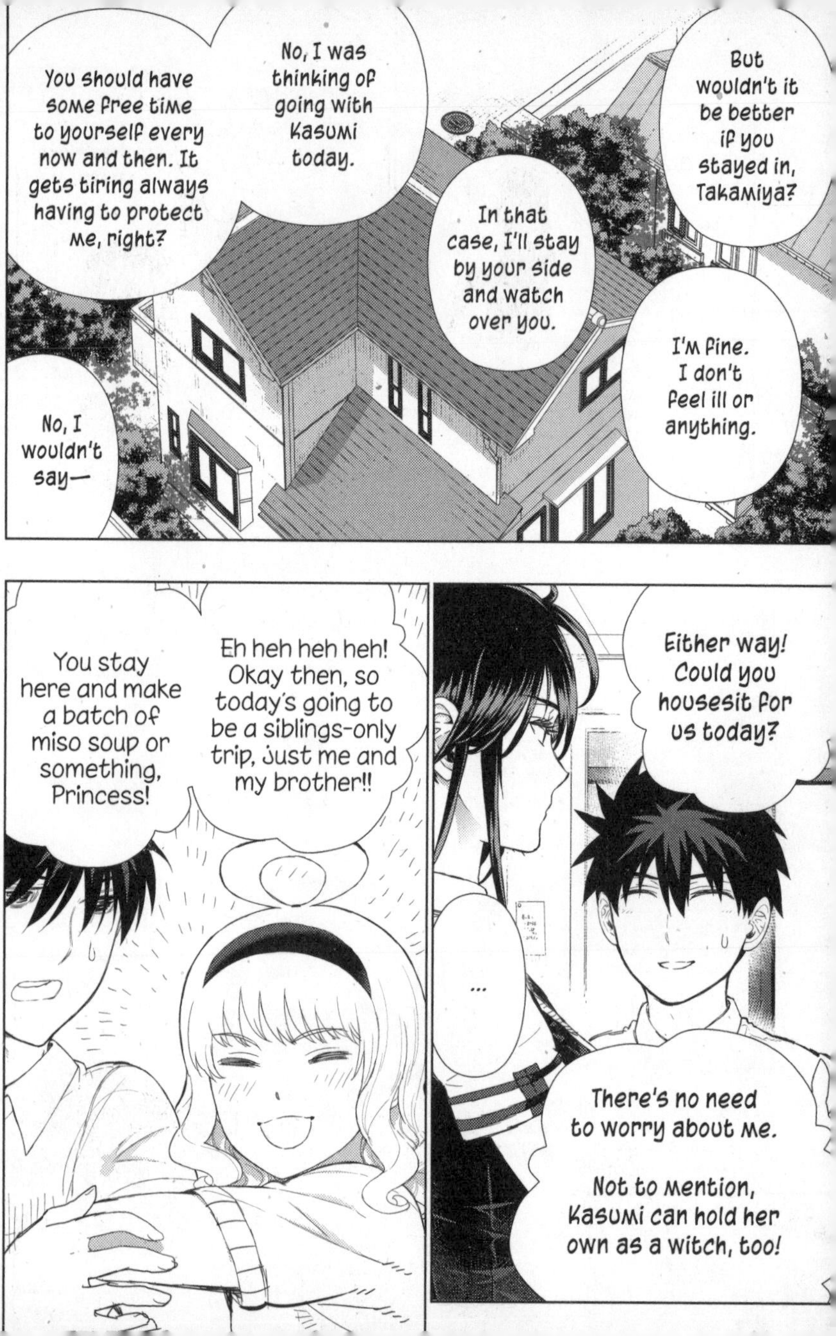
But wouldn't it be better if you stayed in, Takamiya?
I'm fine. I don't feel ill or anything.
In that case, I'll stay by your side and watch over you.
No, I was thinking of going with Kasumi today.
You should have some free time to yourself every now and then. It gets tiring always having to protect me, right?
No, I wouldn't say—
Either way! Could you housesit for us today?
...
There's no need to worry about me.
Not to mention, Kasumi can hold her own as a witch, too!
Eh heh heh heh! Okay then, so today's going to be a siblings-only trip, just me and my brother!!
You stay here and make a batch of miso soup or something, Princess!

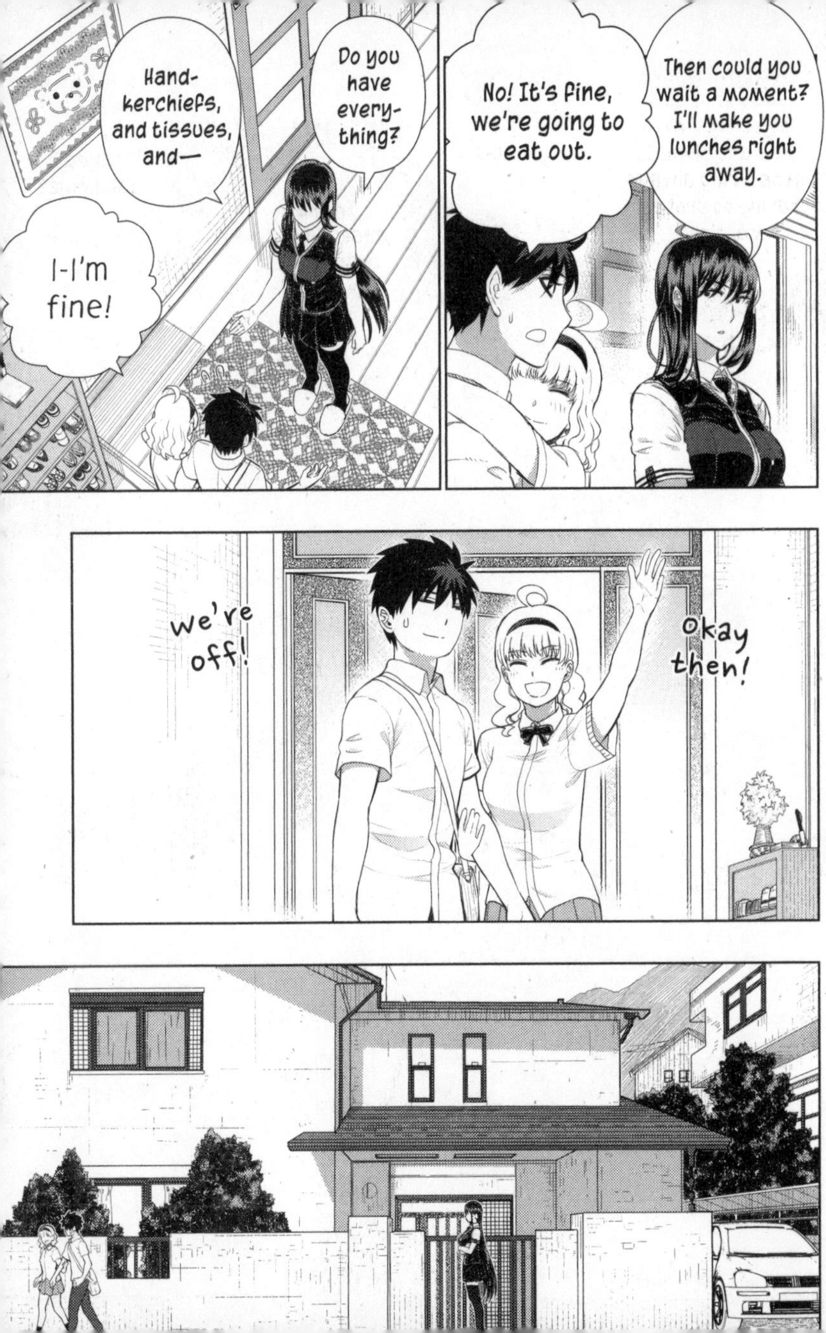
Then could you wait a moment? I'll make you lunches right away.
No! It's fine, we're going to eat out.
Do you have every-thing?
Hand-kerchiefs, and tissues, and—
I-I'm fine!
Okay then!
We're off!

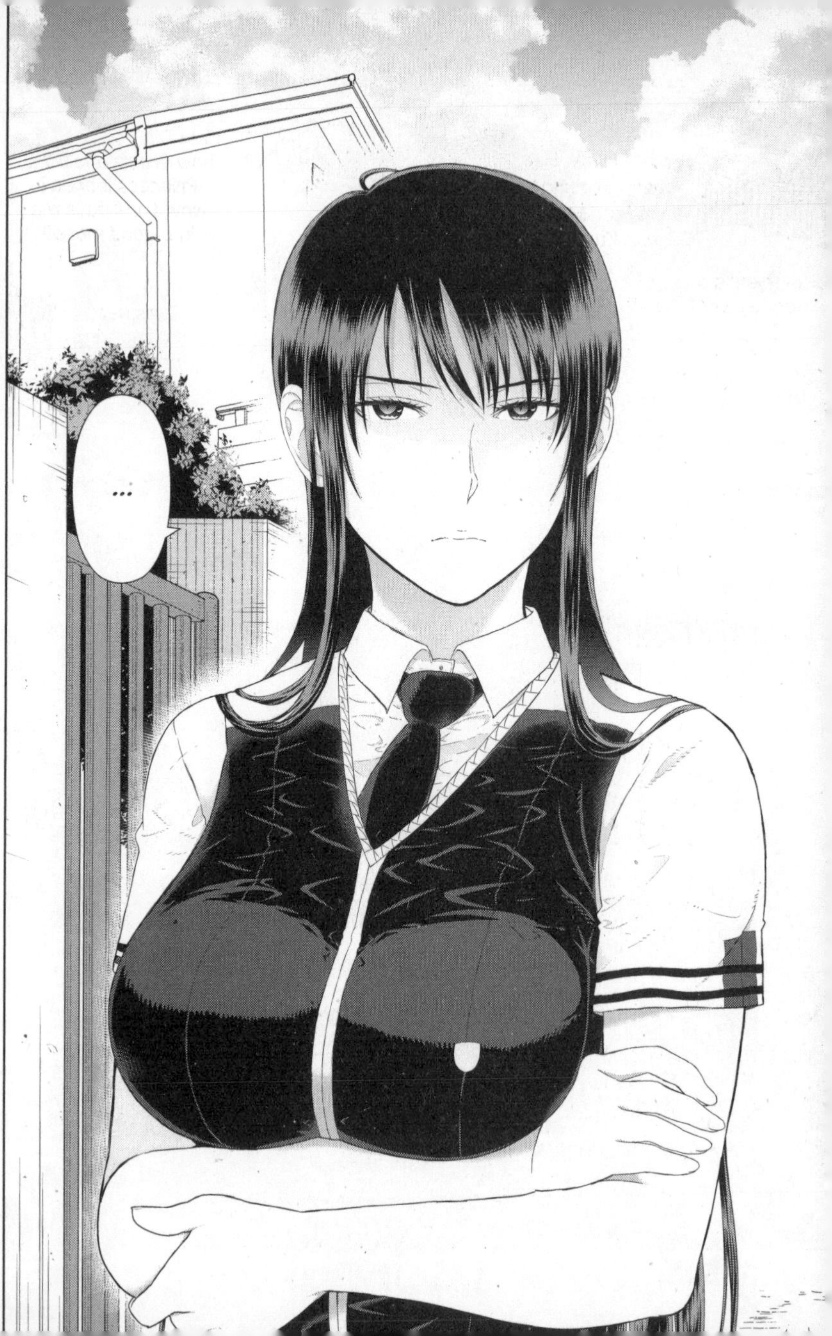
...

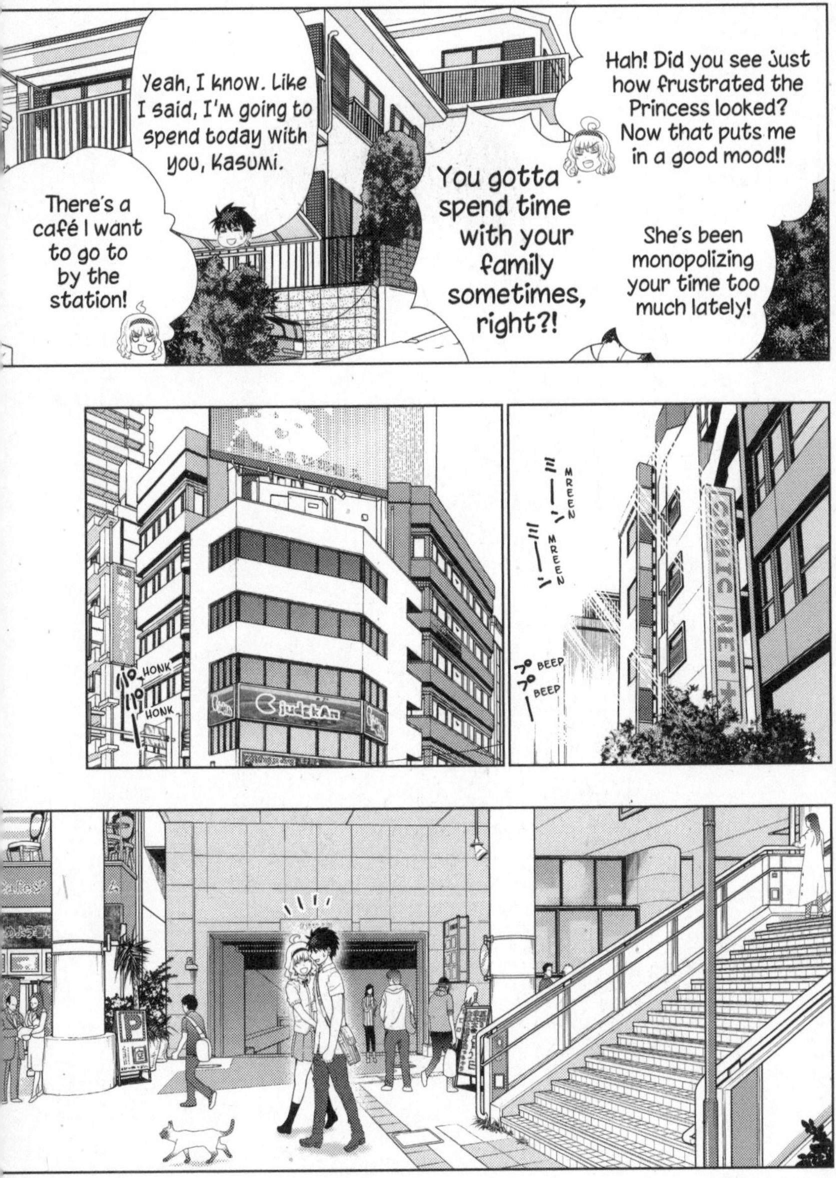
Hah! Did you see just how frustrated the Princess looked? Now that puts me in a good mood!!
She's been monopolizing your time too much lately!
You gotta spend time with your family sometimes, right?!
Yeah, I know. Like I said, I'm going to spend today with you, Kasumi.
There's a café I want to go to by the station!
MREEN
MREEN
BEEP
BEEP
HONK
HONK

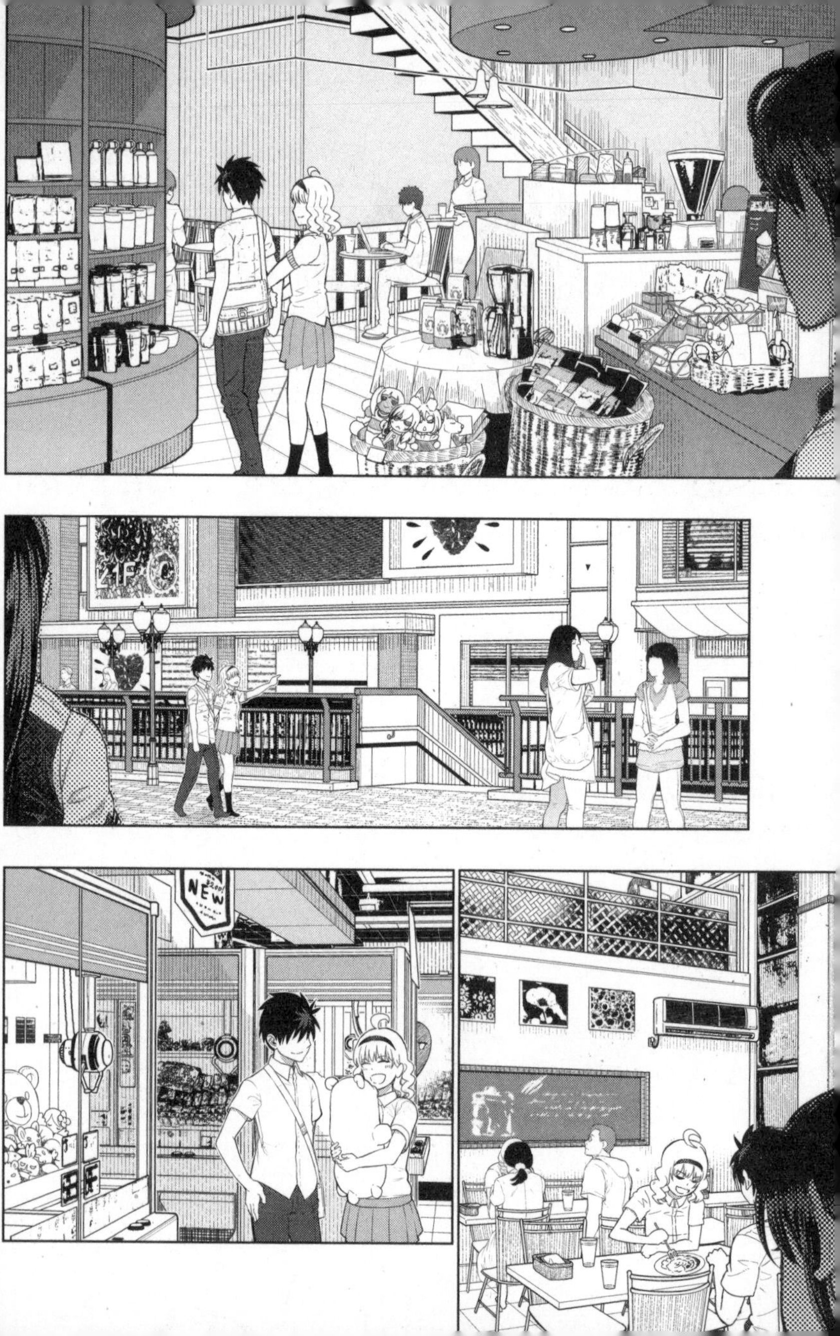
NEW

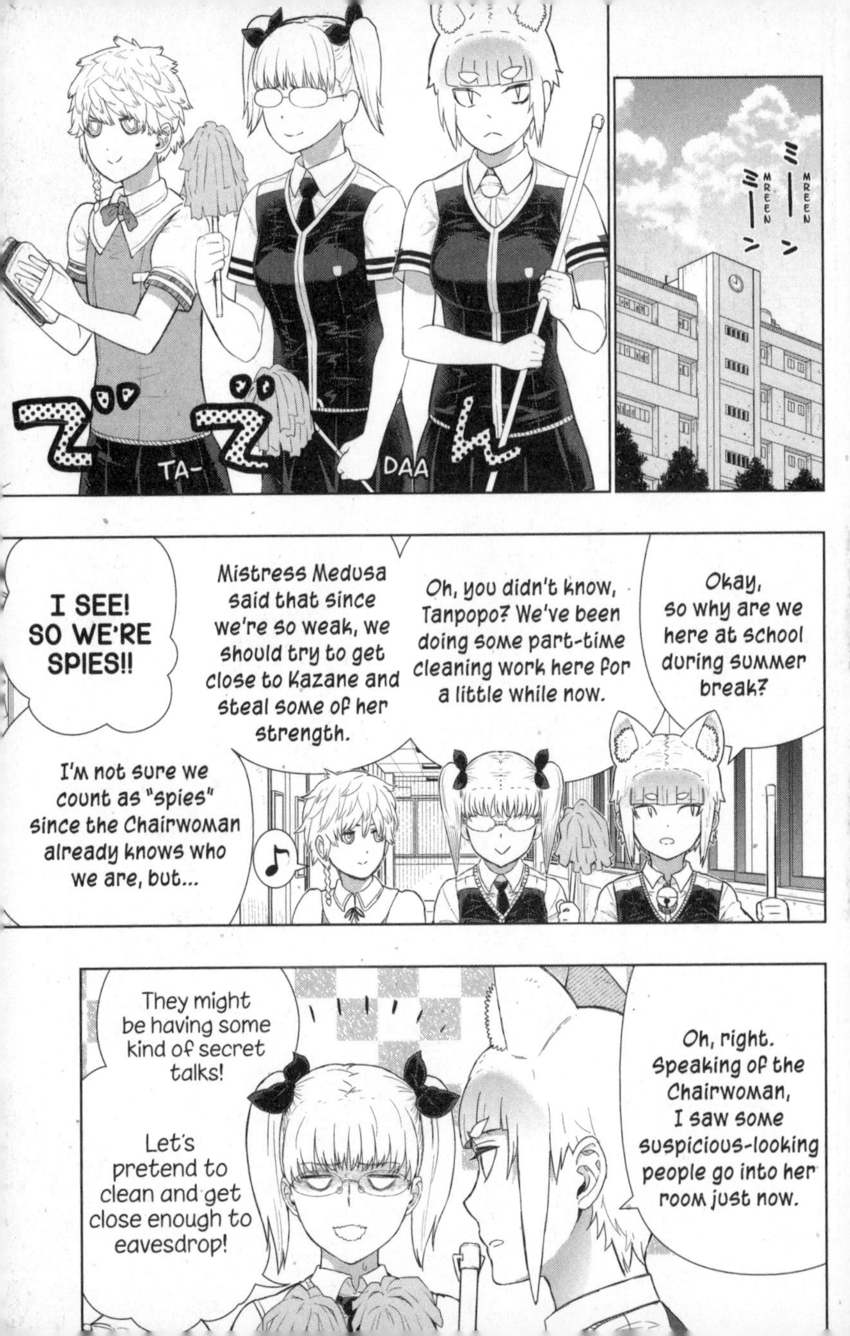
MREEN
MREEN
TA-
DAA
Okay, so why are we here at school during summer break?
Oh, you didn't know, Tanpopo? We've been doing some part-time cleaning work here for a little while now.
Mistress Medusa said that since we're so weak, we should try to get close to Kazane and steal some of her strength.
I SEE! SO WE'RE SPIES!!
I'm not sure we count as "spies" since the Chairwoman already knows who we are, but...
Oh, right. Speaking of the Chairwoman, I saw some suspicious-looking people go into her room just now.
They might be having some kind of secret talks!
Let's pretend to clean and get close enough to eavesdrop!

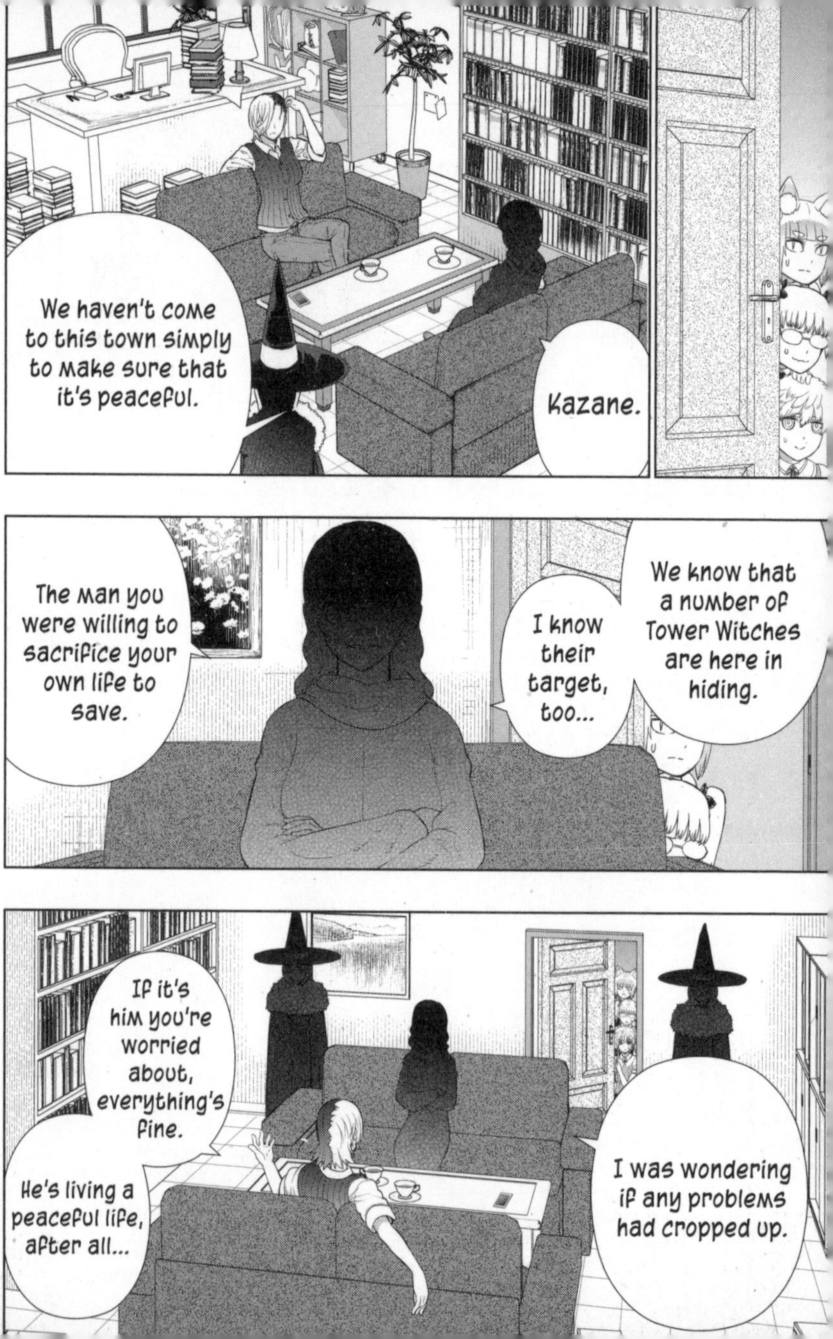
Kazane.
We haven't come to this town simply to make sure that it's peaceful.
We know that a number of Tower Witches are here in hiding.
I know their target, too...
The man you were willing to sacrifice your own life to save.
I was wondering if any problems had cropped up.
If it's him you're worried about, everything's fine.
He's living a peaceful life, after all...

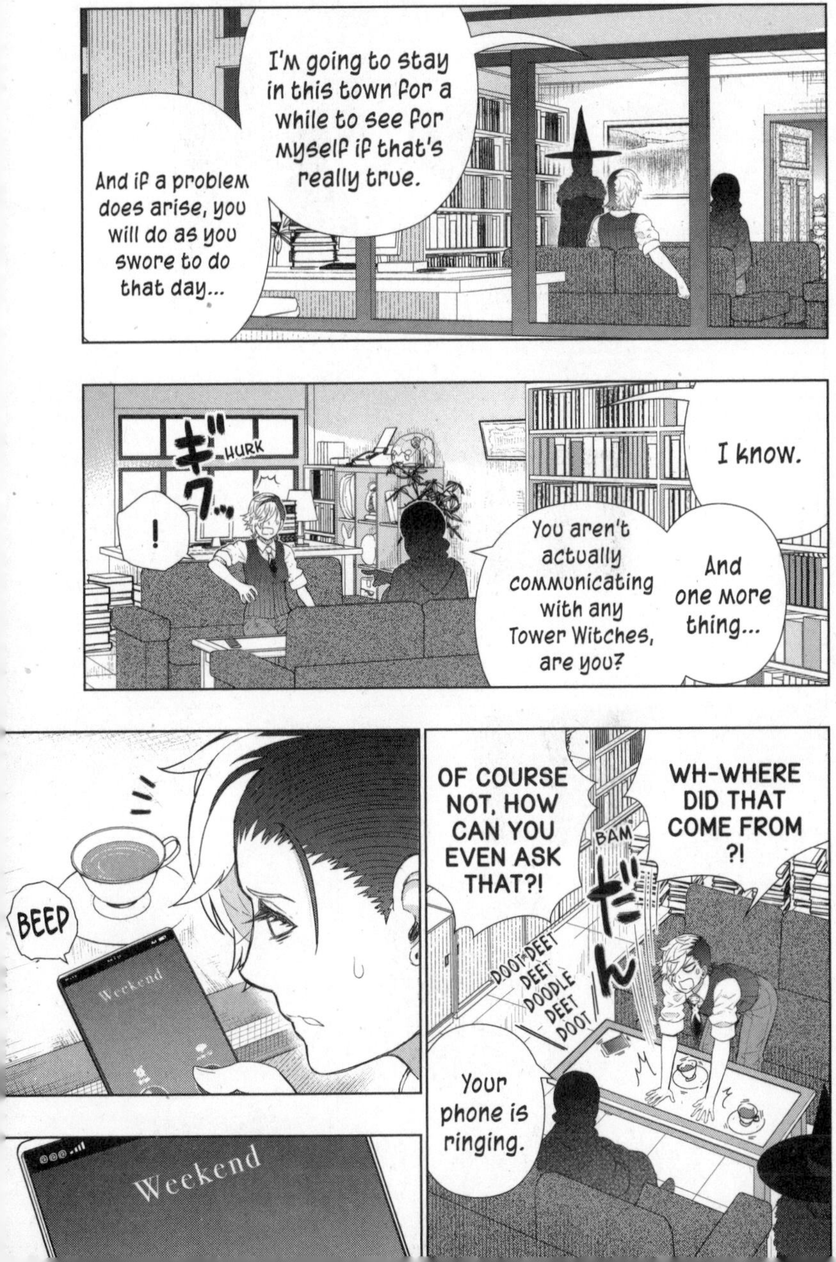
I'm going to stay in this town for a while to see for myself if that's really true.
And if a problem does arise, you will do as you swore to do that day...
I know.
And one more thing...
You aren't actually communicating with any Tower Witches, are you?
HURK
!
WH-WHERE DID THAT COME FROM ?!
OF COURSE NOT, HOW CAN YOU EVEN ASK THAT?!
BAM
DOOT DEET DEET DOODLE DEET DOOT
Your phone is ringing.
BEEP
Weekend
Weekend

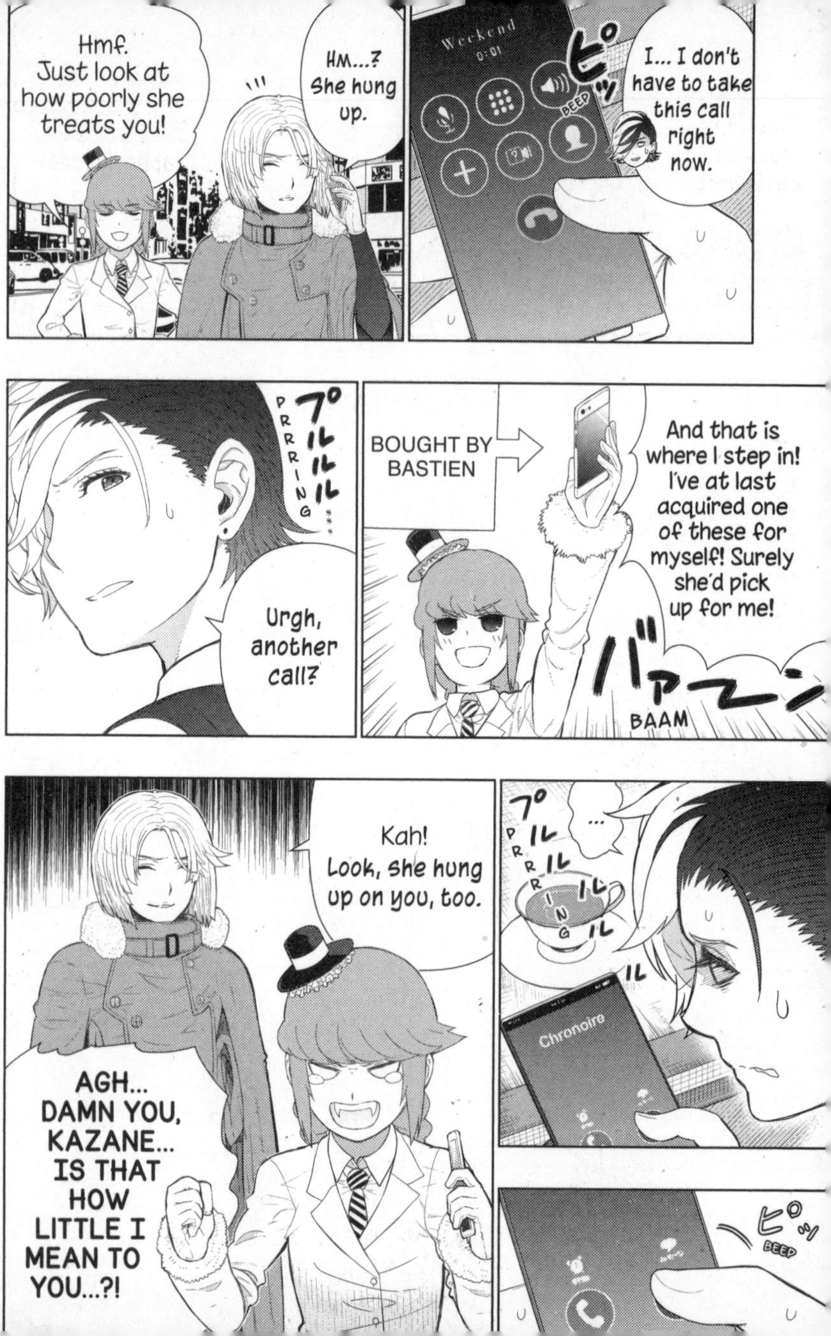

Weekend
0:01
ピッ
BEEP
I... I don't have to take this call right now.
HM...? She hung up.
Hmf. Just look at how poorly she treats you!
BOUGHT BY BASTIEN
And that is where I step in! I've at last acquired one of these for myself! Surely she'd pick up for me!
バァーン
BAAM
プルルルル
PRRRING...
Urgh, another call?
プルルルル
PRRRING
...
Chronoire
ピッ
BEEP
Kah! Look, she hung up on you, too.
AGH... DAMN YOU, KAZANE... IS THAT HOW LITTLE I MEAN TO YOU...?!

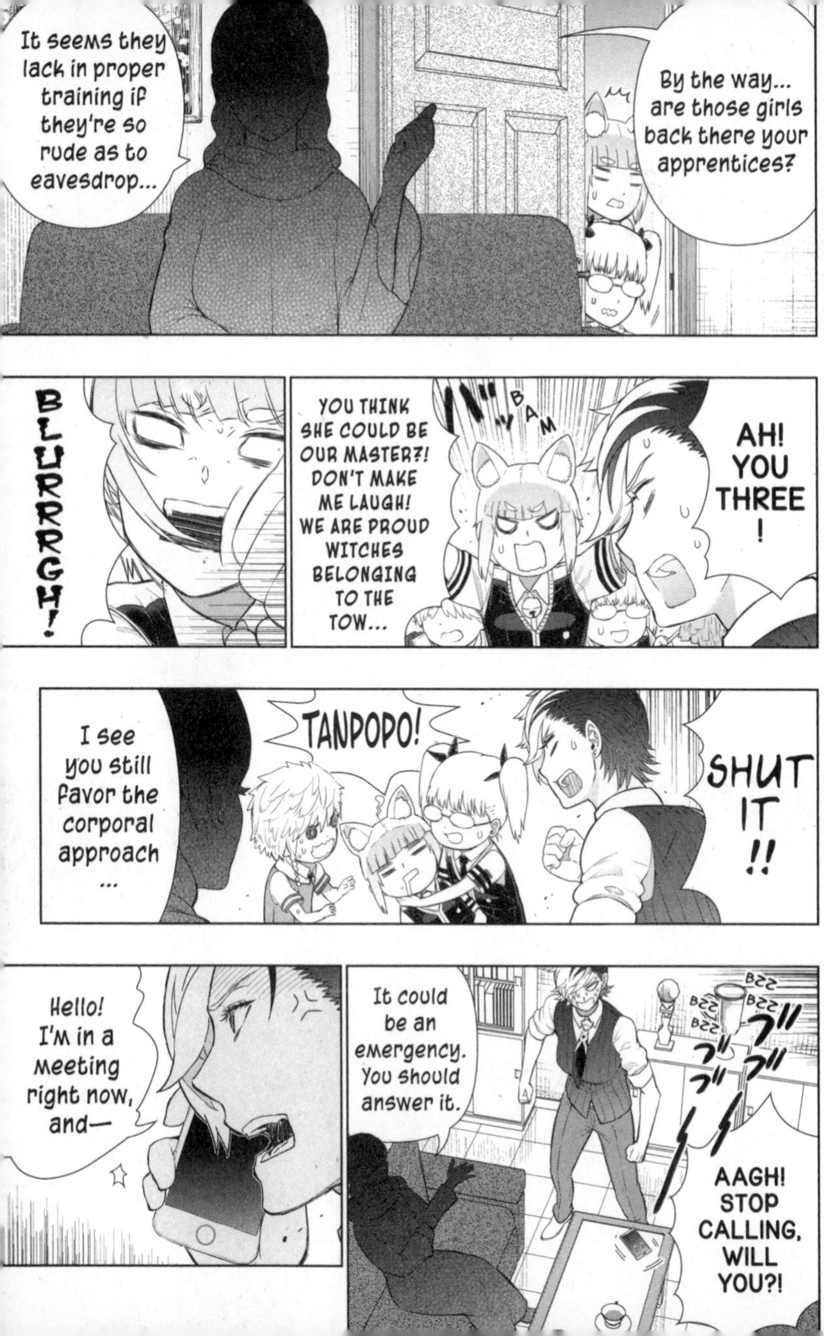
By the way... are those girls back there your apprentices?
It seems they lack in proper training if they're so rude as to eavesdrop...
AH! YOU THREE!
BAM
YOU THINK SHE COULD BE OUR MASTER?! DON'T MAKE ME LAUGH! WE ARE PROUD WITCHES BELONGING TO THE TOW...
BLURRRGH!
SHUT IT!!
TANPOPO!
I see you still favor the corporal approach...
BZZ BZZ BZZ BZZ
AAGH! STOP CALLING, WILL YOU?!
It could be an emergency. You should answer it.
Hello! I'm in a meeting right now, and—

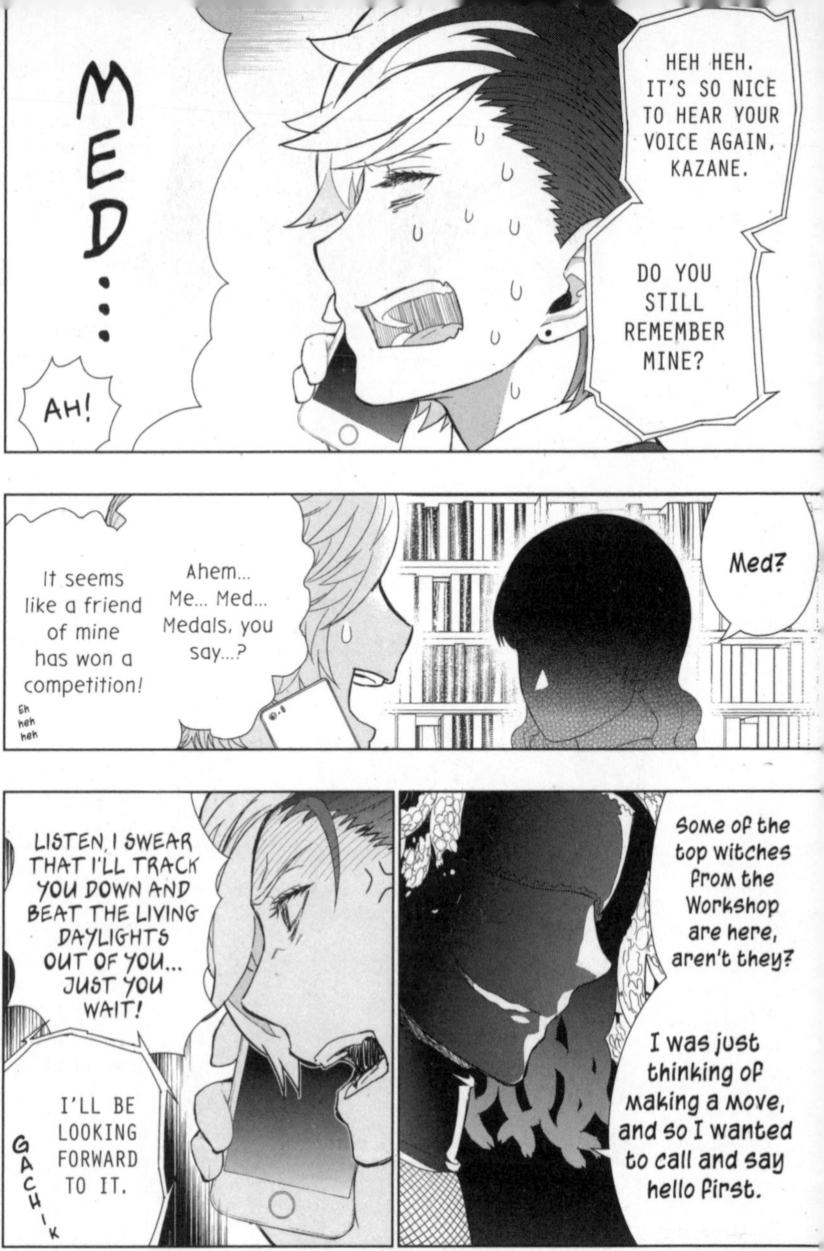
HEH HEH. IT'S SO NICE TO HEAR YOUR VOICE AGAIN, KAZANE.
DO YOU STILL REMEMBER MINE?
MED...
AH!
Med?
Ahem... Me... Med... Medals, you say...?
It seems like a friend of mine has won a competition!
Eh heh heh
Some of the top witches from the Workshop are here, aren't they?
I was just thinking of making a move, and so I wanted to call and say hello first.
LISTEN, I SWEAR THAT I'LL TRACK YOU DOWN AND BEAT THE LIVING DAYLIGHTS OUT OF YOU... JUST YOU WAIT!
I'LL BE LOOKING FORWARD TO IT.
GACHIK

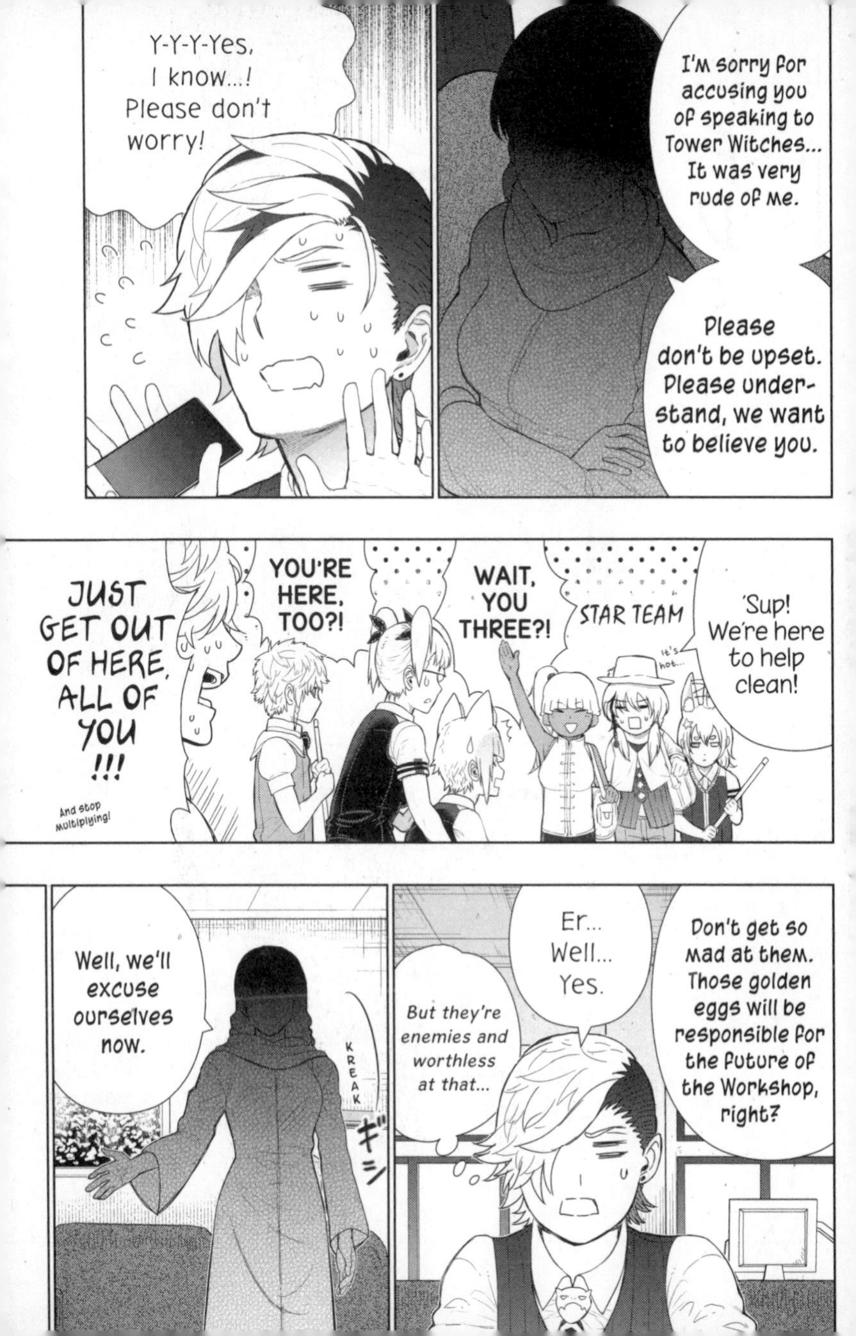
I'm sorry for accusing you of speaking to Tower Witches... It was very rude of me.
Please don't be upset. Please under-stand, we want to believe you.
Y-Y-Y-Yes, I know...! Please don't worry!
'Sup! We're here to help clean!
It's hot...
STAR TEAM
WAIT, YOU THREE?!
YOU'RE HERE, TOO?!
JUST GET OUT OF HERE, ALL OF YOU!!!
And stop multiplying!
Don't get so mad at them. Those golden eggs will be responsible for the future of the Workshop, right?
Er... Well... Yes.
But they're enemies and worthless at that...
Well, we'll excuse ourselves now.
KREAK

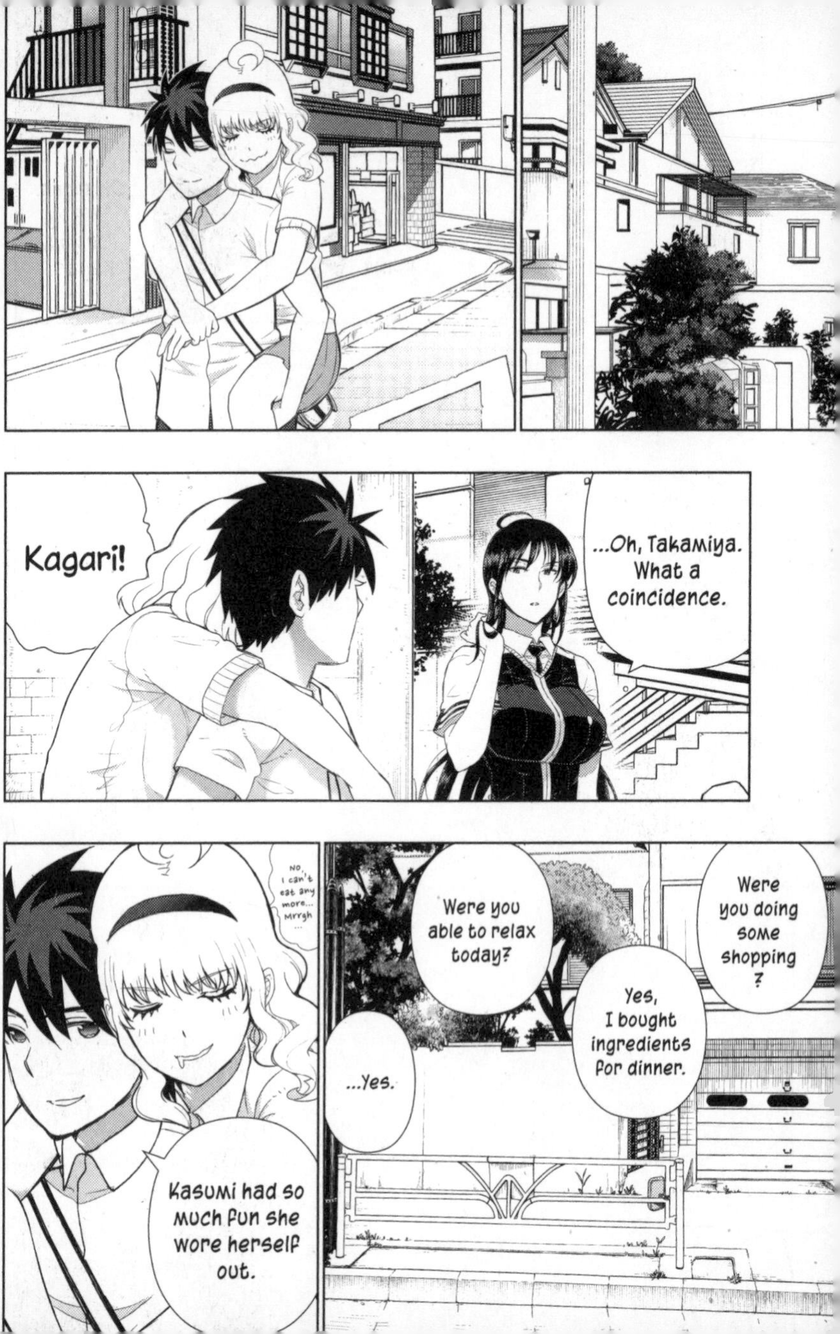
...Oh, Takamiya. What a coincidence.
Kagari!
Were you doing some shopping?
Were you able to relax today?
Yes, I bought ingredients for dinner.
...Yes.
No, I can't eat any more... Mrrgh...
Kasumi had so much fun she wore herself out.

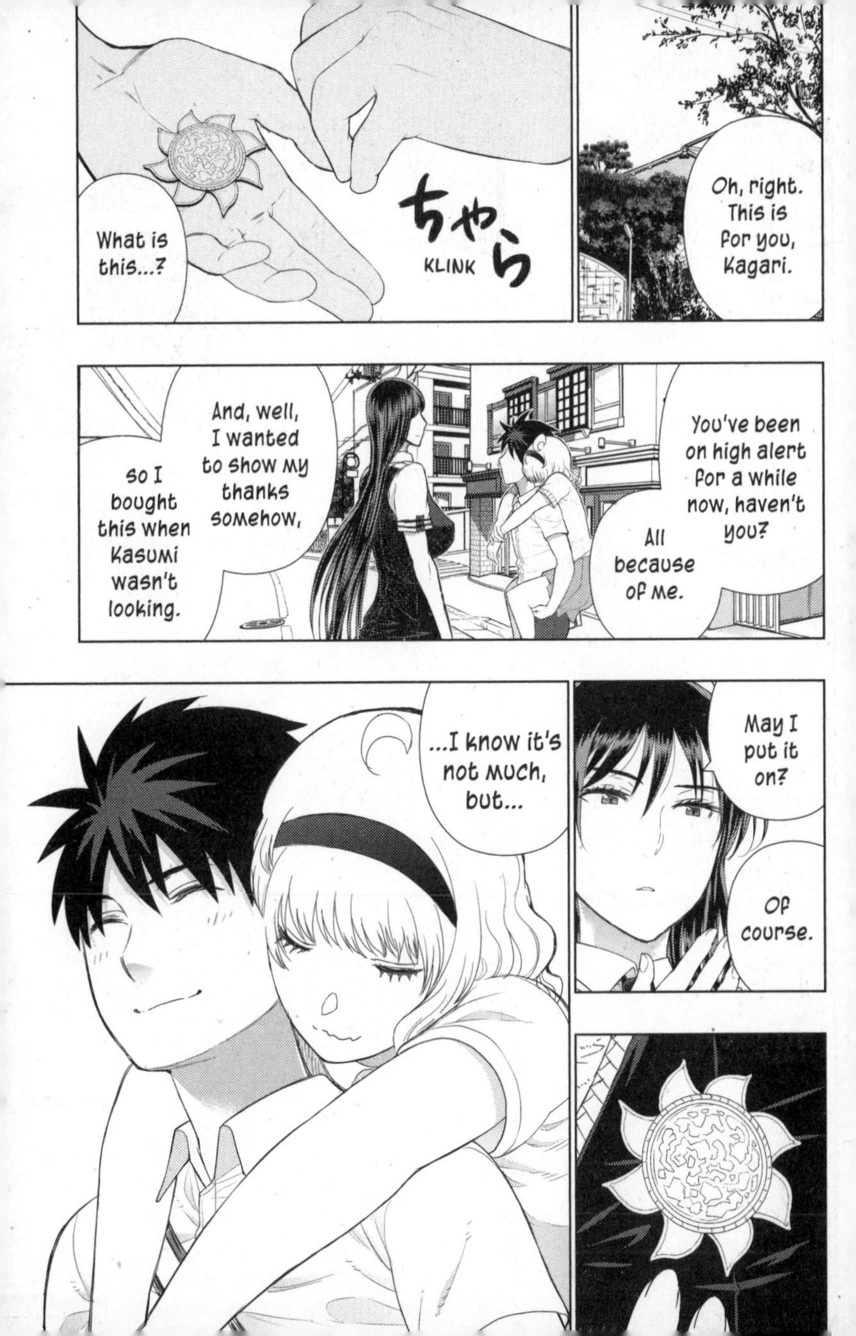
Oh, right. This is for you, Kagari.
ちゃら
KLINK
What is this...?
You've been on high alert for a while now, haven't you?
All because of me.
And, well, I wanted to show my thanks somehow,
so I bought this when Kasumi wasn't looking.
May I put it on?
Of course.
...I know it's not much, but...

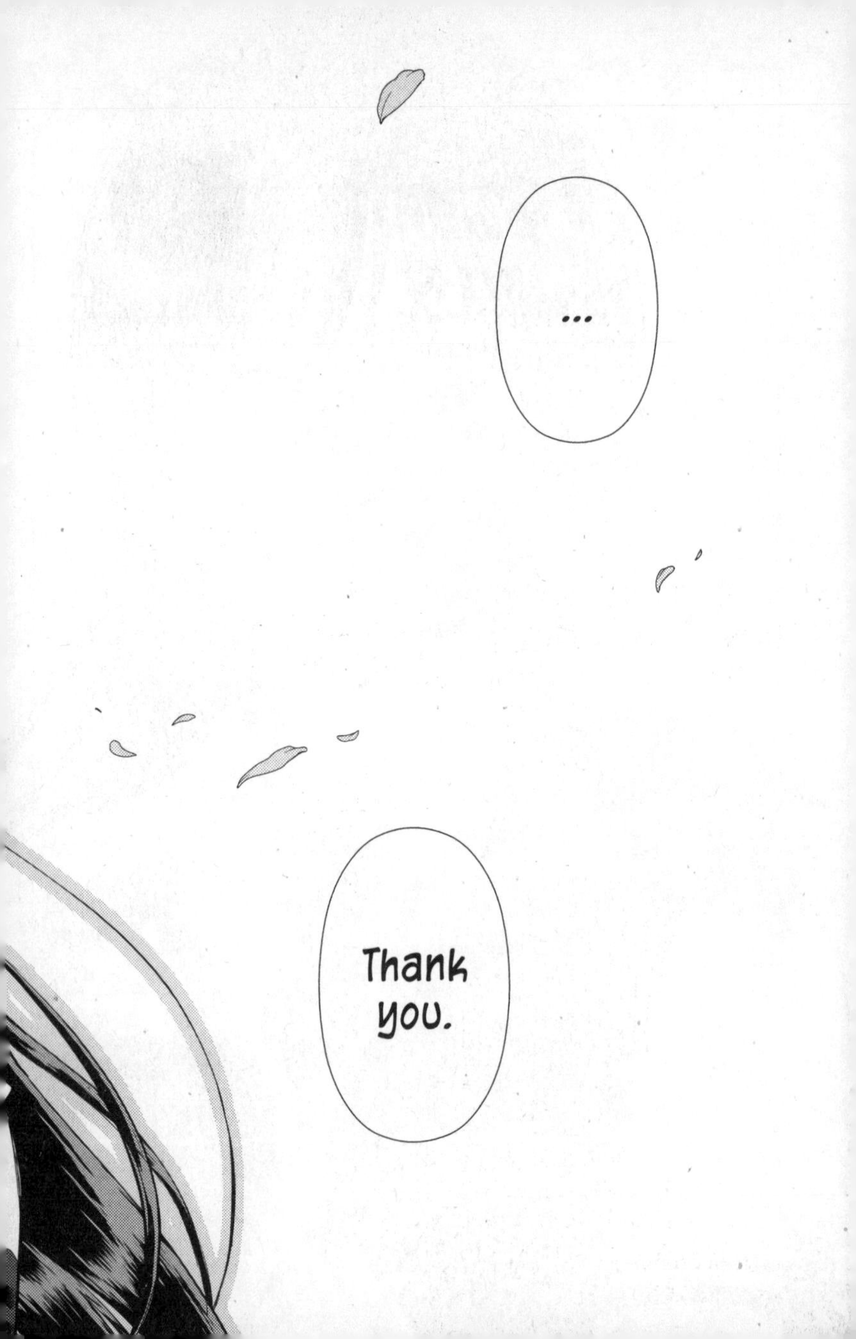
...
Thank you.

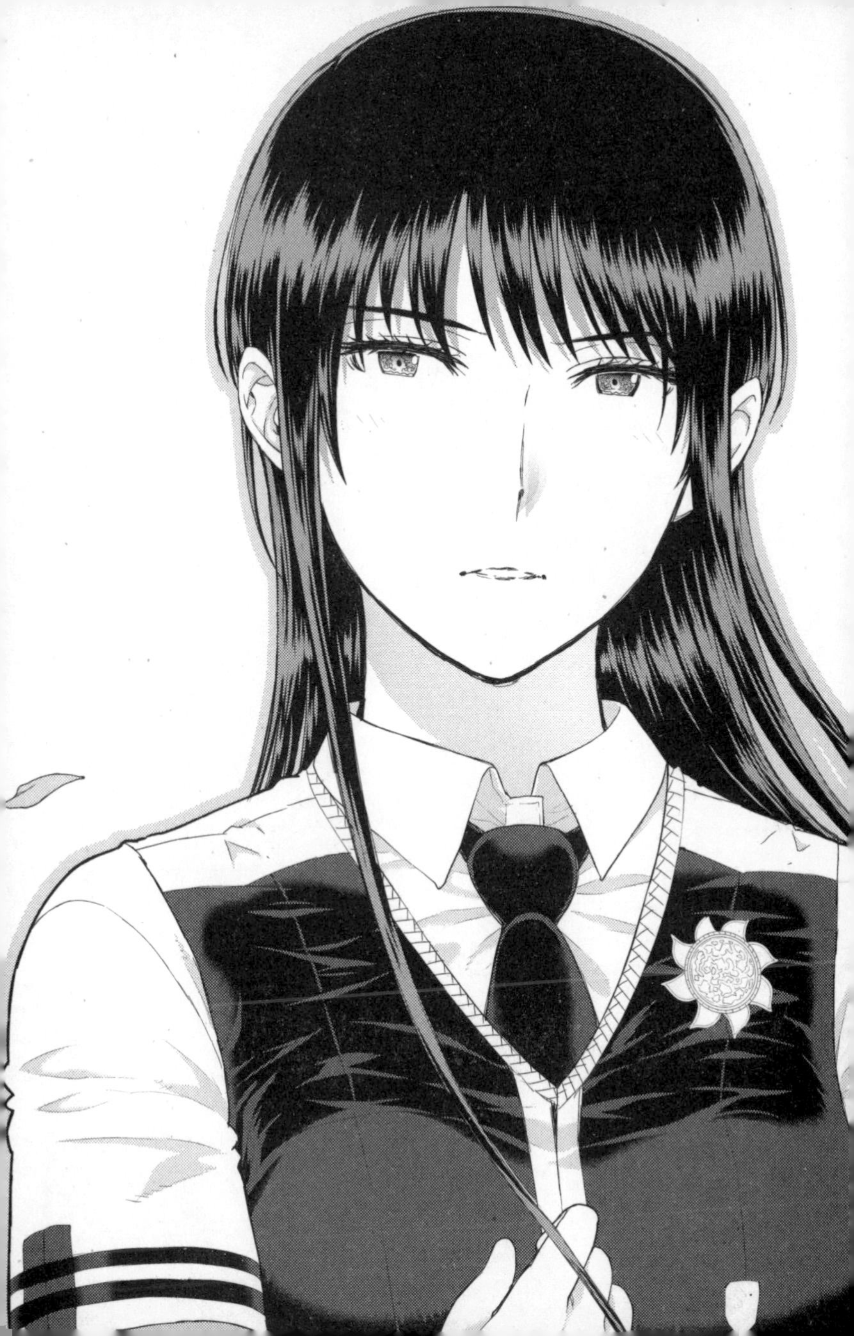

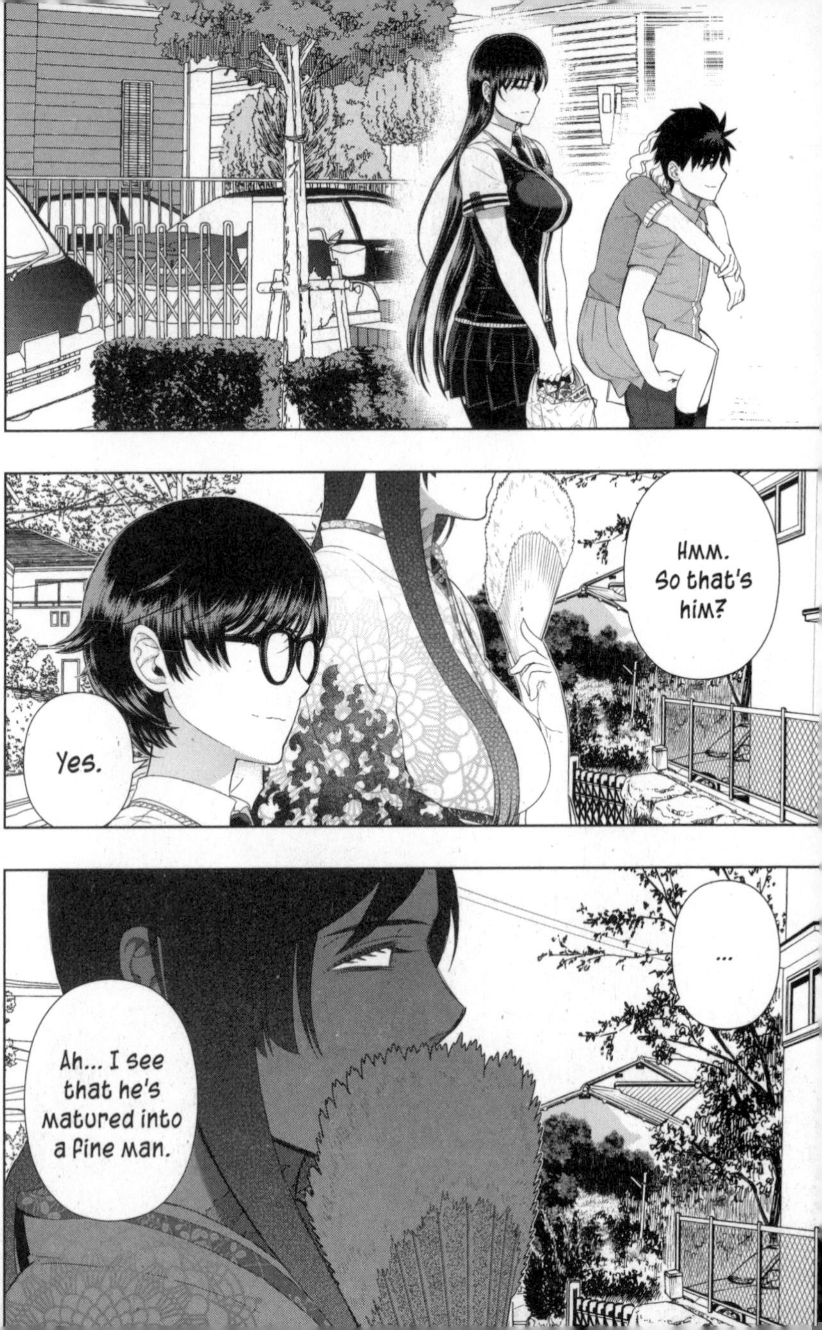
Hmm. So that's him?
Yes.
...
Ah... I see that he's matured into a fine man.

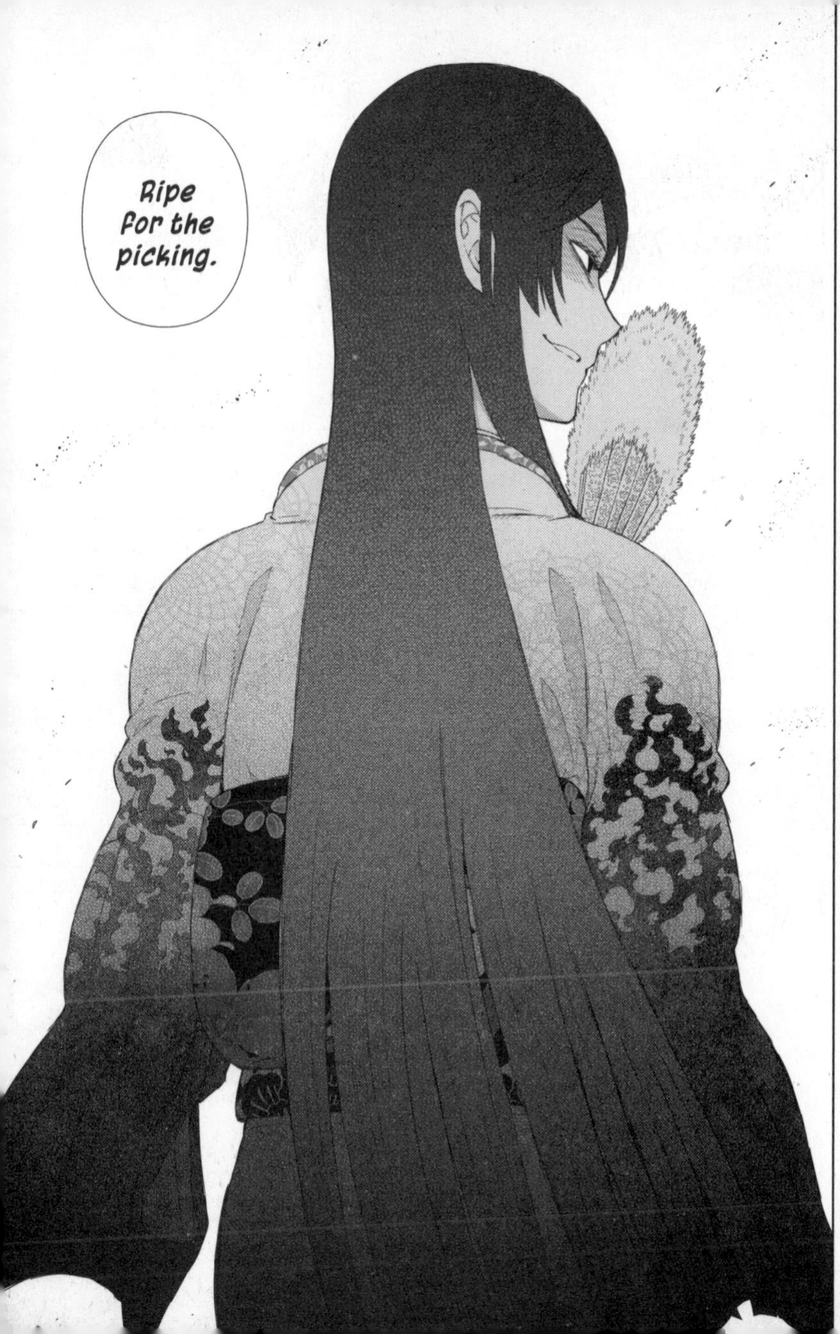
Ripe for the picking.

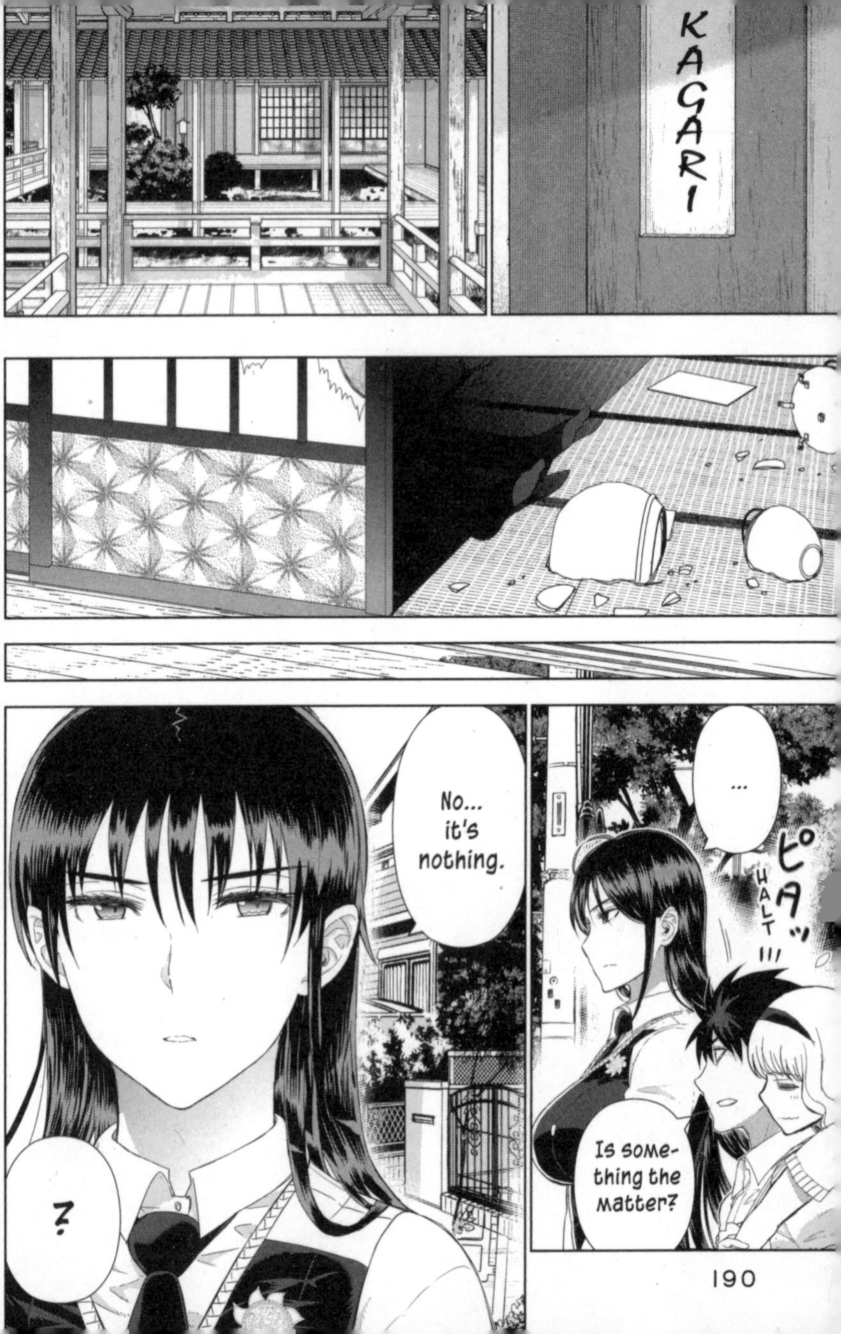
KAGARI
...
ピタッ
HALT!!!
Is something the matter?
No... it's nothing.
?

Afterword

Did you enjoy Witchcraft Works volume 11? In this volume, the past is gradually revealed as our characters head toward a battle against a fated opponent, Kayou (the furry-eared). Do you enjoy getting to see the way that Kasumi and Tanpopo have become good friends now?

I hope you're looking forward to volume 12, where we'll see emissaries from the Workshop, Kayou maneuvering in secret, and Furry-Ear flying all over the place.

Ryu Mizunagi

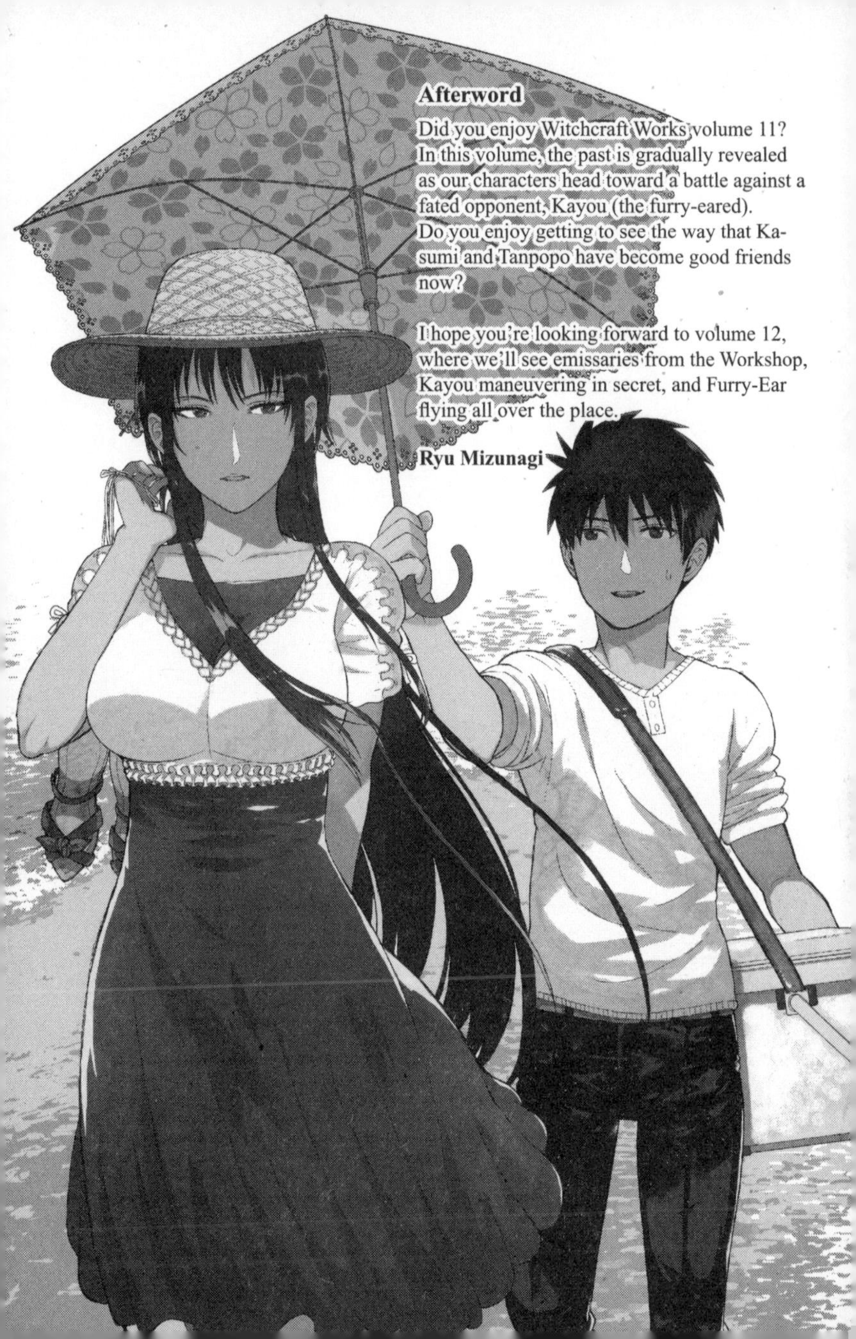

Witchcraft Works

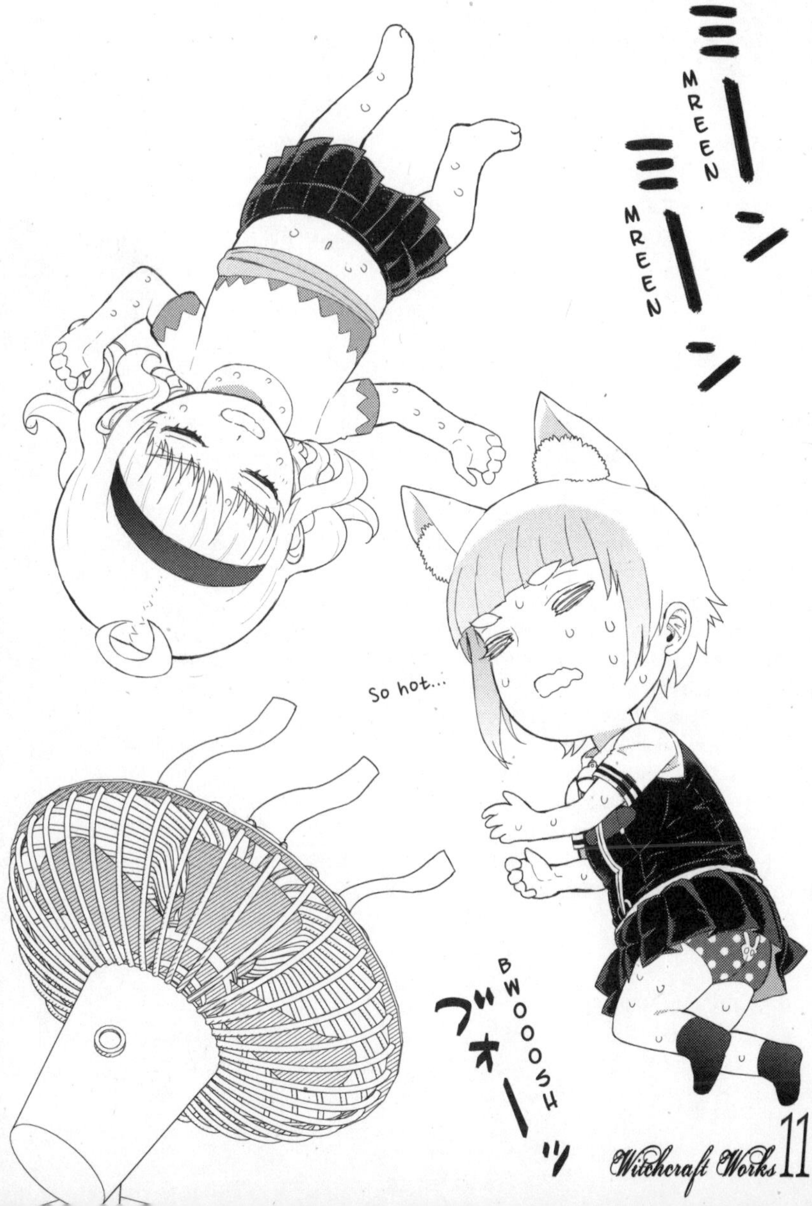
ミーン
MREEN
ミーン
MREEN
So hot...
ブォーーッ
BWOOOOSH
Witchcraft Works 11

Witchcraft Works
SETTING + SECRETS

This page is a collection of behind-the-scenes character and story elements that probably won't affect or appear in the main story, as well as comments by the author. If you finish reading the story and think, "I want to know more!" then we hope you enjoy the information here.

Chapter 55

Takamiya and Kagari meet. Kayou versus Kazane.

• Kayou Kagari

Kagari's birth-mother. The culprit to blame for her own daughter's chaining and imprisonment behind a secret door in the dark research building's library. Judging by these actions, it would be hard to say that she's fulfilling her function as a parent. She describes her own daughter as a "carefully created crystallization of the Kagari family," and "one of many." However, she does at least seem to recognize her as important, as she also calls her "the only one of her kind." We soon learn why she values her this way.

Kayou says that what is important is not Kagari herself, but her body (the vessel). She says that strengthening one's bloodline means everything to a witch, and that a witch and her bloodline are one and the same. She had been giving birth to more and more talented and powerful witches by cross-breeding fire witches for generations. This process eventually created Ayaka Kagari, a witch with unrivaled power but a weak spirit. She is also called "the result of the pursuit of the dark arts," a taboo form of magic practiced by fallen, heretical witches.

★ Marks on Kayou's neck

While the nature of the research conducted by Kayou is still a mystery, those who come in contact with heretical magic are affected by the "Curse of the Unseen Hand" and must constantly suffer a powerful curse. However, she is able to use her mental fortitude to shut the curse out and even use it as her "Dark Thorns," but this is a double-edged spell that ricochets back and damages her every time she uses it.

★ The Wounded White Princess
A fiery beast appears from inside Kagari, and this is the wounded, repulsive form of the White Princess. She is the primal fire magic sealed away inside of her host Ayaka Kagari and bound by the Dark Thorns. A form of Craft that represents the ultimate in fire magic that Kayou herself calls a "great achievement."

Chapter 56

Kayou versus Kazane.

★ Embodied Fireblood Soul
The dark red jewel that Kayou removes from Kagari after banishing the White Princess. This fragment is a concentrated form of the fire witches' life forces. It has taken over a thousand witches' souls to create this gem. It goes without saying that this is a form of heretical magic. Any regular witch would start feeling ill just standing near this cursed item, and touching it would equal death. Handle with caution. However, its effects do not work on men, and so Takamiya is not affected by it here (and even if he was affected by it, he wouldn't die because he has inherited Kazane's blood). While their effects are different, it has a magical power on par with the Siren's Masters created by Chronoire. While Kayou attempts to put it inside her daughter's body, Kazane stops her.

★ Kayou's impression of Kazane
Kazane is a Witch of the End, and Kayou thinks highly of her. However, it seems that she had summoned her to her estate by chance, as she calls their meeting the "gods' idea of a joke." Stories have spread far and wide of Kazane, the witch who brings unhappiness to all other witches who get involved with her, Chronoire being the only exception.

★ The Dark Blade
One of the magical charms hidden inside of Kazane's body. However, it is different from the kinds of heretical charms that Kayou uses. This dark weapon was created long, long ago from solitude and black magic. Over the years, it lost its master, fell into disuse, grew bloodcrazed, then was eventually found by Kazane. This bare sword has lost even its scabbard, and it has neither grip nor

guard. Because of this, though, it possesses special powers.

It seems rare for Kazane to use this blade, as doing so would go against her fighting style of always punching it out with her bare fists. It feels like there's some kind of deep reason behind this, but...

★ Transformation
Kayou reveals her true form after her plans are ruined. She is a transforming female fox who has lived for many years. In other words—a furry-ear.

• Takamiya and Kagari
Takamiya uses his blood as a last resort in order to heal Kagari's injuries. The starving White Princess is lured out by its scent, ready for a meal.

Chapter 57-58

Takamiya's Oath with the White Princess.

• Evermillion
Evermillion calls Takamiya the Witch of the End's disciple. She must have figured this out from his blood. She plots to trick him into making a contract with her and devouring his soul. However, the shining beauty and purity of his soul causes her heart to be cleansed and her own soul to be captured. The peaceful light that comes from him is nothing like what she has seen from any others who attempted to use her before, and so her original form is revealed, a true self that even she had never noticed in the past. Her true form is a lily-white, noble, primeval Fire Princess.

Her personality and appearance reflect the soul of the one she enters into a contract with.

• Takamiya
Takamiya tries to revive Kagari by making her into his follower. He binds her by giving her the character for fire, *ka*, from his name, bringing their two fates together as one. The contract succeeds.

• Kazane
When Takamiya wakes up, Kazane says that she already drove Kayou off. A team is being put together to track and take down the fleeing Kayou. Kazane seems to know about the White Princess, and she's concerned. She also explains to Takamiya that Kagari has lost her memories.

• Kagari

With no memory of what's happened, Kagari spends her days cooped up in the library's hidden cell. Takamiya uses a small bit of magic to try to somehow interest her in the outside world. This causes her to regain her memories. She learns that it was him who freed her from her chains and saved her, and that she is now his follower. She realizes that the ruler she is supposed to serve now stands before her, and that she is a knight reborn in order to protect him. Her heart is filled with joy because she has been given an opportunity to learn the purpose of her life, something that many people never discover.

Bonus: Kasumi and Furry-Ear's Expedition

Kasumi and Furry-Ear's eventful journey as friends.

• Kasumi

Kasumi frantically searches for a way to somehow expose Kagari's schemes. She gets the idea to sneak into Kagari's room in order to confirm her suspicions that she's a stalker. And she's bringing Furry-Ear with her.

• Furry-Ear

Furry-Ear is eating cat food while watching a wildly popular furry-ear TV show, but then the detestable little sister causes her moment of bliss to come crashing down. Though she's caused Furry-Ear a lot of hardship, she's too strong to beat. The only option is to obey. And so, the two recklessly head into the dungeon (room) of the dragon (Kagari) to meet a terrible fate.

However, she ends up back in her own room after Atori moves in secret to rob her of her memories. Then, when Kasumi wakes up, she once again invites Furry-Ear to sneak into Kagari's room. Had this story already happened before? And if so, how many times...?

Prepare to be Bewitched!

Makoto Kowata, a novice witch, packs up her belongings (including a black cat familiar) and moves in with her distant cousins in rural Aomori to complete her training and become a full-fledged witch.

"*Flying Witch* emphasizes that while actual magic is nice, there is ultimately magic in everything." —*Anime News Network*

The Basis for the Hit Anime from Sentai Filmworks!

Volumes 1-5 Available Now!

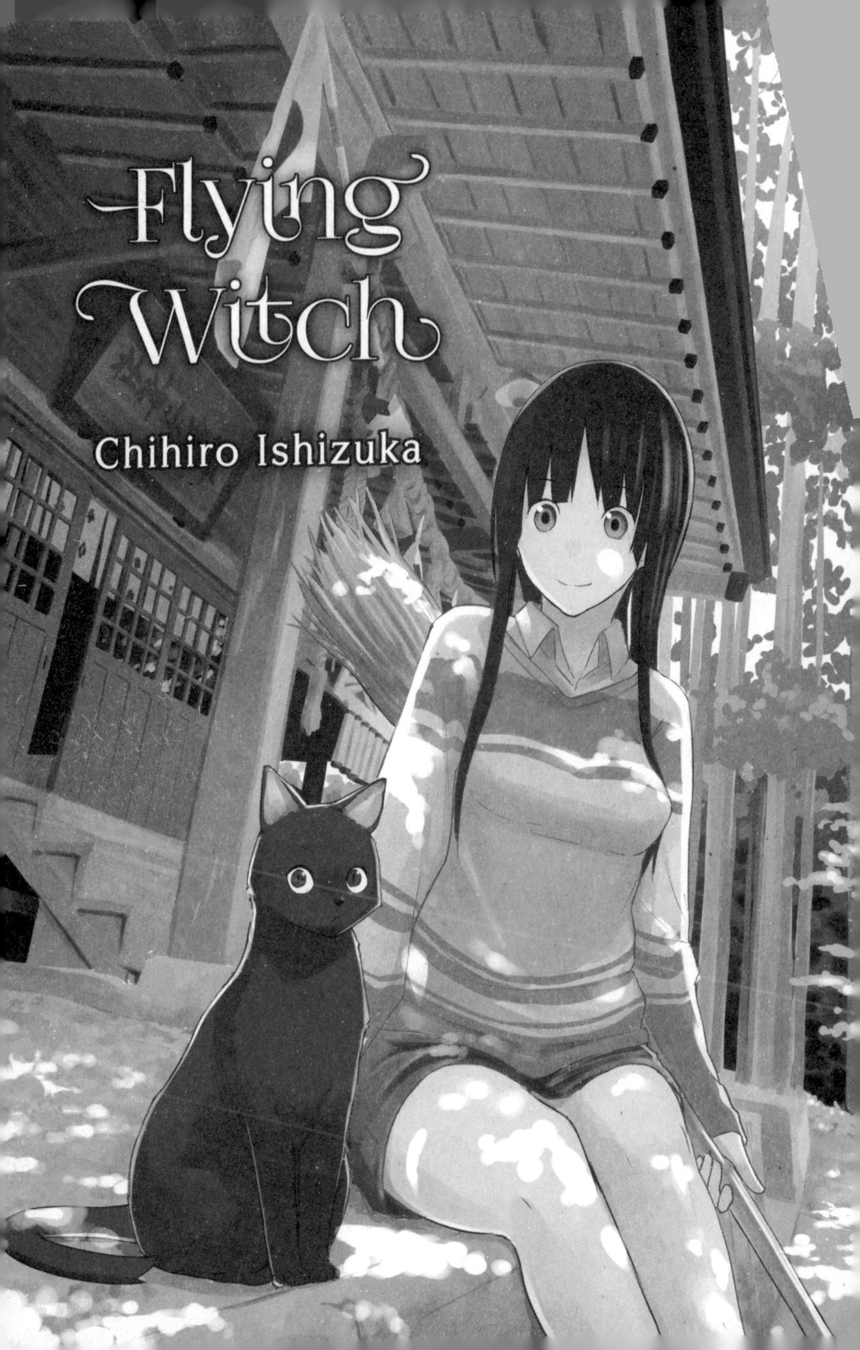
Flying Witch
Chihiro Ishizuka

Witchcraft Works, volume 11

A Vertical Comics Edition

Translation: Ko Ransom
Production: Risa Cho
         Melissa DeJesus

Copyright © 2017 Ryu Mizunagi. All rights reserved.
First published in Japan in 2017 by Kodansha, Ltd., Tokyo
Publication rights for this English edition arranged through Kodansha, Ltd., Tokyo
English language version produced by Vertical, Inc., New York

Translation provided by Vertical Comics, 2018
Published by Vertical, Inc., New York

Originally published in Japanese as *Uicchi Kurafuto Waakusu 11* by Kodansha, Ltd., 2017
Uicchi Kurafuto Waakusu first serialized in *good! Afternoon*, Kodansha, Ltd., 2010·

This is a work of fiction.

ISBN: 978-1-947194-15-1

Manufactured in Canada

First Edition

Vertical, Inc.
451 Park Avenue South
7th Floor
New York, NY 10016
www.vertical-comics.com

Vertical books are distributed through Penguin-Random House Publisher Services.